BOOKS AND THEIR READERS

IN EIGHTEENTH-CENTURY ENGLAND

Books and their Readers in Eighteenth-Century England

EDITED BY ISABEL RIVERS

LEICESTER UNIVERSITY PRESS

ST. MARTIN'S PRESS

1982

First published in 1982 by Leicester University Press
First published in the United States of America 1982
by St. Martin's Press Inc.
For information write: St. Martin's Press Inc,
175 Fifth Avenue, New York, N.Y. 10010
Copyright © Leicester University Press 1982

Designed by Douglas Martin
Text set in 10/12 pt Linotron 202 Baskerville, printed and bound
in Great Britain at The Pitman Press, Bath

British Library Cataloguing in Publication Data
Rivers, Isabel
Books and their readers in eighteenth-century England.
1. Book industries and trade – History
I. Title
686 Z244
ISBN 0–7185–1189–1

ISBN 0–312–09248 (St. Martin's Press)

Library of Congress Card Catalog Number 82–341198

IN MEMORY OF

Ian Hilson

1946–1980

Contents

Notes on the contributors

TERRY BELANGER, A.B. (Haverford), M.A., Ph.D. (Columbia), is Assistant Dean at the School of Library Service, Columbia University. He is the editor of *Bibliography Newsletter*, has written extensively on the history of the eighteenth-century English book trade and on the relationship of rare book cataloguing and computers, and is currently writing a volume entitled *Rare Books and Special Collections in American Libraries, 1876–1976*.

THOMAS R. PRESTON, M.A., Ph.D. (Rice University), is Professor of English at the University of Wyoming. He is the author of articles on Smollett, Johnson, and historiography, and of *Not in Timon's Manner* (1975); he is also the editor of *The Expedition of Humphry Clinker* (forthcoming in the University of Delaware edition of Smollett's works), and is currently writing a book entitled *Biblical Contexts of Eighteenth-Century Narrative*, a study of hermeneutics in fiction and historiography.

JOHN VALDIMIR PRICE, B.A., MA., Ph.D. (University of Texas), is a Senior Lecturer in English Literature at the University of Edinburgh. He is the author of *The Ironic Hume* (1965), *David Hume* (1968), and *Tobias Smollett: The Expedition of Humphry Clinker* (1973); he is also a co-editor of David Hume's *A Letter from a Gentleman* (1967), editor of David Hume, *Dialogues concerning Natural Religion* (1975), and is at present completing a study of sexual manners and *mores* in the eighteenth-century novel.

ISABEL RIVERS, M.A. (Cambridge), M.A., Ph.D. (Columbia), is a Lecturer in English at the University of Leicester. She is the author of *The Poetry of Conservatism 1600–1745* (1973) and *Classical and Christian Ideas in English Renaissance Poetry* (1979), and is currently writing a volume entitled *Reason, Grace and Sentiment: Studies in the Language of Religion and Ethics in England 1650–1760*.

PAT ROGERS, M.A., Ph.D. (Cambridge), is Professor of English at the University of Bristol. He is at present Vice-President of the British Society for Eighteenth-Century Studies. He is the author of *Grub Street* (1972), *The Augustan Vision* (1974), *An Introduction to Pope* (1976), *Henry Fielding* (1979), *Robinson Crusoe* (1979), *Eighteenth-Century Encounters* (forthcoming), and the editor of *Poems of Swift* (forthcoming). Work in progress includes a biography of Sir Joshua Reynolds, and other studies in the Johnson circle.

G. S. ROUSSEAU, B.A. (Amherst), M.A., Ph.D. (Princeton), is Professor of Eighteenth-Century Studies at the University of California, Los Angeles. He is the editor of *The Ferment of Knowledge* (with Roy Porter, 1980), and *The Private Papers and Letters of Sir John Hill* (1982), and the author of (among other works) *Literature and Science in the Age of Newton* (forthcoming).

W. A. SPECK, M.A., D.Phil. (Oxford), is the G. F. Grant Professor of History at the University of Hull. He is the author of *Tory and Whig: The Struggle in the Constituencies 1701–1715* (1970), *Stability and Strife: England 1714–1760* (1977), and *The Butcher: The Duke of Cumberland and the Suppression of the Forty-five* (1981).

PENELOPE WILSON, M.A. (Edinburgh), D.Phil. (Oxford), is a Fellow and Lecturer in English, New Hall, Cambridge. Her special research interest is in the classical tradition, and she is currently completing a book on Pindar in the seventeenth and eighteenth centuries. Other work in progress includes a book on Pope, and an edition of Fielding's *Amelia*.

Preface

The idea for this book arose from a course that my late colleague Ian Hilson and I taught jointly in the English department at the University of Leicester from 1975 to 1980. In this course, on 'Literature and thought in the eighteenth century', we constantly encouraged our students when reading certain eighteenth-century literary and philosophical works to consider the question of readership in a number of different ways: for example, what assumptions about the reader does the author make? What kind of reader does he address himself to? What expectations does the author have of the effect of his writing on his reader? We were anxious that the interpretation of meaning should not be divorced from questions of method, intention, and audience. It seemed to us that these questions had not been widely enough canvassed in eighteenth-century studies, and we decided to bring together a volume of essays that would explore a wide range of books and readers from this kind of perspective.

Ian tragically died in a car accident in June 1980 before he was able to begin work on his essay, which was to have been on the reading of philosophical literature with particular reference to his favourite author, Hume. I am extremely grateful to John Price (who taught Ian at Edinburgh, and who collaborated with him in editing some of Hume's letters) for contributing the essay in his place. Ian was an extraordinarily stimulating friend, colleague and teacher, always interested in hearing the ideas of others, enthusiastic in sharing his own, astute in probing weaknesses, amiable over disagreements. He is very much missed. I hope that he would have been pleased with this book.

Isabel Rivers
Leicester, May 1981

Introduction

ISABEL RIVERS

This collection of essays on writers, books and readers is intended as a contribution to the literary and cultural history of eighteenth-century England. It is not a contribution to literary theory: it does not concern itself with the problems of 'reader-response criticism', nor with the difficulties of the modern reader encountering eighteenth-century books. It is not a contribution to literary criticism: it does not attempt to evaluate by literary criteria the different kinds of books with which it deals. The approach of the essays in the collection is historical; they all investigate ways in which significant kinds of eighteenth-century writing were designed for and received by different audiences. They attempt to answer certain crucial questions about the use of books, for example: what was a religious or philosophical or scientific book considered to be? what kind of reader did the author envisage, and how did he try to influence him? in what ways did different kinds of reader respond to different kinds of book?

The historian can approach these questions in a number of different ways, and some of them are necessarily easier to answer than others. He can concentrate on the book itself, on its author, and on its readers (the last of these being much the most difficult area for research). First, the book itself. Every author makes certain assumptions about his reader, whether the ideal, imagined reader who will respond appropriately to his rhetorical strategies, or the particular class of reader to whose expectations or perhaps limitations he tailors his style or his argument. This is as true of a chapbook as it is of *Tristram Shandy*. By careful study of the text the historian can deduce not only the class of reader the author is addressing (for example the reader's age, sex, social status, or level of education, information about which can often be learnt simply from the title page or preface), but, more important, the moral, intellectual, or social assumptions the author shares with his reader. The author may be confirming the reader's views, extending them, or challenging them; careful consideration of vocabulary, tone and rhetoric will help the historian to decide which is the case. What the author does *not* say may be important; there may be significant matters which he takes for granted, which he assumes his reader already knows and approves. The study of different editions of the same book may be revealing: it is worth investigating any changes the author may have made

I

in the text, whether in response to criticisms or comments by specific readers, or for more general reasons, such as a wish to widen the potential readership of the book. The study of abridgments is an important but neglected field: an author may abridge his own book for a new audience, or an earlier, established book, probably designed for the educated reader, may be abridged for the less educated. A study of what is excluded or retained, in terms of vocabulary, allusion and subject, should tell the historian a good deal about the transmission of knowledge through different classes of reader. Consideration of the book's format, appearance, length and price is obviously relevant.

The second important source of information for the historian of books and their readers is the author. The kind of book he writes and the way in which he writes it may be determined not only by the readership he has in mind, but by the books he has himself read. From the author's private letters, diaries, and reading lists, or from his published statements and recommendations, the historian can learn which books the author considered most important in forming his attitudes (particularly during the formative period of his education), which he took as models, and which he regarded as misleading or pernicious. From the same sources the historian may derive information about not only how the author read other writers' books, but how and by whom he intended his own books to be read. Records of his transactions with his printers and booksellers, though unfortunately these are much less likely to have survived than other sources of evidence, may provide further help. It would seem a useful general rule for the historian of books and readers to try to find out as much as he can about the author's own education, reading habits, predilections, and assumptions as to the uses of books and reading.

The third, largest, and least explored field is the actual reader, that is the reader who in fact read the book, not the reader assumed by the author's rhetoric. There are many different classes of reader, and they may be considered in a number of different ways. How can the historian find out about them? Some are obviously much more accessible than others. It is, for example, very much easier for the historian to find out about the habits and responses of upper-class readers of novels, histories, or sermons, than those of lower-class readers of chapbooks or evangelical tracts. However, it is important to ask two kinds of question about readers, even though in some cases they may be unanswerable. The first concerns distribution. How did the book get into the reader's hands? There were a number of methods: he might buy it, at one end of the scale from the bookseller, or by subscription from the author, and at the other end from the chapman; he might borrow it, from a friend, a book club, or a library (private, university, cathedral, or circulating); he might be given it, either out of friendship, or by a social superior such as a teacher or minister for the good of his mind or his soul. The historian needs to consider the availability of books to different classes of reader in different parts of the country, and whether it would have been possible for a certain reader to know of a certain book. The second question concerns response. What did the reader think of the book? What kind of book did he prefer? These points are much more difficult to establish, particularly if the historian is interested in groups of readers. It may be relatively easy to ascertain the tastes of a certain kind of reader (Horace Walpole, for example); in the case of specified groups, such as dissenters, educated women, undergraduates, or charity-school children, the historian may be able to identify what books were recommended to them or specifically written for them, but not necessarily how they were received by the readers for whom they were intended.

The historian of books and readers may be asking questions such as these for a range of different reasons: he may also be a political, social, or literary historian or a historian of ideas. The contributors to this volume share a common interest in eighteenth-century studies, but the reasons for their interest in and their approaches to the subject of books and their readers are very different. Terry Belanger provides a much-needed map of the state of the book trade in the period; Pat Rogers and W. A. Speck explore different ends of the spectrum of readership, Rogers the process whereby fictional classics were converted into chapbooks, Speck the subscribing habits of politicians. The remaining contributors are concerned with the nature of important kinds of book in the period, and the ways in which they were designed for and read by specific groups of readers: Penelope Wilson investigates classical poetry, Thomas R. Preston biblical criticism, Isabel Rivers dissenting and Methodist books, John Valdimir Price philosophical books, and G. S. Rousseau science books. The volume as a whole breaks new ground, and provides a great deal of information and interpretation not available elsewhere, but it is not meant to be a comprehensive survey of books and their readers in the eighteenth century: important kinds of book which are not considered but which deserve similar treatment are history, political writing, and law. Intending historians of books and readers will in the future find their work made considerably easier by the Eighteenth-Century Short Title Catalogue; the British Library File, which will contain about half the total listings, will be available in 1982. Several contributors to this collection of essays are eager to point out gaps in our knowledge of eighteenth-century books and readers, and it is hoped that the publication of this volume will stimulate further research of the same kind.

3

1
Publishers and writers in eighteenth-century England

TERRY BELANGER

I. INTRODUCTION

At the end of the eighteenth century, aspiring English writers of *belles lettres* had a variety of modes of printed expression open to them. They could, for example, submit prose or verse, anonymous or signed, to a local newspaper or periodical. This they would be likely to do for the glory of it, since their chances of being paid for such occasional contributions, whether in the provinces or in London, would be small. If they were more ambitious, they could submit their material to the national newspapers and magazines, which in the late eighteenth century were, as they had been since their inception, based in London. Unless they became regulars, their chances for payment from these newspapers and magazines would again be small. On the other hand, their potential audience would be large: in the 1790s, monthly magazines like the *Gentleman's Magazine* had a circulation of at least 10,000 copies, and a readership several times larger. If the budding authors preferred to avoid the periodical press, they could attempt to arrange for the separate publication of their effusions, as pamphlets or books. On a modest scale, they could contract with a local printer, dealing with him either directly or through a bookseller, for the production on a fee basis of however many copies they desired and could afford of their work. The authors might then distribute their productions directly, whether gratis or to prepaid subscribers; or they might place copies with friendly booksellers and other shopkeepers, perhaps publicizing the availability of such copies through newspaper advertisements. If the writers were convinced that their writings were likely to attract good sales either locally or nationally, they could of course attempt to secure the interest of a local or London publisher, whose attention they might expect to draw to their work through a patron, through a common acquaintance, or through direct solicitation. If they were able to find such a publisher, they possibly would then be offered a lump sum for the copyright of their works. They might well, on the other hand, be asked instead for a subsidy by the publisher to support production costs, especially if the subject were worthy but of specialist interest. (The practice of paying royalties or employing related profit-sharing schemes was not common in the 1790s when dealing with fledgling writers.) These, then, were the principal options of writers in late eighteenth-century England: publication in a local newspaper or journal, publication in a London newspaper or journal, contracting for local or London printing with a view towards self-publishing, or finding a local or London publisher willing to speculate on the work's chances of reaching on its own a local, national, or international audience.

What were the options of aspiring writers a century earlier, in the late seventeenth century? Until 1695, there was no regularly-published newspaper in England with any interest in *belles lettres*. There were virtually no magazines or periodicals in England in the 1690s. Printing, and therefore publishing, was restricted to London, the university towns of Oxford and Cambridge, and to the archiepiscopal seat of York. The result of these restrictions was that almost every option available to writers in the 1790s was denied to writers in the 1690s. If earlier writers wished to see their works in print, they had to find a London publisher willing to undertake publication, either at his risk or at that of the authors, before their work could see the light of day. Put in simple terms, England in the 1790s was a well-developed print society; in the 1690s, especially once we leave London, we find relatively little evidence of one. It is difficult to overemphasize this point: until the Licensing Act expired in 1695, printing was rigorously restricted to London, the two university towns, and York, and the restriction seems to have been effective; there are few surviving examples of provincial printing, surreptitious or otherwise, in England before the very end of the seventeenth century. Consider the variety of printed ephemera and other pieces, then, that were *not* available in the average seventeenth-century English country town. There were no printed posters advertising estate or agriculture sales; there were no theatre bills or programmes, no newspapers, no printed handbills, bill headings, labels, tickets, or other commercial pieces. There were no printed forms meant to be completed by hand: no marriage certificates, printed indentures, or receipts. From a late twentieth-century point of view, the lack of printed materials is hard to imagine. But it would also have been hard to imagine in 1790, since by the end of the eighteenth century, printing had penetrated very thoroughly into all parts of the British Isles. A great deal had happened very quickly.

Some awareness of the dramatic changes taking place in the English book trade during the eighteenth century is useful in understanding the relationship between eighteenth-century writers and their readers, and it is to be regretted that there is at present no adequate general account of this subject. Both of the two most frequently reprinted general histories of the book trade are seriously defective guides to our period. That part of Mumby and Norrie's *Publishing and Bookselling* (1974)[1] which deals with the period before 1871 derives from Mumby's *Publishing and Bookselling* (1930); subsequent revisions of the 1930 version issued in 1949 and 1956 take little note of twentieth-century scholarship in the field, and the 1974 edition simply reprints without change the 1956 text for the period to the mid-ninteenth century. Plant's *English Book Trade* (1939)[2] was most recently reissued in 1974, but the part of the original 1939 edition that deals with the eighteenth-century book trade has not been significantly changed in the later editions. Whatever their original virtues, both studies are now obsolete and inadequate introductions to the period. Until a satisfactory general book materializes, those interested in learning about the eighteenth-century book trade must from the beginning work with the existing specialist periodical and monographic literature published on the subject, a task complicated by the absence of adequate evaluative guides to this material.[3] The present essay is intended as a small contribution towards the alleviation of this state of affairs. Relying heavily on the considerable body of excellent work in this field published in the past 50 or so years, it attempts to provide a reference structure sufficiently detailed to direct those with particular interests respecting special aspects of the eighteenth-century English book trade to the relevant recent scholarship in those areas; and more generally it attempts to describe the English book trade as it existed in the first half of the eighteenth century in some detail, especially as regards the relationship between publisher and writer.

2. THE PERSONNEL OF THE EARLY EIGHTEENTH-CENTURY BOOK TRADE

The publisher of books in early eighteenth-century England was part of a loosely-knit association of men and women pursuing a variety of inter-related trades. There were papermakers, whose activities during this period were, however, largely restricted to making rough papers intended for industrial and manufacturing purposes (wrapping woollen cloth, for example).[4] Little paper of a quality suitable for printing was made in England till the second decade of the eighteenth century, most of it until then being imported (directly or indirectly) from the Low Countries, France, and Italy. There was some early eighteenth-century English manufacture of cartridge paper, millboard, and other cardboards used in bookbinding. The bookbinding trades were well developed both in London and the provinces at this time.[5] Books might be bound in calf (produced

7

locally) or goat (imported from the Mediterranean); books and pamphlets intended for ephemeral use would usually be issued folded, stitched, and bound in domestic blue paper. The printing types in use in England at the beginning of the eighteenth century were usually cast from continental matrices, especially those sizes used for book work; there were a few establishments in London capable of producing types in display sizes.[6] Throughout most of the second half of the seventeenth century, the number of English printers, and even the number of presses each printer might own, had been tightly controlled, a regulation made feasible by an uneasy partnership between Whitehall and the Stationers' Company.[7] But the capital requirements for setting up a printing business at the beginning of the eighteenth century were modest (probably less than £100), and the necessary skills not difficult to learn; with the expiration of the Licensing Act in 1695, the number of printers and presses both in London and the provinces expanded rapidly.

The distinction between publishing and retail bookselling was not a precise one in the early eighteenth century; most dealers in London, and virtually all those in the provinces, were likely to be concerned with both sides of the business. A relatively small number of London dealers were primarily concerned with acquiring manuscripts, paying for the production of printed books, and establishing mechanisms for their local, national, and international distribution. A large number of London dealers and many provincial ones, while they occasionally participated in such publishing endeavours, were as much or more concerned in maintaining the retail side of their businesses. A still larger number of persons in London and the provinces were primarily concerned in selling, rather than in producing, printed materials; they ranged from substantial owners of London shops to itinerant vendors of news sheets, ballads, chapbooks, pamphlets, and other occasional and ephemeral publications.[8]

In the early eighteenth century, a vocabulary was used to describe the personnel of the book trade which is not always in accordance with modern terminology. In 1700, for example, the word *bookseller* usually signified a person engaged in either, or both, the wholesale and retail aspects of the book trade, whereas *publisher* usually meant what we would today call a *distributor* or *jobber* (though it might also simply mean someone who carried on a retail trade in pamphlets). To avoid confusion, the more careful modern writers on the eighteenth-century book trade tend to avoid using the word *publisher* except in a general context, preferring the word *bookseller* to denote someone whose principal occupation may be either publishing or retail bookselling, but who nevertheless may be concerned, at least to some extent, with both activities. When they do use the word *publisher*, it is in its modern sense: one who pays to have books printed and who distributes them to retail booksellers for sale. Where *bookseller* in its modern sense of a retailer of books is meant, the term *retail bookseller* is used. In the present study, these conventions are adopted: *bookseller* is the general term; *publisher* is used only in its modern sense; and the retailer is always referred to as such.

In 1700, especially in the provinces, one's occupation might combine aspects of both printing and bookselling. A person with a knowledge of printing could commission or otherwise acquire a manuscript, work off as many copies as he thought he could dispose of, and then sell them either directly to the public or indirectly through pamphlet dealers or chapmen.[9] Provincial (and colonial) tradesmen might undertake several different trade activities simultaneously, including printing, publishing, newspaper production and distribution, retail bookselling, and bookbinding, while perhaps engaging as well in the sale of patent medicines and other sundries. Students of the eighteenth-century English book trade have tended to concentrate mainly on the activities of large London dealers, since London was almost the sole place of origin of those major printed works of literature, history, religion, and science for which the century is remembered. But whereas London is overwhelmingly important as regards the production and wholesale distribution of books printed in eighteenth-century England, the provincial trade is of great importance as regards the actual retail distribution of books to readers. Even in 1700, provincial readers tended to acquire their books through provincial dealers, and they did so increasingly throughout the century.

By 1700, both London and provincial booksellers were beginning to interest themselves in newspapers, since they represented a steady source of income.[10] They were, furthermore, a welcome innovation as a vehicle for advertising books, and a useful supplement to the Term Catalogues in making knowledge of the existence of new books available to potential readers.[11] At the beginning of the eighteenth century, the newspaper trade was in its infancy; there were several London papers, but none appearing daily, and while there were sporadic attempts to establish provincial newspapers, none was yet to have much longevity.[12]

Besides papermakers, printers, publishers, bookbinders, retail booksellers, and a wide range of pamphlet sellers, chapmen, and pedlars, the English book trade in 1700 included various specialists, generally based in London, concerned primarily with maps, prints, and music printing and publishing.[13] Maps, prints, and music were usually engraved rather than printed by letterpress, and worked off on special, rolling presses by printers trained for such work.[14] Engraving the plates both for prints meant to be sold separately and for those intended to be used in books was a distinct and highly skilled trade by 1700, one which remained heavily concentrated in London throughout the century.[15] The early eighteenth-century trade supported a small number of printing press and other equipment manufacturers, and an ink maker or two (though many printers made their own), but even the names of such highly specialist tradesmen are hard to discover for this period, as the first separately published directory of the English book trade was published only in 1785.[16]

3. THE LONDON TRADE

By comparison with the end of the century, the London book trade in 1700 was small and closely knit. One reason for the close ties among the booksellers of the earlier years of the century can be seen by a glance at the title-pages of their productions; at this time, several booksellers commonly joined together in the publication of books. The expenses of publishing large works sometimes mounted into hundreds of pounds, and editions of these works often took a decade or longer to sell out. Few booksellers could afford to risk too much of their capital in a single work for too long. Because the copyrights of a large number of earlier eighteenth-century books were jointly owned by varying groups of as many as several dozen booksellers, constant communication among them was necessary in order to work out the arrangements for the publication and reprinting of these books.

A second reason for the comparatively close-knit quality of the London book trade in the first part of the eighteenth century also concerns copyright. With the final expiration of the Licensing Act in 1695, copyright protection in England lapsed. Although the Copyright Act of 1709 attempted to re-establish copyright protection, it did not set up an effective machinery for the detection and punishment of copyright infringement, nor did the limited terms it specified during which copyrights would be valid give the booksellers the perpetual copyright they had thus far enjoyed, and continued to desire. The booksellers had always maintained that literary property could, like any other property rights, be held in perpetuity. In order to protect their investments, and in the face of the Act of 1709, the major booksellers attempted to work together to establish a *de facto* perpetual control over copyright, without recourse either to the Stationers' Company or to the slow and often uncertain forces of the English common law.

The trade's attempt to secure perpetual copyright was finally torpedoed in 1774, when the House of Lords refused to accept contentions that there was a common-law basis for perpetual copyright.[17] But for the first three-quarters of the century, copyright was a major preoccupation of the book trade, and this preoccupation has a direct relevance to the relationship between eighteenth-century booksellers and eighteenth-century writers. It would be fatuous to suggest that there were many booksellers in the early eighteenth century who believed that the only good author was a dead one, but it was nevertheless the case in the eighteenth century (as it still is in the late twentieth) that a strong backlist was a very substantial asset indeed; and a backlist depends upon copyright protection for its very existence. Publishing new works is almost always more risky than reprinting older, proven titles; and publishing new works becomes almost impossible unless the publisher is allowed a sufficient time during which he is the chief beneficiary, in the event of a bestseller, of his own perspicacity. The generosity of booksellers to their authors during the first half of the eighteenth century was always tempered by their fear that a successful work would be pirated, either by Dublin publishers (who were not subject to the terms of the 1709 Copyright Act), or by Scottish or English publishers (whose piratical activities were illegal, but difficult to detect and expensive to prosecute).

4. THE PROVINCIAL TRADE

At the beginning of the eighteenth century, fewer than one hundred London booksellers controlled a large part of the wholesale book trade throughout England; they owned the copyrights of the most important and widely sold books and maintained a near monopoly over their national distribution. Provincial dealers in books generally employed London firms as their agents – indeed, the provincial booksellers absolutely required such representatives. Since most of the books sold in the provinces were published in London, and since the country men needed an uninterrupted supply of these books to be able to continue in business, they had no choice but to accept the regulation of the trade by the booksellers in the capital. The best that the provincial dealer could do was to establish a strong link between himself and one of the large copyright owners in London, in order to assure himself of a supply of the London-owned and London-produced books that he needed for his customers.

Using this method of distribution, the provincial bookseller did not have to establish credit with all the London wholesalers in order to get the books he needed; establishment of credit was often difficult in this period,[18] and the single London agent (who would have easy access to all the books produced in the city) was the best way out of his troubles. Since no agent himself controlled the copyrights of even a substantial part of all the books being produced, the London wholesalers thus had an additional reason to work together, so that they could all supply their individual provincial customers with books, no matter by whom published. Even the Tonsons at the height of their fame owned only a small fraction of all the copyrights of books being printed in London. The Tonsons did own part or all of many of the most valuable copyrights of literary works, but the London booksellers tended to specialize, and there were many other houses contemporary with the great Jacob and his nephew whose names are not so well known to the modern student simply because they specialized in books which are no longer commonly seen or read. William Feales and John Watts, for example, specialized in the copyrights of contemporary plays; the Lintots owned a substantial percentage of the copyrights of law books; the Knaptons owned the rights to many important religious works; William Innys controlled a large part of the trade in medical and scientific works; George Conyers specialized in the copyrights of books of practical instruction; and so forth.

What was true for provincial booksellers in England was even more so for booksellers in the American colonies, where credit matters were complicated by a shortage of hard currency and the risks inherent in shipping an easily damaged commodity overseas. Colonial booksellers had to wait months for their London agents to respond to their requests for books; and, because London and colonial reading tastes did not always coincide, it was difficult for the metropolitan agents to predict successfully the needs of their colonial correspondents in advance of their orders.[19]

Neither the colonies nor the provinces ever seriously challenged London as a publishing centre in the eighteenth century. The entire printed output of the North American colonies in the eighteenth century must have been far less than 10 per cent of that produced in Great Britain. Only after independence was achieved from the mother country did the American book trade begin to come into its own, and not until the 1830s and 1840s did it have much effect on the London trade except in its rôle as a distributor to the American continent of British publications.

Individual country and colonial customers for books produced by the London trade had a variety of ways in which they could acquire these books. Powerful families with connections in the capital could establish contact with a London bookseller, either directly, or indirectly through their own factors, using him as an agent for the acquisition not only of books but also of newspapers and other printed material. Individuals in the provinces with friends in London could impose on them to send new publications into the country. In the absence of a nationwide banking system, it was extremely difficult in the first half of the eighteenth century for the unconnected country customer to deal directly with a London bookseller for the order of a single, or a few, books, the more so in the absence of a national postal system for small packages; and arranging payment was almost impossible, since systems of credit had not yet been established by which strangers could do business with each other over long distances, for relatively small amounts of money.

The country customer was thus thrown on the resources of his local bookseller, an arrangement which probably worked adequately enough throughout the century for newspapers and other locally-published items, but which tended to be less successful for London books, especially as regards specialist material. Ambitious provincial booksellers had their London agents, but these agents were not always willing to acquire and ship whatever was requested, especially if (as tended to be the case) the London agent was himself also a publisher who preferred whenever possible to distribute his own publications to his correspondents rather than those of his rivals.

Still, the emergence of the provincial newspaper press, which contained a great many advertisements for London-published books, ensured that there was a steady pressure growing throughout the eighteenth century which encouraged the widespread distribution of books throughout the country. The nineteenth-century solution to the problem of quick distribution of individual titles was the establishment of London-based wholesale book distributors or jobbers, firms to which any country bookseller could write for any new book published in London. In the eighteenth century, however, especially in the more remote areas of the country, London books were usually acquired with some difficulty except by those with means and influence, with the exception of certain classes of books such as those sold by subscription (where a local agent or friend of the author might be authorized to receive payment and deliver books) or chapbooks, ballads, and other ephemeral material (which were widely distributed throughout the country by itinerant pedlars).

5. THE BOOK TRADE CONGERS

The most substantial profits in eighteenth-century London bookselling did not directly concern retail bookselling at all, whether within London or between London and the provinces. The real money lay in the ownership of copyrights, not in the retailing of books whose copyrights were owned by other men. The booksellers whose names are the most familiar to modern students of eighteenth-century English literature – the Tonsons, the Lintots, the Churchills, Richard Chiswell, the Knaptons, Charles Rivington, Thomas Longman, Robert Dodsley, Thomas Osborne, Andrew Millar, and so forth – were all large copyright owners (and thus wholesalers), even though they all had substantial retail shops as well. The history of the earlier eighteenth-century London book trade is to a degree simply the history of the practices of these and other copyright-owning booksellers. Between 1680 and 1780 they perfected systems by which they attempted to protect their investments from attack both from within the book trade, by pirates, and from without, by legislation.

One of the most important of these systems functioned through the activities of a group of London wholesalers between about 1690 and about

Terry Belanger

1720. The members of this association or (as the booksellers called it) *conger*, which comprised a varying membership of about 15 men, bought large parts of the editions of books produced both by themselves and by other London wholesalers.[20] These books were divided among the members and stored centrally in their warehouses. Various discount prices for these books were set: the price at which the members sold these books to other booksellers for retailing; the partners' price (that is, the price at which the members sold these books to one another, in the event that one member sold his stock of a particular book before another did); the price at which non-conger booksellers were to exchange the books for other books throughout the trade, and so forth. In various ways the conger could help to underwrite the expenses of publishing new books, or – more important – of reprinting old ones. This conger was only the first of a series of formal and informal groups which (though they did not have the same organizational structure as the wholesaling conger) exerted a similar pressure toward the stabilization of copyright. The later organizations were copyright-owning groups (unlike the wholesaling conger, which did not generally own the copyrights of the books it distributed),[21] and they were directly concerned in protecting from piracy their investments – and by extension, those of the whole trade.

The members of the wholesaling conger included Jacob Tonson, Thomas Horne, John Churchill, James Knapton, John Wyat, Robert Knaplock, Daniel Midwinter, Ranew Robinson, Jonah Bowyer, William Taylor, Henry Clements, Robert Gosling, Thomas Varnam and John Osborn, William Innys, William Mears, and Jonas Brown. Each of these men aside from his conger activities was individually a substantial copyright-owning bookseller; together they made up a considerable proportion of the most powerful London wholesalers of their day. The members of the wholesaling and other congers were tightly-knit groups. The Castle Conger, for example, was established shortly before the demise of the wholesaling conger, and the younger group partially absorbed the membership of the latter. There are direct connections between Thomas Horne (wholesaling conger) and Francis Fayram (Horne's successor; Castle Conger); Daniel Midwinter (wholesaling conger) and his son and namesake (Castle Conger); Varnam and Osborn (wholesaling conger) and Osborn and Longman (Castle Conger); James Knapton (wholesaling conger) and John and Paul Knapton (Castle Conger); and so forth.

In some instances the relationship among the members of the various groups is not immediately apparent, since the information necessary to determine these relationships is often inconclusive or hard to find. The Parkers and the Wilkins (both members of the Printing Conger), for example, were very closely associated between 1715 and 1740, with Richard Wilkin succeeding to Richard Parker's business, and William Parker later

14

succeeding to that of Wilkin. The demonstration of such relationships can be complicated, yet for a proper understanding of the operation of the eighteenth-century trade, knowledge of such connections is indispensable. In the 1660–1750 period in particular, the trade carried on its business largely by means of such interlocking sets of personal relationships, working through large and small partnerships and congers for their mutual benefit. For this reason, by far the simplest way to become a successful London bookseller in the first half of the eighteenth century was to be the son, son-in-law, nephew, or other near relation of another one, and a large number of the members of the wholesaling and other congers obtained all or many of their copyrights in this fashion. But there were booksellers who died or retired from trade without heirs to carry on, and copyrights of these men came up for sale either privately or at auction; if the latter, booksellers wishing to add to their own stable of copyrights would have a chance to buy some.

Although a bookseller selling his copyrights might deal directly with another bookseller in a private transaction, by 1718 (and probably for some time before) a very common method of copyright transfer was by means of auctions attended by the London trade.[22] Printed catalogues of books and copyrights sold at such auctions survive from that year. In the period between 1718 and 1768, the years covered by the two most extensive existing collections of eighteenth-century trade-sale catalogues, there is direct evidence for more than 200 sales at which several hundred thousand pounds changed hands. Slightly more than half of these sales were occasioned by the retirement or death of the seller without heirs in the book trade. Approximately another quarter of them were bookseller-sons selling part of their fathers' (or predecessors') copyrights. There were half a dozen bankruptcy sales, and most of the remaining ones were held by active booksellers who were either discarding unwanted copyrights, or else peddling material they had bought low at previous sales in hopes of a later resale at a profit.

These auction sales were a fundamental part of the eighteenth-century book trade (they continued throughout the century and beyond), for they provided a major opportunity for booksellers to purchase copyrights – and thus to become part of the system. From their beginning, the sales seem to have been restricted to London booksellers, but in the period before 1740 there seems to have been almost no exclusion of any established and respectable London trader. Later the sales would become very exclusive indeed, and the increasingly vociferous protests and effective counter-measures taken by those London and provincial booksellers who were refused admittance to the sales contributed towards the end of the century to the breaking up of the control over copyrights once enjoyed almost exclusively by a relatively small group of London monopolists.

The incentive to own copyrights in the first half of the eighteenth century, then, was considerable. One of the easiest ways to acquire them was by purchasing manuscripts from would-be or already-established authors. This was not always the most desirable way of acquiring them, however, since it was likely to be the least profitable: much wiser to acquire the copyrights of books that had already proved themselves, the more so in that in the earlier eighteenth century, the trade in substantial new books was less volatile than is the case today. Standard theology, standard history, standard editions of the classics, standard works of practical instruction, and standard English authors tended to have long and relatively secure sales; and to a considerable extent, the aspiring eighteenth-century author attempting to get a book published (except at his own expense) was competing with the collective backlist of the whole London trade.

6. THE PRICE OF LITERATURE

With this admittedly somewhat recherché information about the London book trade in hand, we can return to the relationship of eighteenth-century English publishers and writers. As regards this relationship, surviving copies of the London trade sale catalogues have important uses. Because they are usually annotated by their orginal owners with the prices fetched at the auctions they describe, we can determine with some precision at any given period what the London trade thought were the financial possibilities of the works of any author, living or dead, whose names appear therein. The names of a great many eighteenth-century writers in whose fortunes modern readers are still likely to be interested do appear in the trade-sale catalogues, as well as other names in English *belles lettres* ranging back to Chaucer and Shakespeare, Milton and Dryden. The Copyright Act of 1709 had spelled out definite terms during which a copyright could be enjoyed, but one would never suspect this fact from the trade-sale catalogues; the various copyrights of Shakespeare's works were sold at the Tonson sale of 1767 right along with the copyrights of the works of Pope and Edward Young, with no indication from the prices fetched that the book trade recognized any difference among these copyrights as regards the likelihood of the rights they represented being open to challenge.

In the first half of the eighteenth century, the most valuable copyrights appearing in the trade-sale catalogues can be divided into two major classes: religious works, and dictionaries. The high values set on the copyrights of such works were partly the result of the physical size of these works and partly the result of the likelihood of their being frequently reprinted. A folio or a fat octavo volume would retail for much more than a small duodecimo, and even if the smaller volume had more frequent editions, the larger work would tend to make more substantial profits for its owners. For example, one of the most valuable copyrights appearing in the trade-sale catalogues is William Burkitt's *Expository Notes, with Practical Observations, on the New Testament*, a large work in folio. The whole copyright was worth roughly £1,000 in the 1730s, though its value fluctuated widely. Shares of this copyright, and of most others, were generally worth most just before a new edition was called for, and worth least just after a new edition had been produced and distributed, since the owners of the copyright made their money from it when – and only when – new editions appeared; some variation in the prices paid for shares of Burkitt on the New Testament (as the trade referred to the work) is thus to be expected.

Burkitt on the New Testament was a large book frequently reprinted, with a correspondingly valuable copyright. Another valuable copyright in the earlier period was that of a smaller book, Elisha Coles's *Dictionary, English-Latin, and Latin-English*, which was worth about £800 in 1740. Various of the Delphin editions of the classics (so called because they were prepared for the use of the Dauphin) had copyrights worth between £200 and £500 in the 1720–40 period, and Boyer's *Royal Dictionary, French and English* in quarto and octavo editions maintained a steady price of more than £500 for many decades after its first appearance in 1699.[23]

But for the most part in the period before 1740, most copyrights sold for well under £200 each. The average London copyright-owning bookseller was likely to own a small share of Boyer's Dictionary; he might own part of at least one of the Delphin classics. He would be likely to have some of his money invested in the copyrights of works of popular devotion, such as Anthony Horneck's *The Happy Ascetick, or Best Exercise*. The average bookseller would often own shares in books of practical instruction, like John Mortimer's book on husbandry. These were the books that were widely sold at this time, and their copyrights were the ones that were the most frequently traded.

Copyrights worth in excess of £400 were substantial properties, far above the average for the period. Certainly the copyrights of the dictionaries (not only Boyer, but also Coles, Ainsworth, Johnson, and others) were worth more than the copyrights of even the major poets of the eighteenth century, with the exception of Pope, whose copyrights sold for more than £5,000 in 1767. In 1746, the whole copyright of *The Spleen* (with 50 copies of the book) was sold at the John Osborn (Senior, of Paternoster Row) sale for only £3 5s. od. In 1756, a third of the copyright of the poems of Stephen Duck sold for a guinea; twenty years earlier, the whole copyright (with 100 books) sold for £22. At the 1759 Lintot sale, half the copyright of Prior's poems sold for about £100, and half of Gay's collected poems fetched £108. At the 1767 Tonson sale, the whole copyright of Steele's *Christian Hero* sold for £10; part of Young's works, including his plays and the *Love of Fame*, sold for about £67; and the whole copyright of the *Faerie Queene* sold for about

£80. One of the few valuable poetry copyrights was that of the first volume of Gay's *Fables*, half of which sold at the Tonson sale for about £220. But except for Pope, the poets generally produced financially second-rate copyrights.[24]

As a class, the playwrights did not fare much better. In 1746, the whole copyright of Lillo's *London Merchant* sold for £7. 15s. od., though by 1759 its value had risen to 20 guineas. Lintot owned the rights to many plays; at his sale in 1746 the whole copyright of Farquhar's *Beaux Strategem* sold for £30. 10s. od. and his *Recruiting Officer* for slightly under £25. At the same sale, Rowe's *Jane Grey* and *Jane Shore* sold together for about 40 guineas.[25]

At the 1767 Tonson sale, the whole copyright of the plays of Congreve (both the collected works and the rights to the individual plays) sold for slightly under £200, and about half the rights to the collected works of Ben Jonson went for about £60. Also appearing at the Tonson sale was about 85 per cent of the copyright of Dryden's collected plays, with the right of publishing most of them individually as well; their copyright sold for about £100. Even Addison's *Cato*, sold at this sale in a lot with his *Miscellanies* and *Travels*, realized only about £300. The £1,200 realized by the Tonsons' two-thirds of the Shakespeare copyright shows very clearly the commanding lead Shakespeare had over his eighteenth-century successors in the copyright auction market.

It is dangerous to tunnel through the catalogues in search of particular copyrights without taking into account all the available evidence, for these copyrights may be tied to other shares, and all of them may have to be worked out in order to understand the history of any one of them. As we have seen, similar dangers are encountered when one extracts single instances of the prices paid for individual copyrights. I have myself been guilty above of a certain promiscuous isolation of individual literary copyrights, and the figures I quote indicating their value should not in every case be taken as an exact index of the price of eighteenth-century English literature. But it may be said with some confidence that the books published in the eighteenth century which are most widely read in the twentieth century were by no means the most valuable part of the London book trade's daily business. The copyright of Chambers's *Cyclopedia*, alone was worth £5,000 in the 1740s,[26] more than half the value of all of Tonson's literary copyrights put together. The prices paid for literary rights must always be viewed in relation to all of the copyrights traded during the period.

7. THE BOOK TRADE IN THE SECOND HALF OF THE EIGHTEENTH CENTURY

The population of England approximately doubled in the eighteenth century, and the number of readers more than doubled. Towns grew rapidly in size especially in the second half of the century, encouraging the growth of schools and the textbook industry, and retail booksellers proliferated in town and country.[27] Transportation improved, and with it the distribution of books from London to the provinces; newspapers proliferated. By mid-century, the English paper trade was well established, and the majority of English books were printed on paper produced domestically; in the second half of the century, indeed, Great Britain began to export printing and other high-quality papers in considerable quantity, especially to the American colonies.

Books continued to be bound in paper or in leather throughout the second half of the eighteenth century; beginning in the 1770s, however, one saw the increased popularity of books bound in paper-covered millboard, a binding which was sturdier than simple paper covers, and sufficiently sturdy to withstand a reading or two before the book was either discarded or sent to the binder for a more permanent, leather cover.[28] In this development may be seen the continuing movement towards trade bindings – that is, bindings executed on all, or on a substantial part, of an entire edition of books before the sale of any of them. Trade bindings in leather were practical only for books for which there was an assured sale, such as bibles, common prayers, and bestselling textbooks. Cloth bindings would be introduced only in the 1820s, with the development of sized cloth capable of being wet on one side during the glueing-up process without staining through to the other side.

By mid-century, the native typefounding industry had edged out most foreign imports of type, and firms like that of William Caslon were cutting punches and producing original designs; with John Baskerville, the English for the first time developed letter-forms with an international impact.[29] The number of printers had grown substantially in both London and the provinces, both book printers and jobbing printers who specialized in occasional work such as printed forms, bill headings, tickets, and handbills.[30] The Stationers' Company continued to lose influence over apprenticeship matters in the printing trade; if a man wished to set up as a printer without a formal apprenticeship, he was free to do so. Newspapers could be found everywhere, daily and weekly, and in the 1780s the Sunday newspaper made its debut. Printing technology did not change substantially during the century, and the late eighteenth-century newspaper looked much like the early eighteenth-century one, with the exception that the physical dimensions of the later one were larger (the simple result of using a larger sheet of paper to print on). Illustrations in newspapers, whether to accompany news stories or for advertising, continued to be rare.

A self-conscious antiquarian book trade became established in the second half of the eighteenth century, first in the shops of London booksellers like

Thomas Osborne of Gray's Inn, who issued frequent and extensive catalogues of his enormous book stock, which he tended to sell at what the twentieth century would call used (as opposed to antiquarian) prices. The market for children's books became more distinct, and both in London and in the provinces, dealers emerged who specialized in such material.[31] This market overlapped that of chapbooks, song sheets, and other cheap printed material intended for the semi-literate. Books in parts issued serially were commonplace throughout the eighteenth century; in the second half of this period, they became ubiquitous, and increasingly appealed to the poorer end of the retail market.[32] Newspapers obliged the growing demand for popular fiction by reprinting old novels and commissioning new ones. Circulating libraries flourished.[33]

The London book trade began increasingly to look towards the west end of town, especially as regards retail shops, but the wholesale trade continued to be concentrated in the area around Stationers' Hall, to the west and north of St Paul's Cathedral.[34] Distinctions between the wholesale book-seller (the forerunner of the modern publisher) and the proprietor of a retail shop were becoming clearer, the more so in that the major copyright owners were making their last stand during the 1750s and 1760s to maintain the principle of *de facto* perpetual copyright – a battle which, as we have seen, they finally lost with the House of Lords decision of 1774. The end of perpetual copyright gave a considerable impetus to provincial publishing, especially as regards editions of classic texts both English and Latin which had formerly been claimed by the London monopolists. Towards the end of the century one sees, published all over England, cheap editions of these classics, regionally printed and regionally distributed. Unaltered reprinting of established bestsellers is the least risky and most profitable sort of publishing, and the provincial trade was enormously stimulated by the sudden wealth of material now open to its individual enterprise.

8. THE IMPACT OF LIMITED COPYRIGHT

During the first three-quarters of the eighteenth century, London book-sellers had no choice but to be more preoccupied with one another than with writers, even living writers whose copyrights they owned. The system of shared copyright, whereby the rights to one book might be owned by more than a dozen men, brought booksellers into constant contact with their fellows. Fraternization was the necessary precondition for carrying on business. The end of *de facto* perpetual copyright (and the death of the hope for perpetual copyright *de jure*) brought about the end of shared copyright, as well. The complicated lists of booksellers' names on the title-pages of English books in the 1750s and 1760s become increasingly rare in the 1780s and 1790s, as single publishers began to contract with individual writers and to undertake sole responsibility for the publication of their work.

Over the long run, the establishment of the principle of limited but secure copyright had a beneficial effect on the relationship between publisher and writer. When copyright is uncertain, publishers have little incentive to pay writers for their work: unsuccessful publications will lose money anyway, and successful ones will be pirated. Only when a publisher could be reasonably sure of a known term of years during which he had the exclusive right to publish a work, without interference, could permanently workable systems of payment and of shared risk be established between publisher and writer. Only then was the stage set for writers to become partners with publishers in the publication process.

Throughout the whole of the eighteenth century, a common form of payment by publisher to writer was the lump sum, whereby the writer received a consideration for which he surrendered the copyright of his work forever. On occasion, such agreements were drawn up so that in the event of a particularly successful sale, an additional payment would be made (one recalls that Milton, who sold the copyright of *Paradise Lost* to his bookseller for £5, was to receive an additional £5 in the event that the first edition sold out – which it did). But of course the most common form of payment between publisher and writer in the eighteenth century was no payment at all. The idea that writers should receive payment for their work gained force during this period, but before mid-century, the transaction might go in either direction. The lack of interest which Thomas Gray displayed in receiving payment from his bookseller for his work probably struck even his contemporaries as somewhat quaint by the 1750s, but it was certainly shared by a great many other writers who came from gentlemanly backgrounds. If to write for money is to be a hack, it is interesting to consider who *did* write for a living in Restoration and eighteenth-century England, and what their contemporary reputations were as a result. It is likely, for example, that almost the only persons earning their living by their pens in seventeenth-century England were playwrights, whose income derived not only from publication but also, and more particularly, from playhouse receipts. This is not to say there were no best-selling works except plays – but the likelihood is that writers of those religious and historical works which sold widely during the seventeenth century received lump-sum payments (if they received payment at all), and that they did not share in the profits caused by their popularity.

The watershed figure is Alexander Pope, who by careful management of his literary productions was able to earn a good deal of money from them. A substantial part of his success came from his translations of Homer and their careful sale by subscription to a carefully assembled circle of patrons, friends, and admirers. Pope is the exception: most writers in the first half of the eighteenth century could not earn their living from *belles lettres*. There were, to be sure, the Samuel Johnsons of the London trade; they begin to make their appearance in the second quarter of the century, or perhaps a decade or so earlier. But there is now work for them in London: by the 1720s, there are a variety of daily, thrice-weekly, and weekly journals requiring editors and contributors. Beginning in the 1730s we have the magazines, voracious devourers of copy, and requiring editorial staffs and contributors. More than anything else, it was the periodical press that gave writers like Johnson the opportunity to earn a living as writers in London – a principle which was to remain true for generations in English and American publishing, and which is probably still true to this day: most writers of non-fiction depend on the market in periodicals, not books, for their principal livelihood.

In the absence of complete evidence one cannot be certain, but it is likely that very few writers before the end of the eighteenth century could earn a good living exclusively from the writing of such works. Fielding began to be paid large sums for his novels only towards the end of his life. Richardson undoubtedly made large sums from *Clarissa* and *Sir Charles Grandison*, but by the time he did so, he was a prosperous printer whose income was substantial; the money he earned as a writer was no doubt welcome, but it was not essential to his domestic economy. Defoe parted with the copyrights of his novels for relatively small lump sums, and though his publishers made a fortune from the sale of *Robinson Crusoe*, Defoe did not. Both Sterne and Smollett made good round sums from their novels, but in neither case was the amount sufficient to support them for any great length of time. Where writers like Smollett did make money was from their histories, not their novels. Indeed, the first writers as a class to make really substantial amounts of money in eighteenth-century England were such authors of popular histories as Hume, Gibbon, and Robertson. What characterizes such writers is their success in securing profit-sharing rather than lump-sum payments from their publishers – thus they shared in the success of their works, not only from the first but also from later editions.

It is characteristic of many writers of all periods that they are frequently in need of money, and that the most apparent way by which they can obtain some is by writing for it. In thinking about eighteenth-century England, it is always useful to remember that at the beginning of the period there were relatively few ways in which a writer could make money, whereas by the end of the period there were a relatively large number of ways; one should not ignore the connection between the sort of work an eighteenth-century writer did, and the sort of money he got paid for doing it. Once royalties were established, the way was paved for the development of an independent, professional class of writers, and though royalty payments did not become common in the eighteenth century, the mechanisms were all in place by the 1770s, and one sees the joint emergence of the recognizably modern writer and publisher by the beginning of the nineteenth century.

NOTES

1. F. A. Mumby and I. Norrie, *Publishing and Bookselling:* Pt 1: *From the Earliest Times to 1870*; Pt 2: *1870–1970* (5th edn, 1974).
2. M. Plant, *The English Book Trade: An Economic History of the Making and Sale of Books* (3rd edn, 1974).
3. Of some use in filling the gap are: T. Belanger and H. G. Pollard, 'Book production and distribution', cols. 249–312, in G. Watson (ed.), *The New Cambridge Bibliography of English Literature*, II, *1660–1800* (1971); and T. Belanger, '100 books on the eighteenth century English book trade', *AB Bookman's Weekly*, 23 June 1975, 3020–50.
4. The most useful general history of the English paper trade during the eighteenth century is D. C. Coleman, *The British Paper Industry 1495–1860* (1958). See also A. H. Shorter, *Paper Making in the British Isles: An Historical and Geographical Study* (1971). For a good, general evaluative bibliography in narrative form of the history of papermaking, see J. Bidwell, 'Paper and papermaking: 100 sources', *AB Bookman's Weekly*, 13 February 1978, 1043–61.
5. There is no adequate history of English bookbinding. A good (if brief) general introduction to the subject is J. P. Harthan, *Bookbindings* (2nd edn, 1961). E. Howe, *A List of London Bookbinders 1648–1815* (1950) has an excellent introduction to the structure of the London bookbinding trades. For information about splendid bindings, see H. M. Nixon, *English Restoration Bookbindings: Samuel Mearne and His Contemporaries* (1974); for non-splendid books, see H. G. Pollard, 'Changes in the style of bookbindings, 1550–1830', *The Library*, 5th ser., XI (1956), 71–94.
6. The standard history of British typefounding is Talbot Baines Reed, *A History of the Old English Letter Foundries* (1887), ed. A. F. Johnson (1952). Important, though badly in need of revision, is W. Turner Berry and A. F. Johnson, *Catalogue of Specimens of Printing Types by English and Scottish Printers and Founders 1665–1830* (1935). For the historiography of English typefounding, see S. Morison, 'On the classification of typographical variations', most easily found in his *Letter Forms Typographic and Scriptorial: Two Essays* (1968).
7. For a good general account of the Stationers' Company, see C. Blagden, *The Stationers' Company: A History, 1403–1959* (1960).
8. Our knowledge of the activities of eighteenth-century chapmen and pedlars of books is imperfect. See, however, L. Shepard, *The History of Street Literature* (1973). Much new information is presented on this subject by D. F. McKenzie in the second of his 1976 Sandars Lectures at Cambridge University, *The London Book Trade in the Later Seventeenth Century* (forthcoming; typescript on deposit at the Cambridge University Library). For a bibliography of the subject, see V. E. Neuburg, *Chapbook Bibliography* (2nd edn, 1972).
9. For a good, autobiographical account of this practice, see B. Wolpe's forthcoming edition of *The Life of Thomas Gent, Printer, of York* (1832).
10. The fullest account of the history of the English newspaper, though badly in need of revision, is S. Morison, *The English Newspaper: Some Account of the Physical Development of Journals Printed in London Between 1622 and the Present Day* (1932). For the provincial press, see G. A. Cranfield, *The Development of the Provincial Newspaper, 1700–1760* (1962).
11. There is no adequate recent account of the history of English book trade catalogues. See A. Growell, *Three Centuries of English Booktrade Bibliography* (New York, 1903). Valuable information may be found in H. G. Pollard and

23

A. Ehrman, *The Distribution of Books by Catalogue from the Invention of Printing to 1800, Based on Materials in the Broxbourne Library* (1965).

12. Michael Harris has begun to explore the growth and management of newspapers during this period; see especially his 'Management of the London newspaper press during the eighteenth century', *Publishing History*, IV (1978), 96–112.

13. There is no good single history of the British map trade, but see J. Howgego, *Printed Maps of London circa 1553–1850* (2nd edn, 1978). For the sale of prints, see R. Paulson, *Hogarth: His Life, Art, and Times* (New Haven, 1971). For music publishing, see D. W. Krummel, *English Music Printing 1553–1700* (1975) and R. J. Wolfe, *Early American Music Engraving and Printing: A History of Music Publishing in America from 1787 to 1825 with Commentary on Earlier and Later Practices* (Urbana, Ill., 1980).

14. I know of no good account of rolling press printing; for an introduction to the subject, see D. W. Krummel, *Guide for Dating Early Published Music: A Manual of Bibliographical Practices* (1974), 83ff.

15. See Hanns Hammelmann, *Book Illustrators in Eighteenth-Century England*, ed. T. S. R. Boase (1975).

16. John Pendred, *The Earliest Directory of the English Book Trade*, ed. H. G. Pollard (1975). Pollard's introduction surveys the history and bibliography of eighteenth-century book trade directories. Modern directories of the eighteenth-century book trade were prepared in the 1920s and 1930s by H. G. Plomer and others and published by the Bibliographical Society; Plomer's work is supplemented by I. Maxted, *The London Book Trades 1775–1800* (1977).

17. A detailed account of this struggle is given in G. Walters, 'The booksellers in 1759 and 1774: the battle for literary property', *The Library*, 5th ser., XXIX (1974), 287–311.

18. H. G. Pollard, 'The English market for printed books', *Publishing History*, IV (1978), 29–30. The text of Pollard's 1959 Sandars lectures, this article is perhaps the best single short introduction to the English book trade.

19. For an evaluative prose bibliography of the colonial book trade in the eighteenth century, see D. Farren, 'The book trades in early America', *AB Bookman's Weekly*, 28 March 1977, 1874–98.

20. For a detailed study of the wholesaling and other congers, see N. Hodgson and C. Blagden, *The Notebook of Thomas Bennet and Henry Clements* (1956).

21. Except in a few instances; see Hodgson and Blagden, *op. cit.*, Appendix 14 (c).

22. For an account of these sales, see C. Blagden, 'Booksellers' trade sales 1718–1768', *The Library*, 5th ser., V (1951), 243–57; and T. Belanger, 'Booksellers' trade sales, 1718–1768', *The Library*, 5th ser., XXX (1975), 281–302; the latter contains a list of surviving sale catalogues.

23. For detailed references to transactions in the catalogues concerning these works, see T. Belanger, 'Booksellers' sales of copyright: aspects of the London book trade, 1718–1768' (Ph.D. thesis, Columbia University, 1970), 109, notes 1–3.

24. For references, see *ibid.*, 122.

25. *Ibid.*

26. *Ibid.*, 123.

27. For an introduction to the trade in the second half of the century, see T. Belanger, 'From bookseller to publisher: changes in the London book trade, 1750–1850', in *Book Selling and Book Buying: Aspects of the Nineteenth-Century British and North American Book Trade*, ed. R. G. Landon (1978), 7–16.

28. A good account of this change may be found in M. Sadleir, *The Evolution of Publishers' Binding Styles 1770–1900* (1930).

29. For the later eighteenth-century typefounding trade, see the introduction to Edward Rowe Mores, *A Dissertation Upon English Typographical Founders and Founderies*, ed. H. Carter and C. Ricks (1961).

30. The growth of English printing is handled by M. Twyman, *Printing 1770–1970: An Illustrated History of Its Development and Uses in England* (1970).

31. There is no single good history of the publishing of children's books in the eighteenth century; but see P. Muir,

English Children's Books 1600 to 1900
(1954), and S. Roscoe, *John Newbery and
His Successors 1740–1814: A Bibliography*
(1973).

32. The standard account of the history of
number books is R. M. Wiles, *Serial
Publication in England before 1750*
(1957).

33. For the history of circulating libraries in
the eighteenth century, see D. P. Varma,
The Evergreen Tree of Diabolical Knowledge
(Washington, D.C., 1972).

34. On the location of the London trade, see
T. Belanger, 'A directory of the London
book trade, 1766', *Publishing History*, 1
(1977), 7–48.

2
Classics and chapbooks

PAT ROGERS

I. FICTION, HIGH AND LOW

We know a little more these days about the reading matter available to the bulk of the population 200 years ago. Students of the subject, notably Victor Neuburg, have alerted us to the range and popularity of 'penny histories' for children and adults; we have come to be aware of the continuing tradition of chapbook publishing which went on alongside the conventional 'literary' production of eighteenth-century England. However, there have been few attempts to explore the connections which occasionally emerge between the high forms and their popular equivalents. In this essay I shall try to investigate one mode of contact, namely the treatment of some classic works of literature in popular abridgments and adaptations.

There are not many candidates for such an inquiry. Neuburg mentions a few authors whose work from time to time appeared in the guise of a chapbook: Bunyan, Deloney, Defoe, Burns, Allan Ramsay and Pierce Egan. (He further observes that few known, that is to say identifiable, authors were responsible for 'original' chapbook texts: Hannah More is the most striking exception to this rule.)[1] Among this group, Deloney should perhaps be excluded in that popular tradition was only reclaiming materials which derive from its own province. *Jack of Newbury* and *Thomas of Reading* are the authentic stuff of orthodox chapbooks; whilst Deloney's ballads and broadsides can be designated 'literary' (if they can be so designated) only on account of some anachronistic distinctions. Egan, in a different way, seems scarcely to be representative of mainstream high literature. In fact, the only authors on Neuburg's list who provided texts that survived both as ordinary classics and as stock items in the chapbook repertoire were Bunyan and Defoe. For much of the eighteenth century, even *Gulliver's Travels* remained impervious to the abridgments. This fact may appear surprising, and some explanation would be in order.

Most of the standard fare of Augustan literature was simply beyond the reach of a chapbook audience. Poetry such as *The Rape of the Lock, The*

Seasons, the *Elegy in a Country Churchyard*, *The Task* – such work was too dense, too allusive, too verbally sophisticated, too independent of 'plot', to be converted easily into popular expression. Drama was seldom the basis of chapbook publications, and the subject matter and style of *The Beggar's Opera* or *The School for Scandal* made each play an unsuitable case for treatment. One might have anticipated that prose fiction would prove a more promising field. In fact, most of the major novelists were equally recalcitrant. Richardson's works, above all *Pamela*, did generate a series of sequels, retorts, dramatizations and parodies. But these were designed for more or less the same audience as had read the original book. There is nothing more remote from the self-consciousness and knowing manipulation of literary technique found in parody than a chapbook. Similarly, Smollett rarely was published in any adulterated form, though the length of *Roderick Random* led to its occasional abridgment. One curious transmigration in 1784 appeared as *The Theatre of Fun, or Roderick Random in High Life*. The same novel was published along with *Robinson Crusoe* as *The Adventurers* early in the nineteenth century. Meanwhile Smollett produced his own bowdlerized version of *Peregrine Pickle*, and *Humphry Clinker* yielded a farce in sequel to the original work.

A more interesting case is *Tom Jones*. Clearly the hero attained within a few years the kind of independent, quasi-mythical status that might have permitted him to become a regular chapbook subject. The evidence for this statement lies in critical comments, but also more concretely in a variety of musical and theatrical derivatives. By the early 1760s Antoine-Alexandre-Henri Poinsinet (1735–69) had compiled a *comédie lyrique* based on the novel. In 1765 J. H. Steffers produced *Thomas Jones: ein Lustspiel nach der Grundlage des Herrn Fielding*. There was another French comedy, *Tom Jones à Londres*, in 1783: this time the author was P.-J.-B. Choudard-Desforges. Meanwhile the first comic opera treatment had appeared in 1769; this version, by Joseph Reed (1723–87), enjoyed moderate success at Covent Garden, though it had the assistance of the expert comedian Ned Shuter in the rôle of Squire Western. Certainly its popularity fell a long way short of that attained by a later comic opera, the treatment by Edward German in 1907, a melodious but not especially faithful version. It should be added that the composer and chess-master Philidor was responsible for an opera produced at the *Comédie Italienne* in Paris (1765), but I have not seen this item.

In addition to these varied ministrations, Tom Jones attained enough celebrity to have a race-horse named after him, and to follow in Pamela's footsteps with the appearance of a sequel detailing his later career in the married state. But the length, or the technical elaboration, of the novel deterred any abridgers. Beauties of Sterne and gleanings from *Tristram Shandy* were features of the publishing world in the second half of the eighteenth century, but Fielding escaped. The time had not yet arrived when he required to be 'edited for the use of modern readers' (a Victorian sub-title), and the unquestionably demotic side of his appeal counted for little in the face of his formal weight, one might almost say the inviolability of his narrative. The British Library contains only one true chapbook version of the book, conjecturally dated 1820, and entitled *The Remarkable History of Tom Jones.* It is a typical production, an undistinguished 32mo crudely laid out; the treatment is without life and energy, and nobody seems to have wished to repeat the experiment.

So much by way of a process of elimination. The texts which did over time enjoy real currency at the lower end of the market are *The Pilgrim's Progress, Robinson Crusoe, Moll Flanders*, and (later and more fitfully) *Gulliver's Travels.* Bunyan's great work was abridged almost from the date of the appearance of the first part in 1678. The first rendition into verse was that of Francis Hoffman, who worked around the world of newspapers and Tyburn ballads: this dates from 1706. Almost a century later George Burder (1752–1832), theologian, engraver and miscellaneous writer, also attempted to versify the work. Burder had been a travelling preacher, and this serves as a reminder that no less a figure than John Wesley had concocted his own abridgment of *Pilgrim's Progress* (1743). Hundreds of editions of Bunyan testify to his enduring renown among all classes of society. If further confirmation of his standing were required, then his enlistment by Mary Godolphin for one of her famous series in 1869 ought to make the point. *The Pilgrim's Progress in Words of One Syllable* followed two years after a similar volume consecrated to *Robinson Crusoe.*

Unquestionably, then, Bunyan survived among the common people, and his masterpiece may properly be regarded as one of the chapbook classics. Only one other book of the period has comparable claims. The staple element continues to be folklore and legend, exemplified by stories such as those of Jack the Giant Killer, Robin Hood, or Tom Thumb. Boswell's allusion to these productions in his *London Journal* (10 July 1763) is well known:

> Some days ago I went to the old printing-office in Bow Church-yard kept by Dicey, whose family have kept it fourscore years. There are ushered into the world of literature *Jack and the Giants, The Seven Wise Men of Gotham*, and other story-books which in my dawning years amused me as much as *Rasselas* does now. I saw the whole scheme with a kind of pleasing romantic feeling to find myself really where all my old darlings were printed. I bought two dozen of the story-books and had them bound up with this title, *Curious Productions*.[2]

It is worth reflecting that the devotee of such 'curious productions' had recently sat with his friends discoursing of Helvétius, Voltaire, Rousseau and Hume. The literary slumming at Bow Churchyard bespeaks a genuine

affection and an unmistakable familiarity, but there is no sign that
Boswell's liking for the popular forms in any way affected his judgment of
what constituted literature, or how the high forms should be assessed.

Yet, as we have seen, *Pilgrim's Progress* managed to bridge this yawning
divide to a remarkable extent. And the case of *Robinson Crusoe* shows that a
secular work could invade the world of the Diceys and establish itself as a
modern legend. In some respects *Crusoe* is the more striking instance. It was
spoken of by literary people in rather less disparaging terms than was
Pilgrim's Progress. Unlike *Moll Flanders*, whose chapbook career I shall take
up briefly later in this essay, it possessed an authentic currency among the
devotees of polite letters. This was more marked after the book had received
the suffrage of Rousseau in *Émile* (1762). Though the popular versions
sometimes attempt to lay particular emphasis on the religious message of
Crusoe (in their final paragraph, if not before), the popularity of the book
among uneducated people seems to have had comparatively little to do with
religion – a statement one could not make, without severe qualifications, in
the case of *Pilgrim's Progress*. Long before the Victorians turned Crusoe into
a hero of self-sufficiency and the work ethic, generations of readers had
responded to the book as a story of survival, as an epic of mastery over the
hostile environment, as a parable of conquest over fear, isolation and
despair. These messages seem to have come through, however the book was
truncated or travestied. It was above all the shipwreck and the early part of
Crusoe's sojourn on the island that drew attention to these aspects of the
myth, and this is a part of the narrative that is never sacrificed, however
abbreviated the text. *Crusoe*'s 'readability' for a mass audience was variously
negotiable, but the *sine qua non* can be firmly located in this crucial episode.

Another significant piece of evidence here lies in the iconography of the
'basic' Crusoe illustration. Virtually all the abbreviated versions have one
initial cut, often as a frontispiece or on the title page itself. This corresponds
to the illustration in the first edition (1719), and the crucial factors in the
design are carried over from one picture to another. First of all, the wrecked
ship is always visible, sometimes in the background, sometimes virtually as
the most prominent feature in the cut. This ship could of course be the
Spanish wreck which Crusoe finds years later: his goatskin dress would,
strictly speaking, preclude the possibility that this is the original vessel on
which Crusoe was cast adrift. But symbolically one does read the illustration in the latter way, and the cut does have the simultaneous effect of much
popular art: the design lays out different portions of the story, almost as a
biblical narrative is shown in stained-glass windows or illuminated manuscripts. Secondly, Crusoe is invariably shown *alone*, without Friday, pirates,
shipmates, or cannibals. He is heavily armed, against no visible predator.
The sea and the land normally conjoin in the design. Crusoe himself is
bearded, unkempt and more heavily accoutred than we expect for a desert

island castaway in a near-equatorial region. All these elements combine to reinforce our sense of Crusoe as a man alone against the elements, threatened by unseen terrors. Above all, we are reminded of the fact of his condition as a castaway.

How the various abridgments handle such a *mythos* will be touched on in the next section. By way of background, let me add that there were perhaps 12 or 15 separate recensions of the narrative between 1720 and 1830. An exact count is hard to make, because a number of the texts overlap in some parts, and then strike out independently in others. Until a comprehensive bibliography is attempted, it will not be possible to specify every discrepant feature in successive editions. My discussion will cover a sample of ten texts, representing rather fewer independent attempts to abridge the text. Some of these are what would normally be described as 'chapbooks', that is they are short, simplified texts, crudely produced for a very low price. Others are not: they are, rather, popularizations and piracies, which evidently assume a level of education and literary sophistication not much inferior to that required by the original work. Others fall in between these categories, and might be regarded as fringe-chapbooks. For the present, it is more useful to compare examples of each category than to refine theoretical distinctions.

2. ADVENTURES OF *Robinson Crusoe*

The immediate success of the first part of *Robinson Crusoe* can be gauged from several pointers. These include the alacrity with which Defoe produced a sequel; the speed with which piracies appeared; the publication of the work in triweekly newspaper parts; the steady run of authentic editions over following years; the buzz of comment in books, pamphlets and periodicals; the considerable sum left by William Taylor, the bookseller who had bought the copyright (for what sum we do not know), when he died in 1724, and the high price these rights brought at auction in 1726. Of these, the last indicator is perhaps the most cogent. The book trade defines a bestseller by the simplest of criteria, and no one would have paid hard cash for a worthless title.

It is in this context that there began the flood of translations, adaptations, imitations and *Robinsonades*. *Crusoe* was first of all a trade success, and then the myth could spread and evolve. By 1723 the proprietor of Don Saltero's famous coffee-house and popular museum in Chelsea was to advertise in Mist's *Weekly Journal*:

> Monsters of all sorts here are seen,
>   Strange things in nature as they grew so;
> Some relics of the Sheba Queen,
>   And fragments of the famed Bob Crusoe.[3]

Such waxworks and collections may have ensured that the name of Crusoe became familiar to wide sections of the public, even those who were totally illiterate. The name 'Crusoe' began to escape from the literal confines of a single printed text.

Within a few weeks of the appearance of the first part of *Robinson Crusoe* in 1719, the bookseller Thomas Cox issued an edition in which the text was said to be 'abridg'd' and made 'more portable'. The identity of the abridger is not known, but it is a fairly competent piece of work, and one candidate who has been suggested is the experienced miscellaneous writer Charles Gildon. Taylor began a suit in Chancery against Cox, the outcome of which I have been unable to discover. Around the same time the *Farther Adventures* appeared: from the outset, this sequel was overshadowed by its predecessor, but there was enough interest in the book to justify new editions every few years during the first half of the century. A year later, in August 1720, Taylor issued the *Serious Reflections* which constitute the third part of the work. This item was never remotely as popular as the original novel. Its later life was confined to its presence in the abridgments. One notable fact is the emphasis that abridgers put on Crusoe's 'Vision of the Angelick World'. Even where they draw on the earlier sections of *Serious Reflections*, they habitually use the phrase just quoted as a sub-title for the section.[4]

The first attempt to reduce all three parts into the compass of a single volume was the most successful. It first came out in 1722 in the form of a duodecimo of 376 pages. The booksellers were all figures of substance in the trade: Bettesworth, Brotherton, Meadows and Midwinter were none of them fly-by-night operators or fringe publishers. This suggests that they considered themselves to possess a defensible right in law to issue abridged editions, though strictly interpreted the Copyright Act of 1709 would not seem to open up this loophole. As we shall see, a similar claim was made in connection with a piracy of *Gulliver's Travels* a few years later. It has been suspected that this particular version was the abridged version of *Crusoe* which Thomas Gent confessed to having made: Gent was apprenticed to Edward Midwinter, printer of the volume, and so the theory is plausible – although another account is that Gent made the woodcuts. It would be safest to say that the abridger is, as usual, an anonymous figure – something pretty well inherent in his rôle.

This abridgment continued to be issued at regular intervals for some decades. It was usually reset, and minor compressions effected to squeeze the text into a still smaller volume. By the fifth edition (c. 1735) the length had been reduced to 336 pages. This was largely a matter of resetting, although the preface was cut: otherwise the proportions remain the same – the first part occupying about 55 per cent of the whole, with the 'Vision of the Angelick World' occupying about a tenth of the text at the end. As usual, the latter subtitle is a misnomer, in that other parts of the *Serious Reflections* are used . The preface is a significant item in the presentation of the work: it confronts the objection 'that there never was such a Man as *Robinson Crusoe*, and that it is impossible such incredible Things should be accomplished in a distant and uninhabited Island.' The answer is to see the entire relation as allegorical. Stress is laid on 'divine Reflections to comfort the afflicted Mind', and on 'such an heavenly Prospect of the Wonderful Providence of God.' Evidently the preface in Taylor's original edition, claiming the work to be 'a just History of Fact', was no longer felt to be a tenable line to defend: Defoe's own preface to the *Serious Reflections* had in any case undermined the editor's ground here. There is naturally some puffing of the 'faithful Abridgment' and a reminder of the popularity which the work had instantly achieved: '*Robinson Crusoe* was in every Body's Mouth, as much as in the Mouth of *Pretty Poll*!'[5]

This version is probably closer to the original than any of the other abridgments, both in its handling of the narrative and in its stylistic character. However, it resembles the others in its habit of shifting words around to no obvious purpose. Particularly noteworthy is the apparent inability of any abridger to leave the opening sentences alone, even though the same information is to be conveyed. One suspects that this may have something to do with legal precautions: the publisher might be able to claim he was not infringing the Copyright Act, since his text was not a literal reprint of the Taylor text. The point can be made simply by comparing the opening lines.

> TAYLOR (1719): I was born in the Year 1632, in the City of *York*, of a good Family, tho' not of that Country, my Father being a Foreigner of *Bremen*, who settled first at *Hull*: He got a good Estate by Merchandise, and leaving off his Trade, lived afterward at *York* . . .

> ABRIDGMENT (1772): In the Year 1632, I was born at *York*, of a reputable Family. My Father was a Native of *Bremen*, who Merchandizing at *Hull* for some time gain'd a very plentiful Fortune . . .

The abbreviated versions nearly all consider it essential to provide all these details, but they display ingenuity in their ways of avoiding the basic text. 'Merchandise' generally defeats them, and in some shape or other this word turns up in most versions.

The present abridger begins his cutting operations from the start, allowing no more than a page to Crusoe's father in his efforts to set his son on the right course. Nevertheless, each considerable section of the plot is covered, however briefly, and this particular version is a paraphrase rather than a précis. In this respect the famous episode of the footprint is representative of the methods employed. That historic paragraph, running to some 250 words in the Taylor edition, is presented in this form:

> But one Day it happen'd that going to my Boat, I saw the Print of a Man's naked Foot on the Shore, very evident on the Sand, as the Toes, Heels, and every Part of it. Had I seen an Apparition, in the most frightful manner, I could not have been more confounded . . .[6]

There is some slight attempt to make the syntax simpler, but the vocabulary is not conspicuously different. Most of the abridger's efforts seem to have gone into reducing the compass of his text, and his paraphrase involves few obvious aids to greater intelligibility. One might summarize the position by saying that this first, and frequently reprinted, abridgment serves some of the purposes of a nineteenth-century pocket edition or a modern paperback text. Compression is achieved not by leaving out whole blocks of the work, but by a steady attrition of the word-count, by removing detail and qualification. The reader gets more for his money in that the significant *events* arrive more promptly, with a consequent diminution of reflection and conjecture. There is thus a literary processing at work, but one rather different from that seen in the chapbooks proper. Here, in the 1722 abridgment, the audience is presumed to have a measure of reading skill, but to be bored by excessive elaboration. In the chapbooks much more is done to alter the basic legibility of the text for a barely literate public.

One of the most striking contrasts to the Bettesworth edition of 1722 is a little book entitled *Voyages and Travels: Being the Life and Adventures of Robinson Crusoe of York, Mariner*, which has been tentatively dated c. 1750. It is found in the British Library in a volume of ballads and broadsides, and resembles such works in its physical dimensions. The formula 'Written by Himself' is retained on the title-page, in black letter: this had been dropped in the Bettesworth edition, no doubt as it contributed to the pseudo-realistic claims that this edition found too embarrassing to sustain. *Voyages and Travels* is a thoroughly naive production, and quite willing to promote such claims of 'authenticity'. The unsophisticated woodcut on the title-page simply conveys the message of Crusoe with his guns and the wreck behind him. Printing is best described as primitive with blunders such as '*Soh*' for '*Son*' and '*doy*' for '*dog*'. All this is understandable when one adds the central fact: this version extends to no more than eight pages. The abridgment in these circumstances cannot be much more than a digest. However, it starts off as though there were all the time in the world; indeed, the opening paragraph survives almost intact. After that, things speed up, but it still takes half the available space to reach the shipwreck. The reluctance of abridgers to cut the pre-island sections is a curious fact which deserves attention.

Despite the narrow confines in which he works, this abridger devotes some space to Crusoe's reactions on finding himself alone on the island. Equally, his efforts to retrieve objects from the wreck are given detailed coverage. After this, an abbreviated rendition of Crusoe's journal (half a dozen extracts) takes us to within two pages of the end of the minute volume. There is just time to mention the pirates: Friday enters the text in the very last paragraph, and the value of Crusoe's property when he regains it at the end is duly recorded. There is obviously no room for the coda recording Crusoe's adventures in the Pyrenees – it might be added that abridgers display far less reverence towards the postlude than to the prolegomena to Crusoe's island adventures. What is much more surprising, both historically and aesthetically, is the total omission of the footprint episode. One might have supposed that this graphic emblem would survive in any popular version, since it appears to us the most imaginative stroke in the entire narrative. It is difficult to be sure whether this absence is a matter of conscious policy: the fierce abridgment on the concluding pages would seem to suggest nothing less than high incompetence. If so, we should be rash to impute the crazy proportions of this chapbook to any sort of planned ordonance. Nevertheless, it is quite evident that the shipwreck and its aftermath are the heart of the book for this compiler. In that judgment he was backed by the title-page woodcut. All the signs are that early readers were captivated by Crusoe's initial trauma, possibly because they were familiar with stories of disaster and delivery in popular theological manuals.

Some twenty years later, a chapbook version allowing itself the luxury of 24 duodecimo pages found room for ten woodcuts. Most of these seem to concentrate on scenes of fighting, not very expertly handled by the artist. At the end we see Crusoe in his new prosperity, dressed in a laced tricorn, a full-bottomed wig and a brocaded jacket; he carries a cane almost worthy of Sir Plume. The text is not so badly mangled as in the previous example. The journal section is presented at greater length, the Pyrenean episode is included (Friday kills the wolves and bear 'with a great deal of Sport'). As in all the chapbooks proper, the material is confined to the first part of *Crusoe*. And as in other cases, a sententious peroration is provided: '. . . And indeed the many miracles of this man's life is very strange and surprising. The events by a serious application, may be as examples to others, and the wisdom of Divine Providence, in all our circumstances, may be justified and honoured, let them occur when they will.' In terms that are genuinely faithful to the original, the compiler refers to the 'very remarkable chain of Providence' evident in the story of Crusoe, and recommends the work's perusal to those who would learn the 'art of patience, in submission to the divine will.' These phrases appear in a new version of the 1770 text, issued by C. Randall at Stirling in 1801.[7] The text has been cut to 16 pages, and three chapters inserted, dealing respectively with Crusoe's early years, the ill-fated voyage and the aftermath of the wreck, and finally the story from

the sprouting of the corn. In other respects this version is very close to the
1770 edition, as regards letter-press. It comes off worse in the matter of
illustration, since only a title-page woodcut of a ship is provided. Where
cuts are present, they tend to be better executed over time: but by no means
all chapbooks contain illustration within the body of the text.

Around 1770 (perhaps even a little earlier) J. Sketchley of Birmingham
produced a so-called 'ninth edition' of the full three parts. This amounts to
408 pages, though it lacks a preface. It is based on the original editions,
possibly with some reference to the Bettesworth paraphrase, but as usual
some variants are present throughout: the opening sentence runs, 'I was
born at York, in 1632, of a reputable family . . .' As far as the first two parts
are concerned, such a text is not very much shorter than Defoe's original,
and one wonders whether the labour of extensive paraphrase would repay
the effort. But verbal detail aside, the reader of Sketchley's does get the
whole of the book, with a customary snatch of the *Serious Reflections*. It is
simply hard to detect a literary purpose in what has been done.

Another item deriving from the West Midlands is a version issued by F.
Houlston of Wellington and Ironbridge. No date is given; one supposes that
the work must postdate the rise of Ironbridge in the late 1770s and 1780s:
an advertisement at the end includes *The Vicar of Wakefield*, another novel
which was less frequently made into a chapbook than one might have
anticipated. The volume contains 189 pages, but in some respects its
procedures recall the chapbook tradition. Unusually, the original preface
from Taylor's edition is included. Defoe's text is treated without reverence,
but also without any great freedom or invention: the degree of alteration
may be judged from the following comparison:

> TAYLOR: It was not till almost a Year after this that I broke loose, tho' in the
> mean time I continued obstinately deaf to all Proposals of settling to Business,
> and frequently expostulating with my Father and Mother, about their being so
> positively determin'd against what they knew my Inclination prompted me to.
> But being one Day at *Hull*, where I went casually, and without any Purpose of
> making an Elopement that time; but I say, being there, and one of my
> Companions being going by Sea to *London*, in his Father's Ship, and prompting
> me to go with them . . .

> HOULSTON: It was almost a Year after this, being one day at Hull, where I
> went casually, and without any design of making an elopement, I met one of my
> companions who was going by sea to London . . .[8]

This time the alternative does seem an improvement. It has got rid of the
straggling detail, and eliminated a few, if not all, of the awkward participles
that clog Defoe's style. (Sketchley, incidentally, had 'I was then, I think,
nineteen years old, when one time being at Hull . . .').[9]

The cuts in this edition, mentioned on the title-page as a major adornment, are distinctly more sophisticated than those in the chapbooks. A notable variant appears in the frontispiece, which for once does not concern the wreck. Robinson is seen as a boy – he looks no more than 11 or 12 – with his parents expostulating to him on the errors of his ways. His father has a crutch and his foot is lifted on to a gout-stool: a nice individuating touch, at long last. Other cuts involve the raft, the rescue of Friday, and Friday dancing with the bear. The wreck is one incident among many, rather than the focus of total attention.

Roughly contemporary is a Dublin version, published in 1799, which covers all three parts in 180 pages. This is one of the more defensive productions, with an anxious preface: 'In this new Epitome . . . all possible care has been taken to preserve the History entire.' The epitomizer asks, 'What if the whole was, as is suggested, a mere fiction?' His answer is predictable:

> Yet the design is so justly carried on, and so interspersed with curious Observations and moral reflections, that all Persons, who have any taste of the metaphorical way of writing, must allow this to be a Masterpiece.

Even at the start of the narrative, this same note is apparent:

> He that pretends to publish to the world an Account of his own Life and Actions, is doubtless under the strongest Obligations, to Confine himself within the strictest Rules of Modesty and Truth, and this I can assure the Public, I most solemnly determine in the following Narration.
>   I was born at *York*, in the Year 1632, of a reputable Family. My Father was a Merchant, born at *Bremen* . . .[10]

It is noticeable that 'reputable' seems to have become a standard replacement for 'good' in popular versions. Otherwise this edition calls for little comment. It naturally omits more than the Houlston text, which had confined itself to the first part of *Crusoe*, and had made only light excisions. The section from the third part in the Dublin 'epitome' ends with verses. There are woodcuts of moderate quality.

Another publication of around 1800 is the volume entitled *The Exploits of Robinson Crusoe*, put out by 'the booksellers': here a new formula, 'written originally by himself', is adopted. The two first parts are covered in 128 pages, with the ratio slightly more in favour of the *Strange Surprizing Adventures* than was customary (roughly eight to five). The frontispiece reverts to the traditional subject, and the cuts are quite good, in contrast to some indifferent printing. It looks as if the compositor was following some earlier printed text, which I have not identified: at all events, on the last leaf of sig. F, the type-face suddenly gets smaller, apparently in order to accommodate the material, whilst on pp. 49–50 an entire page of copy appears to have been omitted. The missing material happens to include the footprint episode, which does not suggest great care was taken with the presswork.

It was not until 1813 that the first identifiable bowdlerized text appeared. This was published by Cradock, Joy and others in London, and is basically devoted to the first part (though hints of the sequel are present at the end). The book is said to have been 'originally written by Daniel Defoe', a fact which only achieved general notice following George Chalmers' edition in 1790. The book has been 'revised for the use of Young Persons', and the text 'corrected and improved'. However, the Podsnappery of the title-page is not really maintained in the bulk of the succeeding volume, once the editor has got a few pious sentiments out of his system:

> Notwithstanding the acknowledged merits of DEFOE's interesting narrative of the Adventures of *Robinson Crusoe*, it will be admitted, that, as he did not address it expressly to Young Persons, it must contain many things which are not well adapted to an early age, and which, when read by them, it were better should be omitted.[11]

It is true that this version passes quickly over the opening scene with Crusoe's parents, and the hero's rebelliousness is muted: but the volume does include the Xury section, Friday, renegade English sailors, and the rest: only tiny adjustments seem to have been attempted. The frontispiece has a suitably young-looking Crusoe returning on his raft laden with provisions from the wreck.

The last item to warrant individual discussion is an Edinburgh publication, *The Wonderful Adventures of Robinson Crusoe* (c. 1815). 'Embellished with Elegant Cuts', this volume manages to cover both the first two parts of *Crusoe* inside 93 pages. In fact, no more than 15 pages at the end are devoted to the *Farther Adventures*, which are reduced to a breathless summary that carries us across continents in a few sentences. An unusual feature is the provision of a caption from the text for each of the cuts. The journal is omitted, and slightly less emphasis is attached to the wreck than in some earlier versions. The degree of paraphrase may be gauged by examining a passage already cited in the original (see p. 36), describing Crusoe's departure from his home:

> As if bent on my own destruction, I hardened myself against the prudent and kind advice of the most indulgent parents; and being one day at Hull, where I met with one of my companions, who was going to sea in his father's ship, he easily persuaded me to go with him.[12]

By contrast, the footprint is presented almost in Defoe's own words, suggesting that by this date the episode had achieved a classic status which discouraged editors from tampering too much with the description.

The 1813 edition for young persons shows that we have reached the eve of Victorianism. It would take us into different aspects of the history of taste if we were to pursue the story further into the nineteenth century. By this date, the novel was beginning to grow in critical esteem; it was firmly associated with Defoe, whose career was better known to the educated public, thanks to Chalmers' biography (1785) and the Ballantyne edition of the works. By 1830 editions had appeared in a diverse range of cities and towns, including Gainsborough, Warrington, Derby, Dunbar, Braintree, Bewdley, Wotton-under-Edge and other provincial localities. There was an edition in Worcester, Massachusetts, in 1795. Some of the chapbooks proper continued to appear in more or less identical guise. The work entered Park's Juvenile Library; there is a version of 32 pages, 'with a Fragment called Begging Sailors.'

The examples taken are, I hope, representative of the publishing history over a century. They range from chapbooks in the strictest sense to popular abridgments aimed at a moderately sophisticated readership. Certain of the books examined may be described as intermediary cases. The Dublin version of 1799 is such an example: it allows itself more room than the highly abbreviated versions, but it simplifies and condenses much more than the full-length editions. Much the same may be said of the *Wonderful Adventures* in 1815, though this incorporates some direct transcript from the original text. It would be possible to assert, by way of general summary, that the book was cut down and stripped according to the space available, the limits of vocabulary applicable to a presumed audience, and the individual skills (or lack of them) possessed by the abridger. The shipwreck and its aftermath in the days, weeks and months immediately following clearly constitute the major point of interest for most compilers. Yet they never feel free to omit the opening sections entirely, and commonly devote more of their space to the pre-island episodes than seems easily justifiable from a literary standpoint. Friday is allowed to wander into the story casually, his education is usually given little emphasis, and the second half of the *Strange Surprizing Adventures* is reduced to a rapid series of events with bloodshed blandly reported. Attempts to cover the *Farther Adventures* are generally made only by those with a good deal of space at their disposal: shorter abridgments can find no effective way of incorporating the sequel. The *Serious Reflections* are usually presented as straightforward didactic material, without any link with what has gone before. A sententious coda is a feature of the chapbooks proper and the intermediate category, rather than the full-scale versions.

3. MOLL AND GULLIVER

Crusoe was not the only novel by Defoe to encounter popularization by the trade. *Moll Flanders*, first published in 1721, indeed survived only in truncated forms: unlike *Crusoe*, it lost almost all its currency in its full and authentic form.[13] Most eighteenth-century editions represented in one way or another a departure from Defoe's model. There are three longer versions of the story. The first is T. Read's piracy, which appeared within about a year of the novel itself. Second, there is a three-part compilation entitled *Fortune's Fickle Distribution*, published in 1730, which imparts an Irish connection to the story. Third, the *History of Laetitia Atkins* (1776) claims that Defoe had doctored Moll's memoirs and offers to print new materials from her own manuscript. Fresh details appear in the second and third of these works, but Read is the main source. His work was highly influential throughout the first century of Moll's existence; he ends with an account of Moll's 'Estate, Penitence, Age, Death, Burial, Elegy, and Epitaph.' This one-shilling piracy could not be described as a chapbook in the ordinary sense, but in its free handling of the story it is something quite different from an abridgment as we should normally understand that term. The novel is divided into nine chapters of markedly unequal length. At the conclusion a third-person narrator breaks in to describe Moll's death, quote an elegy by the 'prime wits' of Trinity College, Dublin, and recount details of her will and her funeral. Read abbreviates the reflections and attempts to provide a more intelligible narrative structure. He was followed by the author of *Fortune's Fickle Distribution*, who adds a brief section on Moll's 'governess', here styled Jane Hackabout, and an even shorter account of James Mac-Faul, the Lancashire husband. (It is characteristic of all adaptations that they provide a fuller identification of Jemmy, the most attractive male in the book.) Finally, *Laetitia Atkins* gives the heroine a new identity, a new parentage, and a less seamy existence – the criminal side is reduced almost to nothing. Jemmy turns up in yet another guise, as James Carrol. This is the most radical adaptation, though it borrows a good deal from Read: the adaptor is not afraid to invent dialogue of his own, and he carries out his aim of cleaning up Moll's career with some energy. *Laetitia Atkins* might be described as an alternative version of the novel, whereas Read supplies a competent transposition, a para-*Moll* for a wider audience impatient with some of the longueurs and moral agonies of Defoe's text. We are unlikely to prefer *Laetitia Atkins* to the original, but within its limits it is a sort of critical reinterpretation of the data.

Nevertheless, it was in the guise of a more orthodox chapbook that Moll most frequently appeared during the eighteenth century. Many editions can be traced, published over a wide span of years and from different addresses. Two basic patterns emerge which underlie all these editions. The main line of descent is the series of editions put out by the Diceys 'in Aldermary Church Yard, London', the firm mentioned by Boswell.[14] Several examples from the second half of the eighteenth century survive: the Dicey standard text has 24 pages, but a Manchester edition of c. 1805 is in essentials the same text squeezed into 16 pages. A slight variant, but fundamentally the same abridgment, was published in Newcastle (c. 1790) and Stirling (1823). It should be noted that the Dicey edition is reset on each appearance, and fresh woodcuts are provided. Standing outside this tradition is a brief précis, only some 2,000 words long, which was published in Newcastle c. 1820.

The various embodiments of the standard chapbook text are garnished with particular enticements to the reader. Changes are routinely made to the title-page, no doubt because this was the most visible element, which a travelling hawker would hold up to a throng of potential buyers. In the case of *Moll Flanders,* we find 'twelve times a Whore' evolving over time into 'seventeen times'. The periods which Moll endures in gaol are variously specified, with a tendency later on to end up lamely 'forty times in other prisons'. The frontispiece varies also: one printing has a four-line snatch of doggerel. Tailpieces and crude ornaments are occasionally used to diversify the presentation. But no great thought was ever put into altering the text. Misprints are sometimes corrected, sometimes carried over from one edition to another. And nothing is done to change the content of the story, which had become fossilized by the third quarter of the century. The style for the most part is just about literate, though a long way from elegant: the word 'personal' is misused for 'personable' and the compiler is no more scrupulous with regard to syntax than Defoe himself. On the whole, we may say that the standard chapbook version of the book does preserve the proportions of the novel in a rough way: the first half gives us marital escapades, the second criminal activity. Beyond that, there is little sense of a human existence – merely a rush of anecdotes, a moralizing conclusion and a trite epitaph. The chapbooks did not have the courage to reinvent the story along the lines of *Laetitia Atkins*. For the chapbook audience, a certain fidelity to the customary succession of events was perhaps necessary. Once a book had joined the company of the Seven Champions of Christendom, it had entered the realms of hagiography. One recalls that Borrow's old fruit-woman in *Lavengro* spoke of the tale of 'blessed Mary Flanders' – and hers, of course, would be likely to be an illicit version – perhaps that of Read.[15]

The final work to be considered is *Gulliver's Travels*. This does not belong to the world of the chapbook proper, but it did increasingly receive the attention of abridgers and editors. Two particularly noteworthy examples from the eighteenth century may be singled out. The first dates from 1727, only one year after Gulliver had come before the world. Two London booksellers were responsible for a shortened version which was published in two duodecimo volumes, generally found bound together. These men, J. Stone and R. King, were not exactly pillars of the book trade, but they were freed members of the Stationers' Company, with a certain amount of reputation to lose. Their decision to produce what was obviously a pirate edition in the guise of an abridgment has interesting implications for the legal and commercial side of publishing. Fortunately, they provided an elaborate justification for what they had done, and this enables us to get some idea of the issues at stake.

The rights in the work were held by Benjamin Motte, a shrewd, even sharp, member of the trade who had paid Swift the £200 he requested. According to John Gay, Motte had contrived to get rid of the whole of the first edition within a week;[16] and it would not be excessive if we were to estimate the total sales within a few months as numbering up to 10,000 copies. However, the pirates who were anxious to gain a foothold in this lucrative market had one possible line of attack: they could argue that Motte had kept the price artificially high. This is the basis of the claims made in the prefatory note by the publisher in the Stone/King edition. However, they concede that an objection may be made:

> It must be confessed, that Undertakings of this Nature are liable to Exceptions, and are frequently charg'd with depriving the Original of those Ornaments which recommend it to the Judicious; because many of them, through ill Management, have neither answered the Intention of the Author, or the Satisfaction of the Reader: But we hope this under Consideration, will answer the Ends of Both. It is true, that some Passages in the Original, which the Generality of Mankind have thought immodest and indecent, are entirely omitted, and many triviall Circumstances contracted into a very narrow Compass: But at the same Time, we may truly say, that Care hath been taken to make the History as uniform, and the Connection as just and smooth, as the Nature of the Performance would allow.

This unconvincing review of the aesthetics of abridgment is followed by a still more strained bout of argument, when the publishers turn to the efforts made by the proprietors of the original work to put a stop to the abridged edition, 'upon a wild Supposition it was the very Copy, and not an Abridgment'. In order to defend their right, they cite a number of titles where such activity has gone on unchallenged, notably the *Philosophical Transactions* [of the Royal Society], 'for 20 Years, *abridg'd* by Mr. *B. Motte*.'[17] Other titles cited are Locke's *Essay*, Camden's *Britannia*, the *State Trials*, Burnet's *History of His Own Time*, and '*Robinson Crusoe's Adventures*'. None of these, apart from the last, appears to have much relevance to the case in question: and after all Taylor had taken Cox to court over the matter. Whatever the legal position over abridgment of a literary work, it could hardly be adequately decided in terms of such imperfect analogies as *State Trials* or the *Philosophical Transactions*. Stone and King, in their anxiety to get one, over on Motte, have surely displayed the weakness of their position.

The volumes which follow are something of an anti-climax. At the outset, one observes the absence of the letter to Sympson and the message from the publishers to the reader, which contribute so much to the rhetoric of mystification surrounding the opening.[18] The entire text is steadily reduced line by line: as with *Robinson Crusoe*, abridgment takes the form of gradual attrition rather than wholesale excision. In the second chapter of Lilliput, Gulliver's phrase about 'the Necessities of Nature' is left out: but in the fifth chapter, perhaps for plot reasons, the voiding of wine is retained. In Brobdingnag, the abridger likewise leaves in the potentially offensive section on the maids of honour in chapter 5. There is some minor bowdlerization in chapter 8 of the voyage to Houyhnhnmland, but excrement still gets thrown around in this book. One is forced to the conclusion that the point of mentioning 'immodest' material in the preface is to remind readers of its existence, in the hope they may buy the book. Very little by way of genuine censorship is apparent in this abridgment. It simply leaves out a lot of small details, and impoverishes the text not by radical surgery so much as by steady dimunition of local point and wit.

In the nineteenth century, immodesty was excised more brutally. The commonest means, of course, was simply to exclude whole chunks of the text, starting with the last voyage. The earliest attempt I have seen to produce a universally acceptable *Gulliver* was that of Francis Newbery, son and successor to John, in 1776. His sixpenny compilation consists of 128 tiny pages, and includes some pleasant engravings to scale. The frontispiece, showing a young lady in dress of the period, has no discernible relevance to *Gulliver* – but that is by the way. One of the illustrations shows Gulliver tied up by the Lilliputians, a motif almost as central to the imaginative trajectory of this work as the wreck is to *Crusoe*.

The most notable feature of this children's version is the decision to put the story into the third person. Only the first two voyages are present, and they are censored with some discretion. The maids of honour are toned down, but Gulliver puts out the fire in his accustomed manner, and the sillier manifestations of bowdlerization are avoided. For some reason, though, Gulliver's amusingly disordered behaviour on his return from Brobdingnag is suppressed almost to nothing.

It was another century before the heyday of censorship, with *Gulliver's Travels* 'revised for family reading' (a representative title from 1873). By that date, the work had become a classic in every sense, and in every corner of our culture. Henry J. Byron produced his 'comic operatic spectacular extravaganza, in five acts and twelve tableaux' at the Gaiety Theatre, London, c. 1880. The action moves from Plymouth to Lilliput, Brobdingnag and then (accountably) the Palace of Comic Song. The Flying Island is followed by an allegorical tableau of the Golden Age. Characters include King Teenyweeny and Queen Petsywetsy. It has certain links with the pantomime versions of *Crusoe* then becoming popular. Gulliver is a *travestie* rôle. In that respect there is a difference from W. M. Ackhurst's *Gulliver on his Travels*, presented at Sanger's National Amphitheatre in 1876, where Crusoe is played by a girl but Gulliver, straying into the same action, is a male rôle. One might add that the same era witnessed the performance of Offenbach's opera (1876) in which the curtain opens to disclose Sir William Crusoe telling the story of the Prodigal Son to his assembled womenfolk – Robinson, as usual, is late.

Such extreme perversions were a thing of the future when the chapbook still dominated popular reading. What this brief survey shows is that popularization could take many forms, and abridgment could be undertaken for a variety of motives. At its crudest, popular adaptation involved formulaic and hasty writing, the mere degutting of a text. At its best, sustained paraphrase could be employed to reproduce a work in simplified but not distorted terms. For a long time, bowdlerization was rather a threat, or a dishonest publisher's claim, than a reality. Only a very few books proved equal to the dual function of literary classic and popular favourite. Leaving aside *The Pilgrim's Progress*, whose appeal was primarily that of a devotional work, we are left with two or three works which regularly survive adaptation: and of these it is *Robinson Crusoe* whose elemental design and stark outlines best fit it to bridge a yawning gap in public taste.[19]

NOTES

1. V. E. Neuburg, *Chapbooks: A Guide to Reference Material on English, Scottish and American Chapbook Literature of the Eighteenth and Nineteenth Centuries* (2nd edn, 1972), 5–6. Neuburg has supplied the only serious modern treatment of the subject that takes proper account of the eighteenth century. See also his *Popular Education in Eighteenth Century England* (1971), esp. chapter 5, 'Chapbooks: origins and distribution', 115–25; and *The Penny Histories: A Study of Chapbooks for Young Readers over Two Centuries* (1968).

2. F. A. Pottle (ed.), *Boswell's London Journal 1762–1763* (1950), 299.

3. Quoted by R. D. Altick, *The Shows of London* (Cambridge, Mass., 1978), 17.

4. For early editions and abridgments, see P. Rogers, *Robinson Crusoe* (1979), 4–10.

5. *The Life and Most Surprizing Adventures of Robinson Crusoe* (2nd edn, 1724), sig. A3r; *The Life and Most Surprizing Adventures of Robinson Crusoe* (5th edn, n.d.), sig. A2v.

6. *The Life and Strange Surprizing Adventures of Robinson Crusoe* (1719), 181–2.

7. *The Life of Robinson Crusoe* (Stirling, 1801), 15–16: compare *The Surprising Life, and Most Strange Adventures of Robinson Crusoe* (n.d.) 24.

8. *The Life and Strange Surprizing Adventures of Robinson Crusoe* (1719), 7; *The Life and Surprising Adventures of Robinson Crusoe* (Wellington and Ironbridge, n.d.), 7.

9. *The Life and Most Surprising Adventures of Robinson Crusoe* (9th edn, Birmingham, n.d.), 3.

10. *The Life and Most Surprising Adventures of Robinson Crusoe* (Dublin, 1799), 5–6.

11. *The Life and Adventures of Robinson Crusoe* (1813), iii.

12. *The Wonderful Adventures of Robinson Crusoe* (Edinburgh, n.d.), 3.

13. I deal with the case of *Moll Flanders* more fully in a separate essay, 'Moll in the chapbooks'.

14. Useful information is supplied by V. Neuburg in his article, 'The Diceys and the chapbook trade,' *The Library*, 5th ser., XXIV (1969), 219–31; see also

his *Chapbooks*, 48–9, and *Popular Education*, 159–60.

15. George Borrow, *Lavengro* (1930), 190
16. *The Correspondence of Jonathan Swift*, ed. H. Williams (1963–5), III, 182.
17. *Travels into Several Remote Nations of the World, by Capt. Lemuel Gulliver* (1727), sigs. A2r-A3r.
18. See A. Ross, *Swift: Gulliver's Travels*

(1968), 19.

19. Since this essay was submitted, I have learnt of the existence of a German monograph dealing with abridged editions of *Crusoe*: namely E. Dahl, *Die Kürzungen des 'Robinson Crusoe' in England zwischen 1719 und 1819* (Frankfurt, 1977). Unfortunately I have so far been unable to locate a copy of this work.

3

Politicians, peers, and publication by subscription 1700-50

W. A. SPECK

Mr Thos. Carte writ to me one day last week to desire I would pay the first year's subscription to his intended History of England. It was about 6 years ago that he desired me to be a subscriber, and with much importunity he obtained of me to set down my name in his roll, but I would not write the sum, telling him I would advise with myself about it, and I persisted in it, when to magnify the expectation the world had of his book, he told me that the late Bishop of Worcester promised twenty pound a year till it was finished, by which I found that Mr Carte expected the like from me. He is a determined Jacobite and fled twice from justice for being concerned in rebellious practices, but by the lenity of the Government he was allowed to return home without prosecution: wherefore, there is reason to believe that his history will be wrote to support the doctrine of indefeasible hereditary right, in order to serve the Pretender. This day, I wrote to him, that so many years had past since he first proposed a subscription, that neither my health nor the years of my age permitted me to hope to live till his book came out, and therefore desired to be excused from subscribing.

The Diary of the first Earl of Egmont, 18 January 1746[1]

I. SUBSCRIPTION LISTS

Quantitative evidence about the book trade in the eighteenth century is notoriously hard to come by. Such questions as how many were printed, how many were sold, and above all who read them, can usually be answered only at a low level of information and a correspondingly high one of intuition. Yet there is one source which provides hard facts, at least about a solid core of purchasers; the lists of subscribers which appear in books published by subscription.

Although the first such list appeared as early as 1617, the method of publishing with the aid of subscribers only became widespread in the eighteenth century. It is generally regarded as a half-way house between dependance on a single patron to underwrite a book and reliance upon sales. A succinct summary of the procedure is given by Sarah L. Clapp: 'the word "subscription" itself when referring to publication signifies an agreement between an author or a bookseller on the one hand and a number of individuals on the other; the author or the bookseller agrees to produce a book of specified content, size and quality, whose publication is financed by the individuals, or subscribers, each of whom receives in return a copy or copies of the book.'[2]

If a writer was well connected the search for subscribers could be fairly straightforward. Alexander Pope's influential friends saw to it that he had no lack of takers for his translation of Homer. It became so fashionable to subscribe to the *Iliad* that 653 copies were bespoken before its publication in 1715. At six guineas a set this was so profitable to the poet that it prompted him to bring out the *Odyssey* ten years later, when 847 copies were underwritten in advance. The whole venture is supposed to have earned Pope the huge sum of £9,000. A more modest enterprise was Joseph Trapp's translation of the *Aeneid,* though as first Professor of Poetry at Oxford he managed to tap the dons of that university, who constituted no fewer than 222 of his 517 English subscribers. Indeed three Oxford colleges, Christ Church, Magdalen and Wadham, account for as many as one-sixth of the total number.[3]

Less fortunately placed authors, however, could find it hard to drum up support for their works. Joseph Morgan, who wrote a two-volume *Complete History of Algiers* (1728, 1729), complained bitterly of the difficulties he had encountered. The first contains an 'Essay upon the comi-tragical history of subscription hunting', in which Morgan explained how he was 'one dwindled to accost, cap in hand, under the scandalous pitiful and contemptible character of subscription hunter. An abject vocation.' He recounted how some of those he approached responded, 'what care we whether there is any such rascally place as Algiers existing upon God's earth?' Morgan, who was asking three half crowns for a first instalment, exclaimed, 'they would not give half of three half crowns for the whole Ottoman dominions.' Although he protested that 'before I would think of again undergoing such fatigue, such scurvy base treatment in hawking about with any work of mine, I here avow, that I would sooner choose to be a hackney horse', he did solicit subscriptions for the second volume. Yet he found the work no more rewarding, and when the book appeared it contained an open letter to one of his first subscribers, which alleged that 'in my almost fruitless trampoosings in search of proper helps and encouragement, I traversed more ground than from hence to Japan; acting all the while very much the part of a common strumpet, or rather of the Devil, roaming about to seek whom I could devour'. In these excursions he came across 'folks who swear desperately they never ran over ten leaves of any sort of History throughout the whole course of their lives . . . what sholes are there not daily to be seen about Cornhill and parts adjacent who scruple not to attest that they seldom or never read a word of anything but letters and newspapers . . . among this last class of thriving men nothing in nature would set afloat this book of mine but a war with the Algerines.'[4]

If authors could find touting for subscriptions wearisome, on the other side of the same coin some of the more obvious targets for their solicitation could be plagued by writers begging money from them. As Mr Wilson explained to Parson Adams in Fielding's *Joseph Andrews:*

> the profit which booksellers allowed authors for the best works was so very small, that certain men of birth and fortune some years ago, who were the patrons of wit and learning, thought fit to encourage them farther, by entring into voluntary subscriptions for their encouragement. Thus Prior, Rowe, Pope and some other men of genius, received large sums for their labours from the public. This seemed so easy a method of getting money, that many of the lowest scriblers of the times ventured to publish their works in the same way; and many had the assurance to take in subscriptions for what was not writ, nor ever intended.[5]

Morgan admitted that one lord he asked offered to sell him subscription receipts, which cost him £60, for 60 pence, so sure was he that the works would never materialize.[6] Some subscribers who had been dunned in this way found a method of avoiding the importuning of alleged authors, which Mr Wilson described thus:

> Subscriptions in this manner growing infinite, and a kind of tax on the public; some persons finding it not so easy a task to discern good from bad authors, or to know what genius was worthy encouragement and what was not, to prevent the expence of subscribing to so many, invented a method to excuse themselves from all subscriptions whatever; and this was to receive a small sum of money in consideration of giving a large one if ever they subscribed; which many have done, and many more have pretended to have done, in order to silence all sollicitation.

When a would-be author approached somebody who had pledged himself thus to subscribe to another writer's work, he would be told that the person whose subscription he solicited was 'tied up'.

Though the vast majority of subscribers undertook to purchase only one copy of a work in advance, some paid for multiple copies. Most of these ran to only two copies, though some pre-empted several, while a few ordered over a hundred. Other ways of subsidizing publication included a special subscription for the printing of one's coat of arms in a book, or an extra sum of money for the purchase of a more sumptuous edition of a work, such as one printed on better quality paper. Subscribers' names were usually listed in the prefatory materials in a rough alphabetical order, with indications of the number of copies or the superior printing ordered. For example, Archbishop Tenison ordered two royal paper copies of John Strype's *History of the Life and Acts of . . . Edmund Grindal*, published in 1710, and heads the list of subscribers under the letter C thus: 'His Grace Thomas Archbishop of Canterbury, 2 books R.P.' Morgan, the unfortunate historian of Algiers, went so far as to indicate with a star the 113 of his 266 subscribers who had actually paid him in advance of the publication of his first volume. 'Such as I have retained, tho they have not my receipts', he wrote optimistically, 'are, I have reason to believe, persons of honour and worth, who design to have their books.' Yet when the second volume appeared with a list of those who had paid for the first attached, very few of those starred in the previous list appear to have paid up. He even exposed one nonpayer, printing against the name of Mr John Southall 'bit us of a book'.[7]

There were over 2,000 subscription lists published during the eighteenth century, containing in all something like a million names. In the past these have been relatively neglected as a historical source. Following the labours of the members of the Project for Historical Biobibliography at the University of Newcastle upon Tyne, who are acquiring copies of every known subscription list and analysing them by computer, this neglect can no longer be justified. Given the dual nature of the evidence, with information about both books and subscribers, it is possible to establish almost any number of associations between them. They do, however, pose certain methodological problems which should caution us against basing broad generalizations upon this evidence. Certainly it would be hazardous to draw conclusions from them about the book trade as a whole. Only a tiny percentage of books published in the eighteenth century were brought out by subscription, and these tended to be fairly expensive productions, confined to the more affluent members of society. We are dealing, therefore, with a small corner of the trade. Deducing the literary interests of the subscribers from the contents of books which bear their names is also dubious. All kinds of pressures could lead a man to advance money for a publication besides its intrinsic merits. The ties of a political party, of a university college, of a profession, or even of simple friendship, might well overcome a complete lack of interest in the subject matter of a book acquired in this way. As Colonel James exclaims in Fielding's *Amelia*, 'Heaven forbid I should be obliged to read half the nonsense I have subscribed to!'[8]

Nevertheless, even though a given name on a list can be suspected of having one of a number of reasons for being there, besides a genuine interest in the contents of the work it precedes, the cumulative patterns created by many subscribers to several books can be regarded as significant. Few if any would subscribe to a work they disliked; most would feel some sympathy for the views expressed by the author. On this basis it seems safe to suggest that one can use subscription lists to find out something about the readership for a certain type of book in the eighteenth century.

There are various ways of analysing this evidence. One is to take an individual title and examine the social status or religious affiliations of its subscribers. Professor Pat Rogers did this with Trapp's *Aeneid* and John Oldmixon's *History of England during the Reigns of the Royal House of Stuart* and showed startlingly that they appealed to entirely different sets of people. Not one name was common to both. Whereas Trapp, as we have seen, drew heavily on his Oxford contacts, Oldmixon got more support from London; Trapp's subscribers were mainly Tories, Oldmixon's Whig; the Professor of Poetry was patronized by several Anglican clergymen, the historian by a significant number of dissenters.[9] Another method is to classify books into genres, such as 'scientific' and 'religious', and to analyse their subscription patterns. The PHIBB project has tentatively essayed this method and suggested some differences in the readerships of various genres.[10]

I have adopted a different approach. Instead of starting with titles I began by isolating two groups of people, and then examined the patterns that their subscriptions established. The first group consisted of 469 members of parliament who sat in the Commons in 1733. The second was the peerage. This enabled me to estimate whether or not people of different political persuasions or social backgrounds differed significantly in the choice of books that they purchased by subscription.

2. SUBSCRIPTIONS AND POLITICS

The group of M.P.s chosen were those who voted for and against the Excise bill in 1733.[11] This was the most controversial issue to divide the Commons during the ministry of Sir Robert Walpole. His scheme to change customs duties on tobacco and wine into inland excises by means of bonded warehouses ran unexpectedly into trouble from the opposition, which claimed that it would be an intolerable extension of the government's power. Although the bill was not actually defeated in the House, the resistance to it both there and in the country was felt to be too formidable to carry it through, so the prime minister withdrew it. Lists were published of those for and against the measure, naming 265 who were in favour and 204 who were opposed to it. The opposition consisted of all the Tories in the House, 106 of whom were named in the lists, and a body of dissident Whigs who were at odds with Walpole's Whig administration, 98 being listed.[12] By thus identifying 265 Whigs who supported the government, 98 who opposed it, and 106 Tories, the division lists provide an excellent opportunity to test whether or not these distinctions are discernible in their subscriptions to books as well as in the way they voted. The Excise division was exceptional, for many Whigs who normally supported the ministry were persuaded to oppose it, on this issue at least. At the same time they reinforced a body of Whigs, led by William Pulteney, which had been opposed to Walpole for some years. Moreover a significant number were to remain in opposition for the rest of the 1730s. By checking the subscriptions of the dissident Whigs over 20 years before the division it might be possible to detect whether the split in Whig ranks came out of the blue or was prefigured by ideological differences before the Excise crisis.

Politicians were a prime target for authors seeking subscriptions, and of these 469 members of parliament only ten appear to have successfully resisted their solicitations. Although some only subscribed to one or two books, the names of many occur in a dozen or more lists, while a prominent politician like Sir Robert Walpole features on no fewer than 64, thus modifying the reputation of being indifferent to literature which the prime minister acquired from writers he chose not to patronize. There was also a great variety in the nature as well as in the number of books they purchased. To some extent this was an inevitable consequence of the passage of time, given the age distribution of the members, the eldest of whom were subscribing to publications before the youngest were born. This 'temporal drift', as PHIBB has termed it, can be offset by statistical techniques,[13] but this was not attempted here, since even the pattern of subscriptions by politicians who might have been expected to overlap significantly in fact proved to be very disparate. For example, ten Tory M.P.s whose careers spanned the entire period 1710 to 1740 subscribed to very different combinations of titles. Their willingness to subscribe itself varied from William Shippen's six subscriptions in those 30 years to Sir Thomas Sebright's 76. Something of the range of their interests can be discerned from the fact that their names appear in the subscription lists to no fewer than 147 books, while not a single title is common to all ten. Indeed the names of all 469 M.P.s are spread rather thinly over the 500 or so subscription lists which appeared between 1710 and 1740. Only 14 titles were common to ten per cent or more of the whole group.

Generalizations from such limited evidence must be made with caution. It seems unwise to seek statistical associations from subscription lists in which fewer than 5 per cent (i.e. 23 or fewer) of the whole group of M.P.s are named. This rules out 29 books where the distribution of names from the 469 M.P.s varied significantly from the proportions of the three political groups into which they can be divided in 1733. A distribution of 56.5 per cent government Whigs, 22.6 per cent Tories and 20.9 per cent opposition Whigs on any subscription list would correspond exactly to the ratios recorded in the Excise division. If a list contained a significant disproportion of government and opposition Whigs it could indicate a book which appealed more to the Whigs than to the Tories. Similarly if it was more inclined towards the Tories than to the other two groups it could be seen as a Tory list. One attracting relatively more supporters than opponents of the Excise scheme could be regarded as a government list, while the contrary ratio might indicate an opposition list. On this basis the 29 subscription lists which contained fewer than 5 per cent of the whole group of 469 M.P.s and which indicated a bias break down into 14 Whig lists, 8 Tory, 5 government, one opposition and one from a combination of Tories and government Whigs.[14]

Despite the statistical doubts induced by the low numbers of subscribers in cases where fewer than two dozen of our M.P.s appear on the subscription lists, some of these associations nevertheless reflect political preferences. Among the Whig lists, for instance, there are several which patently would appeal more to that party than to the Tories. The author of *The Works of the Reverend Samuel Johnson* (published in 1710) had been a leading Commonwealth Whig in the 1690s, along with John Wildman, whose *Life* was prefixed to the volume. Although the subscription list included 'a galaxy of radical families', however, of the 469 M.P.s only ten had subscribed to it.[15] John Strype's *History of the Life and Acts of the Most Reverend Father in God Edmund Grindal* was specifically commissioned by Whigs in 1710 in order to counter the High Church sympathies aroused by the trial of Dr Sacheverell. As William Cole, who noted that no fewer than 34 Whig M.P.s in parliament at the time subscribed to it, observed, 'Mr. Strype no doubt thought the time opportune to publish this false brother's life, which he knew, one way or other, would turn to his advantage. Accordingly the whigs took it well, tho' those who wished well to the interest of the Church of England began to suspect him.' Among the latter were the Fellows of Pembroke Hall, Cambridge. As Thomas Baker warned Strype, 'unless you can make him High Church (which you do not intend) he will be less welcome at that College', even though it had been Grindal's own.[16] John Milton's *Poetical Works* came out under the whiggish auspices of the house of Tonson in 1720. Both the poet and the publisher were regarded as disciples of the Good Old Cause and as such were anathema to Tories, who are under-represented in the subscription list organized by Thomas Tickell for this edition. Tonson also published John Windus, *A Journey to Mequinez* (1725), which was dedicated to Lord Berkeley, the first Lord of the Admiralty, and contained plates inscribed for such Whig politicians as the Duke of Argyll, Viscount Cobham and William Pulteney.[17] John Old-mixon's *History of England* (1729) attracted the subscriptions of some 20 who 'entered parliament at one time or another', all of whom were Whigs, including 13 who voted in the Excise division, eight for and five against the scheme.[18] Joseph Morgan's *History of Algiers* (1728) presumably contains a preponderance of Whig subscribers because he began his somewhat fruitless hunt for subscriptions with the Lords of the Admiralty, while the commissioners of trade and plantations headed the list prefixed to his second volume. By the reign of George II all such officeholders were Whigs. So were knights of the newly created Order of the Bath, which would account for the apparent lack of Tory interest in John Pine, *The Procession and Ceremonies . . . of the Installation of . . . Knights . . . of the Bath* (1730).

The works of the nonjurors Jeremy Collier and Thomas Hearne and the prominent highchurchman George Smalridge all appear on the 'Tory' side, which does not defy expectation. On the contrary, it would have been hard to explain if Whigs had subscribed in any numbers to their books, Richard Fiddes's *Life of Cardinal Wolsey* (1724) became so caught up in party political debate that it is surprising how many Whigs were among its subscribers. Fiddes had been befriended by Jonathan Swift in Anne's reign, having obtained the chaplaincy of Hull garrison by the Dean's intercession. Swift also presumably helped him to become the Earl of Oxford's chaplain. In the preface to his work on Wolsey Fiddes thanked Bishop Atterbury for assisting him in its preparation. These connections with Tories in high places might have dissuaded Whigs from offering their assistance too, in the form of subscriptions, quite apart from the fact that when the biography appeared the author was attacked as a papist, because he took a favourable view of his subject. William Stephens' *Sermons* (1737) drew on the author's local contacts as well as his Tory associates. Stephens is described on the title page as 'sometime Fellow of Exeter College, Oxford, and late vicar of St. Andrews, Plymouth', and it is significant that most of the Tory M.P.s who subscribed to it were connected with Oxford or Devon, while of the three government Whig subscribers, one, John Harris, was member for Okehampton and another, Norton Poulet, had been educated at Exeter College.

The predominance of government supporters among the M.P.s who subscribed to Allan Ramsay's *Poems*, which appeared in two volumes in 1721 and 1728, was because the poems appealed predominantly to Scots, who tended to vote with the ministers when occupying seats in parliament. No similar explanation suggests itself for the singular fact that no Tories or opposition Whigs appear to have subscribed to John Ayliffe's *Parergon juris canonici Anglicani* (1726). His failure to attract Tory subscribers is not surprising, since he was a staunch Whig who had been deprived of his degrees at Oxford for imprudently publishing his views of the University's lack of loyalty to the Revolution Settlement. That opposition Whigs were not forthcoming is, however, curious. There does not appear to have been anything in the work which would be especially unacceptable to them, it being, as the subtitle explained, 'a commentary by way of supplement to the canons and constitutions of the Church of England'. It could be that works of a religious nature were less appealing to them than to the other groups of politicians, for some of them had a reputation for being downright anticlerical. This might also explain their apparent lack of interest in Claude

Fleury's *Ecclesiastical History* (1727) and their failure to subscribe to any of the collections of sermons which attracted subscriptions from their parliamentary colleagues in these years. On the other hand the relative absence of their names from lists with fewer than 5 per cent of all 469 M.P.s in them could simply be fortuitous. Certainly it is difficult to offer any other explanation for the distribution of the remaining titles in this category among the different groups of Members in 1733.

There is more point in analysing the connection between the politics of subscribers and the nature of the works they patronized in the case of lists containing the names of between 5 and 10 per cent of the M.P.s who voted in the Excise crisis. These break down into 11 'Whig' lists, four 'Tory', four 'Government', four 'Tories and government Whigs', and one 'opposition'.[19]

The first Whig list was for Steele's *The Lucubrations of Isaac Bickerstaff* (1710). One of the foremost Whig writers of the age clearly appealed overwhelmingly to his own political kind. So, too, did Nicholas Rowe, whose *Pharsalia* (1718) obtained subscriptions from 26 M.P.s, who later voted for and against the Excise bill, not one of them a Tory. Although the playwright had been a friend of Pope, almost all his other literary associates were Whigs, including Addison, and Halifax to whom he dedicated *The Royal Convert*. He was in fact a 'forthright Whig', whose major play, *Tamerlane*, was virtually banned by the Tory government in the last four years of Anne's reign. After the accession of George I Rowe received his reward, being appointed poet laureate.[20] Giovanni Bononcini's *Cantate e Duetti* (1721) received a disproportionate number of Whig subscribers presumably because he stayed in England as the guest of the Duke of Marlborough, the Earl of Sunderland and other Whig peers. So close was he to the Marlboroughs that he wrote the duke's funeral anthem in 1722. The alleged preference of the Court for Handel is not reflected in the subscription to the work, which was after all dedicated to the king. Charles King's *The British Merchant* (1721) was an edition of *The British Merchant or Commerce Preserved*, a news-sheet originally published between August 1713 and July 1714 to present the Whig case against the then Tory government's policy of attempting to remove barriers to trade with France. In the past it has been cited as having been instrumental in the defeat of the treaty of commerce with France which the ministry had negotiated in 1713, but, as Professor D. C. Coleman has pointed out, it began publication after the bill to make the treaty effectual had been defeated in the House of Commons by a combination of Whigs and 'Whimsical' Tories. Professor Coleman has also demonstrated that it did not enunciate 'mercantilist' doctrines about the need to preserve an overall balance of trade so much as attack Anglo/French commerce for being detrimental to the British economy.[21] But it was its political provenance rather than its economic arguments which led to the lack of Tory interest in its republication. John Breval, whose *Remarks on Several Parts of Europe* (1726) attracted more support from Whigs than Tories, was a notorious roué who had been deprived of his Fellowship at Trinity College, Cambridge for an affair with a married woman which culminated in his assaulting her husband. He also incurred the enmity of Pope, and is preserved in the amber of the *Dunciad*. These personal drawbacks rather than any Tory xenophobia might explain why his work did not appeal to Tories. Although James Thomson received a sum of money from Sir Robert Walpole for his poem 'To the Memory of Sir Isaac Newton', this did not prevent a significant number of opposition Whigs from subscribing to the 1730 edition of his most celebrated poem, *The Seasons*. Not long afterwards Thomson was to go over to their ranks, and it could be that as early as 1730 he was already in transit from government to opposition, though he clearly did not appeal to Tories then. Two Whig historians drew on their political fellow travellers for subscriptions to their work during the 1730s, Christian Cole for his *Historical and Political Memoirs* (1735) and William Maitland for his *History of London* (1739).

Chronologically the first 'Tory' list to contain between 5 and 10 per cent of the names of the M.P.s in the Excise division was Alexander Pope's *Iliad* (1715). The bias was not overwhelming, with as many government supporters subscribing to it as Tories, but since there were well over twice as many of the former in the Excise division list, the latter were over-represented enough to be statistically significant.[22] The next title, Joseph Trapp's *Aeneid of Virgil* (1718), is less equivocally Tory, and as Professor Rogers noted, 'a "subjective" analysis of the Trapp list would probably pick out the strong . . . Tory colouring it wears'.[23] John Barwick, whose *Life*, written by his brother and published posthumously in 1721, also atracted mainly Tory subscribers, had been an eminent royalist in the Civil War, receiving his reward at the Restoration with the deanery of Durham. His brother's biography was edited by Hilkiah Bedford, a prominent nonjuror who had been arrested in 1713 charged with the authorship of *The Hereditary Right of the Crown of England Asserted*. With this pedigree it is surprising that the Latin life received any Whig subscriptions at all. Francis Drake, the author of *Eboracum: or the History . . . of York* (1736) was 'a sturdy Jacobite', who 'could not always disguise his opinions even in the sober pages of his history'.[24] This presumably accounts for the over-representation of Tory M.P.s in his subscription list. It is also significant that of the 11 Whigs who subscribed to it, five represented Yorkshire constituencies, one was a Yorkshireman, while two came from County Durham.

Joseph Mitchell, whose *Poems on Several Occasions* (1729) appealed above all to government Whigs, was one of the few poets actually patronized by the prime minister. Indeed so rare was the distinction that he was known as 'Sir Robert Walpole's poet'. The second of his two volumes was dedicated to Walpole 'as a lasting monument of esteem, gratitude and submission'. A specimen of Mitchell's verse indicates why the opposition to Walpole accused the prime minister of having no discernment for literary talent. Appropriately it is called *The Subscription*.

> Walpole, oracle of sense!
> Prodigy of Eloquence
> Guarantee of Public Credit
> And the very man who made it!
> Best of ministers and friends
> See, O see, your poet bends –
> MITCHELL makes another leg.
> And has something new to beg
> Lo! to curry your Excuse
> In his hand he brings the Muse
> Not for place or pension praying
> Nor his worth and parts displaying
> But most humbly representing
> That his works are now a printing
> Volumes two! Octavo size!
> Royal paper! Guinea price!
> One to Stair and one address'd
> To yourself, his patrons blest!
> Patrons both of noble names!
> MITCHELL's ever sacred themes!
> And whereas he has not yet
> Got the riches he's to get;
> Nor can well defray this charge
> Without a subscription large;
> May it therefore please your Honour,
> (Once a year to him a donor)
> To accept and to dispose
> Ten times ten receipts in prose.[25]

While the reluctance of opposition Whigs as well as Tories to subscribe to Mitchell's poems requires little explanation, it is not so obvious why both were also under-represented on the subscription lists to two works by Samuel Buckley, *A Third Letter to Dr. Mead Concerning a New Edition of Thuanus's History* (1730) and the seven-volume *Thuani historiarum sui temporis* (1733), or in the list accompanying James Anderson's *Royal Genealogies* (1732). These were whiggish works, which would put Tories off. Anderson in particular would not appeal to them, since he was a presbyterian and, possibly worse in some eyes, a freemason. Jacobite Tories would not appreciate his approach to the subject of royal genealogy, since he positively dwelt on the occasions when the hereditary principle had been breached. The book was dedicated to the Prince of Wales, to whose family it was claimed, 'that we of these nations owe our deliverance from all we dreaded, and the enjoyment of all we wish, under the just and benign Government of your Royal father and grandfather'. Even Hanoverian

57

Tories would object to his interpretation of recent English history. Although in the preface he claimed to have 'avoided all terms and expressions that may give offence to any party or person', his potted histories of the later Stuarts gave their reigns a very whig interpretation. When describing Anne's, for example, he observed that by 1707 she 'reigned glorious both at home and abroad', but after Sacheverell's trial things went awry. Notwithstanding his claim to deal 'only with facts and plain truth', these were not facts or truths which Tories found palatable.[26]

The combination of opposition Whigs and Tories on the list accompanying Henry Brooke's *Gustavus Vasa* (1739) is evidence of a concerted effort of opposition politicians against Walpole's ministry. Since the two 'government' Whigs who appear on it, Richard Eliot and Anthony Lowther, had both gone over to the opposition since the Excise crisis, there were in effect no supporters of Walpole's ministry at all among Brooke's subscribers. His play had been one of the first banned by the Lord Chamberlain under the Licensing Act of 1737.

In his prefatory dedication to the subscribers Brooke asserted that 'Patriotism, or love of Country, is the great and single moral which I had in view thro' this play. This Love (so superior in its nature to all other interests and affections) is personated in the character of Gustavus.' It was intended in fact to be opposition propaganda, as the Prologue made even clearer.

> Britons! this night presents a State distress'd,
> Tho' brave, yet vanquished; and tho' great, oppress'd;
> Vice, rav'ning Vulture, on her Vitals prey'd,
> Her Peers, her Prelates, fell corruption sway'd . . .
> Truth, Justice, Honour fled th'infected shore,
> For Freedom, sacred Freedom was no more.
> Then, greatly rising in his Country's right,
> Her Hero, her Deliverer sprung to Light;
> A race of hardy, Northern sons he led,
> Guiltless of Courts, untainted and unread . . .

Just in case his readers might think he was merely discussing the history of Sweden Brooke drove home his message with the lines, 'Such, such of old, the first born Natives were, /Who breath'd the vertues of Britannia's air.' The text in fact geared Swedish history to the contemporary situation in England, a way of drawing parallels with the past which had become a Country cliché. Thus Gustavus Vasa saves Sweden and Swedish liberties from the tyranny of the conqueror Cristiern and his prime minister Trollio, 'Who taught the Throne of Pow'r to fix on Fear; /And raise its safety, from the publick Ruin.'[27] If Brooke thought he could get these thinly disguised opposition stereotypes of George II and Walpole past the Lord Chamberlain he must have been very naive. More likely it was deliberately intended to provoke censorship on the stage, in order to be published by subscription. For, as Bertrand Goldgar has observed, 'to subscribe became a gesture of allegiance to those in opposition to the government'.[28]

Whereas the over-representation of Tories and opposition Whigs on subscription lists can be explained as documenting a concerted effort on the part of Walpole's opponents, it is difficult to know what, if anything, to make of the four which indicate a preponderance of Tories and government Whigs among the subscribers from the 469 M.P.s on the division list. Only one of them, John Stevens' *History of Ancient Abbeys and Collegiate Churches* (1722), was of a 'religious' nature, and therefore, as suggested above, possibly less likely to appeal to an opposition Whig mentality. The others are so heterogeneous that it seems safest to conclude, when fewer than 10 per cent of the M.P.s subscribed to lists, that analyses of them can still turn up statistical anomalies with no real association between titles and political affiliations.

Once the subscription lists overlap with the division list by over 10 per cent such anomalies disappear. At this level there are six 'Whig' lists, one 'Tory', two 'government', one 'opposition' and none with an inexplicable bias towards an alliance of government Whigs and Tories.[29]

Joseph Addison's *Works* (1721), edited by Thomas Tickell and published by Jacob Tonson junior, received the most marked Whig support of any title between 1710 and 1740. Eighty-three of the 469 M.P.s in our group subscribed to it, only five of them being Tories. Although less impressively slanted towards the Whigs, the two volumes of Bishop Burnet's *History of His Own Time* (1724, 1734) were also prefaced by preponderantly Whig lists. There is no need to explain why the Whig Secretary of State and the Whig Bishop of Salisbury appealed, even posthumously, to their fellow partisans. Addison had been identified as a champion of Whig principles at least since the publication of his highly political play *Cato* (1713), while Burnet was regarded as the archetype of the low church bishops whose latitudinarianism had earned the bitter enmity of the High Church Tories. Ariosti's *Alla Maesta di Georgio Re* (1728), Voltaire's *La Henriade* (1728) and William Wekett's *Regni Angliae . . . Reginae Elizabethae* (1729), on the other hand, are less obvious candidates for a Whig constituency. The fact that Ariosti dedicated his six cantatas to the king was enough to put Tories off, though their xenophobia might also have played a part in deterring Tory subscriptions. It could have been partly responsible, too, for their failure to support the definitive edition of Voltaire's epic poem on the martial exploits of Henry IV, even though he was intimate with Bolingbroke and Pope during his English exile. At the same time the London edition of the *Henriade* came out primarily under Whig auspices. It was dedicated to Queen Caroline, the dedication advertising the poem as one which contained 'Bold impartial truths, morality unstained with superstition, a spirit of Liberty, equally abhorrent of rebellion and of tyranny, the rights of kings asserted, and those of mankind never laid aside'. William Wekett was actually the editor of *Regni Angliae sub imperio serenissimae piae et Potetatissimae Reginae Elizabethae*, which had originally been written by Richard Cosin, in Elizabeth's reign, and corrected by John Cosin, the Laudian bishop of Durham in the seventeenth century. Such a pedigree seems more appropriate for a Tory than a Whig title, though the work was very anti-catholic. Wekett, however, was a protégé of the Whig Bishop of Durham, who according to one disgruntled Tory ordained him 'priest and deacon, in three days time, tho' never admitted a member of any University . . . the flagrancy of the fact, of his life and conversation, being matters only fit to come under consideration of a Convocation'.[30] Wekett also dedicated his edition of the text to George II, sycophantically praising the king for having firmly established religion, liberty and the laws rather than the superstition and tyranny of Catholicism which had once threatened Britain.

The 'Tory' list accompanied Matthew Prior's *Poems on Several Occasions* (1718). Prior had been employed as a diplomat by the Tory government in 1711, visiting France to expedite the negotiations that were to culminate in the Treaty of Utrecht, which the Whigs execrated as a betrayal of Britain's allies. Whig poets therefore vilified Prior's embassy, one such poem being called 'Mat's Peace'.[31] In view of this it is noteworthy how many Whigs were prepared to subscribe to his *Poems*, his subscription list containing almost as many M.P.s who voted for the Excise scheme as Tories who opposed it.

The two 'government' lists accompanied Henry Pemberton's *View of Sir Isaac Newton's Philosophy* (1728) and Stephen Duck's *Poems on Several Occasions* (1736). Pemberton had worked closely with Newton in the scientist's last years, and supervised the publication of the third edition of the Principia. Tories were unsympathetic towards Newton, as much for his Whiggism as for his physics, but the only clue to the lack of interest in Pemberton's work on the part of opposition Whigs is the fact that he dedicated it to Sir Robert Walpole. There are no difficulties, however, in accounting for the under-representation of both Tories and opposition Whigs in Duck's list. This was emphatically a government production. Duck, 'the thresher poet' as he is always rather patronizingly called, had been taken up by Queen Caroline and given a pension and a grace and favour house at Windsor. With this background it is remarkable that anybody in the opposition subscribed to the work at all. Yet the subscription list includes both Pope and Pulteney. Nevertheless, M.P.s who subscribed to it came overwhelmingly from the government benches.

The title that attracted relatively more subscribers from opposition M.P.s than from those who supported the Excise scheme was James Gibbs' *Book of Architecture, Containing Designs of Building and Ornaments* (1728).

Although government supporters are under-represented in it, there seems no reason for assuming that the work was unattractive to them on political grounds. On the contrary, it was dedicated to the Duke of Argyll, while one of the subscribers was Sir Robert Walpole himself. The preponderance of Tories and opposition Whigs probably reflects nothing more significant than the fact that most of Gibbs' contacts in England were Tories associated with the Harleys, earls of Oxford, and the Earl of Burlington's associates among opposition Whigs.[32]

Indeed, when the whole range of titles which had, or appear to have had, a bias towards particular political groupings is examined, no connection emerges between types of books and the politics of subscribers. The one exception is a possible disinclination on the part of opposition Whigs to subscribe to religious works. Otherwise the explanation of any connection between a book and the political inclinations of its subscription list, insofar as this is not merely a statistical anomaly, is to be found in the politics of the author or the particular circumstances of its publication. 'Whig' authors like Sir Richard Steele, Nicholas Rowe, John Milton, Joseph Addison, Bishop Burnet and James Thomson attracted Whig subscribers; 'Tory' authors like Jeremy Collier, Thomas Hearne and Matthew Prior appealed to Tories; 'government' poets like Joseph Mitchell and Stephen Duck obtained the subscriptions of government Whigs; 'opposition' playwrights like Henry Brooke received them from opposition politicians. In most cases, that is, there is a political rather than a cultural explanation of the subscribing habits of the 469 M.P.s who voted on the Excise bill.

This information throws some light on a controversy currently exercising political historians of the early eighteenth century. While there is a consensus among them that the last four years of Anne's reign were marked by bitter strife between clearly defined Tory and Whig parties, they differ on the question of how far these divisions survived her death in 1714. Some assert that there was a continuity of party alignments at least until the fall of Walpole, with the Tories retaining a distinct identity and party organization even though the governing party split, with several Whigs going into opposition. Others maintain that, as the period progressed, the Tories and Whigs in opposition combined to promote measures against the government on enough occasions for their joint endeavours to merit another description than Tory or Whig, the contemporary term 'Country' being preferred. For while the old terminology of Tory and Whig undoubtedly survived to describe almost all politicians under the first two Hanoverians, their behaviour was no longer so consistently partisan that it can be fully explained in the vocabulary of politics appropriate to Anne's reign. Contemporaries recognized this, it is claimed, when they used new expressions, such as 'administration' and 'opposition', or fell back on an even older terminology of Court and Country.[33]

When the subscription lists are compared with the division on the Excise bill, there is, as we have seen, little difficulty in describing those which show a statistical slant towards one of the three groups identifiable in 1733 as either Tory or Whig between 1710 and 1720. Thereafter, however, complications arise. While some of these, especially those which indicate a bias in favour of Tories and government Whigs, may possibly be dismissed as statistical anomalies, there is strong evidence that, from the late 1720s at least, some lists are inclined more towards government and opposition than to Tory and Whig. With the subscriptions for Stephen Duck in 1736 and Henry Brooke in 1739 one is in a world of Court and Country rather than Whig and Tory. Indeed, without this dimension much of the literary history of the period can be misunderstood. The satires of Pope and Swift are misrepresented with the term 'Tory'; they are much more explicable as 'Country' writings. Fielding's mentality, too, is as much 'Country' as 'Whig' in his early works.

And yet, towards the end of our period, there is a sharp reminder that, however much they might agree on contemporary issues, Tories and opposition Whigs had been deeply divided in the past and continued to be so about its interpretation. William Maitland's *History of London*, published in 1739, attracted 25 subscribers from Whigs who supported the Excise scheme, nine from those who opposed it, and only two from Tories who appear in the division list. A glance at its contents soon reveals that it was a very Whig history indeed. The first part purported to be 'A compleat history of all the publick transactions, memorable events and other occurrences, which happen'd to the citizens from the foundation of the City by the Romans . . . to the month of December 1737'. Maitland's account of the Exclusion Crisis of Charles II's reign betrays his partiality, for the City's Whig M.P.s are described as 'honorable Patriots', while the Court's move to recall the charter is criticized as 'the iniquitous proceedings of the ministry'. Tory memories were too long to subscribe to such a view of the past. And yet at the same time ministerial memories were too short to allow Maitland's 'Country' version of recent history to dissuade them from subscribing to his book. Although he called the Excise scheme 'a pernicious design', a significant number of M.P.s who had voted for it, including Walpole himself, are named in the subscription list.[34] Perhaps in the end it was the legacy of their bitter quarrels which prevented Tories and opposition Whigs from sinking their differences sufficiently to drop the old distinctions enough to combine in a united Country party against Walpole.

3. SUBSCRIPTIONS AND STATUS

Besides being identifiable by their political affiliations, M.P.s can also be distinguished by their social status and occupations. For example, among those named in the Excise division lists there were 44 lawyers, 35 army officers and 29 merchants.[35] Their subscriptions can therefore be analysed to establish whether these three groups showed any preferences in the choice of works they patronized.

At first sight the prospect seems no more promising than did the pattern for their partisanship. The lawyers subscribed to a total of 217 different books between 1710 and 1740, the officers to 169 and the merchants to 157, while not a single title was common to all the members of a group, or even to 50 per cent of it. One conclusion can be drawn at once from these figures, however, which is that the merchants feature more prominently than the others as subscribers. Their mean average of titles was 13.1 each, whereas the lawyers subscribed to 11.9 and the army officers to 9.8. It is possible that army officers had fewer opportunities to be subscribers since they were away on active service, though between 1713 and 1740 this was so rare that another possibility suggests itself, namely that they were relatively less interested in literary productions.

Where the distribution of subscriptions of these occupational categories to some titles was proportionately higher than that of all 469 M.P.s, the same test of association was used as that employed for the political groups to ascertain if there is a statistical case for assuming that these titles were of particular interest to them. To avoid very low numbers distorting the distribution, only those titles which obtained at least 20 per cent of the names in any one category were checked against the subscriptions from all the M.P.s. In the case of the lawyers there were eight such titles, of the army officers three, and of the merchants 14.

One of the eight common to the lawyers, the second volume of Burnet's *History of His Own Time* (1734), was also subscribed to by approximately the same proportion of all the M.P.s. The names of 22.7 per cent of the lawyers and 19.6 per cent of the M.P.s appear in the subscription list, which indicates no association with the legal profession. The remaining seven lists contained a disproportionate number. Predictably the most notable discrepancy was in the list for a legal tome, Thomas Oughton's *Ordo judiciorum* (1738), 40 per cent of the lawyers subscribing to it compared with only 9 per cent of all 469 M.P.s. Less obvious titles for the patronage of at least a fifth of their number were Thomas Brodrick's *Complete History of the War in the Netherlands* (1713), Addison's *Works* (1721), Henry Pemberton's *View of . . . Newton's Philosophy* (1728), Samuel Buckley's *A Third Letter to Dr. Mead* (1730), Stephen Duck's *Poems* and Pietro Sarpi's *Histoire du Concile de Trente* (1736).

The three lists which contained the names of a fifth or more of the army officers included that for the second volume of Burnet's *History*, about a quarter of them featuring in it. They also figure disproportionately among the subscribers to Voltaire's *La Henriade* (1728) and Alexander Gordon's *The Lives of Pope Alexander VI and his Son Caesar Borgia* (1729).

Burnet's *History of His Own Time* proved to be popular with the merchants too, over a third of them subscribing to the second volume in 1734. Moreover, unlike the other M.P.s they had been conspicuous in the list of subscribers to the first volume in 1724, for nearly a quarter of them are named in it, compared with only 10 per cent of all the M.P.s. The other titles which attracted the subscriptions of at least 20 per cent of the merchants were Addison's *Works* (1721), Pope's *Odyssey* and *Shakespeare* (1725), D. Stanley's *Sir Philip Sidney's Arcadia Modernised* (1725), David Scott's *History of Scotland* (1727), James Gibbs' *Book of Architecture* (1728), Pemberton's *View of . . . Newton's Philosophy* (1728), Joseph Mitchell's, *Poems* (1729), Sarpi's *Histoire du Concile de Trente* (1736), William Maitland's *History of London*, John Motley's *History of Peter I of Russia*, and John Pine's *History of the Tapestry Hangings of the House of Lords* (1739). Why these titles apparently appealed to the merchants among our M.P.s is not obvious. The list of them is more like a bookseller's catalogue than a bibliography of mercantile taste. This cautions against easy generalizations and serves as a reminder that there were myriad motives behind book subscriptions. The prestige of appearing in print as a patron of culture could have given the lists to Pope's works a certain snob appeal. Anybody who ran a business in London could be interested in Maitland's history of the capital. At the same time living in London made one more vulnerable to subscription hunters like Joseph Morgan, who scoured the city in his hunt for subscribers. Whatever their motives for subscribing to these titles, there does not appear to be any immediate connection between them and any particular literary taste.

The business and professional classes are often grouped together into a body which is then defined as the middle class or classes, with distinctly bourgeois attributes. Judging by the books subscribed to by the lawyers, soldiers and merchants among our M.P.s, however, their tastes varied considerably: only the second volume of Burnet's *History of His Own Time* was common to all three, and even that was preferred more by the army officers and merchants than by the lawyers, whose subscriptions did not vary disproportionately from that of all 469 members. The works of Addison, Pemberton and Sarpi also appear to have appealed more to lawyers and merchants than to army officers or M.P.s as a whole. Otherwise there are few, if any, signs in the subscription lists of a specifically bourgeois or middle class culture among the professional and business men who sat in parliament in the reign of George II.

Indeed the very method of publishing by subscription indicates in itself that the market for many books was not exclusively or even predominantly confined to the urban middle classes. Donald F. Bond has shown that when the allegedly 'bourgeois' *Spectator* was published in a separate subscription edition in 1713, in spite of the impressive 'number of names drawn from the financial and mercantile world of London', it nevertheless attracted a substantial number of aristocratic and genteel subscribers.[36] He seems rather to have overestimated the aristocratic element, for he claimed that there were 47 peers in the list, whereas there were in fact 29 English lords and five with Scottish or Irish titles. However, eight sons of noblemen, seven ladies of aristocratic families and three bishops also subscribed to the volume. At the same time he rather minimized the 'genteel' element, for there were 39 baronets and knights and 148 esquires among the subscribers. Some of the titled gentry were 'City knights' like Sir William Ashurt, 'knight and alderman', while many of the esquires were gentlemen in business or the professions rather than country gentry. Yet they also included Sir Richard Temple, future Viscount Cobham, who as well as being an army officer was the owner of Stowe house, and Sir William Wyndham the Tory M.P. for Somerset, together with a sprinkling of Whig members associated at least as much with the country as with the city, from Edward Ashe Esquire, of Heytesbury, Wiltshire, to Robert Walpole Esquire of Norfolk.

In 1710 Richard Steele's *Tatler*, the forerunner of The *Spectator*, was also published by subscription, and attracted even more aristocratic and genteel subscribers. Out of a total of 752 names on the lists which accompany the two volumes of *The Lucubrations of Isaac Bickerstaff Esq.*, no fewer than 71 were of English peers. Since there were only 161 such peers in all at that time this represents 44 per cent of the English aristocracy, a remarkably high proportion of the eligible group. Furthermore there were 35 Scottish or Irish lords, 26 sons of peers and 26 ladies of aristocratic families among Steele's subscribers. With the addition of eight bishops, therefore, the lists contain 166 aristocratic names, or 22 per cent of the total.

Of course the list does not indicate the entire readership of the *Tatler*. Not only were the subscribers a small proportion of the whole, but they were almost certainly the more affluent readers. The subscription edition is therefore no doubt seriously misleading about the nature of the actual audience Steele addressed when the *Tatler* came out as a periodical. Yet one can only speculate about the size and composition of that audience because we simply do not know who read it in that form.

At least subscription lists document a precise readership, enabling scholars to subject generalizations based on deduction to tests of documentation. The widely accepted notion that the reading public in eighteenth-century England was overwhelmingly middle class is one such generalization which an analysis of subscription lists substantially qualifies. The market for the kind of title that was published by subscription was cornered by 'the quality', as contemporaries called them. Indeed, the extent to which subscription lists were dominated by the peerage is remarkable.

Even if we exclude their nearest kin and ignore the Scottish and Irish peers, concentrating only on the English members of the House of Lords, who never numbered more than 180 in the first half of the eighteenth century, they can still be shown to have featured disproportionately among those who subscribed to books. The numbers of subscribers tended to be relatively small anyway, and the proportion of peers correspondingly high. Of 750 subscription lists between 1700 and 1750, as many as 627 contain fewer than 500 names, while 90 have from 500 to 1,000, 28 over 1,000 and only five over 2,000. Even in the few lists where the number of subscribers exceed 500 the peerage could still exert an influence disproportionate to its numbers by dint of purchasing multiple copies. Many lists indicate that subscribers bought more than one copy, and sometimes the additional copies were a substantial fraction of the total paid for in advance. Apart from booksellers, who were presumably acquiring them to resell, the purchasers of multiple copies tended to be the more prominent subscribers, with the peers well to the fore. When Voltaire's *La Henriade* appeared in 1728 the accompanying subscription list named 343 subscribers. Between them they subscribed for 476 copies, the extra 133 being purchased by 32 of the total named. Of the 32 no fewer than 14 were English peers, and moreover they account for as many as 106 of the multiple copies purchased by subscribers.

When to the English peers are added their wives, sons and daughters, and the Irish peerage, which fluctuated between 88 and 103 in number, together with the Scottish peers, who declined from 135 to 100, not to mention their kinfolk, then the preponderance of aristocrats in subscription lists becomes formidable. Far from demonstrating the rise of a middle-class readership, therefore, subscriptions to books document that a significant section of the book trade was dominated by the upper classes of Augustan Britain.

NOTES

This essay has drawn very heavily on the data filed by the Project for Historical Biobibliography at the University of Newcastle upon Tyne, and I wish to thank those involved in it, and above all Dr Peter Wallis, for making it readily available to me. For information about peers I wish to thank Professor John Cannon, and for using it to analyse peerage subscriptions I am greatly indebted to Miss Pat Murrell for her invaluable assistance.

1. Historical Manuscripts Commission, *Diary of Lord Egmont*, III, 312.

2. S. L. Clapp, 'The beginnings of subscription publication in the seventeenth century', *Modern Philology* XIX (1931–2), 204.

3. P. Rogers, 'Book subscriptions among the Augustans', *The Times Literary Supplement*, 15 December 1972.

4. J. Morgan, *A Complete History of Algiers* (1728), I, preface; *ibid.*, (1729), II, 2–5.

5. H. Fielding, *Joseph Andrews*, ed. R. F. Brissenden (1977), 208 (III, 3).

6. Morgan, *op. cit.*, II, 5.

7. *Ibid.*, I, subscription list.

8. H. Fielding, *Amelia*, ed. A. R. Humphreys (1962), 81 (VIII, 6).
9. *The Times Literary Supplement*, 15 December 1972.
10. P. Wallis, *The Social Index* (1978), 34–44.
11. W. Cobbett, *Parliamentary History* (1810), XI, 1308–1313. For the scheme see P. Langford, *The Excise Crisis* (1976).
12. Information on M.P.s in this paper is taken from R. Sedgwick (ed.), *The History of Parliament: The Commons 1715–1754* (2 vols., 1970).
13. Wallis, *op. cit.*, 20–5.
14. Titles are given as in F. G. Robinson and P. J. Wallis, *Book Subscription Lists: A Revised Guide* (1975); *ibid.*, first supplement (1976) compiled by C. Wadham, second supplement (1977), and third supplement (1980) compiled by L. Menhennet. The number of subscribers after each title is given in the sequence: supporters of Excise; Tory opponents; Whig opponents. The X^2 test was used to ascertain if there was an association between a political group and a subscription list. I wish to thank Professor Hugh Berrington for his assistance in this exercise, which followed the method he employed to discern associations between backbench M.P.s and early day motions in S. E. Finer, H. B. Berrington and D. J. Bartholomew, *Backbench Opinion in the House of Commons 1955–59* (1961) and H. B. Berrington, *Backbench Opinion in the House of Commons 1945–55* (1973). Lists with 23 or fewer of the 469 M.P.s which indicate a statistical association were:
'Whig': 710 JOH: 7;2;1.
710 STR: 7;0;4.   720 CHA: 10;1;5.
720 MIL: 9;1;3.   725 CAM: 13;2;6.
725 WIN: 12;1;6.   728 JEA: 16;0;5.
728 MOR: 10;1;4.   729 BRA: 7;0;5
729 OLD: 8;0;5.   730 PIN: 8;1;3.
734 DES: 6;0;4.   735 ROS: 3;0;4.
738 WAR: 8;1;3.
'Tory': 714 COL: 1;5;1.
719 HEA: 3;10;1.   720 HEA: 1;6;0.
720 HEC: 2;6;1.   724 FID: 5;12;5.
724 SMA: 4;9;0.   728 CAS: 4;6;4.
737 STE: 3;12;0.
'Government': 721 RAM: 7;1;1.
726 AYL: 15;0;0.   727 FLE: 12;1;2.
728 RAM: 8;1;0.   732 MAI: 12;1;3.

'Opposition': 732 BUC: 2;8;5.
734 FES: 3;2;5.
'Government Whigs and Tories': 735 ENG: 9;6;2. It must be stressed that the PHIBB files from which the information was obtained are not yet 100 per cent complete, and that more names might in fact be common to both the subscription lists and the Excise division list than are here identified. This also precludes basing confident generalizations on the very small figures obtained from lists containing fewer than 5 per cent of the 469 M.P.s. The more the overlap exceeds 5 per cent, however, the more confidence can be placed in the data, since the occasional oversight should not seriously affect the distribution of names between the political groupings.
15. M. A. Goldie, 'The roots of true whiggism', *History of Political Thought*, I (1980), 204.
16. British Library MS Add. 5853 fos. 83v, 127.
17. K. M. Lynch, *Jacob Tonson Kit Cat Publisher* (1971), 93, 142.
18. Rogers, *op. cit.*
19. 'Whig': 710 STE: 23;3;8.
718 ROW: 19;0;7.   721 BON: 14;2;7.
721 KIN: 19;2;9.   725 SAW: 19;4;9.
726 BRE: 19;3;10.   727 JON: 21;2;12.
728 CUT: 14;2;7.   730 THO: 26;1;11.
735 COL: 21;6;13.   739 MAI: 26;2;9.
'Tory': 715 POP: 14;14;9.
718 TRA: 4;17;1.   721 BAR: 7;21;4.
736 DRA: 6;21;15.
'Government': 729 MIT: 30;3;7.
730 BUK: 30;5;6.   732 AND: 21;1;6.
733 BUK: 17;4;4.
'Opposition': 739 BRO: 2;16;10.
'Government and Tory':
722 STE: 13;10;1.   733 PIN: 20;12;6.
738 BRE: 22;8;2.
738 OUG: 24;16;6.
20. J. Loftis, *The Politics of Drama in Augustan England* (1963), 36, 54.
21. D. C. Coleman, 'Politics and economics in the age of Anne: the case of the Anglo/French trade treaty of 1713', in *Trade, Government and Economy in Pre-industrial England: Essays Presented to F. J. Fisher*, ed. D. C. Coleman and A. H. John (1976), 191.

22. Despite Pope's Catholicism and links with Tories, his works had a universal appeal judging by the subscription lists to his *Odyssey* and *Works of Shakespeare*, both published in 1725. The first obtained 32 subscribers from among the M.P.s who supported the Excise scheme, 23 from Tories and 19 from Whigs who opposed it. Although government Whigs were marginally under-represented on the first list, the distribution of subscriptions on the second was closer to that on the division list: 22;8;11.

23. Rogers, *op. cit.*

24. *Dictionary of National Biography*, sub Drake. The *DNB* contains much useful information about authors of works referred to in this paper.

25. J. Mitchell, *Poems on Several Occasions* (1729), II, 69–71.

26. J. Anderson, *Royal Genealogies* (1732), preface, 768–9.

27. H. Brooke, *Gustavus Vasa* (1739), VI.

28. B. Goldgar, *Walpole and the Wits* (1976), 181.

29. 'Whig': 721 ADD: 50;5;28. 724 BUR: 38;6;13. 728 ARI; 35;8;14.

728 VOL: 30;4;14. 729 WEK: 40;5;19. 734 BUR: 64;13;22. 'Tory': 718 PRI: 33;34;14. 729 WEK: 40;5;19. 734 BUR: 64;13;22. 'Government': 728 PEM: 34;9;9. 736 DUC: 42;6;4. 'Opposition': 726 GIB: 25;24;20.

30. G. Spearman, *An Enquiry into the Ancient and Present State of the County Palatine of Durham* (1727), 120.

31. F. Ellis (ed.), *Poems on Affairs of State* (1975), VII, 504–13.

32. B. Little, *The Life and Works of James Gibbs* (1955), 39–109.

33. I have discussed the historiography of the debate in 'Whigs and Tories dim their glories; English political parties under the first two Georges', *The Whig Ascendancy*, ed. J. Cannon (1981).

34. W. Maitland, *History of London* (1739), 302–3, 345.

35. These were identified by collating the division list with the occupational lists in Sedgwick, *op. cit.*, I, 142–50.

36. D. B. Bond (ed.), *The Spectator*, I (1965), xxxviii–xciii.

4
Classical poetry and the eighteenth-century reader

PENELOPE WILSON

I. 'FOR SCHOOLS AND PRIVATE GENTLEMEN': THE READERSHIP OF CLASSICAL POETRY

> Classical knowledge, that is, Greek and Latin, is absolutely necessary for everybody; because everybody has agreed to think and call it so. And the word *illiterate*, in its common acceptation, means a man who is ignorant of these two languages.[1]

As any student of eighteenth-century literature is aware, within the confines of the literary world demarcated by Lord Chesterfield's wry maxims classical poetry had a special and well-recognized status as a shared fund of reference and connotation. It is not, however, easy to quantify the actual extent of the familiarity of eighteenth-century readers with the classical poets. On the one hand, we have the gallery of gracefully unostentatious closet readers conjured up by Lord Chesterfield in an earlier letter to his son ('if you happen to have an Elzevir classic in your pocket, neither show it nor mention it'). On the other, we must recognize that we are dealing with a badge of status which even then had traditional associations at every level with bluff and false pretences. The nuance is neatly captured by Fielding's mock-nervousness in *Joseph Andrews:* 'I say (but I whisper that softly, and I solemnly declare, without any Intention of giving Offence to any brave Man in the Nation), I say, or rather I whisper, that he is an ignorant Fellow, and hath never read *Homer* nor *Virgil*'.[2]

There are a number of specialist studies in existence of the reception of an individual classical poet, or genre.[3] Perhaps the most straightforward level on which the topic can be approached more generally is that of the individual reader, where substantial evidence about the manner as well as

69

the matter of reading can be gleaned from a variety of sources. Specifically, one thinks of Edward Gibbon's journal with its detailed documentation of his progress through Homer and Juvenal, of Thomas Gray's notebooks and marginalia, of the biographical documentation of Johnson's reading, or of the creative use of classical poetry in Alexander Pope's 'poetry of allusion'.[4] Apart from the numerous letters and journals of the period, we have also the evidence of library sale catalogues. The modest classical library of the poet James Thomson, for example, contained a number of mostly recent editions of Latin poets in the original and in translation, including five editions of Horace and three of Virgil, as well as Terence, Juvenal, Persius, and Lucan. Thomson also owned a Greek primer (in French), Homer, Euripides and the Greek 'minor poets' in editions with a Latin translation, Theocritus and another Homer in Italian, and Brumois's *Greek Theatre* in French.[5] Thomson was not a wealthy man, and his collection is probably quite a reliable guide to the reading habits of its owner; but we cannot always assume, especially with the more impressive collections, that the possession of a book meant that it was also read. As in Timon's villa, prestige and bindings must often have played a part. Subscription lists, like library catalogues, provide a useful but limited source of information. Subscription was a very popular method of publication for translations,[6] but it was not much used for Greek and Latin texts except for some 'fine' editions, such as John Pine's *Horace* of 1733 (the text of which was printed from brass engraving), or Baskerville's famous *Virgil* of 1757.

Such sources apply, of course, almost entirely to a restricted group – a group which for the most part received a strongly classical education under private tutors, at school, and sometimes at university.[7] We are brought closer to a sense of the 'common reader' by the image of classical learning projected by the novelists, especially by Henry Fielding. Knowledge of the classics, particularly the classical poets, is a constant preoccupation in Fielding's novels, where books often function as an important part of the texture of circumstantiality – as, for example, in the scene in *Tom Jones* where Partridge ingenuously offers Jones his choice of his motley collection of 'books in both languages; such as *Erasmi Colloquia, Ovid de Tristibus, Gradus ad Parnassum*'.[8] Parson Adams' manuscript Aeschylus (an unusual taste),[9] and Tom Jones's feeling recitations of odes of Horace are set against a background of classical fraud and simple ignorance, not only in the characters they meet but also in Fielding's recurrent authorial jibes. The motif acquires a new significance, however, in *Amelia*, a novel in which reading in general becomes an important theme. The long-standing joke about the emptiness of most pretensions to classical literacy becomes, in the scene with the author soliciting subscriptions for a translation of Ovid's *Metamorphoses*, a moral castigation. Booth's own classical qualifications are given a new emphasis, demonstrated in this same scene by an ability to converse in critical detail about Lucian, Homer, Lucan, and Ovid, with passing references to Virgil, Statius, Silius Italicus, and Claudian.[10]

The most elaborate use of classical poetry in this novel is, however, in the unequal clash between the good and learned Dr Harrison and the indiscreet Mrs Bennett/Atkinson, whose learning is 'all the fortune given her by her father, and all the dower left her by her husband'.[11] Mrs Atkinson is only one in a long line of satiric representations of the 'learned lady', a tradition stretching back well into the seventeenth century.[12] Fielding accords her a degree of sympathy, but without much certainty. When she is moved to recite half a dozen lines of the *Aeneid,* the ideal heroine Amelia (herself an avid reader of sermons, and of Farquhar's comedies) is, very properly, 'almost frightened out of her wits'. Fielding indulges another – rather recherché – joke at Mrs Atkinson's expense at the end of the novel when, humbled into confessing her need for the help of a Latin translation of Homer, she is made to refer to a non-existent 'Delphin Homer', a solecism with which Dr Harrison is quick to make play.[13] Fielding's obvious bias aside, however, the mechanics of her second confrontation with Dr Harrison are worth noting. Dr Harrison's use of Greek quotation here is a clear signal of male bonding ('the ladies must excuse my repeating the passage to you [i.e. Booth], as I know you have Greek enough to understand it'), and Mrs Atkinson's interception of the signal is met with an automatic aggressiveness, culminating in the following exchange: '"But what is there masculine in learning?" – "Nothing so masculine, take my word for it."'[14]

Indeed there seems to be very little else to do but 'take his word'. Masculinity is so encoded into the language of the subject that in the eighteenth century it is virtually inseparable from it. Johnson told Boswell that he spent the two years before going to Oxford reading 'not voyages and travels, but all literature, Sir, all ancient writers, all manly: though but little Greek, only some of Anacreon and Hesiod'.[15] The heading of this section reflects the ubiquitous formula of title-page and preface to editions of classical texts – 'the whole adapted for the capacities of youth at school, as well as of private gentlemen'. Exclusion on grounds of sex and class is taken for granted. The establishment view did allow women some carefully controlled contact with classical language and literature. Richard Bentley himself is said to have learned his Latin rudiments at his mother's knee,[16] and translations were considered particularly suitable for female consumption. As Robert Potter's preface to his translation of Euripides (1781–3) neatly illustrates, the emphasis almost exactly balances the masculine one associated with the original texts: the translation may, he hopes, 'give an agreeable and rational amusement to the English ladies, whose education does not generally lead them to an acquaintance with the Greek language; and an endeavour to revive the manly simplicity of the antients cannot be unusefull to any persons in any age.'[17] Twenty years earlier the *Monthly Review* had noticed the publication of Ovid's *Metamorphoses* 'epitomized in an English poetical style, for the use and entertainment of the ladies of Great Britain', a volume dedicated to Mrs Charlotte Lennox, herself responsible for the translation into English of some French versions of Greek tragedy. Subscription lists throughout the century show a relatively strong female representation – Joseph Trapp's blank verse translation of the *Aeneid* in 1718 is an early example.[18] Unless feminized through poetical translation or the maternal ideal, however, the classics were very clearly felt to be beyond the bounds of a woman's intellectual sphere.

There were, of course, many exceptional women, of whom the most renowned is Elizabeth Carter, translator of the Stoic philosopher Epictetus. Some, like Jane Barker or Elizabeth Elstob, profited from sympathetic brothers, while others were largely self-taught, like the phenomenal Mrs Grierson in Dublin (the daughter of 'poor illiterate country people'), or – at the opposite end of the social scale – Lady Mary Wortley Montagu, who describes herself, in a revealing phrase, as 'stealing the Latin language'.[19] In fact the arguments and assumptions that lay behind the exclusion of women from classical learning were challenged more frequently and more forcibly than one might expect; but it was a natural result of the absence of any regular channels for women in this area that their studies tended to diversify, in what now seem progressive scholarly directions. Mary Collyer in the mid-eighteenth century, for example, undertook translations from the German poets Gessner and Klopstock, and in 1737 Elizabeth Cooper had published her *Muses Library*, an anthology of early English poetry. Still earlier in the century, Elizabeth Elstob had become a recognized Anglo-Saxon scholar, with a translation of an Anglo-Saxon homily in 1709. The preface to her Anglo-Saxon grammar, published in 1715, is in fact a frontal attack on the classical monopoly of the world of polite learning, an attack directed specifically against the popular little treatise which had been published by Henry Felton two years earlier, *A Dissertation on Reading the Classics, and Forming a Just Style*.[20]

From other directions too there were strong challenges throughout the eighteenth century to the supremacy of a traditional classical education on the public and grammar school model. The curriculum of the dissenting academies, where the influence of Locke was strong, offered a progressive alternative to the established emphasis of the universities, with more attention to English and modern languages.[21] When Thomas Sheridan in 1756 argues in the Locke tradition that more serious attention should be paid to the study of the *English* language, he dismisses 'the absurd notions of so many parents, that Latin and Greek are still the high roads to fortune, because they were so two centuries ago';[22] and in 1762 classical teaching is regretfully but firmly declared an unnecessary luxury for their sons by a group of Glaswegian citizens in a pamphlet with the title 'The Defects of a University Education, and its unsuitableness to a commercial people'. For the partisans of classical learning then, as now, it seemed that the golden age of classical education – when it would, according to William Godwin, have been 'a sort of blasphemy' to question its value – was fast passing away. In 1783 Godwin, defending the study of Latin and Greek on political and educational grounds, suggests that the battle is already lost. 'If [the] works of [the classical authors] were totally annihilated, it would scarcely call forth a sigh from the refined geniuses of the present age.'[23]

Opposition to the traditional course of education comes in the eighteenth century from many quarters. Among the most wide-ranging of the anti-traditionalist arguments are those advanced by John Gordon, later Archdeacon of Lincoln, who opens his critique of 'the present plan of a learned education' with an autobiographical perspective, recalling his own emergence from school with 'a parcel of words' and 'a heap of confused notions about Gods and Heroes, Orators and Poets'.

> Had I been examined in any matter relative to the state of things, which obtains in this earthly system; had I been asked any question in *morality, natural philosophy, metaphysics*, or even *Logic*, beyond a few praedicaments and the structure of a Syllogism, I must have appeared as ignorant as an unlettered *Indian* . . . An imagination accustomed to be for ever straying through enamelled meads in search of flowers and nosegays, must needs look on the rough and uncouth road of rational inquiry with aversion and disgust . . . In short, attending much to words and slightly to things, will probably teach men to substitute elegant expression in place of argument; to give us fine figures for facts; and to treat us with well-turn'd periods instead of proofs.[24]

Gordon's essay, avowedly in the wider tradition of the debate about ancient and modern learning that had occupied writers at the end of the previous century, seems not to have evoked a specific response, but the climate of challenge and innovation was strong enough to force the adherents of the traditional system on to the defensive, and to draw from them some explicit statements about the utility of a classical education.[25]

Over the labouring classes – as, at the other extreme, over those who were destined for the learned professions – there was no debate. No one argued that a classical education would be of any benefit to them as individuals or as members of society, and several writers towards the end of the century made a point of excepting them, using the argument which was to block the progress a century later of Hardy's Jude the Obscure, that they might be tempted to despise or neglect their daily occupations.[26] Advocates for the utility of a classical education did, however, stress that its benefits were by no means restricted to gentlemen and scholars. Joseph Cornish gives an interesting slant to the arguments of James Beattie and Vicesimus Knox by adapting them to a dissenting context and directing them specifically towards those destined for the 'middle ranks of life'. In many of these essays, emphasis is laid on the importance of grammatical study as a rational and philosophical discipline, although Cornish is more sympathetic than Beattie, Godwin, or Knox to the new, more direct methods for learning Latin, which relied heavily on translations.[27] The works of the classical authors are valued especially as providing worthy models for imitation, on the level of both 'style' (a chief preoccupation in Henry Felton's little handbook on reading the classics, and its mid-century successor by John Hill)[28] and morality. As far as the classical poets were concerned, there was some difficulty in reconciling these benefits, since indecency rendered many of them unfit for consumption *in toto* by the innocent young person.[29] The fictions of pagan religion were often, too, seen as an embarrassment, and politically Horace and Virgil themselves were strongly tainted by their acquiescent rôles in the court of Augustus. In general, however, the prevailing image of the classical world was constructed out of all the attributes – military prowess, civic virtue, uprightness, even the 'republican spirit' admired by Godwin – which could be summed up in the one word 'manliness'.[30] In at least one mid-century anthology, published by Charles Hitch in London in 1744, the question of propriety is strongly emphasized on the title-page, which offers a 'florilegium' from Ovid, Tibullus, Propertius, and Martial 'purged of all obscenity, for the use of youths'. It is clear from many other sources that readers tended to compile their own anthologies on moral as well as aesthetic principles, and one school-teacher encouraged his boys to 'set a Mark in the Margin, over against those Passages that convey some excellent moral Instruction, or are otherwise remarkably beautiful', while another accustomed his scholars to learn by heart select passages of Latin poetry to serve as 'ready and agreeable monitors on the conduct of life'.[31]

A related but more pragmatic argument for extending a classical education beyond those who were to make a living out of their learning drew on the need to prepare the mind for 'rational entertainment' in future hours of leisure. The aim of William Foot's essay on the adaptation of a grammar-school education to 'such youth, as are not design'd for the University' is to afford such instruction as will be 'of real service through life, not only to those intended for the learned professions, but to the merchant and tradesman, that when they have done with the business of the counting-house or the shop, they may be disposed, and not be at a loss, to fill up vacant times, in a manner suitable to the dignity of a rational creature.' In Foot's scheme, Latin still holds a central if diminished place. Joseph Cornish relates the want of the tastes acquired through classical reading directly with the need to search for amusement in card-playing, or with 'sauntering from post to pillar, or yawning away tedious hours in an arm chair'. Classical reading as a suitable occupation for the spare time of an army officer is another motif touched on by Fielding in *Amelia*, and we have Gibbon's testimony that 'on every march, in every journey, Horace was always in my pocket and often in my hand'.[32] With commercial prosperity, more and more people were expected to have time on their hands, and this belief provides James Beattie with another important argument. He would not recommend the study of Latin and Greek 'to savages in need of sustenance, or to a wholly martial state', but prosperous modern Europe is a different case: 'I speak of the arts not of supporting, but of adorning human life; not of rendering men insensible to cold and famine; but of enabling them to bear, without being enervated, and enjoy without being corrupted, the blessings of a more prosperous condition.'[33] Classical learning thus becomes, pragmatically and morally, an antidote to the concomitant dangers of luxury. The argument is to become a familiar and often ludicrous refrain in connection with classical publications. We may look, for example, to Edward Burnaby-Greene's presentation of the odes of Pindar as 'lessons to an insect-tribe, who doze/On pleasure's silken couch, and sip the virgin rose';[34] or, for an early example, to the *Monthly Review's* reception of the Foulis edition of Homer in 1757, a hortatory extravaganza of welcome which underlines not only the special status accorded to classical poetry but also the dual aspect of classical learning as a commercial product and incentive as well as a moral control:

> We are sorry to observe, that the little encouragement given to the cultivation of arts and sciences, is not the least instance of the corruption and degeneracy of modern times . . . They who have no *taste* to relish them, would, if they loved their country, patronize them from political principles. The higher perfection the arts attain in any country, the greater will be the demand for its particular productions. The nation that out-rivals its neighbours, will become the mart of commerce: the ingenious and industrious will procure a comfortable subsistence: the inhabitants will multiply: and the kingdom increase in riches, and consequently, in power.[35]

2. THE TEXTS

'The first object that occurs to an ingenuous youth, after having passed the discipline and exercises of a public school . . . is the singular felicity of possessing correct and elegant editions of those writers . . . from which he proposes to derive the most elegant and exalted satisfactions through the subsequent scenes and stages of human life.'[36] Edward Harwood's *View of the Various Editions of the Greek and Roman Classics, with Remarks* (1775), a comprehensive review of the best available editions, with information about second-hand prices where possible, is in itself a testimony to the care taken by eighteenth-century readers over their classical texts. Harwood's judgments now seem rather erratic at times, but the usefulness of his book to contemporaries is beyond question. Small enough to accompany would-be purchasers to sales and bookshops, it went through several editions (including a translation into Italian) within quick succession. From the evidence provided by Harwood, as from the sale catalogues of eighteenth-century private libraries, it is clear that the buyers of classical texts still had a wide international and chronological range to choose from. Amsterdam and Leyden (*Lugd. Bat.*) are the commonest imprints, but it is not uncommon to find sixteenth-century Aldine, Plantin, or Stephanus texts serving apparently as reading copies of classical poetry as well as collectors' pieces. (Coleridge, it may be noted, was still using, and annotating, the 1616 Wittenberg edition of Pindar in 1806, despite the intervention of an Oxford edition and three Glasgow editions, as well as the 1798 Göttingen edition to which he had turned by 1810.)[37] Chesterfield's remark that 'the last editions are always the best, if the editors are not blockheads' is often quoted, and we know that Horace Walpole gave it his mark of approval,[38] but the evidence suggests that the choice of editions was normally much more eclectic, and sometimes, no doubt, if Harwood was serving a real need, random. There were also, of course, the book collectors, of whom James Douglas, with nearly 500 volumes relating to Horace in his library, is a notorious example. Referred to in a note to the *Dunciad*, he stands for Harwood in 1775 as a monument to the excesses of 'bibliomania'.[39]

The writings of the eighteenth century are sprinkled with references to classical texts by code names of which the exact significance is now lost to all but a few – chiefly, the names of the great continental publishing houses such as those referred to in the last paragraph. The Dutch Elsevier classics play an important part in the development of the inexpensive and easily portable text: often reprinted outside Holland, they were particularly popular both as reading texts and with bibliophiles.[40] The 'Delphin' texts of the Latin classics, so called because the series, devised for the education of the son of Louis XIV, was described as 'in usum Delphini', are the commonest of all. With a Latin paraphrase and notes, and copious indices, they were in regular use as school texts throughout the century. After the appearance of the original French editions they were in fact mostly brought out, often with additions, by London publishers, who issued at least 18 'Delphin' editions of Virgil and of Horace before 1800. In the middle of the century there appeared the 'Brindley' classics, a uniform series of Roman authors published in small pot duodecimo by James Brindley in London. Gibbon's travelling library consisted of a 24-volume set of Brindley's classics in a mahogany box with brass handles.[41]

The best editions of the sixteenth and seventeenth centuries were continental. In the eighteenth century, however, the classical presses of Britain were unrivalled, and their achievement is marked by the publication in Stettin in 1797 of a bibliography by Lewis Brueggemann, entitled *A View of the English Editions, Translations, and Illustrations of the Greek and Latin authors.* The demand for fine library editions was high, as can be seen, for example, from the success of Pine's *Horace* and of the editions issued by the Baskerville press in Birmingham, described by Philip Gaskell as 'unusually beautiful, expensive, and incorrect'.[42] A more significant aspect, however, is the emphasis on cheapness and portability. The story is well known of the friend of Lord Chesterfield who tore out pages of a 'common edition' of Horace and other Latin poets to read and then dispose of in the 'necessary house'.[43] There is no other evidence of the demand for a disposable text, but short of that, publishers were clearly anxious to cater for almost every need. The Foulis press in Glasgow, in many ways the most important of the British classical publishers, met the range of demands with a policy of variant issues, printing Greek texts with or without a Latin translation, and texts in different formats and on different qualities of paper. The physical variety of the classical texts of the eighteenth century is one of the most striking features to a twentieth-century reader; copies are often further individualized by being bound with interleaved blank pages.[44]

For Harwood, 'a correct text, and judicious punctuation indeed, are instead of ten thousand notes'.[45] For most eighteenth-century readers of the classics 'correctness' seems to have been just as much a matter of consensus as was the 'elegance' with which it is constantly yoked. When the Foulis press brought out an edition of Horace in 1756 the sheets were actually displayed for six days in the University and a reward of £50 offered to anyone who discovered an error. Communal proof-reading no doubt had its advantages, but the oddness of such a procedure in terms of modern editorial technique is underlined by a comparison with the edition of Horace published in 1711 by Richard Bentley, who had virtually abandoned the notion of the 'received text' for a radical policy of individual editorial decision, resulting in between 700 and 800 new readings.[46] In the absence of a sense of textual criticism as a science based upon an understanding of manuscript tradition, most readers had very little on which to found their assertions about the quality of a text beyond matters of purely typographical accuracy and aesthetic appeal. Bentley himself thought that the work of collating manuscripts was in the past: 'there is hardly anything left, save what is to be extracted, by insight alone, from the essence of the thought and the temper of the style.'[47] It is clear from numerous communications to the *Gentleman's Magazine* and the reviews that one of the chief activities of the learned reader in the second half of the century at least was conjectural emendation. With insight and common sense the only requirements, the field was wide open to the amateur. A corresponding emphasis in the editions, which naturally tended to be more conservative, is on punctuation, an area in which tradition was recognized to count for nothing. 'Although every Reader hath a Right to point an ancient Author as he pleases, since the Art of Punctuation, if it may be so called, is of modern Invention, yet great Exactness is required when it is intended for public Use.'[48] The prominent place given by Harwood to 'judicious punctuation' is not, therefore, as idiosyncratic as it may sound to modern ears. For many editors, improvements in punctuation constitute a primary claim, as in a bookseller's advertisement in 1760 for a new edition of Virgil in which 'many thousand alterations are made in the pointing, different from those hitherto esteemed the best editions'.[49]

Apart from these general concerns – and apart, of course, from the work of individual classical scholars like Bentley – the most interesting developments are to be found in the printing of Greek texts. The eighteenth century saw a major improvement in clarity in the gradual abandonment of contractions, an advance chiefly owing to Alexander Wilson, the type founder for the Foulis press. One of the best examples is the Foulis Homer so magiloquently welcomed by the *Monthly Review* (above, p. 75), and Gibbon's comment upon it, a nice fusion of visual with literary aesthetics, is worth quoting: 'as the eye is the organ of fancy, I read Homer with more pleasure in the Glasgow folio. Through that fine medium the poet's sense appears more beautiful and transparent. Bishop Louth has said that he could discover only one error in that accurate edition, the omission of an *iota* subscribed to a dative. Yet how could a man of taste read Homer with such literal attention?'[50] Another innovation, which did not catch on, was the abandonment in some printed texts of Greek accents – most notably in Thomas Warton's Oxford edition of Theocritus in 1770 – and it is characteristic of the current concern with the implications of typography that this apparently dry philological dispute was widely seen as an issue of what is now called sociolinguistics, the theory being that accents had been introduced in an attempt to stabilize pronunciation at a time when 'conquest, and commerce, and other methods of intercourse brought foreigners into Greece'.[51]

The most far-reaching development in the presentation of Greek texts is, however, the movement towards abolishing the Latin version which had traditionally accompanied them. According to Vicesimus Knox, some editors had long been dissatisfied with the practice but had, perforce, succumbed to what he calls the 'bibliopolian' argument.[52] Greek books without Latin translations were simply not regarded as a saleable commodity. The disadvantages of not only learning but also reading Greek through a Latin medium are too obvious to need discussion; and they had been pointed out in the influential treatise on education by the Frenchman Charles Rollin, translated into English in 1734 as *The Method of Teaching and Studying the Belles Lettres*. The issue is forcefully aired in 1758 by John Burton, in the preface to his *Pentalogia*, a popular selection of Greek tragedies published without the customary Latin version despite the fact that it was designed for schools. Burton's arguments arise partly from a dislike of the habits of idleness induced by any translation, but also from the belief that such 'translation' of Greek into Latin is simply not possible. Not even Greek prose, he argues, can be faithfully represented in Latin – much less the unique qualities of tragic verse style.[53] The practical effect of such arguments seems not to have been great until the beginning of the next century: no doubt the booksellers' case was a strong one. (It is also worth noting that even when an English rather than a Latin crib had become acceptable, the names of Greek gods and goddesses continue to appear in their latinized form.) The protests do, however, add another emphasis to the movement towards a hellenism which was increasingly independent of Rome.[54]

3. THE USES OF TRANSLATION

In 1786 a correspondent suggests in the *Gentleman's Magazine* that there would be much use for a catalogue (preferably with critical comments, on the lines of Harwood's 'view of the editions') of the various English translations that had been made of Greek and Latin authors.[55] The lists which have since been made available (in Brueggemann's bibliography in 1797, and more recently in the *New Cambridge Bibliography of English Literature*) show that the popular demand for literary translations from classical authors had not faltered since the beginning of the vogue at the end of the seventeenth century. In 1696 the anonymous author of the spirited *Essay in Defence of the Female Sex,* claiming that the world of classical literature was now open to women with no access to the originals, lists Ovid, Tibullus, Juvenal and Horace among the poets already available in translation. Dryden's Virgil was on the way.[56] She might also have mentioned Homer, 'Anacreon', Sappho and Theocritus among Greek poets, and Lucretius among the Latin. By the end of the next century, however, the list had grown to include multiple versions of most of the extant ancient poets. The expansion is particularly evident, especially in the second half of the eighteenth century, in the range of Greek poetry available in English – not only Homer and monodic lyric, but Pindar and the Greek tragedians, Bion, Moschus, Tyrtaeus, and even the Homeric 'Hymn to Ceres', first discovered in a manuscript in Moscow in the 1770s.[57] These works, as their contents often suggest, were seen as fulfilling other purposes besides that of drawing the ancients 'from the closet into the world'. The inclusion of a Latin text, for example, or of scholarly notes, was clearly aimed at the learned reader, who ought in any case, according to Joseph Trapp, to be stimulated into a valuable process of comparison: 'he who says he values no translation of this, or that poem, because he understands the original, has indeed no true relish, that is, in effect, no true understanding of either.'[58]

Attached to these works is a vast and repetitious literature, in the form of prefaces and reviews, of the theory of translation, and its various aims and functions. It is from the labours of men like the poet laureate Henry James Pye ('not taking too great a liberty in paraphrasing, on the one hand; nor, on the other, suffering the spirit of the poet to escape me, by adhering too closely to his letter') that the prevailing impression arises of eighteenth-century translation as the great leveller.[59] Some translations may have been undertaken out of a great love of the particular subject (James Grainger, for example, explains what Tibullus had meant to him amid the horrors of war);[60] others were no doubt undertaken in the hope of establishing a reputation and winning preferment; but translations were so popular that the primary motive must frequently have been financial, as indeed Christopher Smart readily acknowledges in the dedication to his verse translation of Horace in 1767. 'I made my version of Horace for the same reason, as he wrote the original, " – *Paupertas impulit audax/Ut versus facerem* – "' ['Bold poverty drove me to writing verses', *Epistles* II. 2.51-2].[61] Smart's case is a sufficient demonstration that such hopes were often unfulfilled, and Pope's case shows that none of these motives precluded the possibility of a translation which was also a major original work; but it was not probable that such productions would challenge the prevailing literary expectations. As might, indeed, be expected, parody and burlesque often present a far more innovative response. In general, we find the ancient poets emerging from the mill of decorum in more or less undifferentiated batches of smooth rhyme, or blank verse, and elegant diction. They are generally met by the reviewers with correspondingly vague commendations such as 'not less faithful than elegant'; and when they are condemned, they are more often condemned on stylistic grounds than on those of accuracy. The reviews sometimes function as a positively reactionary force. Robert Potter, for example, draws attention to the 'simple unraised style' of Euripides, a quality which he signally fails to capture in his decorous blank verse, but even so a reviewer is ready to quarrel with 'several expressions too familiar and prosaic for the tragic Muse, and which by no means were necessary to give a faithful representation of the original'.[62] The failure of integration between scholarly labour and end-product is complete, and it is constantly underlined by the irrelevance of the learning displayed in the footnotes.[63]

The most important developments in eighteenth-century translation are, however, not to be found in these curiously hybrid works, but rather in the emergence into gradual respectability of literal translation (i.e. of prose translation even for poetry). The impetus came from .the French. French prose translations of classical poetry, like André Dacier's Horace and Anne Dacier's Homer, were in common use in England long before the idea of such a version in English was generally accepted. In the literary periodicals of the 1720s and 1730s, notably de la Roche's *New Memoirs of Literature* and its successor *The Present State of the Republic of Letters*, the new French publications are given generous space, and the notices of such works as Sanadon's *Horace*, Brumois's *Greek Theatre*, or Banier's *Ovid* regularly discuss the grounds for translating into prose rather than verse. As early as 1720, John Clarke, schoolmaster at Hull grammar school, had recommended the use of literal English translations in the teaching of Latin, and his recommendations were published as a separate *Dissertation upon the Usefulness of Translations* in 1734. Clarke argued that the use of dictionaries was both unhelpful to beginners and unnecessarily time-consuming. What was obviously a fast-growing demand was met a few years later by the publication of a number of editions of the major Latin poets on the model of Watson's *Horace* (first edition, 1743): *The Works of Horace, translated into English Prose, as near as the propriety of the two languages will admit. Together with the original Latin from the best editions. Wherein the words of the Latin text are ranged in their grammatical order: the ellipses carefully supplied: the observations of the most valuable commentators both ancient and modern, represented: and the author's design and beautiful descriptions fully set forth in a key annexed to each poem; with notes geographical, and historical: also the various readings of Dr Bentley. The whole adapted to the capacities of youth at school, as well as of private gentlemen.* On a more or less identical model are the texts produced by Joseph Davidson, who seems to have been in close and acrimonious competition with Watson for the market, and managed to secure for himself an apparently disregarded royal patent, and by John Stirling, who introduces the possibility that such works will be of service not only to 'the prince, the nobleman, and the gentleman', but to the tradesman and mechanic also.[64]

In these works the issue is seen in very narrowly educational terms: the literal version, like the ubiquitous *ordo* in which the Latin text was re-arranged into the order of construction, is a short-cut to the knowledge of Latin and the enjoyment of Latin poetry, by-passing the laborious consultation of grammars and dictionaries. Needless to say, the method had its critics, who saw it not only as an incitement to indolence but also as a poor substitute for the intellectual discipline of a strict grammatical approach. 'To the use of translations, and to the various modes of facilitating puerile studies, I may venture to attribute the decline of solid learning, and of that just taste which the ancient models tended to establish. Together with translations, I wish it were possible to banish those editions in which the order of construction is given on the same page with the text. . . . It tends to enervate the mind, by rendering exertion unnecessary.'[65] By the time Vicesimus Knox made his protest in 1781, the boom in the publication of such texts seems to have been over. Davidson's Virgil, first published in 1743, had its sixth and final edition in 1790. The editions themselves, like

Knox's criticism of them, are a further testimony to the sense of the rhetoric of typography prevalent in the eighteenth century. The components are variously arranged, with Watson perhaps the most adventurous in his decision, against the common practice, to print the Latin text on the right-hand page and the English version on the left, 'that the reader may cast his eye upon that first, which he understands best.'[66] (The Foulis press has a further variation, presumably for purely aesthetic effect, in several parallel text Greek/Latin editions, where the arrangement of text and version alternates on successive openings.)

In 1756 Christopher Smart published his first translation of Horace, a literal version with Latin text, spurred on by 'the extraordinary success which attempts of this kind have met with, though by men who manifestly did not understand the author, any otherwise than through a French medium; and tho' printed in large volumes, and sold at a proportionable price.' Smart's own two duodecimo volumes are also conceived in terms of those who wish to acquire, or recover, the Latin language, with the novel addition of 'such foreign gentlemen as are already acquainted with the Latin, and are desirous of being masters of the English language'.[67] Smart is as apologetic about the status of such an enterprise as any of his predecessors. The verse translation he was to publish in 1767 is, as its preface makes clear, much more congenial to him, although he does there allow that the power of 'impression' which he perceives in great poetry 'will sometimes keep it up thro' the medium of a prose translation; especially in scripture'.[68] But it is in the response of one reviewer to the literal version that we find the clearest suggestion of a wider view of the subject, where literal translation has its own values apart from those of pedagogic necessity.

> The greatest service that can be done Horace, at least the first, and that which the fewest writers have attempted, is to make him *literally* understood. It is a common thing to hear an author construed, what is called *well*, and *elegantly*, by persons who could not give, neither see, the literal, nor, therefore, his *full* meaning . . . The more finely a man talks, the more is the attention of his audience generally seduced from the weight and accuracy of his reasoning. . . To this fault in education, perhaps, may be ascribed the justice of the general complaint against the English versions of the classic authors: whilst the French, who pursue a contrary plan in this respect, have done more honour to their language by their translations of the Greek and Latin authors, than by any other cause. This was the particular policy of Lewis XIV to make his language spread. . .[69]

At the end of the second section I pointed out the growing dislike in the eighteenth century for the standard Latin versions of Greek poets. Here we see the same matter from a rather different perspective, where even the Latin version is preferable, by its plainness, to the more fashionable poetic rendering in English. William Godwin was something of an extremist in these matters – 'if we will not study the ancients in their own nervous and manly page, let us close their volumes for ever' – but he is a witness less sceptical than Samuel Johnson to the possibility of preferring the Latin version of Homer even to Pope.[70]

4. THE CRITIC'S TASK: COMMENTARIES AND THEIR RECEPTION

For the learned reader in the pre-lapsarian eighteenth century, the classical world was still an international one, whose language was Latin, with subsidiary French. Notes and prefaces to scholarly, as opposed to school, editions of the classical poets were still in Latin, which was generally recognized as a safeguard against geographical and chronological parochialism. When one Thomas Edwards in 1779 adopted the very curious practice, in an edition of Theocritus, of mixing Latin and English notes indiscriminately, Edmund Cartwright in the *Monthly Review* demurred: 'editions of ancient authors ought to be for the benefit of the learned world in general, and not to be confined to the advantage of a particular country.'[71] For 'the world' in another sense, however, the learned no longer had sole or even primary rights to classical literature. Joseph Priestley's extreme diagnosis of 'the great revolution in the state of learning in modern times' reveals a strong historical self-consciousness:

> Time was, when scholars might, with a good grace, disclaim all pretensions to any branch of knowledge but what was taught in the universities . . . the learned world and the common world being much more distinct from one another than they are now. . . . The politeness of the times has brought the learned and the unlearned into more familiar intercourse than they had together before. . . . Criticism, which was formerly the great business of a scholar's life, is now become the amusement of a leisure hour.[72]

The shift towards the vernacular as a medium for classical poetry – one of the most tangible manifestations of this new familiarity of intercourse – was to have far-reaching effects upon poetic commentary as well as upon the availability of the texts in different kinds of translation. Again the French had led the way. It is symptomatic that when Philip Francis, in 1743, attaches to his poetic translation of Horace (with the Latin text) a selection of critical notes translated into English from 'the best Latin and French commentators', chief among the 'Latin' commentators is Richard Bentley, while his contemporaries Dacier and Sanadon appear under their own national colours. (Earlier London editions of Horace had included Dacier's notes translated from French into Latin, although there is a precedent for the provision of English notes with a Latin text in school editions, like Nathan Bailey's Ovid as well as those by Watson, Stirling, and Davidson described in the previous section.)[73] The increase of activity in translating the classics, both catering to and producing an expanded audience for the Greek and Roman poets, is paralleled by a new phase in the demand for poetic commentary and critical guidance. Hitherto, little more had been available in English than such digests of biography and critical *dicta* as Sir Thomas Pope Blount's *Characters and Censures of the most Considerable Poets* (1694) or Basil Kennett's *Lives and Characters of the Ancient Grecian Poets* (1697), and the limited critical debate was dominated by the French neo-classical critics.[74] The availability of the texts themselves, however, even in verse translation, made the reiteration of the old commonplaces anachronistic.

As we saw in the last section, eighteenth-century poetic translations are regularly furnished with not merely the preface and glossary which we might look for today, but also a very detailed and scholarly commentary, sometimes threatening to dwarf the translation itself. The audience for such works is clearly of a very different nature from the traditional one for learned commentaries, and the difference is reflected in a new pre-occupation with issues of language and method. Robert Potter's translation of Aeschylus was first published in Norwich in 1777. In the following year a separate volume of *Notes on the Tragedies of Aeschylus*, inscribed to Elizabeth Montagu and apparently printed at her expense, was distributed *gratis* to the purchasers of Potter's translation. (The notes were subsequently incorporated into the second edition, in 1779.) In reviewing the volume George Colman commends the motive, agreeing that some assistance with such an unfamiliar author was 'absolutely requisite for the information of the English reader', but his criticisms of the end product underline its failure to adapt to the needs of a new audience. The commentator, he notes, seems 'reluctant', and dry; his style is inelegant, with too many 'low expressions' and 'familiar French phrases'. He might have included remarks on ancient drama 'more entertaining and instructive than adjust-ing the difference between Messrs. Pauw and Heath.'[75] Clearly it was not enough simply to produce in English what would before, and for another audience, have appeared in Latin. Classical commentary had been appropriated by the world of 'polite' literature, and it is this brief conflation of what had been two separate worlds that produces the distinctive character of an important eighteenth-century critical debate.

The most notorious example of the resultant clash is the part played by Richard Bentley in the English campaign of the controversy over Ancients versus Moderns, and its sequel in the reception of his great if misguided edition of Horace.[76] One of the most curious of the responses to the edition consists substantially of a translation of the notes into English – with the addition of some 'Notes upon Notes' to broaden the scope – and it was apparently successful enough to have completed its run of 24 monthly parts by 1713. The translation is not a simple aid to the faltering Latinist, despite the odd fact that it is listed in one of Lintot's advertisements under the heading 'proper for schools'. It is a burlesque translation, making the most of the idiosyncrasies of Bentley's racy Latin as well as of the inevitable differences in idiom and propriety between English and Latin an – interesting analogue of the Scriblerus notes to the *Dunciad*. 'But Acron and all his followers are Blockheads for supposing any such thing, as if Horace were Dead, or gone to Hell for Eurydice or some such Doxy; whereas he only speaks of the Woods and Groves of the Muses and Helicon . . . about which the Poets make such a Pother.'[77] The burlesque is pointed at the 'low and mean ways of speech' which Bentley's opponents had objected to in the English style of his essay on Phalaris,[78] but the simple linguistic device of transposing the commentary into English to allow it to parody itself is one which pinpoints the difficulties of producing commentary for an audience attuned to elegance rather than to the particular niceties of scholarship. Oldisworth (the probable author) is also able to pick up some of the more widespread affectations of the manners of international scholarship, for example in the not unfounded comment on a passage which brings in reference to the 'incomparable' Graevius, the 'most elegant' Burmann, and the 'most learned' Heinsius, on the strange rate at which these scholars 'love and compliment one another'.[79] The sense of clique-ishness often, of course, tends in the other direction: Lyttelton, for example, in his *Dialogues of the Dead* has Scaliger declare that 'in my controversies, I had a great help from the language I wrote in: for one can scold and call names with a much better grace in Latin than in French, or any tame, modern tongue.'[80] The same preoccupation with the style of critical language appears time after time in the reviews of commentaries and other works written in English, in the form of criticism of 'errors' or inelegancies. (A particularly piquant example in view of later developments is Owen Ruffhead's condemnation of the usage 'Act one, scene three' instead of the proper 'Act the first, scene the third', in Thomas Francklin's *Dissertation on Ancient Tragedy*.)[81]

Sensitivity to jargon is, of course, closely allied to the amateur's traditional suspicion of professionalism; as Johnson notes, 'every art has its dialect, uncouth and ungrateful to all whom custom has not reconciled to its sound.'[82] Distaste for an appearance of pedantry, one of the recurrent *topoi* of eighteenth-century discussions of classical learning, is epitomized at the most superficial level by Chesterfield's habit of prescribing dancing-masters as an antidote.[83] Pope's attack on Bentley in the *Dunciad* (the title itself has strong etymological connections with pedantry) stands at the other extreme of moral seriousness. ''Tis true', acknowledges 'Aristarchus', 'on Words is still our whole debate':

> In ancient Sense if any needs will deal,
> Be sure I give them Fragments, not a Meal;

What Gellius or Stobaeus hash'd before,
Or chew'd by blind old Scholiasts o'er and o'er.
The critic Eye, that microscope of Wit,
Sees hairs and pores, examines bit by bit:
How parts relate to parts, or they to whole,
The body's harmony, the beaming soul,
Are things which Kuster, Burmann, Wasse shall see,
When Man's whole frame is obvious to a *Flea*.
                                        (*The Dunciad*, IV, 219, 229–38)

The resonances of the *Essay on Man* ('Why has not Man a microscopic eye?'
Epistle I, 193) emphasize the close connection in the set of Pope's mind
between God and Nature in general and the great classical tradition in
particular. To a humanist like Pope, the kind of scholarship represented by
Bentley and his Dutch colleagues – which often itself came under the
heading 'Humanity' or 'Literae Humaniores' – involved not just a petty
obsession with the incidental details of classical literature but also an
abandonment of responsibility for the upholding of established literary
standards. The interest in the fragmentary, in dictionaries and compilations, in ancient commentators, and in the obscure constituted a real threat
to the stable system of literary values expressed in the very concept of the
Temple of Fame. The monolith was being turned into a collection of atoms
(and one might here compare the resistance of a genteel critic like Henry
Felton to the notion that 'the poems of Homer, in each of which appeareth
one continued formed design from one end to the other, were written in
loose Scraps on no settled premeditated scheme').[84] The opposition to
'pedantry' is not in itself a new theme, but it gains a new immediacy in an
age in which the ancient authors, and especially the classical poets, had
been appropriated by literary men as a standard of taste.

A strong moral resistance to the autonomy of words in isolation from
'things' permeates every level of eighteenth-century thinking about the
study of the classics.[85] Despite his image with the wits, Bentley did in fact
play a crucial rôle in the establishment of a historical method – best
exemplified in his *Dissertation upon the Epistles of Phalaris* (1699) – which was to
emerge at the end of the century in the German school of 'Altertumswissen-
schaft', the all-embracing study of the ancient world in terms of its
history, religion, and monuments as well as its literary texts. The edition of
Horace, however, with its copious Latin notes tied strictly to a discussion of
a particular textual reading, and with no gestures towards 'those things
which relate to history and ancient customs' except to throw light on the
text, can be seen, in a century obsessed with weighing the relative merits of
word and thing, as a monument to the verbal.[86] Pope himself, as a
commentator upon Homer, pays only sporadic attention to matters 'philosophical, historical, [or] geographical', and it is in the nature of his
enterprise in making an eighteenth-century *Iliad* that he is less concerned

with the 'otherness' of Homer than with the points of contact in Homer's 'judgment' and imagination. But in the important programmatic note to the commentary (the first note on *Iliad* I), he also dissociates himself from the verbal scholar in pursuit of 'various lections' and 'imaginary amphibologies'. His observations are to be 'critical and poetical', and of his predecessors he singles out for special mention Anne Dacier, who has made 'a further attempt than her predecessors to discover the beauties of the poet'.[87] Pope is fully attuned to the most subtle of verbal effects in Homer – rarely, indeed, has the 'microscope of wit' been better applied than in his commentary – but his eye is always on the appreciation in highly personalized terms of Homer's poetic genius, and it is this appreciation that he sets against what he sees as the hollow speculations of verbal criticism.

Pope's achievement in his 'observations' on the *Iliad* is one of great critical imagination, and deserves to be seen as something more than a mere appendage to the translation.[88] But his view, in the *Dunciad*, of the learning of his age has so over-matched that of the opposition that it may be worth stressing the weakness of his position as far as it concerns classical scholarship at least. The processes of selection and distortion through which classical civilization has reached the modern world demand a radical reconstruction from all the available evidence rather than simple homage to its outstanding monuments, and whatever the rhetorical force of that conscious assent to a unified system of values, it was inevitably the first business of classical scholarship to question, and therefore from some points of view to undermine it. As D. R. Shackleton-Bailey has commented in the same context, 'a subject does not survive on appreciation.'[89] The challenge of an unknown reviewer in the *Monthly Review* to the low estimation in which verbal knowledge was held underlines the dominance of such an attitude in subsequent decades. It seems, he says, the utmost ambition of 'professors of learning in our times . . . to be esteemed men of *polite and elegant taste*'. In a spirited if somewhat overwritten defence, he turns the old jibes boldly back on themselves, with Scaliger and Bentley reinstated as 'the first heroes in the republic of letters'. His central and most emotive theme is an analogy with New Testament criticism:

> It depends therefore intirely on a nice and critical knowledge of words to interpret and investigate what Christ has commanded; and many of those monstrous perversions of scripture, which fix so deep a stain on the history of human nature, derive their origin from the most gross ignorance in [i.e. of] the language and phraseology of the apostles, and are nothing but the crude effusions of unlettered superstition. Let any Christian but reflect a moment on this, and let him bless the days when *Clarke*, *Wetstein*, and *Erasmus* considered the New Testament as critics, not for systems but for sense. . . . We obey not now the edicts of the Pope. We are allowed to think, and want nothing but manly learning and study to think right.[90]

Penelope Wilson

It is a fitting irony that this recommendation of 'verbal knowledge, as the surest defence against the incursions of barbarism, and the absurdities of priests' should appear in a review of an edition of 'Longinus', since the treatise *On the Sublime* was the primary basis for that very concern with 'taste' (and the reviewer is as distrustful of the self-congratulatory aspects of such a concern in 'Longinus' as in his own contemporaries). As Pope himself was one of the first to recognize, the treatise had important implications for the methodology of poetic commentary, as well as for more general matters of criticism and aesthetics.[91] Pope's moral antipathy to modern methods of scholarship did not diminish his awareness of the dangers that attach to the 'appreciative' school. Even in the first note to the *Iliad*, already referred to, he expresses reservations about the Dacier style of commentary, which offers only 'general praises and exclamations' instead of reasons for critical judgments; and by the time he has reached book XV the reservations have become much stronger.

> As this practice of extolling without giving reasons, is very convenient for most writers; so it excellently suits the ignorance or laziness of most readers, who will come into any sentiment rather than take the trouble of refuting it. Thus the complement [sic] is mutual. . . . They may go roundly on, admiring and exclaiming in this manner; *What an exquisite Spirit of Poetry – How beautiful a Circumstance – What Delicacy of Sentiments – With what Art has the Poet – In how sublime and just a manner – How finely imagined – How wonderfully beautiful and poetical –* And so proceed, without one reason to interrupt the course of their eloquence, most comfortably and ignorantly apostrophising to the end of the chapter.[92]

In the same year (1718) as this note appeared in the fourth volume of Pope's *Iliad*, Joseph Trapp published his translation of the *Aeneid*, with notes in which he too saw it as his aim to comment on Virgil as a poet, to offer remarks on his genius and judgment rather than mere 'explanations of his meaning'. But the similarity with Pope's method goes little further. 'In some places I endeavour to give reasons for the beauties of my author: in others I pretend to no more than to mark them . . . it must be remembered, that those beauties are often the greatest, which are capable of no other praise, than that of being shown, and admired.'[93] Trapp's *Praelectiones Poeticae*, the lectures delivered in his capacity as Professor of Poetry in Oxford, which offer an extended example of the pursuit of the *je ne sais quoi*, may have been in Pope's mind – they had been singled out by Henry Felton in 1713 as a prime example of what a 'polite critic' may achieve, as distinct from the 'dry, sour, verbal, study' engaged in by earlier practitioners.[94]

The practice throughout the century of commentators aiming at this wider 'polite' market is as variable as they are numerous. For some, the text of their chosen author does seem to have offered a temptingly open arena for the exercise of a hobby-horse – like Edward Burnaby-Greene's obsession

88

in his translation of Pindar in 1778 with emendation and with relating ancient myths to Biblical prototypes. There is some truth in the verdict of the *Critical* reviewer (perhaps Smollett himself) on the commentary to Grainger's *Tibullus* as 'a huge farrago of learned lumber, jumbled together to very little purpose, seemingly calculated to display the translator's reading, rather than to illustrate the sense and beauty of the original.'[95] It is interesting, however, to note how often this theme recurs, and that it is not restricted to the discussion of works presented in English for the benefit of the less learned reader. Since John Langhorne is one of the most prolific reviewers of classical publications in the *Monthly Review* in the 1760s, it is worth quoting at length from one of his most impassioned contributions, on the notes on Greek tragedians published in 1762 by Benjamin Heath, town clerk of Exeter – one of the century's characteristically extramural Greek scholars. Langhorne's image of the commentator is a striking prototype of that later 'Bat of erudition', George Eliot's Mr Casaubon:

> The task of the Commentator is the most tedious and toilsome of any within the province of literature. The eternal drudgery of collating manuscripts and editions; of tracing the Proteus, conjecture, through all his evasive forms, and wading through the vast profound of Batavian erudition, is dreadful even to think of. . . . But as there is a secret delight even in the pursuit and discovery of geometrical truths, so we suppose some solitary pleasure of the same kind may accompany the wandering commentator through the barren desarts that have been travelled by his predecessors. . . . Would these commentators take it into their heads to enliven their works with sentimental as well as verbal observations, they would be more honourable and more useful; but it is all measuring lines, and weighing syllables. They content themselves with cleaning and scrubbing the picture, without once remarking its particular beauties, or teaching the less skilful beholder the *criteria* which he wants. These sentimental comments would be extremely useful in forming the taste of the young reader, who alone can be supposed to stand in need of a commentator. We cannot indeed but wonder that a person of Dr Heath's erudition should pass silently over so many beautiful scenes without one *euge Poeta!* How could you, Doctor, overlook that animated scene in the first Act of the *Septem apud Thebas*, where the spy describes the appearance and sacrifice of the enemy, without erecting one note of admiration? Not so the acute Longinus. . . .[96]

This is in marked contrast with the endorsement of the severest labours of the textual critic offered by the reviewer quoted on p. 87. In the particular context of Greek tragedy it is an odd stance for 1762, since from a scholarly point of view men like Heath, and Samuel Musgrave who published notes on Euripides in the same year, were pioneers in a study in which the major advances were to be made by Richard Porson, still at this point only three years old; while as far as the general literary public was concerned, Greek drama had met with scant appreciation in the age of Garrick.[97] It is all the more striking to observe how Langhorne's language enacts a kind of appropriation of Greek tragedy, from one point of view a specialized and unfamiliar study, into the less specialist world of literary sensibility. The understanding of Greek tragedy becomes a matter purely of acquiring maturity of taste. The introduction of the word *criteria* illustrates the process by which the function of the critic – a word which in earlier usage tended to have a broad application, to include the philologist and scholar as well as the more generally literary individual – is separated and distinguished from that of, for example, the commentator, as one concerned specifically with the *assessment* of literature.[98]

The antithesis of 'verbal' commentary has modulated here from 'critical and poetical' into 'sentimental', and the use of that elusive and fashionable word suggests one way in which the material of this essay can be brought into a single focus. Six years later Laurence Sterne's sentimental traveller is equally dismissive of the uses of what might be called commentary upon foreign lands, having it as his aim to spy the nakedness of French hearts *through* 'the different disguises of customs, climates, and religion'.[99] Many of the developments I have been tracing in the ways in which classical poetry was becoming available to the English reader can be seen as contributing to just such a confident sense of immediate and unresearched rapport. The proprietorial pride in British classical publications, the emergence of texts from the library to the pocket and from the obscurity of Greek and Latin into the light of French and English, and perhaps especially the growing confidence in the fidelity of a literal rather than an 'improved' poetic version – all these developments were bringing classical poetry into a kind of contemporaneity with the tasteful English reader. Such a reader might well feel in point of access nearly on a level with, and in point of taste well above, the scholar content to spend his life hunting after words in dusty libraries. While classical scholarship was gaining in historical conscious-ness of the otherness of the ancient world and of the contingency and the incompleteness of our material knowledge of it, the non-specialist literary world was able to feel a new confidence in its encounters with the poetic masterpieces of Greece and Rome. The literary periodicals, like the translations of the period, are striking evidence of the apparent unity of the literate world: scholarly excursuses and textual cruces find their places happily alongside accounts of works of political theory or modern novels, with no more than a passing nod towards 'our classical readers' as a special category. M. L. Clarke noted more than thirty years ago that 'when we turn from the eighteenth century to the nineteenth we are conscious of a change in the relations between learning and literature. There is an estrangement between them which had scarcely existed in the previous century.'[100] Perhaps the unity had never gone much deeper than the printed page: but the grounds of that estrangement are clearly to be seen in the very efforts which the eighteenth century had made to build bridges across the gap.

NOTES

1. Philip Dormer Stanhope, fourth Earl of Chesterfield, *Letters*, ed. B. Dobree (1932), III, 1155 (to his son, 27 May 1748). The most important modern study of eighteenth-century classicism is J. W. Johnson, *The Formation of English Neo-Classical Thought* (Princeton, 1967). On classical education, see M. L. Clarke, *Greek Studies in England 1700–1830* (1945) and *Classical Education in Britain 1500–1900* (1959); on classical scholarship in Britain and Europe see R. Pfeiffer, *History of Classical Scholarship from 1300 to 1850* (1976), and the second volume of J. E. Sandys, *A History of Classical Scholarship* (repr. 1967). More specifically literary aspects of the classical tradition in this period are treated by D. Bush, *Mythology and the Romantic Tradition in English Poetry* (Cambridge, Mass., 1937); G. Highet, *The Classical Tradition* (1949); and J. A. K. Thomson, *The Classical Background of English Literature* (1948) and *Classical Influences on English Poetry* (1951). See also R. M. Ogilvie, *Latin and Greek: a History of the Influence of the Classics on English Life from 1600 to 1918* (1964).

2. Chesterfield, *Letters*, III, 1106 (22 February 1748); Fielding, *Joseph Andrews*, ed. M. C. Battestin (1967), 238 (Book III, 6).

3. See the entries under 'Modern studies: foreign sources and influences' in *New Cambridge Bibliography of English Literature*, II, cols. 34–5: K. Simonsuuri, *Homer's Original Genius: Eighteenth Century Notions of the Early Greek Epic (1688–1798)* (1979); and P. B. Wilson, 'The knowledge and appreciation of Pindar in the seventeenth and eighteenth centuries' (D. Phil. thesis, University of Oxford, 1974).

4. Edward Gibbon, *Miscellaneous Works*, ed. John Lord Sheffield, II (1796), 50–70, 94–118. See also G. Keynes, ed., *The Library of Edward Gibbon* (orig. publ. 1940, 1980 repr.); G. Whalley, 'Thomas Gray: a quiet Hellenist', in *Fearful Joy: Papers from the Thomas Gray Bicentenary Conference*, ed. J. Downey and B. Jones

(Montreal, 1974), 146–71; M. N. Austin, 'The classical learning of Samuel Johnson', *Studies in the Eighteenth Century*, ed. R. F. Brissenden (Canberra, 1968), 285–306; R. A. Brower, *Alexander Pope: the Poetry of Allusion* (1959). On Pope's reading for the translations from Homer, see H.-J. Zimmer mann, *Alexander Popes Noten er zu Homer* (Heidelberg, 1966), esp. 13–55.

5. A. N. L. Munby (ed.), *Sale Catalogues of Libraries of Eminent Persons*, I (1971), 45–66.

6. For a discussion of one of the earliest examples, see J. Barnard, 'Dryden, Tonson, and subscriptions for the 1697 Virgil', *Publ. Bibliographical Soc. of America*, LVII (1963), 129–51.

7. See Clarke, *Greek Studies*, and *Classical Education*.

8. M. C. Battestin and F. Bowers (eds.), *The History of Tom Jones*, I (1974), 421 (Book VIII, 5).

9. Until the very end of the century Aeschylus was much less widely read than either Sophocles or Euripides. See Clarke, *Greek Studies*, 151–3.

10. Fielding, *Amelia*, ed. A. R. Humphreys (repr. 1968), II, 77 (Book VIII, 5). In Anthony Blackwall's *Introduction to the Classics* (1718), Statius, Silius Italicus, Claudian, and Lucan are listed among those authors who need only be read once (p. 112). It is interesting that John Hill, in his *Observations on the Greek and Roman Classics*, published two years after *Amelia* in 1753, engages (pp. 253–7) in a ranking procedure similar to Booth's.

11. Fielding, *Amelia*, ed. Humphreys, I, 289 (Book VI, 7).

12. See M. Reynolds, *The Learned Lady in England 1650–1760* (Boston and New York, 1920), 372–419.

13. Fielding, *Amelia*, ed. Humphreys, I, 289 (Books VI, 7) and II, 306–7 (Book XII, 8). Mrs Atkinson's mistake seems the more forgivable for being shared with the Twickenham editors of Pope in 1967 (*The Poems of Alexander Pope*, VII, ed. M. Mack and others, lxxviii). For the Delphin classics see p. 76.

14. Fielding, *Amelia*, ed. Humphreys, II, 185–6 (Book X, 3): cf. II, 166–8 (Book X, 1).

15. Boswell, *Life of Johnson*, ed. R. W. Chapman, with corrections by J. D. Fleeman (1970), 44.

16. J. H. Monk, *Life of Richard Bentley* (second edn, 1833), I, 3.

17. Robert Potter, *The Tragedies of Euripides* (1781–3), I, xvi.

18. See *Monthly Rev.*, xxiv (1761), 154–6; *The Greek Theatre of Father Brumoy*, tr. Charlotte Lennox and others (1759); Joseph Trapp, *The Aeneis of Virgil* (1718); and compare *An Essay in Defence of the Female Sex . . . in a Letter to a Lady*, *written by a Lady* (1696).

19. Laetitia Pilkington, *Memoirs* (1748), I, 27–8; Joseph Spence, *Observations, Anecdotes, and Characters of Books and Men*, ed. J. M. Osborn (1966), I, 303. Examples cited by Reynolds, *op. cit.*, 223 and 196. For Elizabeth Carter and the other women referred to in this paragraph, see Reynolds, *op. cit.*, 137–257.

20. Elizabeth Elstob, *Rudiments of Grammar for the English-Saxon Tongue* (1715).

21. See J. W. Ashley Smith, *The Birth of Modern Education: The Contribution of the Dissenting Academies 1660–1800* (1954). For the impact on classical studies, see esp. 258–61. Cf. John Locke, *Some Thoughts Concerning Education* (orig. publ. 1693; 1970 repr.), 193–212.

22. Sheridan, *British Education* (1756; 1971 facsimile), 221.

23. Godwin, 'Of the study of the classics', *The Enquirer: Reflections on Education, Manners, and Literature* (1797), 36; and *An Account of the Seminary that will be opened . . . at Epsom in Surrey* (1783), 8–9.

24. [John Gordon], *Occasional Thoughts on the Study and Character of Classical Authors, on the Course of Litterature, and the Present Plan of a Learned Education* (1762), 9–11.

25. See especially James Beattie, 'Remarks on the utility of classical learning, written in the year 1769', *Essays* (1776), 489–555; *The Monthly Rev.*, lxi (1779), 434–6; Vicesimus Knox, *Liberal Education* (1781); and Joseph Cornish, *An Attempt to Display the Importance of Classical Learning* (1783).

26. Knox, *Works* (1824), III, 383; Cornish, *op. cit.*, 8; George Chapman, *A Treatise on Education* (fourth edn, 1790), 82. On the socially repressive aspects of eighteenth-century education in general, see R. D. Altick, *The English Common Reader* (Chicago, 1957), 31–3.

27. Cornish, *op. cit.*, 8–9 and 59–66. One of the chief advocates of the new methods was John Clarke, who published several works on the subject, including *An Essay upon the Education of Youth in Grammar-Schools* (1720). See above, p. 81. Contrast Beattie, *Essays*, 506–7; Goodwin, *An Account of the Seminary*, 12–13; Knox, *Works*, III, 430–2.

28. Henry Felton, *A Dissertation on Reading the Classics and Forming a Just Style* (1713, and many later editions); John Hill, *Observations on the Greek and Roman Classics* (1753).

29. A recurrent theme: see, e.g. Felton on Catullus (p. 35) and Hill on Sappho, Alcaeus, Anacreon, Catullus and Ausonius (pp. 184, 187, 190–1, 238, 259–60). Philip Francis, *The Odes, Epodes, and Carmen Seculare of Horace. In Latin and English* (1743), silently omits Horace's eighth and twelfth epodes; Joseph Davidson, *The Odes, Epodes and Carmen Seculare of Horace, Translated into English Prose* (1742 and many later editions), prints the Latin but does not translate; David Watson, *The Works of Horace, translated into English Prose* (1743 and later editions), translates only in part; Christopher Smart, *The Works of Horace, Translated Literally into English Prose* (1756), simply offers, by what he terms a 'pious fraud', a sanitized English version, sensibly rejecting the 'Delphin' policy of asterisks as an invitation rather than an impediment to youthful curiosity.

30. There is clearly something of a gap between the image and the material from which it is constructed. For a full exploration of the political issues, see H. Weinbrot, *Augustus Caesar in 'Augustan' England: The Decline of a Classical Norm* (Princeton, 1978), esp. chapters 4 and 5.

31. *Florilegium Poeticum ex Ovidio, Tibullo, Propertio, Martiali, etc., ab omni verborum*

obscoenitate repurgatum. In usum tyronum
(1744); William Foot, *An Essay on
Education* (n.d., 1750?), 20; Chapman,
Treatise on Education, 197.

32. Foot, *Essay on Education*, 15; Cornish,
op. cit., 36; Fielding, *Amelia*, II, 74
(Book VIII, 5); Gibbon, *Memoirs of my
Life*, ed. G. A. Bonnard (1966), 119.
Cf. James Grainger's translation of
Tibullus (above, p. 80).

33. Beattie, *Essays*, 505.

34. *The Pythian, Nemean, and Isthmian Odes of
Pindar* (1778), xxxviii.

35. *Monthly Rev.*, XVII (1757), 339–40. The
reviewer is identified as Owen Ruffhead
by B. C. Nangle, *The Monthly Review
First Series 1749–89: Indexes of Contributors
and Articles* (1934). On this theme,
compare, from 1712, *The Spectator*, ed.
D. F. Bond (1965), III, 381–2 (no. 367).

36. E. Harwood, *View of the Various Editions
of the Greek and Roman Classics, with
Remarks* (1775), vi. Gibbon's notes on
the fourth edition of Harwood, written
in 1793, were among the new material
included in the expanded *Miscellaneous
Works* (5 vols., 1814, and 3 vols., 1815).

37. For Coleridge's Pindar, see his
Notebooks, ed. K. Coburn, II (1962),
2887 and n., and III (1973), 3721 and n.

38. A. T. Hazan (ed.), *A Catalogue of Horace
Walpole's Library* (1969), I, lii.

39. *The Dunciad*, IV, 394n: *The Poems of
Alexander Pope*, ed. J. Butt (1939–69), V,
380–1; Harwood, vi–viii. A catalogue of
Douglas's Horace collection is
published in David Watson's edition of
Horace (see above, p. 81).

40. See D. W. Davies, *The World of the
Elseviers, 1580–1712* (The Hague, 1954),
142–55.

41. Keynes, *op. cit.*, 288.

42. P. Gaskell, *John Baskerville: a
Bibliography* (1959), xix; and see also
E. J. Kenney, *The Classical Text* (1974),
154.

43. Chesterfield, *Letters*, III, 1066–7.

44. See P. Gaskell, *A Bibliography of the
Foulis Press* (1964); and in general,
P. Gaskell, 'Printing the classics in the
eighteenth century', *The Book Collector*, I
(1952), 98–111.

45. Harwood, *op. cit.*, v–vi.

46. On the importance of Bentley for the

history of scholarship, see R. Pfeiffer,
*History of Classical Scholarship from 1300 to
1850*, 143–63; and Kenney, *op. cit.*,
71–4, 100–1. The final chapter of R. C.
Jebb's *Bentley* (1882) is still a useful
general summary.

47. From the preface to his edition of
Horace (1711) (my translation).

48. P. Francis, *The Odes, Epodes, and Carmen
Seculare of Horace* (1743), xv.

49. Advertisement at end of Joseph
Davidson's *Odes, Epodes, and Carmen
Seculare of Horace* (5th edn, 1760). In
Germany later in the century, J. G.
Herder's review of Heyne's 1773
Göttingen edition of Pindar is almost
wholly devoted to Heyne's
achievements in re-punctuating the
'dithyrambic flights' (*Dithyrambenflüge*)
of his text: Herder, *Sämmtliche Werke*,
ed. B. Suphan, XXXIII (Berlin, 1913),
206–15.

50. Gibbon, *Miscellaneous Works*, III (1815),
579.

51. H. Gally, *A Dissertation Against
Pronouncing the Greek Language According to
Accents* (1754), 105; cf. John
Langhorne's review of the controversy
in the *Monthly Rev.*, XXVIII (1763),
345–9. For an account of the more
scholarly aspects, see S. Allen, *Vox
Graeca: A Guide to the Pronunciation of
Classical Greek* (2nd edn, 1974), 134–7,
and *Accent and Rhythm: Prosodic Features
of Latin and Greek* (1973), 271–4.

52. Knox, *Works*, III, 435–6.

53. Burton, *Pentalogia, sive Tragoediarum
Graecarum Delectus* (1758), 11–15.
Goldsmith expresses his approval in the
Monthly Rev., XIX (1758), 523–4.

54. Various aspects of English Hellenism
before 1800 have been explored in such
works as B. H. Stern, *The Rise of
Romantic Hellenism in English Literature
1732–1786* (Wisconsin, 1940); Clarke,
Greek Studies; T. J. B. Spencer, *Fair
Greece, Sad Relic: A Study of Literary
Philhellenism from Shakespeare to Byron*
(1954); Simonsuuri, *op. cit.* See especially,
for an important general discussion of
the evidence, Johnson, *op. cit.*

55. *Gentleman's Mag.*, LVI (1786), 207.

56. *An Essay in Defence of the Female Sex*,
41–4.

57. For the 'Hymn to Ceres', see the *Monthly Rev.*, LXIII (1780), 481–92, and LXVI (1782), 414–6. The entry for Tyrtaeus in *New Cambridge Bibliography of English Literature*, II (col. 1495) gives no sense of his popularity as a model of patriotic and martial virtue. Brueggemann lists several translations of individual elegies as well as a complete translation in 1761 and *The War-Elegies . . .* imitated by Henry James Pye in 1795. In 1759 the Foulis brothers published *Spartan Lessons; or the Praise of Valour; in the Verses of Tyrtaeus; an Ancient Athenian Poet, Adopted by the Republic of Lacedaemon, and Employed to Inspire Their Youth With Warlike Sentiments*. For a full account of the background to this interest in Sparta, see E. Rawson, *The Spartan Tradition in European Thought* (1969).

58. *The Aeneis of Virgil* (1718), I, xxxix.

59. H. J. Pye, *Six Olympic Odes of Pindar* (1775). On translation, see in general L. Kelly, *The True Interpreter: a History of Translation Theory and Practice in the West* (1979); J. W. Draper, 'The theory of translation in the eighteenth century', *Neophilologus*, VI (1921), 241–54; and the excellent brief study by R. A. Brower, 'Seven Agamemnons', reprinted in *Mirror on Mirror* (Cambridge, Mass., 1974), 159–80. Smart's verse translation of Horace's *Odes* has recently been edited, with an introduction, by A. Sherbo (Victoria, B. C., 1979). There are interesting eighteenth-century discussions of Pope's method in translating Homer, e.g. in the *Gentleman's Mag.*, XI (1741), 599–601, and in Thomas Twining's dissertation 'On poetry considered as an imitative art', in *Aristotle's Treatise on Poetry translated* (orig. publ. 1789; 1972 repr.), 30–34; more recently, see the introduction to Pope's *The Iliad of Homer* in the Twickenham edition, VII, xxxv–ccxlix, and H. A. Mason's *To Homer through Pope: An Introduction to Homer's Iliad and Pope's Translation* (1972).

60. James Grainger, *A Poetical Translation of the Elegies of Tibullus; and of the Poems of Sulpicia. With the Original Text, and Notes Critical and Explanatory* (1759), I, vii.

61. *The Works of Horace, Translated into Verse. With a Prose Interpretation, for the Help of Students.*

62. Potter, *Euripides*, I, xv; *Monthly Rev.*, LXVII (1782), 242.

63. In some, like Grainger's *Tibullus*, the awkwardness is greatly increased by the fact that all the notes, even the most detailed discussions of the text, are keyed in by line number to the translation rather than to the original (see, e.g. II, 63, where the note on I. 48 actually refers to I.39 of the Latin text, on p. 60).

64. The first edition of Davidson's Virgil was published in 1743; Horace in 1746; Ovid, *Epistles* in 1746, and *Metamorphoses* in 1748. Stirling's Virgil (*Pastorals* and *Georgics*) first appeared in 1741; Horace in 1752–3; Ovid, *Tristia* (second edition) in 1752; and Juvenal in 1760.

65. Knox, *Essays*, III, 437–8. Other advocates of the 'plain text' include William Godwin (see above, p. 83) and, at the end of the seventeenth century, the celebrated Dr Richard Busby, headmaster of Westminster School (see Felton, *op. cit.*, 56–7).

66. Watson, *Horace*, (4th edn, 1760), vi.

67. *The Works of Horace, Translated Literally into English Prose; for the Use of those who are Desirous of Acquiring or Recovering a Competent Knowledge of the Latin Language* (1756), v.

68. *The Works of Horace* (1767), I, xii.

69. *Monthly Rev.*, XVI (1757), 34–5. There are valuable, if rather disorganized, hints on 'interlinearity' as a Romantic ideal in Kelly, *The True Interpreter*, e.g. 92–4.

70. Godwin, *An Account of the Seminary*, 12–3: 'were I to search for a true idea of the style and composition of Homer, I think I should rather recur to the verbal translation in the margin of the original, than to the version of Pope.' Cf. Johnson, 'Life of Pope', *Lives*, ed. G. Birkbeck Hill (1905), III, 114; and Boswell, *Life of Johnson*, 921, 979.

71. *Monthly Rev.*, LXI (1779), 321–2.

72. *An Essay on a Course of Liberal Education for Civil and Active Life* (1765), 21–3.

73. Francis, *Horace* (4 vols., 1743–6). For

Bailey, see e.g. *Ovid's Tristia . . . With Arguments and Notes of J. Minellius Translated into English; to which is Added a Prose Version, viz. the Very Words of Ovid Digested into the Proper Ordo They Ought to be Taken in Construing* (1726). His frequently reprinted edition of the *Metamorphoses* is attacked by Gordon, *op. cit.*, 53–4.

74. See *New Cambridge Bibliography of English Literature*, II, cols. 65–8 for a list of the works of French criticism translated into English; and A. F. B. Clark, *Boileau and the French Classical Critics in England (1660–1830)* (Paris, 1925).

75. *Monthly Rev.*, LIX (1778), 466.

76. On the reception of Bentley's Horace, see J. H. Monk, *op. cit.*, I, 316–24.

77. *The Odes, Epodes, and Carmen Seculare of Horace . . . with a Translation of Dr Ben-ley's Notes. To Which are Added Notes upon Notes. In 24 Parts Complete* (1713), part 12 (on *Odes* 3.4.7).

78. Cf. R. C. Jebb, *Bentley* (1895), 70–71.

79. *Odes, Epodes, and Carmen Seculare*, part 5, 20.

80. George Lyttelton, *Dialogues of the Dead* (1760), 107; and cf. Twining, *Aristotle's Treatise on Poetry*, x–xi, on the 'disgusting, though privileged, language of emendatory criticism on ancient authors'.

81. *Monthly Rev.*, XXIII (1760), 9.

82. *The Rambler*, CLXXIII (12 November 1751); *The Yale Edition of the Works of Samuel Johnson*, V, ed. W. J. Bate and A. B. Strauss (1969), 151.

83. E.g. to his godson, 5 October 1768: 'I would have you understand Greek and Latin as well as Graevius, Gronovius, and Gruterus ever did, but at the same time I would have you dance and dress better than I am apt to think they did' (*Letters*, VI, 2863). Cf. also Felton, *op. cit.*, 47–9.

84. Felton, *op. cit.*, 27–8. The importance of the microscope and related images for Pope and his contemporaries is usefully explored by P. Fussell, *The Rhetorical World of Augustan Humanism* (1965), ch. 10.

85. Cf. John Gordon, above, p. 73. It is a central theme in most of the discussions of classical education – e.g. Clarke,

Essay, 8–9; *Monthly Rev.*, LXI (1779), 434; Beattie, *Essays*, 494–502; Godwin, *Enquirer*, 52–4.

86. *Q. Horatius Flaccus*, ed. Bentley (1711).

87. Pope, *The Iliad of Homer*, ed. M. Mack and others (1967): *Poems*, VII, 82.

88. There are fuller treatments of the commentary in Zimmermann, *op. cit.*, and F. Rosslyn, 'The making of Pope's translation of the *Iliad*' (Ph. D. thesis, University of Cambridge, 1979).

89. 'Bentley and Horace', *Procs. Leeds Philosophical and Literary Soc.*, X (1962), 115.

90. *Monthly Rev.*, LX (1779), 376–7. According to B. C. Nangle's *Index of Contributors*, the historian John Gillies had some part in the review.

91. Cf. also Edward Gibbon's notes on his reading of 'Longinus', *Miscellaneous Works*, II (1796), 72–87. The standard account is S. H. Monk, *The Sublime: A Study of Critical Theories in Eighteenth Century England* (New York, 1935).

92. *Poems*, VIII, 231.

93. Trapp, *The Aeneis of Virgil*, I, 313.

94. Felton, *op. cit.*, XV–XVI.

95. *Critical Rev.*, VI (1759), 477. Grainger – a contributor to the rival *Monthly Review* – responded in a letter to Smollett, discussed at some length in the seventh number of the *Critical Review*, 140–58.

96. *Monthly Rev.*, XXVI (1762), 321–5.

97. On tragic scholarship, see Clarke, *Greek Studies*, 61–3 and 72–5, and on taste, the same work, 147–53.

98. Edward Gibbon makes a similar point in his *Essai sur l'Étude de la Litterature* (1761), an exceptionally interesting analysis from a French perspective of the impact of the debate over ancients and moderns on learning and criticism: 'On a ôté à cette étude [the study of ancient literature] le nom de Belles-Lettres, qu'une longue préscription sembloit lui avoir consacré, pour y substituer celui d'érudition. Nos littérateurs sons devenus des érudits' (*Miscellaneous Works*, II, 452).

99. Sterne, *A Sentimental Journey through France and Italy*, ed. G. D. Stout Jr (Berkeley and Los Angeles, 1967), 217–18. For a detailed study of the uses

of the word, see E. Erametsa, *A Study of the Word Sentimental and of Other Linguistic Characteristics of the Eighteenth-Century* *Sentimentalism in England* (Helsinki, 1951).

100. Clarke, *Greek Studies*, 164.

5
Biblical criticism, literature, and the eighteenth-century reader

THOMAS R. PRESTON

I. INTRODUCTION

After escaping from the house of the 'roasting squire', the main characters in Fielding's *Joseph Andrews*, Parson Abraham Adams, Fanny Goodwill, and Joseph, retire to a nearby inn. Here Adams enters into a discussion with a 'grave Man' he supposes a Church of England clergyman, but who is actually a Roman priest in disguise. The piety of the priest's discourse evokes a typically enthusiastic response from Adams: '"Give me your Hand, Brother," said *Adams* in a Rapture. . . . "I believe I have preached every Syllable of your Speech twenty times over: For it has always appeared to me easier for a Cable Rope (which by the way is the true rendering of that Word we have translated *Camel*) to go through the Eye of a Needle, than for a rich Man to get into the Kingdom of Heaven."'[1] Adams' translation of the phrase from Matthew 19:24 and Mark 10:25 reflects an old debate in biblical criticism. The translation had been suggested as a possibility since patristic times, and although usually rejected, continued to be at least discussed in most of the late seventeenth- and eighteenth-century commentaries on the New Testament.[2]

For an understanding of the novel, the correct translation of the disputed passage holds little importance. What is important, however, is that by so casual and passing an allusion Fielding implies his general readers will know of the problem in translation and understand the terms of the biblical debate. It is doubtful that many general readers today, including the most highly educated, would catch an allusion to problems in current biblical interpretation, never mind understand the debate about them. Fielding, however, clearly expects quite the contrary from his contemporary readers. His expectations, I think, were certainly not unreasonable, and in this essay I will try to justify them. The discussion will indicate briefly the popularity of biblical criticism in eighteenth-century England; give a synoptic view of the variety and major works of biblical criticism, regrettably often merely a list of titles and names with brief comments; explain the consolidation of biblical criticism into a body of received interpretation; and finally suggest significant relationships between biblical criticism and eighteenth-century literature.

2. THE VARIETY AND POPULARITY OF BIBLICAL CRITICISM

Biblical criticism covers a number of different but related aspects of biblical study, including textual criticism and the so-called 'Higher Criticism' that deals with such problems as authorship, genuineness of the text, or canonical authority. In this essay, however, I use the term primarily to designate hermeneutics, that area of biblical study concerned with the art or science of interpreting the meaning of biblical texts.[3] One of the main hermeneutic problems, the determination of the historical context behind the language used by the biblical writers, began to be explored seriously in the late seventeenth century. In practice, this aspect of hermeneutics focused on biblical exegesis and exposition, the most important of which survives in major biblical commentaries, general guides to interpretation, and studies of ancient Hebrew history and antiquities. Taken together these works of late seventeenth- and eighteenth-century biblical criticism, whether written by dissenters or members of the Established Church,[4] comprise a kind of 'received interpretation' of the Old and New Testaments. In turn, this body of received interpretation forms a considerable portion of the religious literature published in eighteenth-century England and read by the general reader.

There have been several studies of eighteenth-century reading habits and vogues, and all the evidence points to an almost astonishing interest in religious works generally and biblical criticism specifically. I. W. J. Machin has assembled many important statistics in 'Popular religious works of the eighteenth century: their vogue and influence'.[5] As might be expected, sermons dominated religious publishing from the Restoration to the middle of the eighteenth century. According to Sampson Letsome's *An Index to the Sermons, Published since the Restoration* (1751), 8,800 sermons were published from 1660 to 1751, about 96 a year.[6] In the decades from 1700 to 1790, an average of 230 books on religion (including Bibles and Prayer Books) was published annually.[7] Excluding Bibles and Prayer Books, the Term Registers for 1700–1708 show the publication of 144 new religious works every year.[8] In public libraries, like those at Bristol, Bedford, and Bamborough Castle, religious works dominated the holdings.[9] From 1731 to 1779 the *Gentleman's Magazine* devoted about 20 per cent of its reviews or 'books mentioned' to religious works, and in discussions of religious topics presented in the *Gentleman's* and the *Monthly Review*, the Bible equals the topics on general Christianity and the question of subscription to the Thirty Nine Articles.[10] Biblical commentaries (I include annotated editions of the Bible) went though an astonishing number of editions: there were ten editions of Matthew Henry's *An Exposition of All the Books of the Old and New Testament* within the eighteenth century, and five of Bishop Simon Patrick's *Old Testament Commentary*. Biblical commentaries covering both Testaments, including Henry's, totalled 123 editions.[11]

New Testament commentaries enjoyed equal popularity, totalling 71 editions during the course of the century. William Burkitt's commentary went though 8 editions, Henry Hammond's 7, Daniel Whitby's 7, Philip Doddridge's 7, Samuel Clarke's 9, John Wesley's 5, and George Stanhope's *Paraphrase and Commentary upon All the Epistles and Gospels Appointed to be Read in the Church of England on all Sundays and Holy-Days* 5.[12] Borrowings from public and cathedral libraries reflect the publishing figures; books on religious subjects and biblical commentaries top the list.[13] This borrowing and buying trend extends to provincial England. Roy Wiles has recently shown that the range of books offered for sale in the provinces was large, but the most frequently advertised were 'travel books, biography, history, geography, descriptions of England and Wales, commentaries on the Bible'.[14] With the rise in the number of printing presses in England from 75 to 150 between 1724 and 1757, quadrupling the annual publication of books,[15] it is clear that the amount of religious publication, especially of biblical criticism, also continued to rise or at least maintain its own.

Before consulting a variety of specialized works and the biblical commentaries themselves, the eighteenth-century reader could refer to a number of shorter works that introduced him to the contents of the Bible and provided him with the basic methods for interpretation. As early as 1678 John Wilson had published *The Scripture's Genuine Interpreter Asserted: or, A Discourse concerning the right Interpretation of Scripture*, while in the same year appeared John Owen's *The Causes, Ways, and Means of Understanding the Mind of God as Revealed in his Word, with Assurance Therein*. These two works remained available, and a number of similar introductions were published, but the most popular throughout the century were Samuel Blackwell's *Several Methods of Reading the Holy Scriptures in Private* (1718), a pamphlet in its fourth edition by 1736, and William Lowth's *Directions for the Profitable Reading of the Holy Scripture*, first published in 1708 and still in use in the mid-nineteenth century. Blackwell's little pamphlet is less a guide to interpretation than a series of procedures for covering the biblical text. For example, his first 'method' consists of following the biblical readings outlined for daily use in the Prayer Book; his third 'method' comprises the frquent reading of the most remarkable passages from the Bible, the majority of which he lists for the reader. Only his second 'method' suggests a critical approach – to read each book of the Bible in succession with a commentary at hand.[16]

In contrast to Blackwell, Lowth offers a basic method of interpretation that well serves as an emblem of the many other works introducing the reader to the Bible. Underlying Lowth's *Directions* is the often repeated argument that all things necessary for salvation are plainly stated in the Scriptures. Yet Lowth explains, 'no book can be so plain, but that it is requisite for the perfect understanding of it, that men should be acquainted with the idioms and proprieties of the original language, and the customs and notions which were generally received at the time when it was written. This is a difficulty common to Scripture with all other books of antiquity'.[17] With this caveat, Lowth gives his 'directions': read the plainest books first – the Gospels, Psalms, Proverbs, Ecclesiastes, Job, Acts, Epistles, the books of Moses, Joshua, Judges, Kings, Chronicles, Ezra, Esther, and lastly Canticles. As he reads, the reader should interpret according to the 'analogy of faith'. The concept of the analogy of faith, a reference to Romans 12:6, informs eighteenth-century biblical criticism, and it meant primarily that no biblical text should be so interpreted that it contradicted fundamental Christian doctrine. In practice, interpreting according to the analogy of faith meant following the third 'direction' of comparing one place of Scripture with another, similar place.[18]

It was a truism (from Luther) that 'Scripture doth best interpret itself',[19] and as John Wilson wrote, Paul himself probably meant by the analogy of faith the art of deciphering a 'dark or difficult Scripture' by comparing it with another 'wherein the same Truth or Doctrine is more clearly and perspicuously delivered'.[20] Finally, Lowth urges his readers to maintain a special regard to the opinions and interpretations of those who lived closest in time to the Apostles.[21] Lowth provides other observations to help the reader in his reading of Scripture, but his 'directions' form the core of his book. In slightly different forms Lowth's methods repeated those of earlier writers and were themselves repeated.[22] John Owen, for example, had already written that in interpreting Scripture the reader should keep in mind: '1. A due consideration of the *analogy of faith* ...; 2. A due examination of the *design and scope of the place*; 3. A diligent observation of *antecedents* and *consequents*'.[23]

The popularity of such guides to biblical interpretation as those provided by Lowth and Blackwell indicates that eighteenth-century readers found them very useful. But as Lowth and others also suggested, the reader would also need some historical information and some general reference tools.

Proper interpretation of Scripture, according to John Owen, required knowledge and skill in the languages of the original writings, acquaintance with the history and geography of the world and with chronology, and proficiency in the ordinary ways and methods of reasoning.[24] The general reader would not necessarily have knowledge and skill in the original languages, but for historical background, geography, and chronology, he could consult a number of good works, of which the most important were translations from the writings of two French priests. The most exhaustive was Dom Augustin Calmet's *Historical, Geographical, Critical, Chronological, and Etymological Dictionary of the Holy Bible*, translated in three volumes in 1732, but equally a standard work of reference was Father Claude Fleury's *The Customs of the Israelites*, translated by Richard Gough in 1750.

English writers offered a survey of sacred (Jewish) and secular antiquities in three well-known works attempting to 'connect' biblical and 'profane' history. Probably the most celebrated was *The Old and New Testaments Connected; in the History of the Jews and Neighbouring Nations, from the Declension of the Kingdoms of Israel and Judah, to the Time of Christ* by Humphrey Prideaux, dean of Norwich. Published in two folio volumes in 1716–18 and frequently thereafter in several sizes and volumes, it had achieved 16 editions by 1808. In 1759 Percival Stockdale was reading it as a standard work.[25] Samuel Shuckford attempted to complete Prideaux in *The Sacred and Profane History of the World Connected, to the Dissolution of the Assyrian Empire; and to the Declension of the Kingdoms of Judah and Israel*. Published in 1728, Shuckford's work also achieved great popularity and was still in use in the mid-nineteenth century, a new edition having been issued in 1808.[26] Finally, in 1737 Thomas Stackhouse tried to rival Prideaux and Shuckford with two folio volumes entitled *A New History of the Bible, from the Beginning of the World to the Establishment of Christianity*. This work, although at first well received and perhaps even influencing a passage in Fielding's *Joseph Andrews*,[27] never enjoyed the popularity of Prideaux and Shuckford.[28] It went through only four editions in the eighteenth century.

General and more comprehensive aids for interpreting Scripture also flourished during the eighteenth century. Extraordinarily popular was David Collyer's *The Sacred Interpreter; or a Practical Introduction towards a Beneficial Reading and Thorough Understanding of the Holy Bible*. Published in two volumes in 1732, *The Sacred Interpreter* went though several editions, including one at Oxford as late as 1831.[29] Collyer provides, among many things, a brief history of the ancient, 'profane' monarchies, a general view of Jewish religion to the fall of Jerusalem in 587 B.C., remarks on most of the biblical books, showing their general design and scope, a chronology of the Scripture, and explanations of difficult biblical texts. A superficial book, it nevertheless gave the general reader a kind of overview of the several kinds of hermeneutic questions. Central to Collyer's interpretive method is typology, for despite the fact that typology was under attack by deism, as will be discussed below, it remained a regular hermeneutic device, even into the nineteenth century.[30] In brief, typology consists in the interpretation of Old Testament persons, events, and things as historical foreshadowings or prefigurings that are fulfilled or completed in New Testament counterparts or antitypes. Typology formed the basis of sixteenth- and seventeenth-century hermeneutic practice, even carrying over extensively into the metaphoric structures of secular literature. The importance of typology lay in its apparent demonstration of the unity of the two Testaments, and this unity was an assumption shared by all Christians. In the words of William Lowth, 'So we find one and the same design pursued from one end of the Bible to the other; and all the sacred writers agree in displaying the great mystery of godliness by various steps and degrees, from the promise of the blessed seed in paradise to the end and consummation of all things.'[31]

Two typological works dominated the popular aids for interpreting Scripture during the eighteenth century. *Moses Unveiled*, by William Guild, which was first published in 1620 and continued through many editions, was republished in the first edition in 1740. *Grace and Truth*, by a Scottish divine, William McEwen, although first published as late as 1763, went through 13 editions before the end of the century. Both works are essentially handbooks taking the reader through the traditional types and their fulfilments in the New Testament. Guild's entire book, in fact, merely comprises a short-hand list of types and antitypes arranged in biblical order with a summary of the 'disparities' between type and antitype after each section. For example, under a list of various Abraham types he includes: '*Abraham* went out of his native Country, and Father's House, at God's Command, *Gen.* xii. 4.' Directly opposite, on the same page, he gives the antitype: 'So Christ, according to the Decree of the Father, left the Heavens, and took painful Journeys on Earth, to work Man's Redemption, Luk. ii. 31.'[32] On a larger scale and encompassing other things besides typology was Benjamin Keach's *A Key to the Scripture Metaphors*. First published in 1682, the *Key* remained available throughout the eighteenth century, a new edition appearing as late as 1779. This enormous work, which includes several essays on parables, metaphor, simile, and other literary terms, examines in practical detail the meaning and application of hundreds of New Testament tropes, thus justifying its bulk and utility. Collyer, Guild, McEwen, and Keach by no means exhaust the list of writers of general aids to interpretation, but they are typical, and by and large they outsold their competitors.

3. BIBLICAL COMMENTARIES AND RECEIVED INTERPRETATION

It is clear from the above survey, which is intended to be representative rather than exhaustive, that eighteenth-century readers possessed a large variety of general reference works to aid their interpretation of Scripture, and the number of editions these reference works achieved indicates their fairly widespread use. But the real heart of biblical criticism available to the reader was the large collection of biblical commentaries that began to appear from about the time of the Restoration. In *Practical Discourses upon Reading the Scriptures* (1717), a series of Friday-evening lectures delivered by 'several ministers' at the Weigh-House in Eastcheap, the Rev. Mr Harris urged the use of commentaries.

> Reading the Scriptures is made more *profitable* by some Exposition upon them. The Reading some Portion of Scripture with a short Explication; giving the Sense of the Place; opening the Meaning of peculiar Idioms, and difficult Expressions; pointing out the Course of the Argument, and Order and Connection of Things; making some proper Remarks and practical Observations; accommodating the Scripture to the common Purposes of Life; is certainly very advantagious, and not without Countenance from the Scripture.[33]

James Boswell's query of Dr Johnson suggests that reading Scripture with a commentary was indeed commonplace: 'I asked him whether he would advise me to read the Bible with a commentary, and what commentaries he would recommend. JOHNSON. "To be sure, Sir, I would have you read the Bible with a commentary; and I would recommend Lowth and Patrick on the Old Testament, and Hammond on the New." '[34]

Under the guidance of Bishop John Pearson the great scholarly Latin commentaries of the Reformation and post-Reformation period, both English and continental, had been collected together into nine volumes and published in Amsterdam in 1660 under the title of *Critici Sacri*. Between 1669 and 1674 Matthew Poole published a five-volume condensation and consolidation of this collection with the title *Synopsis Criticorum*, adding more commentary from famous English scholars like Henry Hammond and John Lightfoot; Lightfoot's works, especially *Horae Hebraicae* (1658), made him probably the most noted Hebraist and rabbinical scholar of the seventeenth century. The *Critici Sacri* and the *Synopsis* were, of course, available to any reader, as were several histories of ecclesiastical and biblical writers,[35] but the general reader would instead turn to the commentaries intended for popular use, where he could find the scholarly discoveries and debates distilled and adapted to exegesis in English. The Rev. Mr Harris obviously refers to this body of commentary in English when he urges the use of biblical commentary. Earlier he had stated, 'there are many excellent Writings fitted for common Use, and of singular Advantage; as larger *Commentaries* and *Expositions*, and shorter *Paraphrases* and *Notes* upon the principal Parts of the Scripture.' In a note Harris specifically refers the reader to '*Mr* Pool's Annotations. *Mr* Burkett, *and Mr* Henry's Expositions,

Bp Patrick's *and Dr* Clark's Paraphrases'.[36] In this essay I cannot even note all the biblical commentaries available to the eighteenth-century reader, but in order to give local habitation and a name to this large body of material, I will mention briefly at least the major ones.

The biblical commentaries fall into three major areas: those covering the entire Bible, those covering the Old Testament, and those covering the New Testament. In the area of commentary on the entire Bible, four works from the late seventeenth century continued in general use during the eighteenth century. John Mayer's *A Commentary upon the Whole of the Old Testament, Added to That of the Same Author upon the Whole New Testament*, published between 1631 and 1653, provided the reader with a useful summary of patristic and Reformation interpretation, as indicated in a variant title announcing that Mayer will propound and examine the 'Divers Translations and Expositions, Literall and Mysticall, of the most famous Commentators, both ancient and modern'.[37] John Trapp provides a similar collection of earlier commentaries in *A Commentary on the Old and New Testaments* (1646–56), but his observations, objects a nineteenth-century critic, 'are for the most part expressed in uncouth language'.[38] In response to the directions of the Westminster Assembly, a number of English scholars, working under the general editorship of John Downame, finally produced in 1645 a useful one-volume commentary known as *The Assembly's Annotations*. They were republished again in two volumes in 1657, the same year that *The Dutch Annotations* appeared in English. These annotations were first ordered by the Synod of Dort in 1618 and pubished in 1637. Theodore Haak made the translation, dedicating it to Oliver Cromwell. Parliament recommended it 'to the authors of the Assembly's Annotations; and [it] is very similar in its plan and character to that work'.[39]

Despite the importance of these earlier commentaries, they were largely overshadowed by three other major works. The first of these, Matthew Poole's *Annotations upon the Holy Bible* (1683–5), remained a standard commentary, even though Poole himself wrote the annotations only to the end of the 58th chapter of Isaiah, other divines completing the work. Perhaps the most read commentary, however, was Matthew Henry's *An Exposition of All the Books of the Old and New Testaments* (1708–14). Achieving ten editions, as noted earlier, during the eighteenth century, and still in print, Henry's commentary received the highest praise from Philip Doddridge: it 'deserves to be entirely and attentively read through. The remarkable passages should be marked: there is much to be learned in this work in a speculative, and still more in a practical way.'[40] In a sense the only major rival to Henry was *A Critical Commentary and Paraphrase of the Old and New Testaments* (1727–60), better known as 'Patrick, Lowth, Whitby, and Arnald'. The commentaries of these divines were all published separately and, except for Arnald's, before 1727. Bishop Simon Patrick

covered the historical and poetical books of the Old Testament, William
Lowth the prophets, Daniel Whitby the New Testament, and William
Arnald the Apocrypha. Again Philip Doddridge suggests the high esteem
this commentary received. 'Patrick', he writes, 'is the most considerable [of
commentators on the Old Testament], from Genesis to Solomon's Song: he
has made use of many former writers, some Jewish and others Christian.'
Lowth, maintains Doddridge, 'has compiled a judicious commentary on
the Prophets . . .; in which there are some good critical notes and a
fine collection of parallels.' Doddridge accords Whitby the highest acco-
lade of all: 'On the whole New Testament, Whitby is preferable to any
other'.[41]

In the area of commentaries covering the Old Testament, only Henry
Ainsworth need be mentioned. Although published as early as 1627, his
Annotations on the Pentateuch remained, in Doddridge's terms, 'a good book,
full of very valuable Jewish learning'.[42] Of commentaries covering only the
New Testament, however, several achieved prominence during the eighteenth century. Henry Hammond's *A Paraphrase and Annotations upon All the
Books of the New Testament*, although published as early as 1653, continued to
be read, as Dr Johnson testifies, and indeed Doddridge claimed he was 'in
great and growing reputation'.[43] Dr Samuel Clarke's *A Paraphrase on the Four
Evangelists* (1702), recommended by the Rev. Mr Harris, also received high
praise from Doddridge: 'Dr. Clarke's Paraphrase on the Evangelists deserves an attentive reading. He narrates a story in handsome language, and
connects the parts well together'.[44] Except for Doddridge's own *Family
Expositor*, however, no New Testament commentary achieved the popular
success of William Burkitt's *Explanatory Notes with Practical Observations on the
Four Evangelists* (1700) entitled in subsequent editions *Expository Notes . . . on
the New Testament*. Doddridge disparages Burkitt thoroughly: 'Burkit has but
few valuable criticisms; but he has many schemes of old sermons. His
sentiments vary in different parts of his work, as the authors from whence
he took his materials were orthodox or not.'[45] Doddridge's criticism may be
apt, but in this case beside the point. The *Expository Notes* went through
eight editions in the course of the century, according to Machin, but the
British Museum Catalogue lists 17. Several of these were probably impressions, which were also called editions. The volume published in 1753, for
example, claimed to be the 14th edition, while that of 1772 announced itself
as the 17th edition. Whether editions or impressions, the sheer number of
reprintings is astonishing, and these continued into the mid-nineteenth
century.[46]

The capstone of commentaries on the New Testament was undoubtedly
Philip Doddridge's own *The Family Expositor* (1738–55). This famous work
became a household word, and even though Doddridge was a dissenter, the
Expositor achieved the status of a classic within the Church of England as

well as in dissenting circles. Perhaps the best description and praise of this famous work comes in the early nineteenth century from Shute Barrington, Bishop of Durham:

> In reading the New Testament, I recommend Doddridge's Family Expositor, as an *impartial interpreter and faithful monitor*. Other expositions and commentaries might be mentioned, greatly to the honour of their respective authors, for their several excellencies; such as elegance of exposition, acuteness of illustration, and copiousness of erudition: but I know of no expositor who unites so many advantages as Doddridge; whether you regard the fidelity of his version, the fulness and perspicuity of his composition, the utility of his general and historical information, the impartiality of his doctrinal comments, or, lastly, the piety and pastoral earnestness of his moral and religious applications. He has made, as he professes to have done, ample use of the commentators that preceded him; and in the explanation of grammatical difficulties, he has profited much more from the philological writers on the Greek Testament than could almost have been expected in so multifarious an undertaking as the *Family Expositor*. Indeed, for all the most valuable purposes of a Commentary on the New Testament, the Family Expositor cannot fall too early into the hands of those intended for holy orders.[47]

Few, if any, eighteenth-century readers would have disputed the Bishop of Durham's comments.

This group of commentaries, along with George Stanhope's commentary on the epistles and Gospels used in the Church of England and a series of commentaries on the epistles by John Locke, George Benson, and James Peirce, comprised the most important and most popular exposition of Scripture.[48] Less significant writers freely and widely borrowed from them. John Marchant, for example, published New and Old Testament commentaries in 1743 and 1745 respectively, and John Lindsay published *A Critical and Practical Commentary on the New Testament* in 1737, but both men largely provided extracts from the major commentaries, as did the editor of *The Universal Bible*, published in 1765. As suggested earlier, the primary and secondary commentaries, taken together with the other works of biblical criticism, form a body of received interpretation of Scripture.[49] The commentators and critics echo each other, sometimes expanding and sometimes condensing the exposition or exegesis. The commentaries on the camel-cable problem alluded to in Fielding's *Joseph Andrews* offer an excellent example of this exegetical consolidation.

The Assembly's Annotations treat the problem succinctly, indeed cryptically, quoting the patristic references: 'Theophylact saith that some say that κάμηλον signifieth not here the living creature (that is a *Camel*) but τὸ παχυοι οινον, etc. a great rope, etc. That is, a cable, but indeed this is a proverbial manner of speaking, which *Caninius* noteth out of the *Talmudists*; though they the Elephant; and Christ mentioneth the *Camel*, a beast better known in *Syria*, and likely according to their usual proverb.'[50] This preference for the camel is carried over by Matthew Henry, who ignores the cable or rope, but instead moralizes the text:

> He saith, That the conversion and salvation of a rich man is so extremely difficult, that *it is easier for a camel to go through the eye of a needle.* . . . This is a proverbial expression, noting a difficulty altogether unconquerable by the art and power of man. . . . *First,* The way to heaven is very fitly compared to a *needle's eye,* which is hard to hit, and hard to get through. *Secondly,* A rich man is fitly compared to a *camel,* a beast of burthen, for he has riches, as a camel has his load, he carries it, but it is anothers, he has it from others, spends it for others, and must shortly leave it to others; it is a burthen, for *men load themselves with thick clay,* Hab. 2. 6. A camel is a large creature, but unwieldy.[51]

In Henry's moralization, the only bow to the historical context appears in the assertion, 'This is a proverbial expression'.

Like Henry, William Burkitt does not mention the rope or cable, but alludes to the proverbial nature of the saying. He also focuses on drawing the moral, as he does again in the annotation to Mark 10:25.[52] Daniel Whitby, on the other hand, translates camel in the text, but gives 'cable-rope' as an alternative in parenthesis, and in the annotation leans towards the latter translation.

> There is no necessity of reading κάμιλος for καμηλος, for that both signify a 'cable,' or thick rope used by the mariners in casting anchors, Euthymius, Theophylact, and Phavorinus testify; and that a camel is not here to be understood, Bochartus argues, (1.) because the Hebrew proverb speaks only of an elephant, not of a camel. (2.) Because the Syriac and Arabic versions here mention not a camel, but a cable. (3.) Because the Jews, as Buxtorf notes, use the same proverb of a cable rope; and (4.) because there is some analogy betwixt drawing a thread and a rope through the eye of a needle, but none at all between a camel and a thread. . . .[53]

Whitby is almost the only commentator to prefer the 'cable-rope' to the camel.

Some of the secondary commentaries, especially those of John Gill, John Lindsay, and John Marchant, present a very elaborate history of the problem, with all the patristic arguments and those based on the *Talmud* set out in detail.[54] As might be expected, however, Doddridge provides the convenient summary of the case. In his text, which is actually a harmony of the Gospels and a paraphrase, Doddridge gives both cable and camel as translations: 'it is *easier* for the huge cable of a ship, or even *for a camel to go through the eye of a needle,* than it is *for a rich man* to conquer the snares of his estate and the corruptions of his heart so far as *to enter into the kingdom of God,* and become the faithful, obedient subject of his Son.' Doddridge's annotation, however, and despité his praise of Whitby, comes clearly down on the side of the camel:

> Theophylact, and after him some other critics, for καμηλον read καμιλον, which they explain of a *cable rope*, which might appear more fitly to be mentioned as what *could not pass through a needle's eye*. Others very precariously assert that there was near Jerusalem a low gate called the Needle's eye, through which a camel could not pass unless his load were taken off. But I see no reason for departing from the received reading and interpretation: nor is there any thing in this proverbial expression, as it here stands, but what is very agreeable to the Eastern taste, and may be paralleled in other Jewish writers. See Dr. Lightfoot's *Hor.[ae] Hebr.[aicae]* on Matt. xix. 24 where it is shown there was a Jewish proverb to the same purpose of the elephant.[55]

Although stated with the utmost economy of words, Doddridge's annotation presents the basic terms of the problem, including the possibility of a special gate in Jerusalem, and then refers the reader to the scholarly materials, which, as noted above, were conveniently summarized in several of the secondary commentaries.

This consolidation of exposition into a body of received interpretation, although highlighting historical and rational criteria for interpretation, nevertheless also carried with it a strong tendency to moralize the text, to provide what the divines called 'practical observations'. Two main kinds of moralizing inform the commentaries. One takes the form of an exemplary reading of biblical characters, translating Old and New Testament characters into models – both positive and negative – for the reader to imitate or avoid. The other extends exposition into moral instruction or, in the manner of Doddridge, inserts it into a paraphrase and perhaps, again like Doddridge, intersperses separate, self-contained sections of 'improvement'. To use E. D. Hirsch's terms, the commentators readily (and happily) confused the possible significance that could be drawn from a text with its meaning.[56] Exemplary reading was commended on all sides. In his commentary on Romans 4:23, Matthew Henry states the rationale of searching Scripture for exemplary models: 'In the close of the chapter, he [Paul] applies all to us; and having abundantly proved that Abraham was justified by faith, he here concludes that his justification was to be the pattern or sampler of our's'. The story of Abraham's justification by faith 'was not intended only for an historical commendation of Abraham, or a relation of something peculiar to him'; instead it is like all the 'accounts we have of the Old Testament saints', which 'were not intended for histories only, barely to inform and divert us, but for precedents to direct us, for ensamples'.[57]

The practice was heavily reinforced by recommendations in such popular works as Collyer's *Sacred Interpreter* and Richard Theed's *Sacred Biography, or Scripture Characters Illustrated* (1714), and by the example of Bishop Joseph Hall's *Contemplations on the Historical Passages of the Old and New Testaments*

(1612–26).[58] Moreover, the pulpit added weight to the practice, as many sermons of the time illustrate. Doddridge, for example, urges it on preachers:

> Examples of Scripture Characters, and pieces of sacred history. These are very interesting and entertaining subjects, and will often afford you natural occasions of saying useful things in a very inoffensive way. Sometimes a virtue is better represented by such an example than by a topical discourse. Thus, submission to the will of God will be better illustrated by the example of Aaron, Eli, Job, Samuel, etc. than by general observations on the nature, advantages, and reasonableness of such a temper.[59]

The practice of exemplary reading had been, in effect, canonized by the saintly Bishop Jeremy Taylor, whose *The Great Exemplar of Sanctity and Holy Life* (1649), a moralized version of the life of Christ, had achieved the status of a classic before the end of the seventeenth century.[60]

Exemplary reading inevitably incorporated Old and New Testament characters into the received interpretation of Scripture as a kind of gallery of positive and negative examples for the practical use of the reader. Emphasis naturally fell on positive models like Abraham and Joseph. The commentaries on Nimrod from Genesis, however, will illustrate the process of absorbing biblical characters into received interpretation as well as exemplifying the rarer, negative model. Genesis gives very little information on Nimrod:

> And Cush begat Nimrod: he began to be a mighty one on the earth. He was a mighty hunter before the Lord: wherefore it is said, Even as Nimrod the mighty hunter before the Lord. And the beginning of his kingdom was Babel, and Erech, and Acad, and Calneh, in the land of Shinar. Out of that land went forth Asshur, and builded Nineveh, and the city Rehoboth, and Calah. And Resen between Nineveh and Calah: the same is a great city.
>
> (Genesis 10:8–12)

The Dutch Annotations, recalling the patristic interpretations of 'before the Lord', explain the phrase as meaning 'openly, dareingly, without either fear of God, or shame before men'. With this understanding of 'before the Lord', it inevitably followed that Nimrod's apparent empire building should be interpreted as evil. Nimrod was a hunter 'not only of the wilde beasts, but of men also, with whom he dealt little otherwise, then the hunters did with Deer, killing and subduing them at their own pleasure.'[61]

The outline of the tyrant suggested in *The Dutch Annotations* emerges more clearly in Bishop Patrick. Using a variety of patristic and ancient writings for support, [62] Patrick identifies Nimrod as the person 'whom the Greek writers call Belus, that is *Lord*'. He was 'the first great warrior and conqueror' and was 'the first that put down the government of eldership, or paternity (as Sir Walter Raleigh speaks), and laid the foundation of sovereign rule.' Nimrod's skill as a hunter, the basis of his fame, was also the means he used to become a great monarch: 'He hardened himself to labour by this exercise (which was very toilsome), and drew together a great company of robust young men to attend him in this sport: who were hereby also fitted to pursue men, as they had done wild beasts. For this was looked upon, in all ages, as the rudiment of warfare'. In effect, by performing a service to his fellow men Nimrod secured power over them:

> For it must be further noted, that in this age of Nimrod, the exercise of hunting might well be the more highly esteemed, and win him the hearts of mankind; because he delivered them, by this means, from those wild beasts whereby they were much infested, and very dangerously exposed, while they were but few, and lived scattered up and down, in the open air, or in tents but weakly defended. The destroying of wild beasts (and, perhaps, of thieves whom he hunted also) was a great service in those times, and made many join with him in greater designs, and make himself master of the people who were his neighbours, in Babylon, Susiana, and Assyria.

From these humble beginnings, Nimrod, who was also probably the same person 'the Greeks call Bacchus', along with his son Ninus, built Babel and several other cities, including Nineveh, and conquered Assyria.[63]

Bishop Patrick fleshes out the picture of Nimrod, but his carefully chosen words do not quite transform him into a model of villainy. This was achieved in other commentaries, especially Matthew Henry's long commentary on Nimrod. Those that went before Nimrod

> were content to stand upon the same level with their neighbours, and though every man bare rule in his own house, yet no man pretended any further; Nimrod's aspiring mind could not rest in this parity; he resolved to tower above his neighbours, and not only so, but to Lord it over them. . . . Note, there are some, in whom ambition and affection of dominion seem to be bred in the bone.

Henry acknowledges that some scholars think Nimrod performed a service to men by hunting wild beasts, but he also notes that 'Others think, under pretence of hunting, he gathered men under his command, in pursuit of another game he had to play, which was, to make himself master of the country, and to bring them into subjection.' Henry clearly agrees with the villainous interpretation. Nimrod was indeed a mighty hunter, but primarily in the sense of a 'violent invader of his neighbours' rights and properties, and a persecutor of innocent men, carrying all before him, and endeavouring to make all his own by force and violence.' His power as a ruler and his building of cities exemplified the tyrant.

> Observe in Nimrod the nature of ambition. 1. It is *boundless*; much would have more, and still cries, *Give, give*. It is *restless*; Nimrod, when he had four cities under his command, could not be content, till he had four more. 3. It is *expensive*; Nimrod will rather be at the charge of *rearing* cities than not have the honour of

ruling them. The spirit of building is the common effect of a spirit of pride. 4. It is *daring*, and will stick at nothing; Nimrod's name signifies *rebellion*, which, (if indeed he did abuse his power to the oppression of his neighbours) teaches us, that tyrants to men are rebels to God, and their *rebellion is as the sin of witchcraft.*[64]

Henry's presentation of Nimrod dominates the biblical criticism. Henry himself echoes earlier writers, and his views in turn reappear in the secondary commentaries, the histories, and the aids to interpretation. In John Gill's words, 'besides his being in a literal sense an hunter, he was in a figurative sense one, a tyrannical ruler and governor of men'.[65]

The extension of exposition into moral instruction offered commentators opportunity for more variety of moralizing, but even here the consolidating process was at work. Some of the commentaries on the camel-cable problem have already indicated the general way commentators moralized the text, but a few examples from commentaries on the parable of the talents in Matthew 25:14–30 will, I think, bring the art of 'practical observations' into clear focus. The trading metaphor in the parable was suggestive, and Henry picks it up, offering his own parable of the Christian tradesman.

A true Christian is a spiritual tradesman. Trades are called *mysteries*, and *without controversy great is the mystery of godliness*; it is a manufacture trade; there is something to be done by us upon our own hearts, and for the good of others. It is a merchant-trade: things of less value to us are parted with for things of greater value. . . . A tradesman is one who, having made his trade his choice, and taken pains to learn it, makes it his business to follow it, lays out all he has for the advancement of it, makes all other affairs bend to it, and lives upon the gain of it. Thus does a true Christian act in the world of religion; we have no stock of our *own* to trade with, but trade as factors with our master's stock.[66]

William Burkitt also saw the value of the trading metaphor, but he keeps it more submerged in his commentary. Annotating verses 14 and 15, Burkitt first notes that the talents are really the 'Goods of Providence, Riches and Honours; Gifts of Mind, Wisdom, Parts of Learning: Gifts of Grace'. He then turns to exhortation:

Learn, 1. That Christ is the great Lord of the Universe, and Owner of all his Servants Goods and Talents. 2. That every Talent is given by our Lord to improve and employ for our Master's Use and Service. 3. That it pleases the Lord to dispense his gifts variously among his Servants, to some he commits more, to others fewer Talents. 4. That to this Lord of ours every one of us must be accountable and responsible for every Talent committed to us and entrusted with us.

The annotations to verses 16–18, however, allow more play with the trading metaphor.

The former Verses gave an Account of the Lord's Distribution; these acquaint us with the Servants Negociation. Some traded with, and made Improvement of their Talents, others traded not at all; yet it is not said, they did embezzle their Talent, but not improve it. *Learn*, It is not sufficient to justify us, that we do not abuse our Talents; it is Fault enough to hide them, and not improve them; the slothful Servant shall no more escape punishment, than the wasteful Servant.[67]

Like Burkitt, Doddridge plays down the trading metaphor, focusing instead on diligence and sloth. In the 'Improvement' section following the parable, he writes: 'What can excite us to a becoming care and activity in the duties of life, if we are deaf to those various and important motives which this excellent parable suggests? We have each of us received our talents, whether five, or two, or one. . . . Our acceptance and reward will be proportionable to our diligence'. Later he exhorts, 'Whatever our particular snares in life may be, let us think of the doom of the slothful servant, to awaken our souls, and to deter us from every degree of unfaithfulness.'[68] After a discussion of the monetary value of a talent in Christ's time, John Gill, a secondary commentator, returns to the trading metaphor, but applies it primarily to the clergy. Gill acknowledges that the talents stand for 'the gifts of nature and of providence', but he wants to focus on 'ministerial gifts, such as fit and qualify men to be preachers of the Gospel'. Following this bent, he concludes: 'The ministers of the Gospel are traders, not in their own name, nor on their own stock, and for themselves, but for Christ, and for the good of immortal souls: they closely attend unto, and work at, their business and employment'.[69] In effect, Gill has merely applied Henry's general metaphor of the 'spiritual tradesman' specifically to the clergy, thus including their work as part of the 'business' of life.

4. BIBLICAL CRITICISM AND LITERATURE

This essay began by quoting Fielding's allusion in *Joseph Andrews* to the camel-cable problem in biblical criticism. Inevitably the question arises of how eighteenth-century biblical criticism relates to secular literature. There are, in fact, two questions: how far did the biblical critics regard the Bible as a work of literature, and what influence, if any, did the biblical criticism have on secular literature? The great figure of Robert Lowth looms large in any response to the first question. His *Lectures on the Sacred Poetry of the Hebrews*, published in Latin in 1753 and in English in 1787, are to many modern readers, perhaps, the only eighteenth-century work that treats the Bible as literature. In fact, however, Lowth, the son of the biblical critic William Lowth, was mainly carrying out in detail and in a sustained fashion a tradition very prominent in biblical criticism since the Reformation. Grotius and other post-Reformation critics had commonly compared the style of Scripture with the best Greek and Roman writers,[70] and in the second half of the seventeenth century several biblical critics dwelt on the literary value of the Bible. In 1693–5 John Edwards published *A Discourse concerning the Authority, Stile, and Perfection of the Books of the Old and New Testaments* in three volumes. This work provides a thorough analysis of the great variety of rhetorical figures in the Bible, ranging from hyperbole to metaphor. Edwards carefully delineates and relates to the Greeks and Romans major metaphors like the path or way of life, man a traveller on a journey, the life of man a warfare, the world as an inn. He also examines in detail the nature and structure of the parable, relating it to the Hebrew mashal and the fable.[71]

Edwards was actually following in the footsteps of Henry Lukin, who published in 1669 *An Introduction to the Holy Scripture*,[72] and the tradition continued throughout the eighteenth century, beginning in 1727 with Anthony Blackwall's two-volume *The Sacred Classics Defended and Illustrated*. Blackwall focuses on the New Testament, and some of his conclusions well deserve quoting.

> There is in the sacred writers of the New Testament such an agreeable and instructive variety of surprizing and important histories and narrations, sublime doctrines, and styles, that must highly entertain and improve any man that is not indispos'd by vice and brutality to relish the things, or by ignorance to understand the language. In the precepts and command there is a venerable and majestic brevity; in supplications, entreaties, and lamentation the periods are larger, and the style more flowing and diffusive. The narration is clear; the stronger passions are express'd with majesty and terror, the gentler and softer affections in the smoothest and most moving terms: and all this agreeable to *nature*, and the rules of the greatest masters, tho' in a manner excelling their best *compositions*.[73]

Invariably, of course, critics compared the Bible with the Greek and Roman classics, the standard of great literature. Literary criticism also pervades the biblical commentaries, especially through discussions of tropes and the parable. Some of the commentators even give a kind of running literary analysis along with their exposition and moral observations. Here is Matthew Henry on the sacrifice of Isaac: 'Hitherto, this story has been very melancholy, and seems to hasten towards a most tragical period; but here, the sky, of a sudden, clears up, the sun breaks out, a bright and pleasant scene opens'.[74] Lowth's celebrated *Lectures* essentially expanded partial and fragmentary literary evaluation into a piece of sustained literary analysis of entire Old Testament poems in formal literary terms such as epic, tragedy, ode, elegy. But he was primarily extending a well entrenched tradition of biblical criticism.[75]

Arnold Williams shows in *The Common Expositor* that much of the material in post-Reformation biblical commentaries, which contain a wide range of secular literature, science, pseudo-science, philosophy, and theology, served as sources for a great deal of Renaissance literature based on biblical themes.[76] Numerous recent studies have also demonstrated the rich use seventeenth-century poets made of biblical typology, and most recently Barbara Lewalski has brilliantly explored the flowering of the religious lyric in England and America in terms of the poetics Renaissance biblical critics applied in their literary evaluations of Scripture.[77] Such an immediate and direct transfer from biblical commentary to secular literature did not, for the most part, occur during the eighteenth century.[78] Biblical criticism does figure importantly in eighteenth-century literature, but generally in indirect ways that are just beginning to be perceived. The literature of the period felt the impact of biblical criticism most significantly, I think, through biblical quotation and allusion, which pervade eighteenth-century literature, especially the novel. Moreover, very often these quotations and allusions expand to include the biblical criticism, thus importing into the narrative the received interpretation of the biblical texts. In effect, the received interpretation generates contexts of Christian meaning more extensive than the surface of the narrative in any one place or than biblical quotation and allusion alone immediately suggest.

These expanded biblical allusions, if derived from a variety of biblical texts, may simply effect a fairly straightforward Christian evaluation of particular themes, characters, scenes, or events in literature. At times, however, expanded biblical allusion can be quite complex, especially if a whole work, or a large part of it, invokes the received interpretation of an entire book of the Bible. Such is the case with Dr Johnson's use of the received interpretation of Ecclesiastes in *Rasselas*, as I have tried to demonstrate in 'The biblical context of Johnson's *Rasselas*'.[79] The biblical context evoked by Fielding's quotation of Matthew 19:24 in *Joseph Andrews*, however, more briefly illustrates the literary process. The biblical text itself, with its emphasis on the difficulty of a rich man entering heaven, points to one of the main themes of the novel. But the quotation, I think, also recalls the extended exposition or moralizing of the text acquired in the received interpretation. Parson Adams' choice of cable perfectly fits his ironic and comic charcter, for the camel translation is undoubtedly more appropriate to the novel.

The extended exposition of Matthew Henry on the text of Matthew, cited earlier, focuses, for example, on riches as a 'burthen' or 'load' that metaphorically transforms the rich man into a camel, 'a beast of burthen'. In William Burkitt's less colourful terms, rich men

> do certainly meet with more Difficulties in their Way to Heaven, than other Men: It is difficult to withdraw their Affections from Riches, to place their supreme Love upon God in the midst of their Abundance. . . . yet the Fault lies not in Riches, but in rich Men; who, by placing their Trust, and putting their Confidence in Riches, do render themselves uncapable of the Kingdom of God.

Later Burkitt relates riches to happiness: 'It is hard for a rich Man to become happy, even by God, because he thinks himself happy *without God*.'[80] Without giving a detailed analysis of the novel, I think it neverthe-less seems clear that Fielding's quotation invokes this context of received interpretation to support the narrator and assist the reader's evaluation of the Lady Boobys, Peter Pounces, and 'roasting squires' that heavily populate the novel. They carry their riches and desire for riches as a 'burthen'; they cannot 'withdraw their Affections from Riches', and they think themselves 'happy *without God*'.

By alluding to the camel-cable problem in the biblical quotation, Fielding also adds further insight into the comic character of the one person who most clearly has withdrawn his 'Affections from Riches', Parson Adams. The innocence, naiveté, and benevolence of Adams place him in conflict with the majority of persons in the novel. The context of received interpretation, however, reveals the further irony that this man of God is also in the minority among the biblical critics. His preference for the cable translation, in effect, pits him, with Daniel Whitby, against the mainstream of received interpretation. But his choice of translations is perfectly consistent with his character, for later in the novel he joins the minority again in defending Bishop Hoadly's unorthodox and much attacked *A Plain Account of the Nature and End of the Sacrament of the Lord's Supper* (1737).[81] The context of received interpretation helps the reader see that Parson Adams is nearly always in the minority, and that from Fielding's perspective such a position may be normal for the true Christian. Even the clergy, Adams asserts, alluding to John 18:36, seek riches and power, when 'Surely those things, which savour so strongly of this World, become not the Servants of one who professed his Kingdom was not of it'.[82] Without examining how the received interpretation of this allusion might enlarge the meaning of the passage, I would suggest that Parson Adams' minority position, even among professed Christians, and comically enhanced by the context of received interpretation, reinforces the novel's larger comic concerns with the Christian conflict between living in this world and seeking first the kingdom of heaven.

As another, brief example of expanded biblical allusion I will use a scene from Tobias Smollett's *Humphry Clinker*. Matthew Bramble and his entour-age, on their tour from Wales to Scotland, make a detour to visit Matt's cousin, Squire Burdock. Matt writes to Dr Lewis that 'our Yorkshire cousin has been a mighty fox-hunter *before the Lord*; but now he is too fat and unwieldy to leap ditches and five-bar gates; nevertheless, he still keeps a pack of hounds, which are well exercised; and his huntsman every night entertains him with the adventures of the day's chace'. Matt's biblical allusion, of course, is to Nimrod, and the immediate description of Burdock focuses on the hunting parallel in the Genesis story. But the allusion is really much richer, for Smollett invokes the context of received interpretation that includes the whole background of commentary treating Nimrod as a tyrant. The Nimrod allusion precedes Smollett's comic revelation that Burdock is essentially a vicious tyrant. Burdock's tyranny is checked only by his equally tyrannous wife. Burdock hates his wife,

> but, although the brute is sometimes so very powerful in him that he will have his own way, he generally truckles to her dominion, and dreads, like a school-boy, the lash of her tongue. On the other hand, she is afraid of provoking him too far, lest he should make some desperate effort to shake off her yoke. – She, therefore, acquiesces in the proofs he daily gives of his attachment to the liberty of an English freeholder, by saying and doing, at his own table, whatever gratifies the brutality of his disposition, or contributes to the ease of his person. The house, though large, is neither elegant nor comfortable. – It looks like a great inn, crowded with travellers, who dine at the landlord's ordinary, where there is a great profusion of victuals and drink, but mine host seems to be misplaced; and I would rather dine upon filberts with a hermit, than feed upon venison with a hog.[83]

Through the biblical context Smollett suggests that Nimrod, now reduced and petty, is still playing the tyrant; he is alive and well in eighteenth-century Yorkshire. In effect, the tyrant of the received interpretation is a type of Burdock, not in the sense of a prefiguring or foreshadowing, but in the sense of a pattern that Burdock comically apes and reflects on a minor scale among his family and neighbours.

The literary use of biblical allusion is, of course, an old artistic device, but its popularity and expansion to include the received interpretation in eighteenth-century literature derived in large part from the redefinition of typology Christian apologists developed during the height of the wearying deist controversy. In *A Discourse of the Grounds and Reasons of the Christian Religion* (1724), Anthony Collins sought to undermine the unity of the two Testaments by arguing that the Old Testament prophecies cited in the New Testament as proofs that Christ is the Messiah are not literal predictions of Christ at all, and can be applied to him only in a typical, mystical, allegorical, or enigmatical sense. Therefore they are 'not Proofs according to Scholastick Rules'.[84] In *The Scheme of Literal Prophecy Considered* (1726), his reply to the first Christian counter-attack, Collins continued to define type theologically as a prefiguring, but was forced to acknowledge that its primary meaning, as biblical criticism had always asserted, was 'a mould or pattern of a thing'.[85] This acknowledgement reflects Collins' awareness that Christian apologists, in the heat of the controversy, had begun to shift ground. While defending literal prophecy and theological typology in some instances, they began to emphasize, as many earlier biblical critics had pointed out,[86] that a great number of the New Testament citations were intended merely as 'accommodation' (adaptation to an Old Testament text). They were, in essence, resorting to the primary meaning of type, and

Arthur Ashley Sykes, as Collins himself commented,[87] doubtless carried this line of argument to its extreme.

Sykes, a leading participant in the deist controversy, accepted Collins' argument that the prophecies cited in the New Testament were not literal predictions, but in his various responses he almost entirely jettisons the whole theological meaning of type. A type, he insists, 'signifies originally any natural *Model*, or *Pattern*, or *Impression*'. Paul expands the term to mean, in general, '*a moral Example*, or *Pattern*', except in Romans 4:14, where 'the Metaphor is carried a little further' and the 'Word is put for a *General Likeness*, or a *Similitude*'. Based on these definitions, the term *antitype*, the supposed New Testament fulfilment of the type, then really means 'Any thing therefore formed according to a *Model*, or *Pattern*'. Sykes proceeds to examine the New Testament citations of the Old Testament as basically rational arguments in which types appear 'only by way of Illustration, Analogy, and Similitude'. Paul, for example, generally argues 'from a Similitude of particular Circumstances; and this very much tended to help his Readers to an easy Conception of what he was reasoning about.' Usually 'the Apostle proceeds according to the Rules of strict Reasoning and argues analogically, and explains his Sentiments by Similes, which exactly suited the Case'. Sykes concludes his discussion of Matthew by noting, 'If the Prophet cited be speaking of himself, or of his Contemporaries, or of his own Times, or of Past Times, the Application of such Citation to our Saviour ought to be deem'd no more than Allusion, or Resemblance of Facts'.[88] For Sykes, and to a lesser extent the other Christian apologists, the idea of type had already evolved to its modern meaning, a pattern of representative traits, persons, or events that are predictive (but not prefigurative) in the sense that the behaviour or activity of instances fitting the type can be predicted, will follow the pattern.

The older theological meaning of type continued, of course, and the typological reading of Scripture also continued well into the nineteenth century, but the modern meaning began to dominate as the idea of type was irrevocably caught up in the eighteenth-century predilection for analogical reasoning that is, perhaps, best represented by Bishop Joseph Butler's famous *Analogy of Religion Natural and Revealed* (1736). Certainly by 1741 David Hartley could complacently assert, 'It may be added in favor of typical reasoning, that it corresponds to the method of reasoning by analogy, which is found to be of such extensive use in philosophy. A type is indeed nothing but an analogy, and the scripture types are not only a key to the scriptures, but seem also to have contributed to put into our hands the key of nature, analogy.'[89] In eighteenth-century literature, as Paul Korshin has shown, this 'abstracted type', to use Korshin's term, merged with the older 'character', the literary term originally meaning 'representative specimen', to produce 'character types', fictional persons whose representative nature

allowed a reader to predict consequent behaviour. Not every fictional
person becomes a character type, of course, but a great many do, as the
great variety of Lady Boobys and Matt Brambles testify. Character types in
eighteenth-century literature, Korshin continues, 'are not so much *prefigurative personages* as they are *predictive structures*, a knowledge of which
serves to foreshadow information about the novel to its audience. The
character type, then, becomes a standard eighteenth-century fictive entity
whose behaviour could be predicted, whose place in a work of fiction an
audience would probably understand without special authorial commentary.'[90] Whether referring to persons, traits, or events, a type provided a
pattern of predictive behaviour or action that persisted and was repeated in
time. This is certainly the idea meant by the narrator of *Joseph Andrews*
when he describes the perennial lawyer: 'I question not but several of my
Readers will know the Lawyer in the Stage-Coach, the Moment they hear
his Voice. . . . The Lawyer is not only alive, but hath been so these 4000
years, and I hope G— will indulge his Life as many yet to come.'[91]

If the Christian apologists in the deist controversy gave a new meaning to
type, one that literature quickly adapted, they also further enhanced the
practice of biblical allusion. Their vision of the New Testament writers
turning to the Old Testament for patterns of meaning analogous to New
Testament situations reinforced the tendency of eighteenth-century literature to consider the entire Bible and its received interpretation as a
repertoire of timeless patterns that provided Christian meaning to the
situations of the contemporary world. Contemporary situations become, in
essence, antitypes of the biblical types, but in the new sense of repetitions of
the pattern. Certainly this is how Smollett uses Nimrod and the received
interpretation in *Humphry Clinker*, and Fielding follows the same procedure,
as Martin Battestin has demonstrated, when he models Abraham Adams
and Joseph Andrews on the received intepretation of the biblical Abraham
and Joseph.[92] The literary use of expanded biblical allusion occurs quite
extensively, I think, in eighteenth-century literature, and its significance
has only begun to be explored. As noted earlier, I have tried to explain its
large scale meaning in Johnson's *Rasselas*, and more recently Martin
Battestin has initiated a debate over how the received interpretation of Job
applies to the theme and structure of Oliver Goldsmith's *The Vicar of
Wakefield*.[93]

Biblical criticism may have helped to shape eighteenth-century literature
in two other important ways that need extensive investigation. Here I will
merely suggest the possibilities. The development of exemplary characters
in sentimental fiction and drama, the latter properly discussed by Robert
Hume as exemplary drama,[94] may have as its context the exemplary
reading of biblical characters and events in biblical criticism. As Sykes
recalls in his reference to Paul's practice, while the biblical types may be

patterns in the sense of predictive representatives, they could also serve as patterns in the sense of models to be imitated or avoided. Bishop Taylor had reminded his readers that even in pagan Rome 'It was not without great reason advised, that every man should propound the example of a wise and vertuous person; . . . and by a fiction of imagination to suppose him present as a witness, and really to take his life as the direction of all our actions.' But the best of the pagans were grossly defective, so that only Christian history provides the best examples: 'But how happy and richly furnished are Christians with precedents of Saints, whose faith and revelations have been productive of more spiritual graces, and greater degrees of moral perfections.' Even the saints were, of course, somewhat defective; only Christ can be the perfect 'exemplar'.[95]

In some way the idea of the exemplary pattern also informs the character type even in non-sentimental works. Fielding, of course, has great fun in the opening chapter of *Joseph Andrews* ridiculing the idea of exemplary characters like Pamela, and in the course of the novel the comedy increases as Joseph acknowledges his biblical namesake and Pamela as the examples helping him preserve his chastity.[96] Moreover, as often noted, part of Joseph's development requires him to see that even Parson Adams cannot be a complete model for his imitation. And yet, despite all the comedy, Adams and Joseph do remain somehow examples of imitation, just as their namesakes remain in the received interpretation. Part of the comedy arising from many of these exemplary character types derives from the mixture of the imperfect with the perfect, for example, the often noted vanity informing the benevolence of Adams. The precedent for this very mixture, however, as Bishop Taylor intimates, may also come from the received interpretation. Except for Christ, no biblical 'saint' was considered perfect, and while biblical criticism naturally highlighted the moral and religious perfections of biblical persons, it also reminded the reader of their failures, offering these as warnings and admonitions. As Matthew Henry writes, 'The Scripture is impartial in relating the miscarriages of the most celebrated saints, which are recorded, not for our imitation, but for our admonition.'[97] Samuel Richardson, in the pompous concluding editorial note to *Sir Charles Grandison*, urges that fictional character types be presented as exemplary, and, as might be expected, he wants them to be the most perfect patterns consistent with the 'frailties of mortality'. Richardson is clearly thinking in terms of biblical criticism, for he quotes from a sermon in which Archbishop Tillotson, echoing the biblical critics, urges writers to portray models of eminent moral virtue.[98]

Finally, I will suggest that the eighteenth-century delight in the moral tale or apologue, whether it appeared as a short story in *The Rambler* or other literary journals and magazines, as a novella such as *Rasselas*, or as an interpolated tale in a novel, may also stem from biblical criticism. One important precedent for such tales was clearly the Graeco-Roman Fable, and Aesop remained popular throughout the century.[99] But I suspect eighteenth-century literary writers also thought of the apologue as a particularly Christian kind of narrative. The model here was the parable, which received extensive discussion in the biblical commentaries as well as in biblical criticism generally. Of primary importance is the fact that the parable was identified as the Christian form of the pagan fable or apologue. Robert Lowth may serve to summarize the many discussions of this notion.

> Another kind of allegory is that, which, in the proper and restricted sense, may be called Parable, and consists of a continued narration of a fictitious event, applied by way of simile to the illustration of some important truth. The Greeks call these allegories αvoι (or *apologues*), the Latins *fabulae* (or fables): and the writings of the Phrygian sage, or those composed in imitation of him, have acquired the greatest celebrity. Nor has our Saviour himself disdained to adapt the same method of instruction, of whose parables it is doubtful, whether they excel most in wisdom and utility, or in sweetness, elegance, and perspicuity.

Because of Christ's use of the parable, however, the term now has a particularly Christian or 'more confined sense'.[100]

The peculiarly Christian overtones of the term probably prevented it from supplanting fable or apologue in literary discourse, but its relevance as a Christian underpinning of the moral tale could hardly be lost. The parable may use historical facts at times, but, as Lowth indicates, its narrative is primarily fiction. Yet these fictions are based on the fact of typical occurrence, explains Matthew Henry, commenting on the parable of the rich man and Lazarus in Luke 19:19–31:

> we need not call it a history of a particular occurrence, but it is a *matter of fact* that is true every day: that poor godly people, whom men neglect and trample upon, die away out of their miseries, and go to heavenly bliss and joy, which is made more pleasant to them by their preceeding sorrows: and the rich epicures, who live in luxury, and are unmerciful to the poor, die, and go into a state of insupportable torment.[101]

The importance of parables, according to Henry, is their 'use, not only for the explaining of Christian doctrines, but for the pressing of Christian duties; for they make and leave an impression'.[102] Benjamin Keach reiterates the moral purpose of parable in his *Gospel-Mysteries Unveil'd* (1701). Parables, he writes, 'in their main Scope and Design, intend not Matter of Fact . . . but are principally Doctrinal, and are brought to open the Mind of God the better to our Weak Capacities, move upon our Affections, and convince the Conscience, as the Parable of *Nathan* in *David's* Case.' Indeed, because of their importance in enforcing moral duty, Keach encourages the clergy to write their own at times: 'Moreover, a Minister may use other Parables and Similitudes of his own framing, besides what are mentioned in the Scriptures for Illustration sake; which is found by Experience very useful to the Hearers.' At the end of his discussion of Christ's use of parables, Keach presents sample outlines of possible parables a clergyman (or other author) could write, thus encouraging imitation of the biblical form.[103]

5. TOWARDS THE DECLINE OF BIBLICAL CRITICISM AS POPULAR
READING – A QUESTION

In his *The Eclipse of Biblical Narrative*, Hans W. Frei uses the deistic writings of Anthony Collins to symbolize the emerging, modern crisis of belief in biblical narrative as a story into which the secular world and its concerns – the world of the reader – could be incorporated, as it had been in the Renaissance and early seventeenth-century Christian tradition: 'It is no exaggeration to say that all across the theological spectrum the great reversal had taken place; interpretation was a matter of fitting the biblical story into another world with another story rather than incorporating that world into the biblical story.'[104] In one way this reversal is reflected in the steady application of historical and rational criteria to biblical interpretation, and in an important sense the reversal is also reflected in the heavy use in literature of expanded biblical allusion. This literary practice does not attempt to fit the secular world into the course of biblical history, but rather uses biblical history to provide a Christian meaning for events in the secular world. The progress of the deist attack on revealed religion, however, struck at the very historicity or facticity of the characters and events portrayed in the Old and New Testaments. Following the debate over prophecy and typology, the controversy shifted to the facticity of Christ's miracles. The miracle stories inevitably became a focal point of discussion, because many of the Christian apologists, in responding to the typological problem, moved to the argument that miracles rather than prophecy proved Christ to be the Messiah. Thomas Sherlock, later Bishop of London, protested in *The Use and Intent of Prophecy in the Several Ages of the World* (1725) that the interpretation of prophecy must be understood in a retroactive rather than a prefigurative sense. There is no point, Sherlock claims, for example, in asking whether the prophecies of the Messiah's death and resurrection apply to Jesus, 'unless we are first satisfied that Jesus dy'd and rose again'. Therefore, 'the Truth of the Resurrection, consider'd as a Fact, is quite independent of the Evidence or Authority of Prophecy'.[105] Such arguments opened the door to the questioning of whether Jesus did indeed die and rise again, whether the biblical story was fact or fiction.

This is not the place to rehearse the deist controversy, but a few important points should be made. The immediate effect of the controversy on the general reader of biblical criticism could not have been great. In fact, by 1756 he could follow it step by step, from a Christian perspective, of course, in John Leland's three-volume *A View of the Principal Deistical Writers* (1754–6). Many of the most popular hermeneutic reference works, including the republication of *Moses Unveiled* in 1740, appeared during the height of the controversy. The long-term results, however, were undoubtedly devastating. As biblical scholars began the long quest for the historical Jesus, the body of received biblical interpretation disintegrated. The one exception, perhaps, was the tradition of typological reading, which continued, despite the deist controversy, well into the nineteenth century. It could still form a context of meaning for the Victorians, as George P. Landow's new study of typology in Victorian literature and art testifies.[106] But biblical criticism in general quickly became the reading matter of biblical specialists, not of the ordinary reader, although pious books and pamphlets continued to abound.[107] I cannot fix a definite date for this disintegration of received biblical interpretation, but it was certainly well under way in the early part of the nineteenth century. Perhaps the major biblical publishing event of 1788–92 was Thomas Scott's edition of the Bible, containing both Testaments, original notes, practical observations, and copious marginal references.[108] This work became the standard biblical commentary in English throughout the nineteenth century and well into the twentieth. Editions of it could be found in nearly every English and American home. But except for typological references, could nineteenth-century writers make a biblical allusion with the expectation that the general reader would include even this commentary? The answer to that question remains to be given, but I suspect it will be in the negative.

NOTES

This essay is based on current research that has been generously supported by several groups. I wish to thank especially the University of Wyoming Division of Basic Research, the National Endowment for the Humanities, and the American Council of Learned Societies.

1. Henry Fielding, *Joseph Andrews*, ed. M. C. Battestin (Middletown, Conn., 1967), Book III, viii, 253.
2. See the discussion of this biblical text on pp. 106–8.
3. For a good, if old fashioned, text book on hermeneutics, see M. S. Terry, *Biblical Hermeneutics* (orig. publ. in New York, 1883; repr. in Grand Rapids, Mich., 1974). See R. E. Palmer, *Hermeneutics* (Evanston, Ill., 1969) for an introduction to modern theories of hermeneutics, especially in relation to non-biblical texts. General histories of hermeneutics, usually dismissing the late seventeenth and eighteenth centuries rather quickly, include E. C. Black, *Biblical Interpretation* (New York, 1966); R. M. Grant, *A Short History of the Interpretation of the Bible* (revised edn, New York, 1963); J. D. Wood, *The Interpretation of the Bible: A Historical Introduction* (Naperville, Ill., 1958). Still useful is F. W. Farrar, *History of Interpretation* (1886).
4. Except for noting unusual sectarian doctrines and making occasional outbursts against some Roman doctrines, especially papal supremacy

and transubstantiation, eighteenth-century biblical criticism enjoyed a remarkable ecumenicism free of sectarian controversy.

5. Ph.D. thesis, University of London, 1939.

6. See I. W. J. Machin, 'Popular religious works of the eighteenth-century: their vogue and influence', 17.

7. *Ibid.*, 16.

8. *Ibid.*

9. *Ibid.*, 30.

10. *Ibid.*, 33, 134.

11. *Ibid.*, 165–7.

12. *Ibid.*

13. See P. Kaufman, *Libraries and Their Users* (1969), especially 31, 80, 94–5; *idem*, 'Reading vogues at English cathedral libraries of the eighteenth century', *Bull. New York Public Library*, LXVII–LXVIII (December 1963; January, February, March 1964), 643–71, 48–64, 110–32, 191–202.

14. R. M. Wiles, 'The relish for reading in provincial England two centuries ago', in *The Widening Circle*, ed. P. J. Korshin (Philadelphia, 1976), 99.

15. L. Lowenthal, *Literature, Popular Culture, and Society* (New Jersey, 1961), 56. I am not concerned here with the state of literacy, but the general public that could read. For the former, see R. D. Altick, *The English Common Reader* (Chicago, 1957), 30–77. Altick's pessimistic figures are somewhat revised by L. Stone, 'Literacy and education in England 1640–1900', *Past and Present*, LXII (1969), 69–139. See also Wiles, *op. cit.*, 112.

16. See S. Blackwell, *Several Methods* (4th edn, 1736), *passim*. Two indispensable guides to the biblical criticism, both annotated, are T. H. Horne, *A Manual of Biblical Bibliography* (1839) and W. Orme, *Bibliotheca Biblica* (1824). For works cited in the text, short titles only are used in the notes. Unless indicated otherwise, references and quotations are from first editions whose dates are given in the text. Several biblical commentaries lack or use eccentric pagination. Where useful, page numbers are given; otherwise references

are to biblical book, chapter, and verse.

17. W. Lowth, *Directions* (1821), 46–7.

18. *Ibid.*, 50–60.

19. *Ibid.*, 56.

20. J. Wilson, *Scripture's Interpreter* (1678), 168.

21. Lowth, *Directions*, 60–70.

22. See, for example, Jean Ostervald, *The Necessity and Usefulness of Reading the Holy Scriptures*, transl. John Moore (1750); *Practical Discourses upon Reading the Scripture* (1717), 97–204; Dom Bernard Lamy, *Apparatus Biblicus*, transl. R. Bundy (1723); David Collyer, *The Sacred Interpreter* (2nd edn, revised, 2 vols., 1732), I, 64–6, 219–309.

23. Owen, *Works*, ed. W. H. Goold (1852), IV, 201.

24. *Ibid.*, 210–26. The movement in biblical criticism was definitely away from the older allegorization and towards interpretation according to historical and rational criteria. See on this subject, V. Harris, 'Allegory to analogy in the interpretation of scriptures', *Philological Quarterly*, XLV (January 1966), 1–23.

25. P. Stockdale, *Memoirs* (1809), II, 13. See Orme's comments on Prideaux, in Orme, *op. cit.*, 326.

26. See Orme, *op. cit.*, 403.

27. See *Joseph Andrews*, Book III, i, 189, n. 1. (The passage is quoted on p. 118 above.)

28. See Orme, *op. cit.*, 418.

29. *Ibid.*, 111.

30. See Collyer, *op. cit.*, I, 219–309.

31. Lowth, *Directions*, 74.

32. W. Guild, *Moses Unveiled* (1740), 15.

33. *Practical Discourses*, 157.

34. Boswell, *Life of Johnson*, ed. G. B. Hill, rev. L. F. Powell (1934), III, 58.

35. The most famous were L. E. Du Pin, *A New History of Ecclesiastical Writers*, 3 vols. (1722–24) and J. L. Mosheim, *An Ecclesiastical History* (transl. A. Maclaine, 2 vols., 1764).

36. *Practical Discourses*, 140. During the course of the century many new translations of the Bible were also proposed. See S. I. Tucker, 'Biblical translation in the eighteenth century', *Essays and Studies*, n.s., XXV (1972), 106–20.

37. Horne, *op. cit.*, 253–4.
38. *Ibid.*, 254.
39. Orme, *op. cit.*, 223.
40. P. Doddridge, *Lectures on Preaching* (1821), 90. They were transcribed by students in 1739.
41. *Ibid.*, 85–6.
42. *Ibid.*, 86.
43. *Ibid.*
44. *Ibid.*, 88.
45. *Ibid.*, 87.
46. See Horne, *op. cit.*, 301.
47. Quoted in Horne, *op. cit.*, 302. While preparing the *Family Expositor*, Doddridge was in correspondence with such famous members of the Church of England as George (later Lord) Lyttleton, the friend of Fielding. In a letter of 16 April 1750 Lyttleton begged Doddridge to avoid phrases which 'most readers of our Church will call *Cant*'. See G. F. Nuttall, *Calendar of the Correspondence of Philip Doddridge* (1979), 327.
48. George Stanhope, *A Paraphrase and Commentary* (4 vols., 1714); John Locke, *A Paraphrase and Notes on the Epistles of St. Paul* (1705); George Benson, *A Paraphrase and Notes on the Epistles of St. Paul* (1734); James Peirce, *A Paraphrase and Notes on the Epistles . . . to the Colossians, Phillipians and Hebrews* (1727).
49. Some of the other secondary, but important, commentaries include: John Richardson, *Choice Observations and Explanations upon the Old Testament* (1657); John Gill, *An Exposition of the Old Testament* (6 vols., 1763); Edmund Wells, *Paraphrases of the Old and New Testament* (1718–23); Edward Leigh, *Annotations upon All the New Testament* (1650); John Gill, *An Exposition of the New Testament* (3 vols., 1746–8); Joseph Trapp, *Explanatory Notes upon the Four Gospels and the Acts of the Apostles* (2 vols., 1747); John Guyse, *The Practical Expositor: Or, An Exposition of the New Testament* (3 vols., 1739–52).
50. *Assembly's Annotations* (1657), II, Matt. 19:24.
51. M. Henry, *Exposition* (1808), IV, Matt. 19:24.
52. W. Burkitt, *Expository Notes* (1772), Matt. 19:24 and Mark 10:25.
53. Whitby, *Commentary* (Philadelphia, 1844), IV, 140.
54. See Gill, *New Testament*, I, 195; J. Lindsay, *A Critical and Practical Commentary on the New Testament* (1737), 75; J. Marchant *A Commentary on the New Testament* (1743), 111.
55. Doddridge, *Family Expositor* (1825), 270.
56. See E. D. Hirsch, *Validity in Interpretation* (New Haven, 1967), 8, 38, 57, 62ff, 127, 141, 216, 255.
57. Henry, V, Romans 4:23.
58. Collyer, *op. cit.*, II, 111–26; R. Theed, *Sacred Biography* (1714), *passim*; J. Hall, *Contemplations* (1822 edn.), for example, 'Of Abraham', 15.
59. Doddridge, *Lectures*, 40.
60. On imitation and examples see also Burkitt, 'The Close' to the Gospel of John and James 5:10–11.
61. *Dutch Annotations*, I, Genesis 10:9. The evil character of Nimrod began with St Gregory's commentary on Genesis and continued throughout the middle ages and Renaissance. Milton's depiction of Nimrod in *Paradise Lost*, XII, 24–63 derives from the standard biblical commentaries of his time. See the note to these lines in John Milton, *Complete Poems and Major Prose*, ed. M. Y. Hughes (New York, 1957), 454.
62. These are summarized in the *Assembly's Annotations* (1657), I, Genesis 10:8–12. Patrick's outline of the tyrant can also be found there.
63. S. Patrick, *Commentary*, I, 49–50.
64. Henry, I, Genesis 10:8–12.
65. Gill, *Old Testament*, I, 68. For further commentaries on Nimrod as exemplary tyrant, see J. Richardson, *op. cit.*, Genesis 10:9; H. Stackhouse, *History of the Bible* (1752), I, 176–7, 201. Samuel Shuckford gave almost the only positive portrayal of Nimrod: see *Connections*, ed. J. Creighton (1824), I, 125–6.
66. Henry, IV, Matt. 25:14–30.
67. Burkitt, Matt. 25:14–18.
68. Doddridge, *Family Expositor*, 332.
69. Gill, *New Testament*, I, 277.
70. See the discussion in John Edwards, *Discourse*, II, 68–70.
71. *Ibid.*, 114–55, 70–1, 19–30.
72. See especially pp. 1–11, 39, chapters 4, 7.

73. A. Blackwall, *Sacred Classics* (orig. publ. 1727, repr., New York, 1970), I, 404–5.
74. Henry, I, Genesis 22:14.
75. For further literary evaluations of the Bible, see Collyer, *op. cit.*, I, 75ff; Robert Boyle, *Some Considerations Touching the Style of the Holy Scriptures* (4th edn, 1675); Thomas Leland, *A Dissertation on the Principles of Human Eloquence: With Particular Regard to the Style and Compostion of the New Testament* (1764).
76. See A. Williams, *Common Expositor* (Chapel Hill, North Carolina, 1948), 26–39, and *passim*.
77. See B. Lewalski, *Protestant Poetics and the Seventeenth-Century Religious Lyric* (Princeton, 1979). Lewalski conveniently lists the major literary studies of typology, 449–50, n. 1. See also S. Bercovitch, 'Annotated bibliography', in *Typology and Early American Literature*, ed. S. Bercovitch (Amherst, 1972) 245–337. Also useful, especially for the medieval and Renaissance periods, is the short bibliography in Harris, *op. cit.*, 2, n. 1. *Literary Uses of Typology*, ed. E. Miner (Princeton, 1977), comprises for various periods an important collection of essays on typology and literature. Lewalski gives a detailed analysis of the major biblical criticism from the Reformation to the Restoration, 31–250. She also includes excellent discussions of Guild (pp. 452–3), Lukin (pp. 82, 446, 452), and Keach (pp. 83, 446, 453).
78. Typology was still important for Restoration and early eighteenth-century literature. See, for example, S. Zwicker, *Dryden's Political Poetry: The Typology of King and Nation* (Providence, 1972). It declined soon, however, into minor religious poetry for the most part. See D. Morris, *The Religious Sublime* (Lexington, 1972).
79. See *Publications Modern Language Assoc.* xxxxiv (1969), 274–81. See also my 'Johnson's *Rasselas* continued', *Publications Modern Language Assoc.* xxxxvii (1972), 312–14; and *Not in Timon's Manner* (Alabama, 1975), ch. 5.
80. Burkitt, Matt. 19:23–24.
81. *Joseph Andrews*, Book I, xvii, 83.
82. *Ibid.*, 82.
83. *The Expedition of Humphry Clinker*, ed. L. Knapp (1966), Matthew Bramble to Dr Lewis, Harrogate, 26 June, 164–5.
84. A. Collins, *Discourse* (1741), 35–6.
85. A. Collins, *Scheme of Literal Prophecy* (1776), 345.
86. See Edwards, *op. cit.*, 11, 15–16 for an early discussion of 'accommodation' that also cites other biblical critics.
87. Collins, *Literal Prophecy*, 348.
88. A. A. Sykes, *An Essay upon the Truth of the Christian Religion* (1725), 179–82, 193, 196, 249. For excellent dicussions of type as analogy by divines who did not abandon the theological meaning, see Edward Chandler, *A Defence of Christianity from the Prophecies of the Old Testament* (1725), 282–7, 340–69; Samuel Chandler, *A Vindication of the Christian Religion* (1725), 259, 338–53.
89. Quoted in Harris, *op. cit.*, 22.
90. P. J. Korshin, 'The development of abstracted typology in England, 1650–1820', in *Literary Uses of Typology*, 161–2. See also my 'Smollett and the benevolent misanthrope type', *Publications Modern Language Assoc.* lxxix (March 1964), 51–7; and *Not in Timon's Manner*, *passim*.
91. *Joseph Andrews*, Book III, i, 189.
92. M. C. Battestin, *The Moral Basis of Fielding's Art* (Middletown, Conn., 1959), especially ch. 3. Battestin relies primarily on sermons rather than the biblical criticism many of the sermons were reflecting. Seventeenth-century literature, following Renaissance biblical interpretation, would view the reader, in Barbara Lewalski's terms, as a 'correlative type', i.e., a person 'undergoing much the same kind and quality of spiritual experience' described in the biblical presentation ('Typological symbolism and the "Progress of the Soul" in seventeenth-century literature', in *Literary Uses of Typology*, 83). The eighteenth-century translation of type into pattern markedly shifts the reader's involvement away from the experience of the biblical person or event, a distancing process that foreshadowed the eventual loss of a received

interpretation of Scripture, as discussed
on p. 122.

93. See M. C. Battestin, *The Providence of
Wit* (1974), ch. 7; and J. H. Lehman,
'*The Vicar of Wakefield*: Goldsmith's
sublime, oriental Job', *English Literary
History*, XLVI (1979), 97–121.

94. R. Hume, *The Development of English
Drama in the Late Seventeenth Century*
(1976), 38–48, 61–2. Aubrey Williams
has made an admirable and
controversial start on the drama in *An
Approach to Congreve* (New Haven, 1979).
Like Battestin, however, Williams relies
primarily on theology and sermons.
Biblical criticism may provide support
for the more strained parts of his
argument. See also his 'Interpositions of
providence and the design of Fielding's
novels', *South Atlantic Quarterly*, LXX
(1971), 265–86.

95. J. Taylor, *The Great Exemplar* (1653), 10.

96. *Joseph Andrews*, Book I, i, 17–20; Book I,
viii, 41; Book I, x, 46–7.

97. Henry, I, Genesis 12:10–13.

98. S. Richardson, *Sir Charles Grandison*
(1902), VIII, 330–1.

99. See P. J. Korshin, 'Abstracted
typology', in *Literary Uses of Typology*,
174–9.

100. Lowth, *Lectures* (1787 edn., repr. New
York, 1971), I, 224.

101. Henry, IV, Luke 19:19–31.

102. *Ibid.*, Matt. 20:1–16.

103. Keach, *Gospel Mysteries*, 2, 5–6.

104. H. Frei, *Eclipse of Biblical Narrative*
(New Haven, 1974), 130. The first part
of Frei's study is extremely important as
background to eighteenth-century
hermeneutics.

105. Sherlock, *Use and Intent of Prophecy* (5th
edn, 1749), 39. See also S. Chandler,
op. cit., 162.

106. G. P. Landow, *Victorian Types, Victorian
Shadows* (Boston, 1980). I have not seen
this study, which appeared just as this
essay was going to press. Typology has
been cautiously reentering current
biblical scholarship. See, for example,
Essays on Typology, ed. G. W. H. Lampe
and K. J. Woolcombe (Naperville, Ill.,
1957); W. Eichrodt, 'Is typological
exegesis an appropriate method?', in
Essays on Old Testament Hermeneutics,
ed. C. Westerman (Atlanta, Georgia,
1963), pp. 224–45; and G. von Rad,
'Typological interpretation of the Old
Testament', *ibid.*, 17–49.

107. See Altick, *op. cit.*, especially ch. 5.

108. See Orme, *op. cit.*, 393–4.

6

Dissenting and Methodist books of practical divinity

ISABEL RIVERS

Knowledge and affection should go hand in hand, in all the affairs of religion.
Isaac Watts[1]

I. INTRODUCTION

Eighteenth-century Christian authors of all denominations Roman Catholic, Anglican, dissenting, and Methodist – placed religious literature in three main categories: doctrinal or speculative (concerned with establishing the truth of specific doctrines and the evidences, natural and revealed, for Christianity), controversial (concerned with demolishing on rational or historical or scriptural grounds the beliefs and practices of rival denominations), and practical (concerned with helping the individual to practise the Christian life). No one doubted that the last category was the most important. The subject matter and method of practical literature varied a good deal; it included guides for the individual's private or 'closet' devotions, and warnings to the drunkard or fornicator to abandon his favourite sin under threat of damnation. The audience for such literature might be defined in either social or spiritual terms: thus specific books, chapters, or even paragraphs were addressed to women, families, various trades, clergy or ministers, the unlearned and the learned, the reader being defined by sex, education, and social status; or such books were addressed (in the typical phrases of dissenting and Methodist practical literature) to the ungodly, the unconverted, formal or almost Christians, young Christians, backsliders, advanced Christians, the reader being defined by his stage on the path to salvation. Strenuous efforts were made to ensure that the books came to the hands of their defined readers. The scale of distribution ranged from the individual minister who gave books away to his parishioners (as Baxter urged in *The Reformed Pastor*), to organizations engaged in publishing and distributing religious literature, such as Dr Bray's Society for Promoting Christian Knowledge and Wesley's Book Room. The format, length, and price of a book depended on its audience and function. It might be a beautifully bound duodecimo pocket book for private devotion (like the first edition of Taylor's *The Rule and Exercises of Holy Living*), a heavy folio for the minister's study or the householder's parlour (like Baxter's *Christian Directory*), a handsomely printed quarto for the gentleman's library (like Law's *Serious Call to a Devout and Holy Life*), or a paperbound duodecimo pamphlet for mass distribution, priced at 4d. (like the majority of Wesley's publications).[2]

It is not possible to make straightforward distinctions between the practical literature of different churches: the writer's intentions and audience must be taken into account. Some practical literature was interdenominational: Catholic and Anglican books of devotion were widely used by Methodists, and to a lesser extent by dissenters. However, one of the many sources of the self-scrutiny of dissent in the 1730s and 1740s and the rise of Methodism in the same period was dissatisfaction with contemporary Anglican literature. It was thought that Anglican speculative theology concentrated too narrowly on natural religion, and that Anglican practical literature only stressed ceremonial observance and social duties. Dissenters and Methodists wanted a religious literature that was experimental, affectionate, and evangelical as well as practical: it could not be the last without being the former. By 'experimental' they meant that it must be based on the personal religious experience of the writer, or appeal to that of the reader, or narrate that of others; by 'affectionate' that it must be directed at the reader's heart and excite his passions; by 'evangelical' that it must teach the gospel doctrine of salvation by faith. Only then could it be practical, and effect a radical change in the life of the reader. With this end in view dissenters and Methodists wrote, edited, and abridged a number of influential books which were to be widely read and distributed for the next hundred years.

This essay is largely concerned with the work of Richard Baxter, Isaac Watts, Philip Doddridge, and John Wesley. It is an account of the most important dissenting and Methodist books of practical divinity, the sources from which they were drawn, the readers to whom they were addressed, and their publishing history; it also explores two important related topics, the theory of the place of the affections in religion, which is the essential underpinning of dissenting and Methodist practical divinity, and the theory of the Christian's need for books, which directly shaped dissenting and Methodist educational practice.

2. DISSENTING THEORY OF THE PASSIONS AND CHRISTIAN ORATORY

In 1730 Strickland Gough, a dissenter who subsequently conformed to the Church of England, published an anonymous pamphlet called *An Enquiry into the Causes of the Decay of the Dissenting Interest*, which galvanized his contemporaries into defining the qualities and characteristics of dissent in contrast to those of the Established Church. By 'decay' was meant the falling membership of dissenting congregations and the conforming to the Church of many young middle-class dissenters.[3] Gough attributed this decay to '*ignorance* of their own principles, and *ill conduct* and management of their own interests'. Writing as a rationalist, Gough defines the 'fundamental principle of the dissenters' as 'a *liberty* for every man to form his own sentiments, and to pursue them by all lawful and regular methods; to disclaim the *impositions* of men, and to worship God according to the dictates of his own conscience.'[4] Gough here points out the damaging effect of the disputes between the orthodox Calvinist, Baxterian, and Arian branches of dissent – disputes that were to continue throughout the century.[5] Writing as a gentleman, Gough attacks dissenting ministers for their anachronistic adherence to the manners of their Puritan forbears and their lack of politeness; dissenting ministers, he argues, should be chosen from the families of gentlemen, and not from 'low and mechanical persons'. 'There are many Gentlemen,' he claims, 'who can give no other reason, for leaving us, but that they are asham'd of our interest.'[6]

Among those rallying to the defence of dissent were Doddridge (anonymously) in *Free Thoughts on the Most Probable Means of Reviving the Dissenting Interest* (1730) and Watts in *An Humble Attempt towards the Revival of Practical Religion among Christians* (1731). Although Doddridge begins by agreeing with Gough's strictures he soon subverts Gough's position. Doddridge's title, *Free Thoughts*, suggests sympathy with Gough's rational, free-thinking approach, but he insists that the basis of dissent is not just a sense of liberty '(which may warm the breast of a deist or an atheist) but a religious reverence for the divine authority.'[7] While agreeing that intending ministers should be taught 'genteel and complaisant behaviour', Doddridge insists that the choice between the Established Church and dissent is not one of taste, and that the dissenting interest should be supported by methods 'most subservient to the cause of practical religion, and vital holiness in all its branches'. Doddridge's portrait of the ideal minister is therefore very different from Gough's. Because the minister's responsibility is to his people, he must be in the fullest sense popular: 'He who would be generally agreeable to dissenters, must be an evangelical, an experimental, a plain and an affectionate preacher.'[8]

Watts' *Humble Attempt*, divided into 'An Exhortation to Ministers' and 'A

Serious Address to the People', deals more systematically with the same question. In the first part Watts explains the aims and methods of 'sacred oratory',[9] the steps by which a minister can become an evangelical, experimental, plain and affectionate preacher. The terms 'affectionate' and 'experimental' are particularly worth exploring: they have reference to both a theory of human nature and a religious and literary tradition. Watts exhorts the ministers:

> Remember that you have to do with the understanding, reason and memory of man, with the heart and conscience, with the will and affections; and therefore you must use every method of speech, which may be most proper to engage and employ, each of these faculties or powers of human nature, on the side of religion and in the interests of God and the gospel.

Watts goes through these faculties in turn, explaining their function and how the preacher can appeal to them. He concludes with an account of the passions. The understanding can be persuaded of what is right, but the will is prevented by the world and the flesh from putting it into practice:

> The God of nature therefore has furnished mankind with those powers, which we call passions, or affections of the heart, in order to excite the will with superior vigour and activity to avoid the evil and pursue the good. Upon this account the preacher must learn to address the passions in a proper manner.[10]

Watts is here summarizing in the context of advice to preachers a theory of the passions which he develops much more fully elsewhere. In some respects this division of the faculties of the soul into understanding, will and passions (or affections – Watts uses the terms synonymously) is a traditional one, going back to classical oratory; thus in his account of the parts of rhetoric in *The Improvement of the Mind*, part I (1741), his handbook 'for the Attainment of Useful Knowledge', Watts puts forward Cicero and Demosthenes as models. Watts treats rhetoric here as an instrument that every educated man should be able to employ in disputation on any subject. He explains how the speaker appeals to the understanding, will, and passions of the hearer, and how the hearer responds by being convinced in his understanding, making a choice with his will, and, impelled by the passions, pursuing or avoiding the object.[11]

Watts expounded his theory of the religious use of the passions most fully in *The Doctrine of the Passions Explained and Improved* and its companion volume *Discourses of the Love of God, and the Use and Abuse of the Passions in Religion* (1729, revised and enlarged in 1732). In the first volume Watts gives a systematic analysis and classification of the passions, their different kinds and functions, and their place within the human constitution. The passions belong to both the mind and body: they create 'sensible commotions of our whole nature'. They are 'active and sprightly powers' because 'they have a tendency to excite the person to lively and vigorous actions', and this tendency 'is the chief design of them in the nature of man'. 'The heart, in the common sense of mankind, is reckoned the seat of the passions.' This meaning of the heart as the seat of the passions and hence the source of action should be noted: when Watts or Doddridge or Wesley talked of heart religion they did not mean feeling divorced from action. The passions are limited in function, but essential to human nature. They assist the reason, which is capable of judgment but too weak to incite one to action:

> Though [the passions] were not given to tell us what is good, and what is evil, yet when our reason, upon a calm survey, has passed a just judgment concerning things, whether they are good or evil, the passions . . . are those lively, warm, and vigorous principles and powers in our nature, which animate us to pursue the good, and avoid the evil.[12]

In the Preface to the second volume, *Of the Love of God*, Watts explains that his motive in making this analysis is the current decay in 'vital religion', and the tendency of preachers to rely on rational explication of religious duties without 'a pathetic address to the heart'. Watts' object is to distinguish the true use of the passions in religion from the extremes of enthusiasm, which is affection divorced from reason and hence incapable of issuing in action (since it cannot know what is good), and cold reasoning religion, which is divorced from affection and similarly incapable of action (since it has no motivating 'springs'). But when the understanding, will, and affections, or the head and heart, are fully engaged the whole man will commit himself to vital religion. 'Now if the passions are strongly engaged for God, the world will have but little power to call off the heart from religion.'[13] In the terms of the title of Discourse VI, the affectionate Christian is vindicated.

In his emphasis on the integration of head and heart Watts consciously followed the Baxterian tradition. In the fourth part of *The Saints' Everlasting Rest* (first published in 1650), 'Containing a Directory for the getting and keeping of the Heart in Heaven', Baxter describes the preferred method of meditation. He is concerned (as is Watts) with the crucial problem for practical religion of converting understanding into action, and the process is described in psychological and physiological terms. All the human faculties must be involved:

> The understanding is not the whole soul, and therefore cannot do the whole work: . . . the understanding must take in truths, and prepare them for the Will, and it must receive them, and commend them to the Affections: The best digestion is in the bottom of the Stomack; the affections are as it were the bottom of the soul, and therefore the best digestion is there. . . . Therefore this is the great task in hand . . . to get these truths from thy head to thy heart, and that all

the Sermons which thou hast heard of Heaven, and all the notions that thou hast conceived of this Rest [i.e. the everlasting rest] may be turned into the blood and spirits of Affection.[14]

Watts' American contemporary Jonathan Edwards, working within a similar Puritan tradition, carried the theory of the religious use of the passions to its furthest extent. Both Watts and Wesley took a keen interest in the Great Awakening in New England of 1734–43 and in Edwards' accounts of it. It was in the context of the Awakening that Edwards developed the theory published as *A Treatise Concerning Religious Affections* (1746).[15] He wished to dissociate himself on the one hand from rationalists who, drawing on classical philosophy, regarded the affections as brutish, having no place in religion, and needing to be suppressed, and on the other hand from enthusiasts who divorced Christian experience from practice, whose affections did not issue in practical holiness. Edwards therefore had a twofold task, to explain the function of the affections in human psychology, and to distinguish between false and 'truly gracious and holy' affections. Edwards' account is much fuller and more discriminating than that of Watts, but his fundamental distinction between the faculties of the understanding, which discerns and judges, and the will, which approves or disapproves and expresses its inclination through the affections, is very similar, as is his argument that the test of true religious affections is that they issue in practice.[16]

Doddridge, in his work as tutor and pastor, made Watts' theory of the passions his own. He used *The Doctrine of the Passions* as a textbook in his lectures on 'The Powers and Faculties of the Human Mind',[17] and in his *Lectures on Preaching* explained the practical application of the theory. The sixth lecture analyses the 'Different Strains of Preaching', including the argumentative, pathetic, insinuating, evangelical, spiritual and experimental, and scriptural; under the pathetic, Doddridge restates the function of the passions and urges his pupils to 'make your sermons addresses to your hearers, rather than general essays or speculative harangues'.[18] In the Preface to *Ten Sermons on the Power and Grace of Christ*, Doddridge justifies the warmth of his own style:

> I hope I shall always remember, how unworthy the character of a man and a christian it is, to endeavour to transport men's passions, while the understanding is left uninformed, or the judgment unconvinced: But so far as is consistent with a proper regard to these leading powers of our nature, I heartily pray, that I, and all other gospel ministers, may so feel the energy of divine truths on our own souls, as to preach and write concerning them with an holy fervency and ardour.[19]

It is worth emphasizing the belief of Doddridge and Watts that the passions must not be divorced from the understanding. Thus in his extremely sympathetic pastoral advice to Miss Scot, a friend suffering from severe religious depression, Doddridge urged her 'To lay it down as a certain principle, *that religion consists more in an intelligent, rational, and determinate choice of the will* than in any ardent transport of the affections.'[20] This advice is not inconsistent with the doctrine of the passions; on the contrary, it is true to its rational and practical implications.

Watts and Doddridge, Baxter and Edwards almost always link 'affectionate' with 'experimental'. In seventeenth- and eighteenth-century religious literature the term usually means 'experiential', appertaining to the experience of God in the soul, but it also becomes associated with the scientific usage in 'experimental philosophy', so that it can come to mean 'verifiable by appeal to the evidence of experience'. Edwards specifically links the two usages at the conclusion of *Religious Affections*: 'As that is called experimental philosophy, which brings opinions and notions to the test of fact; so is that properly called experimental religion, which brings religious affections and intentions, to the like test.'[21] In Puritan and dissenting works on the ministerial function 'experimental' is used more specfically: it means making a direct address to the capacities and experiences of different kinds of hearers or readers.

In *An Humble Attempt* Watts recommends John Jennings' *Two Discourses*, 'Of preaching Christ' and 'Of particular and experimental Preaching', both addressed 'to Younger Ministers'.[22] Jennings' aim is to revive the Puritan habit of preaching in scriptural language, on evangelical themes, and especially by making particular application 'to the several Cases, Tempers, and Experiences of the Hearers'. Jennings argues that the Puritan divines imitated the example of the prophets and apostles, 'suiting their Discourses to all the Variety of the Hearts of Men, and Sorts and Frames of Christians, according to the true Precepts of Oratory and Christianity'.[23] (One of Jennings' epigraphs is from Baxter's *Reformed Pastor*.) In the Preface to Jennings and *An Humble Attempt* Watts seizes on the point that the dissenters' Puritan fathers were careful to distinguish the characters of their hearers.[24] He argues young ministers to address on different occasions 'saints and sinners, the converted and the unconverted, the sincere christian and the formal professor, the stupid and the awakened, the diligent and backsliding, the fearful or humble soul, and the obstinate and presumptuous', and he lists the methods that dissenting congregations expect from their preachers: they must search their hearers' souls and consciences, enter 'into the various turnings of the heart of man' (Doddridge's 'insinuating strain'), 'pass through the various parts of spiritual experience, and the several scenes and stages of the christian life. Surely,' Watts continues,

> this was the fashion and practice of our fathers amongst the puritans and protestant dissenters in their ministry: I hope this is the present mode of

preaching amongst us, and I wish with all my soul this sort of ministration, this manner of *dividing the word of God, and giving to each their due*, may never grow out of fashion in our places of worship.[25]

What for Gough was unfashionable awkwardness, for Watts, Jennings, Doddridge, and Doddridge's pupils was the essence of the dissenting tradition, a ministry based on knowledge of the human heart, demonstrating its validity through its practical results. For one sinner converted by a preacher 'who is generally entertaining the audience, with a long and weighty chain of reasoning from the principles of nature, and teaching virtue in the language of heathen philosophy, Watts promised to show ten 'who have become holy persons and lively christians by an attendance upon a scriptural, affectionate and experimental ministry.'[26]

3. DISSENTING EDUCATION AND THE USE OF BOOKS

For Baxter, books were essentially a superior method of preaching.[27] True, the preacher knew the individual needs of his congregation, but in other respects the book had the advantage. In *A Christian Directory* (1673), designed as 'A Summ of Practical Theologie' to guide the individual in all his duties, private, domestic, ecclesiastical, social and political, Baxter makes this point explicit:

> The Writings of Divines are nothing else but a preaching the Gospel to the eye, as the *voice* preacheth it to the ear. Vocal preaching hath the preheminence in moving the affections, and being diversified according to the state of the Congregations which attend it: This way the Milk cometh warmest from the breast. But Books have the advantage in many other respects: you may read an able Preacher when you have but a mean one to hear. Every *Congregation* cannot hear the most judicious or powerful Preachers: but every *single person* may read the Books of the most powerful and judicious; *Preachers* may be silenced or banished, when *Books* may be at hand. . . . If Sermons be forgotten, they are gone. But a Book we may read over and over till we remember it: and if we forget it, may again peruse it at our pleasure, or at our leisure. . . . Books are (if well chosen) domestick, present, constant, judicious, pertinent, yea, and powerful Sermons.[28]

After the ejection of the nonconformist ministers in 1662, reading became a necessary substitute for preaching for those congregations who could not attend secret prayer meetings and would not attend their parish churches. Baxter, the most prolific author of his day,[29] explained in *Reliquiae Baxterianae* (published posthumously in 1696) how he was once inclined to blame himself for overloading the world with books, but now saw the importance of his work: 'I now bless God that his poor Servants have the private help of Books, which are the best Teachers, under God, that many thousand Persons have.'[30]

Baxter knew from his own early experience that books could be a much more powerful influence than ministers. Edmund Calamy records how Gilbert Burnet extolled Baxter's practical works and owned to Calamy 'that, if he had any acquaintance with serious vital religion, it was owing to his reading them in his younger days.'[31] In turn, Calamy told Burnet of Baxter's account of being awakened in his youth by Bunny's *Resolution*. Baxter goes on to admit of his early reading that 'the use that God made of Books, above Ministers, to the benefit of my Soul, made me somewhat excessively in love with good Books.'[32]

Denied the opportunity of a university education, Baxter taught himself.[33] His early reading included scholastic and controversial works, but he stressed that it was all directed to the end of his salvation. He was convinced that he would die young, and it was this conviction, he says, that 'caused me to study *Practical Divinity* first, in the most *Practical Books*, in a *Practical Order*; doing all purposely for the informing and reforming of my own Soul.' By this means 'my *Affection* was carried on with my Judgment.'[34]

Baxter always insisted on this conjunction of feeling and understanding, practice and learning. Hence a crucial part of the minister's function was to encourage Christians of all social classes to read. In *Gildas Salvianus*, his handbook for 'the reformed pastor' based on his own experiences at Kidderminster in the 1640s and 50s, Baxter expressed this idea in a striking metaphor: 'All Christians are Disciples or Schollars of Christ, the Church is his School; we [the ministers] are his Ushers, the Bible is his Grammar.' The basis of Baxter's pastoral method was that the minister should know, visit, hear and teach each member of his flock.[35] Between the Acts of Uniformity (1662) and Toleration (1689) this method could only be put into practice intermittently ('since Bishops were restored this Book is useless,' said Baxter pessimistically in 1664), but it remained the ideal of the dissenting tradition, and exercised great influence on Doddridge and Wesley.[36] The minister should see that each family owns 'some profitable moving book (besides the Bible)'; if they are too poor, the minister or some charitable gentleman should give them books free.[37] Baxter himself gave away Bibles and copies of his own works because, he said, 'I had found my self the benefit of reading to be so great, that I could not but think it would be profitable to others.'[38]

Baxter also provided guidance for those who wanted not simply practical handbooks for the religious life but a thorough knowledge of theology. In *A Christian Directory* there are three reading lists:[39] the first is intended for 'young Christians' (in experience rather than age), the next 'especially' for 'Masters of Families'; the third, provided in answer to the question, 'What Books Especially of Theologie should one choose, who for want of money or time, can read but few?' is much the longest. These lists, which demand an extraordinary commitment on the part of the reader to the idea of the

Christian life as achieved through the study of the printed word, constitute a very full guide to moderate Puritan literature of the early and mid-seventeenth century, and must have been invaluable for later generations of dissenters.

For what books meant to dissenting ministers in the mid-eighteenth century, we have ample evidence in the works of Doddridge. In his private diaries, correspondence with his friends and mentors, lectures to his academy, and the memoirs compiled by his pupil Job Orton, there is a detailed record of what Doddridge read, taught and disseminated in his rôles as student, tutor, and pastor (the rôles under which in his diaries he always analysed his past activities and planned his future ones), and what he thought the function of education to be. Doddridge was a student at Jennings' academy at Kibworth and Hinckley in Leicestershire.[40] After Jennings' death, and a period of intensive study while minister at Kibworth, Doddridge with the encouragement of Watts reestablished the academy in 1729, first briefly at Harborough and then at Northampton. Until his death in 1751 Doddridge energetically combined the rôles of tutor to his academy, minister to his church in Northampton, and author of books of practical divinity. He drew on the educational ideas of Watts and the practice of Jennings, and in turn exercised considerable influence through those of his students who themselves became tutors. We have several sources of information as to what was taught and how: Doddridge's letter to his friend Thomas Saunders of November 1725,[41] describing Jennings' system, a letter which was read and commented on by Watts, and which suggested to Watts that Doddridge was the right man to head the academy; *Some Account of the Life and Character of the Rev. Thomas Steffe*, a student of Doddridge who died in 1740 shortly after entering the ministry, and whose death was used by Doddridge as an occasion for both celebrating the exemplary minister and describing his own teaching methods; *A Course of Lectures on the Principal Subjects in Pneumatology, Ethics, and Divinity*, published posthumously in 1763 by Doddridge's student Samuel Clark jr, and used as a text book in other academies; *Lectures on Preaching*, first published in the collected *Works* of 1802–5; many passages in letters (especially to his mentor Samuel Clark sr) and diaries on his preparation for particular courses of instruction; and the sixth chapter of Orton's *Memoirs of the Life, Character and Writings of the Late Reverend Philip Doddridge* (1766).

Doddridge commented in a letter on Jennings' tutorial methods: 'He furnishes us with all kinds of authors upon every subject, without advising us to skip over the heretical passages for fear of infection. It is evidently his main care to inspire us with sentiments of CATHOLICISM, and to arm us against that zeal, which is not according to knowledge.'[42] Doddridge took over both Jennings' fundamental principle of encouraging 'the greatest freedom of inquiry',[43] and the substance and structure of much of his teaching. In their course at Northampton, as described by Orton, Doddridge's students covered a great range of subjects, including classics, science, history, and 'polite literature'. The central part of the course was Doddridge's system of divinity (published as *A Course of Lectures*) – 'the *Author's* capital Work, as a *Tutor*'.[44] In addition the ministerial students were given lectures on preaching (including elocution) and pastoral care. The system of divinity (containing 230 lectures in 10 parts) begins with the faculties of the human mind, goes on to the being of God, the nature of moral virtue, and the immortality of the soul, and then (the basis of natural religion having been established) turns to revelation, the scriptures, and the gospel doctrines. Doddridge's lecturing method clearly illustrates his principle of free enquiry:[45] he assembled from several authors arguments pro and con a particular subject, discussed their merits, and indicated his own position; the students took down the references, and followed them up in the library; at the next lecture Doddridge questioned them on their reading and heard their points of view before proceeding to the next subject. The students thus acquired at first hand a wide-ranging and up-to-date knowledge of contemporary moral and religious thought; for example, for the lectures on the nature of moral virtue and the moral attributes of God (lectures LII–LXII) they were required to read passages from among others Clarke, Hutcheson, Balguy, Shaftesbury, Wollaston, Cumberland, and Pope. Doddridge introduced them not only to deist but also to sceptical thought; thus in lecture XXIII, after considering arguments in favour of 'a self-existent being' Doddridge continues: 'Yet it must be owned that a late writer, who seems determined to carry scepticism to the greatest excess, has presumed to call this matter into question.' The reference is to Hume's *Philosophical Essays*.[46]

The correspondence, particularly with Samuel Clark, provides fascinating evidence of how Doddridge acquired and passed on information about new books. In May 1724 he told Clark that he had joined a book society, and a year later he explained its rules to his brother-in-law: 'For little more than a crown a year, I have the reading of all that are purchased by the common stock, amounting to sixteen pounds yearly.'[47] In the period of his Kibworth ministry Doddridge's non-theological reading included history and a good deal of classical literature. He was utterly opposed to superficial reading; while at Jennings' academy he wrote in shorthand in the fly leaf of his New Testament 'Rules for the Direction of my Conduct while a Student', containing this injunction: 'Never let me trifle with a book with which I may have no present concern. In applying myself to any work, let me first recollect what I may learn by it, and then beg suitable assistance from God; and let me continually endeavour to make all my studies subservient to practical religion and Ministerial usefulness.'[48] He obviously did not always follow this rule, and he later rebukes himself for 'meddling with books in which I had no concern'.[49] The instructions about reading scattered through Doddridge's diary should be compared with Watts' more systematic advice in the chapters 'Of Books and Reading' and 'Of Study or Meditation' in *The Improvement of the Mind*; Watts urges in the second that every speculative study should be applied to practical use.[50]

For all his emphasis on free enquiry, on the rational scrutiny of arguments and evidence, Doddridge was certain that this activity was a subordinate one. Thus his *Course of Lectures* concludes:

> To cultivate a devotional temper, and study as much as possible to enter into the spirit of the gospel, and to conform every action and every sentiment to the tenour of it, must be one of the most important branches of a proper furniture and preparation for the ministerial work. And God grant, that *this* remark may be deeply fixed on the memories and hearts of all that have studied this various course of Theological Lectures, *whatever else* be disputed or forgotten![51]

One of the references here is to Watts' *Humble Attempt*. Doddridge agreed with Watts on the supreme importance of practical literature. In his comments on Doddridge's letter to Saunders describing Jennings' academy, Watts pointed out that at the academy where he had studied, the students were encouraged to read books of practical divinity in private from the beginning of their studies. Doddridge added a note hoping that his pupils would 'allow some time to Practical Writers *every day* as I have done, unless when accidentally prevented, for more than ten years.'[52] According to Orton, Doddridge insisted on this habit for his students.[53] Doddridge's letters, diaries, and especially his *Lectures on Preaching* indicate which authors he thought most important. Among the divines of the Established Church he recommends especially Tillotson ('my principal favourite')[54] and Barrow; the Scottish Episcopalians Robert Leighton ('his works ought to be reckoned among the greatest treasures of the English tongue')[55] and Henry Scougal. Among the nonconformists he recommends John Howe ('He seems to have understood the Gospel as well as any uninspired writer; and to have imbibed as much of its spirit')[56] and especially Baxter. Among contemporary dissenters he recommends Watts. Doddridge's great love among practical writers was Baxter. He received a set of his works in 1724, and observations in his letters and resolutions in his diaries up to 1732 indicate how carefully he read them.[57] He took *Gildas Salvianus*, together with Burnet's *Discourse of the Pastoral Care*, as a model for his ministerial conduct.[58] Doddridge's judgment of Baxter in his *Lectures on Preaching* shows both sides of Doddridge's own activities and his view of their relative merits. The academy tutor finds fault with Baxter's learning, but the minister and practical writer extols his powers of persuasion:

> He is inaccurate because he had no regular education, and always wrote in haste, as in the views of eternity; but generally judicious, nervous, spiritual, and

evangelical. . . . He discovers a manly eloquence, and the most evident proofs of an amazing genius; with respect to which he may not improperly be called The English Demosthenes. . . . Few were ever instrumental of awakening more souls.[59]

4. DISSENTING BOOKS OF PRACTICAL DIVINITY

Since dissenting practical literature is concerned with appealing experimentally to the reader, with converting evangelical knowledge into practice, it is frequently self-conscious about its own rhetorical methods, about the relation between author and the variety of readers it addresses, and about the most effective ways in which it can be read. Of the many kinds of such literature – the sermon, conversion treatise, experimental biography and autobiography, handbook of domestic and social duties, guide to the devotional and spiritual life – it is the last which illustrates this self-consciousness most clearly. Two of the most influential dissenting books are of this kind: Baxter's *The Saints' Everlasting Rest* (first published in 1650, but revived in the eighteenth century) and Doddridge's *The Rise and Progress of Religion in the Soul* (first published in 1745).

In the Preface to *A Call to the Unconverted* (1658) Baxter describes a plan for a series of practical books addressed to specific groups of Christians. Baxter says that the idea was suggested to him by Archbishop Ussher, who 'was oft, from first to last, importuning me to write a Directory for the several ranks of professed Christians, which might distinctly give each one their position; beginning with the unconverted, and then proceeding to the babes in Christ, and then to the strong.' Baxter initially refused, but after Ussher's death he thought again. Having decided to write a 'Family Directory' (the work that was to become Part II of *A Christian Directory*), he realized that Ussher's scheme would make a suitable introduction, so he resolved to proceed as follows:

> First, to speak to the impenitent, unconverted sinners, who are not yet so much as purposing to turn; or at least are not setting about the work. And with these, I thought, a wakening persuasive was a more necessary means than mere directions; for directions suppose men willing to obey them. . . . My next work must be for those that have some purposes to turn, and are about the work, to direct them for a thorough and a true conversion, that they miscarry not in the birth. The third part must be directions for the younger and weaker sort of Christians, that they may be established, built up, and persevere. The fourth part, directions for lapsed and backsliding Christians, for their safe recovery.[60]

The first part of this scheme was filled by *A Call to the Unconverted*. This little book, only rivalled by Joseph Alleine's *An Alarm to Unconverted Sinners* (published with a preface by Baxter in 1672), was the most popular conversion treatise of the seventeenth century. Writing in 1664, Baxter reckoned that it had sold over 30,000 copies. 'Through God's mercy I have had Information of almost whole Housholds converted by this small Book, which I set so light by.'[61] It is presumably these results Watts had in mind when he said, 'I had rather be the author of *Mr Baxter's Call to the unconverted* than the author of *Milton's Paradise Lost*.'[62]

The preface is important because it indicates Baxter's intention to adapt method and tone to the requirements of particular categories of readers, and because in some ways it anticipates the structure of *The Rise and Progress of Religion*. But Baxter's writing, always hastily executed, usually at inordinate length, was rarely so schematically planned. The development of *The Saints' Everlasting Rest* was much more haphazard, but it illustrates superbly his concern with experimental knowledge, his appeal to the affections, and his desperate urge to break the restrictions of literary form so as to convert reading into a kind of action. The genesis of the book is described in the dedication of the first part to the inhabitants of Kidderminister, and in 'A Premonition' prefixed to the second edition of 1651. Baxter began writing it during the first Civil War, when he was far from home, with no book but his Bible, and expecting shortly to die. It was intended as his own funeral sermon, as 'the legacy of a dying man'.[63] It is in four parts, the first describing the saints' rest, what its 'excellencies' are, and the people for whom it is designed; the second demonstrating the truth of that rest from scripture; the third illustrating the practical 'uses' of the doctrine of rest; and the fourth (the most important) directing how to keep the heart in heaven, by means of meditation. Baxter explains in 'A Premonition' 'that the first and last Part were all that I intended when I begun it; which I fitted meerly to my own Use.' The second part he added because of his own doubts on the subject and because he thought it of 'exceeding necessity', while the third was intended for different kinds of readers – the beginning for 'secure and sensual sinners', the end for the godly, and the middle chapters for both.[64] The title page of the first edition tells us that it 'was 'Written by the Author for his own use . . . and afterwards Preached in his weekly Lecture.' To the second and subsequent editions Baxter added copious marginal quotations from Seneca, the Fathers, and scholastic and protestant authors, completely transforming the original text as written by a dying man bereft of books.[65]

Baxter urges the reader in 'A Premonition' not simply to read and approve but to 'set upon this work'.[66] He sometimes joins himself with his reader as 'we' in the heavenly search, sometimes hectors and berates him; the act of reading is interrupted by the author, who stops to question the reader whether he has understood and been convinced by what he has read, and whether he intends to act on it:

> Reader, stop here while thou answerest my Question: Are these Considerations weighty, or not? Are these Arguments convincing, or not? Have I proved it thy

duty, and of flat necessity, to keep thy heart on things above, or have I not? Say, Yea, or Nay, man![67]

He also urges the reader to use the method of soliloquy, which 'is a Preaching to ones self'.[68]

Just as he appealed through the reader's affections to urge him on to practice, so Baxter stressed that his writing was the fruit not of his understanding only but of his heart. In the conclusion to part IV he prays that author and reader may be united through the transforming influence of the book,

> That those who shall read these Heavenly Directions, may not read only the fruit of my Studies, and the product of my fancy; but the breathings of my active Hope and Love; . . . That so these lines may not witness against me; but proceeding from the heart of the Writer, may be effectual through thy Grace upon the heart of the Reader; and so be the savour of Life to both.[69]

In spite of its enormous length, *The Saints' Everlasting Rest* went through 12 editions of about 1,500 copies each between 1650 and 1688.[70] Some of the practical works (including *The Saints' Rest*) were issued in four volumes in 1707 – this is the set that Doddridge owned. Thereafter it was not to be reprinted in full until Orme's edition of 1830. However, Benjamin Fawcett, one of Doddridge's students, ensured the continuation of the Baxterian tradition by abridging and making available to a wider reading public some of Baxter's most popular practical books. Of Fawcett's ministerial work Doddridge wrote in 1747, 'Nor must I reckon among the smallest of my mercies the opportunities I have had of seeing how eminently [God] has blessed the labours of good Mr. Fawcett . . . in consequence of which I can truly say, I should think all my labours, as a tutor, well repayed to have been instrumental in raising up but one such person to the service of the sanctuary.'[71] In 1745 Fawcett became pastor at Kidderminster, where Baxter had himself ministered a hundred years earlier. Influenced perhaps by this association as much as by Doddridge's teaching, Fawcett published abridgments of *The Saints' Everlasting Rest* (1759, often reprinted up to the mid-nineteenth century), part III of *The Divine Life* as *Converse with God in Solitude* (1761), *The Poor Man's Family Book* as *Dialogues on Personal and Family Religion* (second edition, 1776), and *The Dying Thoughts of the Reverend . . . Mr. R. Baxter* (1761).

However, Fawcett was not the first eighteenth-century abridger of Baxter. Wesley published *An Extract of Mr. Richard Baxter's Aphorisms of Justification* (1745, from Baxter's first published work), and abridgments of *The Saints' Everlasting Rest* (1754, in volume XXXVII of *A Christian Library*, and separately in 1776) and *A Call to the Unconverted* (1782).[72] In their editions of *The Saints' Rest* both Fawcett and Wesley reduce the book to about a quarter of its original size by eliminating Baxter's annotations and contemporary references, cutting paragraphs, sections, chapters, and even parts, simplifying the subdivisions, and pruning the style. In general, Fawcett's treatment is much freer. In one respect he is closer to Baxter's original intention than Wesley: he dedicates the book (as Baxter did the first part) to the inhabitants of Kidderminster, because 'it contains the substance of what was first preached in your parish-church, and was first published from the press with a dedication to your worthy ancestors'. Fawcett is deliberately invoking the Puritan origins of the dissenting tradition, with its stress on practical piety; his one wish is 'to see the same holy and heavenly conversation in himself, and in those around him, now, as Mr. Baxter saw in his day'.[73] Fawcett's most drastic piece of editing is the running together of chapters; there are 16 consecutive chapters with new titles, with no division into parts. The whole has logical continuity and is very much a private devotional handbook. Wesley's edition, on the other hand, is more faithful to Baxter's broader plan. It contains the opening of the original dedication to the first part, with Baxter's account of how he came to write the book, and is divided into three parts (Wesley totally omitted Baxter's part II), with six chapters from part I, 12 from part III, and ten from part IV; chapters are omitted but not run together, and Wesley keeps close to Baxter's titles. Of the two abridgments, Fawcett's seems to have been the most influential (perhaps because Baxter was more popular with dissenters than with Methodists), reaching a thirteenth edition by 1815; Orme remarked in 1830 that it had greatly diminished the circulation of Baxter's version.[74]

Although Fawcett's edition of *The Saints' Rest* reached a wide audience among dissenters, it was outstripped in popularity by Doddridge's *The Rise and Progress of Religion in the Soul*, a work which was planned to fill a carefully defined need and which therefore tells us a great deal about the function of practical literature and the way in which it was designed to be read. The idea for *The Rise and Progress* came from Watts, who had intended to write it himself. Doddridge's dedication to Watts describes it as 'a book, which owes its existence to your request, its copiousness to your plan, and much of its perspicuity to your review.' Doddridge goes on to say that Watts had projected it as 'one of the most considerable services' of his life.[75] This judgment is interesting in the light of the great range of Watts' writings. Unlike Doddridge, who deliberately restricted himself in his writing, though not his teaching, to practical religious works, Watts as an educationalist and philosophical publicist interested himself in theoretical questions. It seems that Watts regarded Doddridge as an instrument for putting many of his ideas into practice.[76] Doddridge points out in the dedication how Watts through the variety of his writings – catechisms, educational textbooks, sermons, hymns – has reached a huge audience of children, students, ministers, families, in the Established Church as well as among dissenters, in Scotland and America as well as England. Clearly Watts felt a single work was needed that would cater for all the ranks of Christian readers (the 'Exhortation to Ministers' in *An Humble Attempt* in effect provides the heads of such a work), and in age and ill health he suggested it to Doddridge. The younger man was somewhat defensive about the fact that almost all his writings (including sermons, hymns, exemplary biographies, and his popular biblical commentary *The Family Expositor*) were practical: in the introduction to *The Rise and Progress* he says that he has laid aside 'many of those curious amusements in science which might suit his own private taste, and perhaps open a way for some reputation in the learned world.'[77] But in the preface to *Ten Sermons* (dated 1741, while he was working on *The Rise and Progress*) there is no hint of this temptation to a more worldly fame: 'If any ask, why I publish so many things on these practical subjects, so often handled by a variety of writers; I answer in a few words. . . . "Because I know the gospel to be true . . .".'[78]

The Rise and Progress follows the method of *The Saints' Rest* of addressing different categories of reader, holding a dialogue between author and reader, and encouraging the reader to converse with himself, but in a clear and helpful way so that a given reader can turn to the section of the book that is relevant to his own psychological or spiritual state. The subtitle indicates that it is 'a Course of Serious and Practical Addresses, suited to Persons of every Character and Circumstance: with a Devout Meditation or Prayer added to each Chapter'. In chapter I Doddridge explains the method and how the book is to be read. He tells the reader 'he would, as it were, enter with you into your closet, from day to day; and with all plainness and freedom, as well as seriousness, would discourse to you of the great things which he has learnt from the christian religion, and on which he assuredly knows your everlasting happiness to depend.' This awkward third-person characterization of the author is soon dropped. Doddridge goes on to explain that he will not assume the role of a preacher of sermons:

> I shall here speak in a looser and freer manner, as a friend to a friend, just as I
> would do, if I were to be in person admitted to a private audience, by one whom
> I tenderly loved, and whose circumstances and character I knew to be like that,
> which the title of one chapter or another of this treatise describes.[79]

After this conversation between friends, the author then leaves the reader to meditate alone, having provided him with the text of a suitable meditation. (The meditation at the end of each chapter for each Christian character and situation is a logical extension of Baxter's 'Example of this Heavenly Contemplation, for the help of the unskilful' at the end of *The Saints' Rest*.) Thus when a reader has finished a particular chapter and followed its instructions a drama of therapeutic pastoral care will have been enacted.

Doddridge begins with the character of the careless sinner. He is not here addressing 'a prófane and abandoned profligate', not a deist, nor a sceptic; he assumes the sinner to be a nominal Christian. After the careless sinner has been awakened, six chapters are devoted to cautioning him, arraigning and convicting him, stripping him of his pleas, and condemning him. The drama of the heavenly tribunal is consistently maintained, and the reader's terror is deliberately aroused. (The aim is identical to Baxter's in the first four chapters of part III of *The Saints' Rest*.) In chapter VIII the tone suddenly changes, and Doddridge brings to the terrified sinner on the brink of destruction the news of salvation. He is taught how to obtain salvation, and urged to accept it. At this point (chapter XI) Doddridge faces the 'infidel reader', and challenges him to write a dated memorandum of renunciation of and opposition to Christianity, confident that none of his readers would dare to do so; it is the negative counterpart of the form of self-dedication that the converted Christian is asked to transcribe and sign (XVII). The second part of the book, from chapter XII on, is more interesting because more psychologically subtle: Doddridge is concerned here not with the alternatives of damnation and salvation, but with the varieties of Christian experience. Hence he addresses a soul 'overwhelmed with a Sense of the Greatness of its Sins' (XII), 'The doubting Soul' (XIII), the soul suffering from 'spiritual Decay and Languor' (XXII), 'The Christian under the Hidings of God's Face' (XXIV), and so on. The convincing tone with which Doddridge handles these cases derives partly from his insistence on his 'intimate and frequent view of facts' as a pastor, which qualifies him to give advice. He points out that desolation and distress may have physical or social rather than spiritual causes, and that in such a case a physician rather than a divine is needed.[80] The directions in chapter XIX 'for maintaining continual Communion with God' derive from Doddridge's own experience, and he quotes at length from one of his own letters for illustration. Indeed Doddridge's letters and especially his diaries (consisting chiefly of meditations after communion and annual reviews of his life) show how important to him were the devotional practices which he here advocates for others. The final part of the book is for the 'advanced', 'established' and 'experienced Christian', and it concludes with advice on how such a Christian should die.

A weakness of this scheme is that although the reader is encouraged to turn to the chapter appropriate for his condition, the book has a chronological development, so it appears that to become an established Christian he must go through the horrors described in the first part. Doddridge admitted that it was not necessary for everyone to go through these steps to conversion, or to have experienced the state of sin that he describes.[81] (It is worth comparing Wesley's objection to Bunyan's account of the Valley of the Shadow of Death in *Pilgrim's Progress*: 'I cannot learn, either from scripture or experience, that every Christian passes through this.')[82] A further limitation is that although Doddridge writes, as he says in the preface, as plainly as possible in order that the lowest class of reader may understand him,[83] he takes no account of different social, as distinct from spiritual, capacities, except in the chapter addressed to the established Christian (xxviii), which assumes a reader of some social importance. Here he differs from Watts, who in *An Humble Attempt* is aware of the 'Special Advantages' for piety accruing to those Christians who have access to religious books, can retire to their own closets, and are not overburdened with business.[84]

But these limitations did not impede the great success of the book. Although Watts had originally envisaged 'a small Book for the Poor, like Baxters *Call to the Unconverted*', he was certain of its usefulness: 'I am not ashamed, by what I have read, to recommend it as the best treatise on practical religion which is to be found in our language.'[85] Doddridge sent several copies to friends (among them members of the Church of England), and it was uniformly well received. He had intended that the book should be produced as cheaply as possible, in order that the charitable might give it away,[86] and an example is provided by the Countess of Somerset, Watts' one-time correspondent, who wrote to Doddridge in 1750: 'I could not be easy till I had given one to every servant in my house who appeared to be of a serious turn of mind.'[87] Doddridge recorded how it was instrumental in converting the local physician (i.e. James Stonhouse, who became an Evangelical clergyman); Stonhouse, obviously Doddridge's ideal reader, 'read it again and again, and marked . . . some hundreds of passages'.[88] By 1748, Doddridge told his wife, the fifth edition in large octavo was being prepared, though the fourth in duodecimo was still available; his bookseller judged it 'proper to have them always ready in both sizes'.[89] The popularity of the book was not restricted to England: in his 'Reflections on the Opening of the New Year, 1749' Doddridge lists translations made or to be made of several of his works, including *The Rise and Progress*, into French, Dutch, and German.[90] It remained widely read in evangelical circles until the third quarter of the nineteenth century.[91]

5. WESLEY'S EDUCATIONAL SCHEME AND THE DISSENTING TRADITION

The links between Methodist and dissenting literary culture are various and complex. Whereas the dissenters were consciously continuing the tradition of 'our fathers' in distinction to that of the Established Church, Wesley, himself a life-long member of that church (in spite of the legally anomalous position of his Methodist societies), was an eclectic in religion, drawing on whatever tradition – Roman Catholic, Anglican, or dissenting – he believed contributed to the central question of vital, practical, scriptural holiness.[92] From one point of view Wesley was as much entitled as Watts or Doddridge to call the Puritans 'our fathers', though it was some time before he recognized this fact. Both his parents came from nonconformist families, but themselves conformed and became strongly High Church in their sympathies.[93] As a result, the young Wesley was prejudiced against and largely ignorant of the dissenting tradition.

At Oxford, during the late 1720s, Wesley read the books of practical divinity that were to form the core of his educational and publishing schemes: Thomas à Kempis's *The Imitation of Christ* (or *The Christian's Pattern*), Jeremy Taylor's *The Rule and Exercises of Holy Living*, William Law's *Christian Perfection* and *A Serious Call to a Devout and Holy Life*, and Henry Scougal's *The Life of God in the Soul of Man*. Wesley testifies to the way the first three authors determined his view of religion in the account of his life up to 24 May 1738 published in the second part of his *Journal*,[94] and especially in *A Plain Account of Christian Perfection* (first published in 1766). He was particularly affected by the section in Taylor relating to purity of intention: 'Instantly I resolved to dedicate all my life to God, all my thoughts, and words, and actions.' The effect of reading à Kempis was that 'the nature and extent of inward religion, the religion of the heart, now appeared to me in a stronger light than ever it had done before.' Law's books 'convinced me, more than ever, of the absolute impossibility of being half a Christian.'[95] It is worth stressing that the authors who influenced Wesley most at this period, and who were to exert a life-long influence, were a medieval Catholic, an Anglican, a non-juror, and a Scottish Episcopalian. Studies made of Wesley's reading at Oxford, during the voyage to Georgia, and in Georgia indicate a close sympathy with Catholic, Anglo-Catholic, non-juring, mystical, and pietist authors.[96] It is clear that by the time Wesley returned from Georgia in 1737 he had already chosen many of the books that were to figure prominently in his educational and publishing schemes,[97] that many of these were of a High Church, mystical, or pietistic tendency, and that at his point he owed nothing to and indeed knew very little about the dissenting tradition.

Wesley had two main reasons for disapproving of dissenters: in terms of discipline, he objected to their separation from the Church of England, and always insisted (as in the *Large Minutes*) that Methodists were not dissenters because they were not thus separated;[98] in terms of doctrine, he objected to their Calvinism. He consistently maintained these objections after he had become familiar with the dissenting tradition and more sympathetic towards Puritan attitudes. It seems that he did not begin seriously to read dissenting books until he was in Georgia (1735–7); here he read Watts' hymns, and a work that was to become one of the most important exemplary biographies in his canon of practical divinity, *Memoirs of the Life of . . . Thomas Haliburton*. The second edition of the *Memoirs* was published in 1718 with an epistle by Watts, and Wesley himself published and wrote a preface for an *Extract of the Life and Death of Mr. Thomas Haliburton* in 1739.[99] This is the first example of a convergence of the editorial interests of Wesley and his dissenting contemporaries. Wesley did not really begin systematically to investigate Puritan and dissenting literature until the distinctive features of Methodism had become established; we learn from the *Journal* that in 1739 he read Bunyan's *Grace Abounding, Pilgrim's Progress, The Law and Grace* and Daniel Neal's *History of the Puritans* (published 1732–8), and in 1741 Baxter's *Life* (it is not clear whether this refers to *Reliquiae Baxterianae* or Calamy's *Abridgment*, both of which Wesley read in 1757).[100] There seem to be three reasons why Wesley became interested in the Puritans at this time: under the influence of the Moravians, he discovered the evangelical doctrine of salvation by faith, still the essential doctrine of the orthodox wing of dissent; his adoption of the irregular methods of field preaching and employing lay preachers brought him into contact with members of other churches and made him question his own assumptions about the constitution of the Church of England; his conflict with Whitefield and Howel Harris who were now teaching extreme Calvinist doctrine led him to investigate the origins of predestinarianism.[101] As a result, he relinquished his early prejudices against Puritans and nonconformists, and was shocked to learn of the barbaric behaviour of members of his own church towards them.[102]

The events in New England were a further stimulus to Wesley's interest in dissent. There were direct links between Methodism and New England. Although Wesley never went to America again after the Georgia episode, Whitefield made repeated visits to North and South from 1738 on, and in 1740 was himself responsible for initiating another revival in New England. Wesley tended to compare the rise of Methodism in England favourably with the awakenings in Scotland and America: he thought the New England revivals, though led by ministers, were sporadic, whereas the work of the English Methodists, though the majority of them were laymen, was continuously successful.[103]

However, like Watts and Doddridge, Wesley was principally interested in the psychology of the revivals, and in the evidence they provided for experimental religion and the visible work of the spirit. All three men, working separately, spread knowledge of the Great Awakening by publishing in England the works of Edwards and his missionary friend David Brainerd. In 1738 Wesley read Edwards' *A Faithful Narrative of the Surprising Work of God in the Conversion of Many Hundred Souls in Northampton*, and was much affected by it: 'Surely, "this is the Lord's doing, and it is marvellous in our eyes."' As a result, he began to analyse again his own concepts of faith and holiness.[104] The first publication of this work was in England in

1737, edited and with a preface by Watts and John Guyse. Watts was sent the manuscript by Benjamin Colman, a Boston minister with whom he corresponded, and he published it with some misgivings as to the enthusiastic tendency of Edwards' style.[105] Edwards' next work on the revival was *The Distinguishing Marks of a Work of the Spirit of God* (Boston, 1741, reissued by Watts, London, 1742). Edwards followed this with *Some Thoughts Concerning the Present Revival of Religion in New England* (Boston, 1743, not reissued by Watts). The results of Edwards' observations of the Great Awakening were contained in his *Treatise Concerning Religious Affections* (Boston, 1746).

Wesley published much abridged editions of all four of these works: *A Narrative of the Late Work of God, At and near Northampton, in New England* (1744, reprinted 1755, also in vol. xvii of Wesley's *Works*, 1773); *The Distinguishing Marks of a Work of the Spirit of God* (1744, reprinted 1755, also in vol. xvii of *Works*); *Thoughts Concerning the Present Revival of Religion in New England* (1745, also in vol. xvii of *Works*); and *An Extract from a Treatise Concerning Religious Affections* (in vol. xxiii of *Works*, 1773).[106] There was much in Edwards of which Wesley disapproved: doctrinally, Edwards was a Calvinist, and Wesley attacked him unfairly in his preface to his extract from *Religious Affections* for not allowing that backsliders might have been true believers. Wesley claimed that in this extract he had selected 'much wholsome food' which in Edwards' heap of 'curious, subtle, metaphysical distinctions' was mixed with 'much deadly poison'.[107] However, the evidence Edwards accumulated and his attitudes towards it corroborated Wesley's own experience in England: particularly important was Edwards' insistence on the varieties of conversion, the complete change effected in the life of the individual, the importance of the heart and affections, and especially on fruit in Christian practice as the true mark of conversion.[108]

Though Edwards' accounts were thus directly relevant to Methodists, the experience of his friend Brainerd was more important to Wesley in that it provided a model for his preachers. In this case there was a convergence of Wesley's interests with those of Doddridge. In 1748 the Scottish S P C K published *An Abridgment of Mr. David Brainerd's Journal among the Indians*, with a dedicatory letter to the Society from Doddridge, who was a corresponding member. Doddridge had been sent by a friend a manuscript extract of the original American edition of 1746, entitled *Mirabilia Dei inter Indicos: or, The Rise and Progress of a Remarkable Work of Grace*. Doddridge was so impressed with the extract (he had not seen the original) that he sent it to the Society for publication, with the object of awakening the interest of ministers in missionary work to the Indians and of stimulating readers to join the Society.[109] In 1749 Wesley read this abridgment, 'the surprising *Extract of Mr. Brainerd's Journal*', and while rejoicing in the conversions and recognizing Brainerd's qualities criticized him for narrow views and self-applause.[110] At some later date Wesley came across Edwards' *An Account of the Life of the late Reverend Mr David Brainerd* (first published Boston, 1749), which is an edition of the remainder of Brainerd's journals. The Scottish S P C K published unabridged both Edwards' *Account* and Brainerd's *Journal* in 1765. Wesley published an abridgment of the *Account* in 1768 as *An Extract of the Life of the Late Rev. Mr. David Brainerd* (reprinted in 1771, and in vol. XII of *Works*, 1772). (It appears from a letter from Doddridge to Fawcett of June 26 1750 that Fawcett had a similar intention.)[111] Wesley recommended the *Life* to all his preachers, and urged them to follow Brainerd's 'deadness to the world, and . . . fervent love to God and man'; similarly, Doddridge tried to live a life of greater strictness by fasting secretly in imitation of 'that faithful and zealous servant of Christ, Mr. David Brainerd.'[112]

Wesley had the greatest respect for the educational and practical work of Watts and Doddridge, and applied directly to the latter for advice about the education of his itinerant lay preachers. He was particularly concerned with this question at the first annual Methodist Conferences in the years 1744–7, at which the organization of the Methodist Societies and the function of the preachers was being defined.[113] Wesley regarded his preachers as university students nominally under his supervision, requiring them to spend seven hours a day reading the Bible, practical divinity, some doctrinal theology, religious poetry, and ecclesiastical history, and forbidding them to read any books not recommended by him.[114] They were to read wherever possible the books that Wesley had himself edited, and though he had already published many of the important practical authors (e.g. à Kempis, Scougal, Law, Bunyan, Haliburton), some of the books he recommended must have been difficult to obtain. Wesley decided to edit and publish a complete collection of practical divinity, *A Christian Library*, that would furnish virtually all his preachers' needs, and with this end in view he applied to Doddridge for advice.

Relations between Wesley and Doddridge were cordial. Indeed, Doddridge was much criticized by other dissenters for friendliness to the Methodists, particularly Whitefield. Most dissenting ministers thought the Methodists irrational and enthusiastic, irregular in their modes of worship, and socially disruptive; they particularly objected to the pretensions of the lay preachers.[115] Doddridge himself had doubts about the intellectual quality of the movement: he thought Whitefield a weak man,[116] and hoped that a proper education would moderate the preachers' excesses. According to Orton, he blamed their errors on 'the Want of being led thro' a regular Plan of *Lectures in Divinity*'.[117] However, he urged his ministerial students to show charity and humility: 'Do not contend with them, nor inveigh against them. God has used many of them for excellent purposes, and we must not tie him to our rules.'[118] Of Wesley's capacities Doddridge had no doubts: in

September 1745 Wesley visited Doddridge at Northampton and at his request took his place in expounding Scripture to his students.[119] In June 1746 Doddridge wrote Wesley a long letter, 'giving you my thoughts on that little collection of books, which you seem desirous to make for some young preachers.'[120]

The books in Doddridge's list are based essentially on his *Lectures on Preaching* (in his recommendation of Howe, for example, the wording in the list and the *Lectures* is virtually identical).[121] Thus Doddridge was proposing to Wesley for his preachers a course of reading which his own ministerial students only reached after a thorough grounding in other subjects, especially ethics and theology. He would certainly have regarded an education consisting entirely of practical divinity as an inadequate one for a preacher of the gospel, even though he regarded theoretical and secular subjects as a stepping stone to it. Hence in his letter he lists as a preface to practical divinity several books under the headings of courses taken by his own students: logic, metaphysics, ethics, Jewish antiquities, history (civil and ecclesiastical), natural philosophy, astronomy, and proofs of natural and revealed religion. He divides practical authors into four categories (as in the *Lectures on Preaching*): 'Divines of the established church', Puritans, 'Nonconformists of the last age', and 'Dissenters of the present age'. Authors recommended by Doddridge whom Wesley had already edited or was to edit in *A Christian Library* include Tillotson, Barrow, Norris, Scougal, Law and Leighton in the first category; Bolton, Hall (wrongly classed as a Puritan by both Doddridge and Wesley) and Sibbes in the second; Owen, Baxter, Flavel and Howe in the third. In the fourth category Doddridge included works by Watts, Jennings and himself (tentatively suggesting *The Rise and Progress*), but Wesley did not issue editions of any of these. Doddridge concludes with a list of scripture commentaries. The critical study of scripture is important, he says, because 'it may prevent those *extravagant reveries* which have filled the minds of so many, and *brought so great a dishonour* on the work of God.' At the end of the letter, Doddridge makes an important point about the way in which the books are to be used:

> You will not by any means imagine that I intend to recommend the particular notions of all the writers I here mention, which may, indeed, sufficiently appear from their absolute contrariety to each other in a multitude of instances; but I think that, in order to *defend the truth*, it is very proper that a young minister should know the chief strength of error.[122]

Doddridge is here reasserting his basic principle of free enquiry in education, a principle Wesley by no means shared.

Although there is some overlap between the authors Doddridge recommended and those Wesley included in *A Christian Library*, Wesley did not rely on it exclusively; rather, he drew on a far wider range of authors, of various religious persuasions, and even when choosing Puritans he went beyond Doddridge's suggestions.[123] Wesley's debt to Doddridge and contemporary dissent is difficult to assess. A brief comparison of the two men as educationalists and Christian publicists may be helpful. They had much in common. Both had the task of educating pastors, Doddridge by taking his ministerial students through his academy course, Wesley by controlling the reading and discipline of his lay preachers. Both aimed at reaching a wide popular audience through their practical writings, though Wesley did this on a much larger scale than either Doddridge or Watts, because through the Methodist societies he had his own organization for publishing and distribution, and his working life covered a much longer span.[124] Wesley's four important serial publications – his *Journal, A Christian Library, Works*, and *The Arminian Magazine* – had general educational as well as practical religious ends (for example, in the *Arminian* vols. v–vii he serialized extracts from Watts' *Doctrine of the Passions* and Locke's *Essay Concerning Human Understanding*). Like Doddridge, Wesley wrote a popular scripture commentary (he drew on Doddridge's *Family Expositor* for his *Notes on the New Testament*);[125] like Watts he published popular scientific works. The religious temper of Doddridge and Wesley was very similar: both were relatively catholic in their approach to other churches, both stressed the importance of affection, experience and practice in religion, both thought practical literature the most valuable. Yet there were many differences. In one way Wesley was freer to create his own literary culture; because he did not have the responsibility, as Doddridge did, of continuing one particular tradition, he could draw impartially on many. In other respects Wesley's intellectual position was much more authoritarian and restricted than that of Doddridge. The polities of Methodism and dissent were completely different. Dissenting congregations were autonomous, electing their own ministers; Methodist organization was hierarchical, with preachers imposed on circuits from above. Doddridge thought truth was established through free enquiry and controversy, and he encouraged his students to read unorthodox books for this reason; Wesley abhorred controversy, and in the Preface to *A Christian Library*, in total opposition to the spirit of Doddridge's advisory letter, he wrote, 'I have . . . particularly endeavoured to preserve a consistency throughout, that no part might contradict any other.'[126] There may have been some conflict between the rationalist intellectual and practical religious aims of Doddridge. The kind of speculative freedom that he encouraged in his academy led in the period after his death to a widespread attack by Arian dissenters or Unitarians on those evangelical doctrines which were the basis of his concept of practical religion. Wesley's singlemindedness, his rigid control of the intellect in the interests of religion, sets him apart from the dissenting tradition as it developed in the eighteenth century, and in this respect he owes more to his early High Church mentor, William Law.

6. WESLEY'S BOOKS OF PRACTICAL DIVINITY

Wesley's principal collections of practical divinity were *A Christian Library* (50 vols., Bristol, 1749–55) and *The Works of the Rev. John Wesley* (32 vols., Bristol, 1771–4). The first did not contain any of his own writings; the second consisted of works either written or edited by him. *A Christian Library*, designed for the preachers, had only a limited circulation (in a letter of 1748 describing the scheme, Wesley said he would 'print only an hundred copies of each'); the *Works*, available in weekly parts as well as volumes, had a wider distribution among society members.[127] Wesley printed over the years many individual editions of the works he considered most important, and in this way they achieved their widest circulation. However, the collections as such reveal both the range and the varied method of Wesley's practical divinity. First, Wesley drew on a number of religious traditions. He edited works by members of the several branches of the Church of England, including High Churchmen, such as Ken and Law; Cambridge Platonists, such as Smith, Cudworth, and More; orthodox Anglicans of no particular grouping, such as Taylor, Sanderson, and Barrow; and Latitudinarians (the group with whom Wesley was least in sympathy), such as Patrick and Tillotson.[128] Outside the Church of England, he edited works by Roman Catholics, such as à Kempis, Pascal, and Fénelon;[129] the Scottish Episcopalians Leighton and Scougal; the Scottish Calvinists Haliburton; Puritans, such as Bolton, Preston, and Sibbes; Nonconformists, such as Bunyan, Alleine, Baxter, and Calamy; the New England Presbyterians Brainerd and Edwards; and the German pietist Francke. Much of this literature is not evangelical in content. Second, a number of kinds of practical divinity is represented: sermons, spiritual biographies and autobiographies, letters, rules for social and moral conduct, devotional handbooks. Works of practical divinity by Wesley himself include sermons, rules for conduct, and, most important, his *Journal* (in vols. XXVI to XXXII of the *Works*). The *Journal*, in its careful observation and analysis over many years and in hundreds of cases of the nature and meaning of experimental religion, may well be the most important work of practical divinity of the century. Wesley, however, unlike Doddridge, wrote no devotional handbook; there is no exact Methodist equivalent of *The Rise and Progress of Religion*. Wesley obviously felt that there was no need for him to provide an original book of this kind; instead, he edited, abridged and popularized the handbooks that had influenced him so profoundly at Oxford, those of à Kempis, Taylor, Scougal, and Law.

His editions of Kempis and Law reached enormous audiences, and may be considered the most influential of Wesley's books of practical divinity.

Wesley's editorial principles are explained in the Preface to the first volume of *A Christian Library*. He claims that 'there is not in the world, a more complete body of Practical Divinity than is now extant in the English tongue, in the writings of the last and the present century.' However, this 'very plenty' contains many faults: truth and falsehood are mixed, many works are largely controversial, the style of some is 'scarce intelligible to the bulk of mankind', some are too superficial, some too mystical, many contradict themselves. Wesley says he has 'endeavoured to extract such a collection of *English Divinity*, as (I believe) is all true, all agreeable to the oracles of God: as is all practical, unmixed with controversy of any kind; and all intelligible to plain men'. With this aim in view, he has not only abridged and excised material but added it.[130]

Wesley's criteria as an editor are truth, usefulness, brevity, and clarity; he always has in mind the needs of the reader. He in effect stands at the reader's elbow to jog his attention by asterisking passages he considers particularly important.[131] He reduced bulky works to the requirements of a 350 page duodecimo pocketbook ('if Angels were to write books,' he said, 'we should have very few Folios'),[132] and abbreviated short works further. All Wesley's publications could be easily carried and referred to at any time; thus the reader was not confined to his study, and reading was not necessarily separate from other activities (Wesley himself did much of his reading while travelling).[133] Wesley envisaged that his editions would be read both in private and in public. Thus his preachers were to study them carefully in private, at set hours of the day, and also to read them aloud and expound them to the societies. He attached particular importance to the latter: 'I wish all our preachers . . . would herein follow my example, and frequently read in public and enforce select portions of *The Christian Library*.'[134] The members of his societies, in addition to hearing books expounded both at meetings and in their own homes (the latter according to 'Mr. Baxter's plan' of afternoon visiting),[135] were to keep such books for private and family reading. But reading was never to be an end in itself: the handbooks Wesley selected were all designed to effect a methodical, disciplined transformation in the reader's life.

In the *Large Minutes* Wesley specified that à Kempis 'ought to be in every house';[136] he thus gave *The Christian's Pattern* greater authority than any of the other handbooks. Its importance is attested by the number of different editions he issued. The first complete edition of 1735 is Wesley's revision of John Worthington's seventeenth-century translation of the Latin text. This finely-produced illustrated octavo edition has a very full preface, extracted by Wesley from the prefaces to three seventeenth-century editions. In the same year he issued a pocket edition (24mo, reprinted 1750) with a shortened preface. In 1741 he issued an abridged duodecimo version of less than half the full length, *An Extract of the Christian's Pattern*, again with the shortened preface. This, the most widely-circulated version, was reprinted many times, and abridged slightly more for its inclusion in vols. VII and VIII of the *Works* (1772). In addition, Wesley printed separately *A Companion for the Altar* (1742, reprinted many times), extracted from Book IV of the abridged version, and an abridged Latin edition for Kingswood School (1748).[137]

The preface to the complete edition makes important observations on the work itself, on the temper of appropriate readers, on the way it is to be read, and on the style of Wesley's version. The shortened preface contains only the third of these. The value of the book for Wesley is that it teaches the meaning of Christian perfection and how it is to be attained. The appropriate reader is one 'who desires direction and assistance in the several exercises of his Christian warfare'. But the book cannot communicate knowledge that the reader has not already experienced:

> It must be remember'd, that the great practical truths of religion . . . cannot be fully discerned, but by those readers, who have read the same things in their own souls. These cannot be clearly known, but by those who derive their knowledge, 'not from commentaries, but experience'. . . . This is that inward, practical, experimental, feeling knowledge, so frequently commanded by our author.[138]

Wesley attached especial importance to the proper way of reading. In the shortened preface he lists 'a few plain directions, how to read this (or indeed any other religious book) with improvement'. The reader should set aside a stated time every day, and prepare himself by 'purity of intention' and by praying for his understanding to be enlightened and his heart made receptive. He should read slowly and attentively, with pauses 'for the enlightnings of Divine Grace'. He should stop now and then to recollect his reading 'and consider how to reduce it to practice'. His reading should be 'continued and regular, not rambling and desultory', but he should often reread those passages that concern him directly, and learn 'any remarkable sayings or advices' by heart. Wesley stresses again the connection between reading and practice: 'Labour for a temper correspondent to what you read; otherwise it will prove empty and unprofitable, while it only enlightens your understanding, without influencing your will, or inflaming your affections.'[139]

Wesley explains that he has sought to avoid the faults of other editors who have paraphrased rather than translated the original. He attacks 'those paraphrastical expressions, so highly injurious to the nervous brevity of the author', which are intended 'to polish his style, and refine his simplicity into eloquence'.[140] Wesley here has in mind the popular version of George Stanhope, first published in 1696.[141] Comparison between Stanhope's and

Wesley's versions reveals Wesley's stress on the function of practical literature, and his fear that it may become an end in itself. Stanhope's is set out in long paragraphs, is wordy and pompous, and uses fashionable moral terminology. Wesley's is set out by sentences, aphoristically, and its language is plainer, simpler, and more biblical. One sentence, from Book I, chapter III, must illustrate the difference:

> The better acquainted any Man is with himself, the more he converses with, and retires in his own Breast; and the less he wanders abroad, and dwells upon things without him, the more extensive and sublime is his Knowledge, and the easier attained; because this Man receives immediate Illumination, and is directed by a Ray darted from Heaven into his Soul.[142]

> The more simple any one is, the more doth he understand without labour: because he receiveth the light of knowledge from above.[143]

Wesley has compressed and sharpened the Latin aphorisms so that they will be more readily memorable and will provoke the reader: 'expect no softening here', he says of his version, 'no mincing or palliating of evangelical truths.'[144] His aim is to enforce the hortatory tone of the original, expressed in the first two books by direct address to the reader, and in the last two by dialogue between Christ and the disciple. Wesley's own habit of quoting from à Kempis in his letters (usually in Latin) and applying the aphorisms to particular situations shows that he himself had much of the text by heart and used it in his daily life.[145] By contrast, Stanhope's version would be difficult to remember, and a reading which attended to its literary devices would distract the reader from its practical end.

Wesley always aimed to reduce practical works to their essentials, by cutting literary ornament, controversial matter and repetition. It was perhaps because he thought Taylor's work contained too many such excrescences that he did not attempt to make it widely popular. Wesley's abridgment of Taylor's *The Rule and Exercises of Holy Living* and its companion volume *The Rule and Exercises of Holy Dying* appeared only in volume XVI of *A Christian Library* (1752).[146] Though Wesley had some misgivings about Taylor's teaching on faith and repentance he had no doubts about the extent of Taylor's influence on himself. This influence manifested itself both in Wesley's thinking about intention and perfection and in his application of rules to every aspect of life (for example, in *Advice to the People called Methodists*, 1745). In his abridgment of *Holy Living* Wesley not only drastically simplified Taylor's rules, he also undermined the meditative, literary, scholarly tone of the work by omitting most of Taylor's narrative illustrations from history and classical literature and all his classical quotations, and by simplifying the style. Wesley may well have felt that the essence of Taylor's teaching was adequately conveyed in other practical works, and that this truncated and somewhat distorted version was not worth reprinting.

These difficulties did not apply to Scougal's *The Life of God in the Soul of Man*. This brief work, which was to be enormously popular throughout the eighteenth century, was first published anonymously in 1677 with a preface by Gilbert Burnet, who described it as 'a Transcript of those divine Impressions that are upon [the author's] own heart.'[147] Wesley published an abridgment in 1744, reprinted it several times, and included it in vol. VIII of the *Works* (1772). He also published Scougal's *Discourses on Important Subjects* and the funeral sermon preached for him by George Garden in vol. XLV of *A Christian Library* (1755).[148] Scougal, like his fellow Scottish Episcopalian Leighton, was much influenced by à Kempis and the Cambridge Platonists. In the first part of *The Life of God in the Soul of Man* Scougal defines true religion not as a matter of opinion or duty or emotion, but as 'an union of the soul with God; a real participation of the divine nature'.[149] (Scougal's Platonic, mystical language seems to have influenced Wesley considerably, for example in his *Journal* account of his 'new judgment of holiness'.)[150] After defining the nature of divine love, Scougal sets out under headings the means by which it may be obtained, here associating himself with the reader in the pursuit, for example 'We must strive to put ourselves out of love with the world.'[151] Wesley must have valued Scougal for the same strong, aphoristic style, the 'nervous brevity' he found in à Kempis.

The handbooks of à Kempis and Scougal envisage the reader as an isolated, individual soul, seeking God and shunning the world, not as a social being with practical duties in the world. It is worth stressing the paradox that three of Wesley's favourite devotional writers, à Kempis, Scougal, and Law, had mystical leanings, whereas Wesley himself strongly disapproved of what he regarded as the self-obsession of the mystics, their slighting of 'social holiness', and their ignorance of the doctrine of justification by faith.[152] This paradox is most evident in the case of Law. The majority of Wesley's editions of practical works were from seventeenth-century authors; very few were from contemporaries (Edwards, not an English author, is an exception). In the very interesting case of Law, Wesley took the works of a contemporary and made them the handbooks of a movement with which the author was not in sympathy. Wesley began publishing Law's works after he had made explicit the extent of their disagreement and in effect destroyed their friendship. During the Oxford and Georgia periods Wesley's admiration for Law was wholehearted. The breach between them in 1738 coincided with Wesley's introduction to the doctrine of salvation by faith; it widened when Law revealed his increasing interest in mysticism in his later works.[153] Nevertheless, Wesley remained unshaken in his admiration for Law's singlemindedness and his belief in the practical value of Law's writings. *A Serious Call* he regarded as 'a treatise which will hardly be excelled, if it be equalled, in the English tongue, either for beauty of expression, or for justness and depth of thought'.[154]

A Practical Treatise upon Christian Perfection was first published in 1726. Wesley abridged the first chapter in 1740 as *The Nature and Design of Christianity*, and reprinted it many times. In 1743 he abridged the whole work, reducing it to about a quarter of its size, and reprinted it in vols. IV and V of the *Works* (1771). Law's second and best known practical work, *A Serious Call to a Devout and Holy Life*, was first published in 1729. Wesley published his abridgment, reduced by about a half, in 1744, and reprinted it, abridged further, in vols. V and VI of the *Works* (1771–2). The *Nature and Design* and *Serious Call* were included in the tracts published in 1782 to be given away to the poor.[155] In addition, Wesley issued abridgments of many of Law's later works, both as single volumes and in vols. VI and VII of the *Works*.

Unlike à Kempis and Scougal, but like the practical writers of the dissenting tradition, Law carefully defined and appealed to specific assumed readers. But whereas the reader of the dissenting handbook is defined by his position on the path of spiritual progress, Law's reader is defined as a member of a specific social class. The subtitle of *A Serious Call* (omitted in Wesley's abridgment) is 'Adapted to the State and Condition of All Orders of Christians'. This resembles the subtitle of *The Rise and Progress of Religion*, but it turns out to mean something very different.[156] Law's reader may be a gentleman of leisure, a clergyman or scholar, he may even be engaged in business or politics, but he certainly has substantial private means and cultivated tastes. Law's object is to demonstrate to the socially privileged reader that his life, however much he may regard himself as a useful member of society pursuing laudable goals, is as thoroughly unchristian as that of a heathen or libertine. He must learn the true function of his life:

> You are no *labourer*, or *tradesman*; you are neither *merchant* nor *soldier*; consider yourself therefore as placed in a state, in some degree like that of *good angels*, who are sent into the world as *ministring spirits*, for the general good of mankind, to *assist*, *protect*, and *minister* for them who shall be heirs of salvation.[157]

He must deny himself, renounce the world, submit himself to the demands of the gospel in all their rigour, and devote himself totally in intention and action to God. This is the unremitting theme of Law's two books.

His method, applied haphazardly in *Christian Perfection*, much more systematically and effectively in *A Serious Call*, is to present a series of characters who exemplify on the one hand the favourite sins of the leisured and on the other the holy and useful lives they might lead if they responded to Law's appeal. Thus he portrays characters enslaved to their pursuit of false goals – Classicus to classical learning, Negotius to amassing wealth,

Flatus to amusements – and others who embody his ideal of devotion – Paternus the Christian educator, Ouranius the country priest, Miranda the philanthropic gentlewoman. It may seem surprising that Wesley popularized handbooks that assume a class of reader to which the majority of the members of the Methodist societies did not belong. Within Wesley's circle of friends it is clear that Law's characters provided models for self-definition – indeed we find the names used as a kind of shorthand. Thus James Hervey, objecting to Wesley's itinerant preaching, urged him to fix in one parish and be 'a living *Ouranio*'.[158] Whitefield, deputizing as curate for a friend, reconciled himself to the task of ministering to the poor and illiterate by reading the character of Ouranius.[159] Wesley urged his friend Miss Ritchie, 'I would have you just such an one as Miranda.'[160]

Law's method, however, involves more than the delineation of exemplary characters. *A Serious Call* is a work of definition, illustration, and practical guidance. In addition to defining the nature of a devout life and illustrating it through his characters, Law shows the reader how to organize his own life according to rule by following the canonical hours of devotion and allotting a specific subject to each hour. The most important chapter in this respect is entitled 'Concerning that part of devotion which relates to times and hours of prayer. Of daily early prayer in the morning. How we may improve our forms of prayer, and increase the spirit of devotion' (XII in Wesley's abridgment, XIV in the original). *A Serious Call* is from one point of view a handbook of devotion in the old sense, a guide to prayer. But prayer is only an aspect of devotion: 'Devotion signifies a life *devoted* to God.'[161] It is the essence of Law's concern with the real meaning of devotion to show that there can be no distinction between prayer and action, or between books and life. Hence there runs throughout *Christian Perfection* and *A Serious Call* a significant self-consciousness about the status of books of devotion. Law was resolutely opposed to all forms of reading – whether scholarly or for amusement – that were ends in themselves. His anti-intellectualism was toned down by Wesley, notably in chapter v of *Christian Perfection* (x in the original), '. . . wherein is shewn the great danger and impiety of reading vain and impertinent books'. Yet Wesley certainly upheld Law's basic distinction between vain and true learning:

> When men retire into their studies to *change* their nature; to *correct* and *reform* their passions; to find out the folly, the falseness, the corruption and weakness of their hearts; to penetrate into the vanity and emptiness of all worldly attainments; when they read and meditate, to fill their souls with heavenly affections, and to raise their hearts unto God; when this is *learning*, (and what else deserves the name?) then learning will lead men unto God; then learned men will be devout, and great *scholars* will be great *saints*.[162]

Law was well aware of the danger that religious literature may be self-defeating by becoming an end in itself, that devotional books may become a substitute for devotion: many 'hope to be devout merely by reading over books of devotion: which is as odd a fancy, as if a man should expect to be happy, by reading discourses upon happiness'.[163] This danger is repeatedly brought to the reader's attention; it is a habit to which Law's false characters are prone. Flavia, Miranda's selfish sister, 'will sometimes read a *book* of *piety*, if it is a short one, if it is much commended for *stile* and *language*, and she can tell where to *borrow* it'.[164] Law wryly seems to anticipate this kind of recognition befalling his own devotional books.

This self-conscious, almost self-mocking treatment by Law of the genre to which he made such an important contribution draws attention in a very direct way to its inherent difficulties. The writers and publicists of the dissenting and Methodist traditions assumed that they could best serve the cause of Christianity by disseminating on a wide scale books of experimental, affectionate, practical divinity. In the course of a hundred years a great deal was learned about making these books practical in a professional sense: Wesley's cheap abridgments, prepared for mass publication, could reach a far wider audience than Baxter's bulky folios. In a religious sense the practical value of these books depended entirely on the effect they had on their readers. Hence the importance that their authors and editors attached to rhetorical method and knowledge of the human heart. On its own terms a book of practical divinity can only be considered successful if it ceases to be simply a book and becomes a motivating force in its reader's life. Hence it is that many of these books, from *The Saints' Everlasting Rest* to *A Serious Call*, seem to be trying to escape from the limitations of their own literary form, by breaking down the barrier between author and reader and the distinction between reading and doing.

NOTES

Research for this article was aided by a grant from the University of Leicester Research Board. I would like to thank the Rev. G. F. Nuttall, John Walsh of Jesus College, Oxford, Neil Keeble of the University of Stirling, and R. K. Biswas of the University of Leicester for helpful comments.

1. *Of the Love of God, and the Use and Abuse of the Passions in Religion*, in *The Works of the Rev. Isaac Watts*, ed. E. Parsons (1800) II, 330, (hereafter cited as Watts, *Works*).
2. For various aspects of devotional literature see C. J. Stranks, *Anglican Devotion* (1961); H. R. McAdoo, *The Structure of Caroline Moral Theology* (1949), ch. 6; G. S. Wakefield, *Puritan Devotion* (1957); H. Davies, *Worship and Theology in England From Andrewes to Baxter and Fox* (Princeton, 1975), ch. 3; J. H. Overton, *Life in the English Church 1660–1714* (1885), ch. 8; W. K. L. Clarke, *Eighteenth Century Piety* (1944), ch. 1.
3. For figures see E. D. Bebb, *Nonconformity and Social and Economic Life* (1935), 45, 57.
4. *An Enquiry into the Causes of the Decay of the Dissenting Interest* (2nd edn, 1730), 5–6.
5. D. Coomer, *English Dissent under the Early Hanoverians* (1946), 63ff.
6. Gough, 34ff, 42, 36.

7. *Free Thoughts on the Most Probable Means of Reviving the Dissenting Interest* (1730), 6.
8. *Free Thoughts*, 7, 21, 38.
9. Watts, *Works*, IV, 29. See also Watts on the oratory of Scripture, *Works*, IV, 31; 'Dedication to the First Volume of Sermons', *Works*, I, xxvi; *Of the Love of God*, *Works*, II, 312–13.
10. Watts, *Works*, IV, 26, 29.
11. *Ibid.*, VI, 305–6.
12. *Ibid.*, II, 220, 240, 244.
13. *Ibid.*, II, 272, 298.
14. *The Saints Everlasting Rest* (seventh edn, 1658), part IV, ch. 6, sect v, 698–9. Cf. Wesley's abridgment of this passage in *A Christian Library*, XXII (2nd edn, 1825), 288–9. For Baxter's application of this theory to preaching, see *Gildas Salvianus: The Reformed Pastor* (1656), ch. 3, sect. i; ch. 4, sect. v.
15. Watts was unlikely to have known this work, but Wesley published an abridged version in 1773. See section V below.
16. *Religious Affections*, ed. J. E. Smith (New Haven, 1959), part I, 96–7; part III, 450–2. Cf. Wesley's abridgment of these passages in *The Works of the Rev. John Wesley*, XXIII (Bristol, 1773), 182, 272–4.
17. Doddridge, *A Course of Lectures on the Principal Subjects in Pneumatology, Ethics, and Divinity*, ed. S. Clark (1763), lecture XIV, 27.
18. Doddridge, *Lectures on Preaching* (1821), 44.
19. *The Works of the Rev. P. Doddridge*, ed. E. Williams and E. Parsons (1802–5), II, 212 (hereafter cited as Doddridge, *Works*).
20. *The Correspondence and Diary of Philip Doddridge*, ed. J. D. Humphreys (1829–31), IV, 414–5 (hereafter cited as Doddridge, *Correspondence*).
21. Edwards, *Religious Affections*, part III, 452. (Not included in Wesley's abridgment.)
22. Published posthumously in 1723 with a preface by Watts. Jennings was Doddridge's tutor, and after his early death Doddridge took over his academy.
23. *Two Discourses* (1723), 36, 44.
24. Watts, Preface to *Two Discourses*, viii.
25. Watts, *Humble Attempt*, *Works*, IV, 21, 68.
26. Watts, *Works*, IV, 31.
27. A very good account of Baxter's attitude to books is given by N. H. Keeble, 'Some literary and religious aspects of the works of Richard Baxter' (D. Phil. thesis, University of Oxford, 1973) ch. 3.
28. *A Christian Directory* (1673), part I, ch. 2, 60.
29. See the appendix to G. F. Nuttall, *Richard Baxter* (1965), listing 140 volumes.
30. *Reliquiae Baxterianae* (1696), part I, 106.
31. Calamy, *An Historical Account of My Own Life*, ed. J. T. Rutt (1829), I, 468.
32. *Reliquiae Baxterianae*, part I, 3, 5. On Bunny see *The Autobiography of Richard Baxter*, ed. N. H. Keeble (1974), 280.
33. On Baxter's library see Nuttall, *Baxter*, 116, and *idem*, 'A transcript of Richard Baxter's library catalogue', *J. Ecclesiastical History*, I (1951), 207–21, and II (1952), 74–100; and Keeble, *thesis*, 89–92.
34. *Reliquiae Baxterianae*, part I, 5–6.
35. *Gildas Salvianus*, ch. 2, sect. iii, 59; sect. v.
36. *Reliquiae Baxterianae*, part I, 115. Cf. Doddridge's letter of instruction to the 'Elders of the Church of Christ at Northampton' on visiting and teaching families, Doddridge, *Correspondence*, V, 85–90, and Wesley's instruction to his preachers in the *Large Minutes* to 'follow Mr. Baxter's plan', Wesley, *Works*, ed. T. Jackson (3rd edn, 1831), VIII, 302–3, 315 (hereafter cited as Wesley, *Works*, ed. Jackson).
37. *Gildas Salvianus*, ch. 2, sect. v, 85.
38. *Reliquiae Baxterianae*, part I, 89.
39. *A Christian Directory*, part I, ch. 2, 60–1; part II, ch. 21, 580–1; part III, quest. 174, 922–8. See Keeble, *thesis*, 92ff.
40. Dissenting academies for both the training of ministers and the liberal education of dissenters intended for the professions played an extremely important rôle throughout the eighteenth century in continuing and transforming the dissenting tradition. The principal accounts are David Bogue and James Bennett, *History of*

Dissenters (1808), II, ch. 5; III, ch. 5; IV, ch. 4; I. Parker, *Dissenting Academies in England* (1914); H. McLachlan, *English Education under the Test Acts* (1931); O. M. Griffiths, *Religion and Learning* (1935), on Presbyterians only; J. W. Ashley Smith, *The Birth of Modern Education* (1954). Particularly useful for Doddridge are Parker, Smith, and A. V. Murray, 'Doddridge and education', in *Philip Doddridge*, ed. G. F. Nuttall (1951); and G. F. Nuttall, *New College, London, and Its Library* (1977).

41. Doddridge, *Correspondence*, II, 462–74 (where the date is given wrongly as 1728). See G. F. Nuttall, *Calendar of the Correspondence of Philip Doddridge* (1979), 32.

42. 27 February 1723, Doddridge, *Correspondence*, I, 198–9. In this use of the term 'catholicism' Jennings and Doddridge were firmly in the tradition of Baxter's moderate nonconformity. See G. F. Nuttall, *Richard Baxter and Philip Doddridge* (1951).

43. To Mr Clark, September 1722, *Correspondence*, I, 155 (editor's italics omitted).

44. Job Orton, *Memoirs of the Life, Character and Writings of the Late Reverend Philip Doddridge* (1766), 94.

45. The scholastic format of Doddridge's lectures derived from Jennings and was criticized by Watts. See Doddridge, *Correspondence*, II, 480.

46. *A Course of Lectures*, 44. Doddridge probably learnt of Hume from Warburton. See Doddridge, *Correspondence*, V, 167, 15 June 1750.

47. *Ibid.*, I, 378; II, 57. See also Nuttall, *Calendar*, Appendix III.

48. Doddridge, *Correspondence*, I, 97.

49. *Ibid.*, V, 310.

50. Watts, *Works*, VI, 253.

51. *A Course of Lectures*, 595.

52. Doddridge, *Correspondence*, II, 481.

53. *Memoirs*, 98.

54. Doddridge, *Correspondence*, I, 44. Doddridge's admiration for Tillotson may seem unexpected in view of his own preference for evangelical and affectionate preaching; what he admired was the easiness, simplicity and clarity of Tillotson's style (*Lectures on Preaching*, 25).

55. *Lectures on Preaching*, 31. Doddridge edited and write a preface to Robert Leighton's *Expository Works* (2 vols., Edinburgh, 1748). For Leighton's writings see E. A. Knox, *Robert Leighton, Archbishop of Glasgow* (1930), ch. 16.

56. *Lectures on Preaching*, 19.

57. Doddridge, *Correspondence*, I, 368, 378, 426, 460; II, 58; III, 9; V, 282, 291, 296, 298, 320.

58. *Ibid.*, I, 460; see Orton, *op. cit.*, 63.

59. *Lectures on Preaching*, 18–19.

60. *Practical Works of the Rev. Richard Baxter*, ed. W. Orme (1830), VII, cccxxxi–ii. Keeble, *thesis*, 199–202, discusses Baxter's schemes for books of practical divinity. Compare Watts' comments on 'the practice of our fathers', p. 133 above.

61. *Reliquiae Baxterianae*, part I, 115.

62. T. Gibbons, *Memoirs of the Rev. Isaac Watts* (1780), 157.

63. *The Saints Everlasting Rest* (seventh edn, 1658), A verso. Subsequent references are to *The Saints Rest*.

64. *The Saints Rest*, C3 verso.

65. Cf. Keeble, *thesis*, 256.

66. *The Saints Rest*, f.

67. *Ibid.*, part IV, ch. 3, sect. xv, 657.

68. *Ibid.*, part IV, ch. 10, sect. ii, 744.

69. *Ibid.*, 815. Cf. Wesley's abridgment of this passage, *A Christian Library*, XXII (1825), 357.

70. F. J. Powicke, 'Story and significance of the Rev. Richard Baxter's "Saints' Everlasting Rest"', *Bull. John Rylands Library*, V (1919–20), 470; J. T. Wilkinson (ed.), *The Saints' Everlasting Rest* (1962), 'Handlist of Editions'. Both Powicke and Wilkinson state that there is little trace of *The Saints' Rest* between 1690 and 1754. This seems unlikely in view of Doddridge's interest. On Doddridge's set of Baxter's works, see Nuttall, *New College, London*, 34, and a facsimile of the title page in *idem*, *Baxter and Doddridge*.

71. Doddridge, *Correspondence*, V, 469–70.

72. R. Green, *The Works of John and Charles Wesley* (1896), nos. 67, 363; also pp. 88, 187. See also F. Baker, *A Union Catalogue of the Publications of John and Charles*

Wesley (Durham, N. C., 1966), which uses Green's numbering.

73. B. Fawcett (ed.), *The Saints' Everlasting Rest* (Romsey, 1816), v-vi.
74. Orme, *op. cit.*, I, 740.
75. Doddridge, *Works*, I, 211.
76. Cf. A. Smith, *The Birth of Modern Education*, 129, 144.
77. Doddridge, *Works*, I, 219.
78. *Ibid.*, II, 211.
79. *Ibid.*, I, 219, 223.
80. *Ibid.*, I, 407-8.
81. This weakness was pointed out by Nathaniel Neal (Doddridge, *Correspondence*, IV, 396), and Doddridge took note of it in the Preface to the second edition (Doddridge, *Works*, I, 215).
82. Wesley, *Works*, IX (1772), 79.
83. Doddridge, *Works*, I, 215.
84. Watts, *Works*, IV, Part II, sect. vi, 94-6. Cf. the account of Law's *Serious Call* in Section vi below.
85. Nuttall, *Calendar*, 194-5; Doddridge, *Correspondence*, IV, 356-7.
86. Doddridge, *Works*, I, 215.
87. Doddridge, *Correspondence*, V, 185.
88. Doddridge, *Correspondence*, IV, 528. Bogue and Bennett, *History of Dissenters*, I, 366-80, tell the story of a churchman who becomes a dissenter, partly influenced by *The Rise and Progress*.
89. *Correspondence*, V, 73.
90. *Ibid.*, V, 479.
91. It was reprinted in the USA in 1977 as a cheap paperback. For some accounts of *The Rise and Progress* and its influence, see A. Gordon, 'Philip Doddridge and the catholicity of the old dissent', in *Addresses Biographical and Historical* (1922); F. W. Harris, 'The life and work of Philip Doddridge' (B. Litt. thesis, University of Oxford, 1950), 71ff; E. A. Payne, 'The Rise and Progress of Religion in the Soul', *Congregational Quarterly*, XXV (1947), 9-20.
92. G. R. Cragg, *Reason and Authority in the Eighteenth Century* (1964), 163, calls Wesley 'an evangelical Catholic'.
93. For Wesley's Puritan origins see J. A. Newton, *Methodism and the Puritans* (1964) and *Susanna Wesley and the Puritan Tradition in Methodism* (1968). For his father Samuel's rejection of his dissenting education see McLachlan, *op. cit.*, 77-9.
94. *The Journal of the Rev. John Wesley*, ed. N. Curnock (1909-16), I, 466-7 (hereafter cited as Wesley, *Journal*).
95. Wesley, *Works*, ed. Jackson, XI, 366-7. Wesley has in mind Ch. I, sect. ii of *Holy Living*.
96. A. W. Harrison in *Procs Wesley Historical Soc.*, XIII (1922), 25-9; XV (1926), 113-17; 161-5. V. H. H. Green, *The Young Mr Wesley* (1961), Appendix I, lists Wesley's reading from 1725 to 1734. He read Watts' *On Predestination* and *The Strength and Weakness of Human Reason* (in 1725 and 1732 respectively), but these are exceptions.
97. Harrison, *op. cit.*, XV (1926) 163, suggests that the germ of the idea for *A Christian Library* came from a book Wesley read in 1725, Bull's *Companion for the Candidates of Holy Orders*. F. Baker, *John Wesley and the Church of England* (1970), 33-4, quotes the document of 1733 which 'reveals the genesis of his amazing publishing career'. Curnock suggests that 'no inconsiderable portion of *The Christian Library* had its beginnings in Georgia' (Wesley, *Journal*, I, 424).
98. Wesley, *Works*, ed. Jackson, VIII, 321; Baker, *Wesley and the Church of England*, 133-5.
99. R. Green, *op. cit.*, no. 10.
100. Wesley, *Journal*, II, 205; 215; 312-13, 472; IV, 93, 221.
101. See Curnock's note, *ibid.*, II, 473.
102. See e.g. his comment on the treatment of the Elizabethan Puritans, letter to 'John Smith', 25 March 1747, *The Letters of the Rev. John Wesley*, ed. J. Telford (1931), II, 94 (hereafter cited as Wesley, *Letters*), and his comment after reading Calamy on the treatment of the nonconformists, Wesley, *Journal*, IV, 93.
103. E.g. *ibid.*, IV, 54, 122-3.
104. *Ibid.*, II, 84, 89-91. Cf. Doddridge's reaction to the book, Doddridge, *Correspondence*, III, 279, 30 October 1737.
105. Jonathan Edwards, *The Great Awakening*, ed. C. C. Goen (New Haven, 1972), 136. On the relationship between

Watts and Edwards see the editor's introduction, 32–45, also A. P. Davis, *Isaac Watts* (1948), 49–52, and A. S. Pratt, *Isaac Watts and His Gifts of Books to Yale College* (New Haven, 1938).

106. R. Green, *op. cit.*, nos. 49, 54, 66, 294; pp. 172, 174. The Yale editors of Edwards' *Works* give an incomplete account of Wesley's abridgments, omitting those in Wesley's *Works* (*The Great Awakening*, ed. Goen, 90–1; *Religious Affections*, ed. Smith, 80).

107. Wesley, *Works*, XXIII (1773), 178.

108. E.g. *Works*, XVII (1773), 127ff, 147, 252–3; XXIII, 259ff.

109. *An Abridgment of Mr. David Brainerd's Journal* (1748), i–ii, v.

110. Wesley, *Journal*, III, 449. He is not here referring to Edwards' *Account*, as is wrongly assumed by Green, no. 253, and I. Rivers, '"Strangers and Pilgrims": sources and patterns of Methodist narrative', in *Augustan Worlds*, ed. J. C. Hilson, M. M. B. Jones and J. R. Watson (1978), 196.

111. Doddridge, *Correspondence*, V, 171. Fawcett was evidently not intending to abridge Brainerd himself, since Doddridge recommends Caleb Ashworth as the suitable person to execute Fawcett's scheme.

112. Wesley, *Works*, ed. Jackson, VIII, 328; Doddridge, *Correspondence*, V, 49. Cf. Doddridge's letter of 2 February 1751 recommending Brainerd, V, 189. On the importance of Brainerd as a model for Methodists, see Rivers, *op. cit.*

113. See 'John Bennet's copy of the minutes of the conferences of 1744, 1745, 1747 and 1748; with Wesley's copy of those for 1746', *Publ. Wesley Historical Soc.*, I (1896); J. S. Simon, *John Wesley and the Methodist Societies* (1923); T. E. Brigden, 'The reading of Wesley's preachers', *Wesleyan Methodist Mag.*, CXXVI (1903), 457–65; W. L. Doughty, *John Wesley: His Conferences and His Preachers* (1944).

114. 'John Bennet's copy of the minutes', 1746, 36; 1747, 50.

115. See the critical letters from Nathaniel Neal and John Barker, Doddridge, *Correspondence*, IV, 274, 278, 283–4; also Coomer, *op. cit.*, 109ff, and Harris, *op. cit.*, 108–13.

116. Doddridge, *Correspondence*, IV, 56.

117. Orton, *op. cit.*, 179.

118. Doddridge, *Lectures on Preaching*, 131.

119. Wesley, *Journal*, III, 206.

120. Doddridge, *Correspondence*, IV, 484. Wesley published Doddridge's letter in *The Arminian Mag.*, I (1778), 419–25.

121. Doddridge, *Correspondence*, IV, 488; *idem Lectures on Preaching*, 19.

122. Doddridge, *Correspondence*, IV, 491–3.

123. R. C. Monk, *John Wesley: His Puritan Heritage* (1966), Appendix I, identifies the authors in *A Christian Library* which are recommended by Doddridge, by Baxter in *A Christian Directory*, part III, and by John Wilkins in *Ecclesiastes*.

124. On Wesley as publisher see F. Cumbers, *The Book Room* (1956) and T. W. Herbert, *John Wesley as Editor and Author* (Princeton, 1940), though neither is adequately detailed.

125. Wesley, *Works*, ed. Jackson, XIV, 237.

126. Wesley, *A Christian Library*, ed. Jackson (2nd ed., 30 vols., 1819–27), I, ix. This edition contains Wesley's revisions.

127. *Letters*, II, 151. R. Green, *op. cit.*, nos. 131, 276.

128. By including extracts from Tillotson (vol. XLV) and *The Whole Duty of Man* (vol. XXI) Wesley dissociated himself from Whitefield's violent attacks on both (for these see L. Tyerman, *The Life of the Rev. George Whitefield*, 1876, I, 360–3). Wesley thought Tillotson 'as far from being the *worst*, as from being the best of the English writers' (*Christian Library*, XXVII (1826), 3). He approved of the moralism of *The Whole Duty*, and did not think it contradicted the doctrine of salvation by faith (*Christian Library*, XII (1821), 25–6). *The Whole Duty of Man*, first published in 1657, was the handbook most widely distributed by Anglicans, especially the Society for Promoting Christian Knowledge, in the eighteenth century. See Stranks, *op. cit.*, ch. 5.

129. Cf. Watts' recommendation of à Kempis, Fénelon, and de Renty in *An Humble Attempt*, Watts, *Works*, IV, 53. On Wesley's reading and editing of Catholic authors see the important articles by J. Orcibal, 'Les spirituels français et espagnols chez John Wesley

et ses contemporains', *Revue d'Histoire des Religions* (1951), 50–109, and 'The theological originality of John Wesley and continental spirituality', in *A History of the Methodist Church in Great Britain*, ed. R. Davies and G. Rupp (1965), I.

130. *Christian Library*, I (1819), v–ix.
131. See F. Baker, 'John Wesley, literary arbiter: an introduction to his use of the asterisk', *Procs Wesley Historical Soc.*, XL (1975–6), 25–33.
132. *Arminian Mag.*, IV (1781), iv.
133. F. Baker, 'A study of John Wesley's readings', *London Quarterly and Holborn Rev.*, CLXVIII (1943), 143.
134. Wesley, *Journal*, IV, 94. Cf. the letter to Doddridge from R. Pearsall describing his reading aloud of Doddridge's *Life of Colonel Gardiner, Correspondence*, IV, 573.
135. See n. 36.
136. Wesley, *Works*, ed. Jackson, VIII, 319.
137. R. Green, *op. cit.*, nos. 3, 26, 36, 114. See F. Baker, 'John Wesley and the "Imitatio Christi"', *London Quarterly and Holborn Rev.*, CLXVI (1941), 74–87.
138. *The Christian's Pattern* (octavo edn., 1735), xix–xx.
139. *An Extract of the Christian's Pattern, Works*, VII (1772), 308.
140. 1735 edn, xxiv–v.
141. For the various versions see W. A. Copinger, *On the English Translations of the Imitatio Christi* (1900).
142. Stanhope, *The Christian's Pattern* (2nd edn., 1700), 7.
143. Wesley, *Works*, VII (1772), 313.
144. 1735 edn., xxvi.
145. E.g. to John Fletcher, 20 March 1768, Wesley, *Letters*, V, 84.
146. R. Green, *op. cit.*, 79. See H. T. Hughes, 'Jeremy Taylor and John Wesley', *London Quarterly and Holborn Rev.*, CLXXIV (1949), 296–304; Stranks, *op. cit.*, ch. 3; Baker, *Wesley and the Church of England*, 26.
147. *The Life of God in the Soul of Man* (1677),

A7 verso. See the edition by W. S. Hudson (Philadelphia, 1948); D. Butler, *Henry Scougal and the Oxford Methodists* (1899); G. D. Henderson, *Religious Life in Seventeenth-Century Scotland* (1937), chs. 6 and 10.
148. R. Green, *op. cit.*, no. 51; p. 93.
149. Wesley, *Works*, VIII (1772), 292.
150. 14 October 1738, Wesley, *Journal*, II, 90.
151. Wesley, *Works*, VIII (1772), 341.
152. E.g. letter to Samuel Wesley, 23 November 1736, Wesley, *Letters*, I, 207–10; Preface to John and Charles Wesley, *Hymns and Sacred Poems* (5th edn., 1756), iii–v; Wesley, *Journal*, V, 46, 5 February 1764.
153. See E. W. Baker, *A Herald of the Evangelical Revival* (1948). The principal documents are in Wesley, *Journal*, IV, 410; VIII, 319–24; Wesley, *Letters*, I, 239–44; III, 332–70.
154. 'On a single Eye' (1789), Wesley, *Works*, ed. Jackson, VII, 297. Wesley links à Kempis, Taylor and Law in this passage.
155. R. Green, *op. cit.*, nos. 17, 45, 48; p. 217. On *A Serious Call* see Stranks, *op. cit.*, ch. 7.
156. See p. 143 above. For Doddridge's attitude to Law see *Correspondence*, III, 231.
157. Wesley, *Works*, V (1771), 112–13; Law, *A Serious Call to a Devout and Holy Life* (1729), 69.
158. Wesley, *Letters*, I, 333.
159. *Whitefield's Journals*, ed. W. Wale (Gainesville, 1969), 71.
160. Wesley, *Letters*, VI, 84.
161. Wesley, *Works*, V (1771), 62; Law, *Serious Call*, I.
162. Wesley, *Works*, V (1771), 7; Law, *A Practical Treatise upon Christian Perfection* (1726), 427.
163. Wesley, *Works*, V (1771), 8; Law, *Christian Perfection*, 433.
164. Wesley, *Works*, V (1771), 135; Law, *Serious Call*, 96.

7
The reading of philosophical literature

JOHN VALDIMIR PRICE

I. 'WHAT PASSES IN A MAN'S OWN MIND'

In one of his more exuberant moments, Tristram Shandy had no doubt about the definition of a philosophical book. Referring specifically to John Locke's *Essay concerning Human Understanding* (1690), he asserts, 'I will tell you in three words what the book is – It is a history – A history! of who? what? where? when? . . . It is a history-book . . . of what passes in a man's own mind.'[1] By the time Sterne was writing *The Life and Opinions of Tristram Shandy* (1759–67), Locke's *Essay* had infiltrated literary consciousness in the eighteenth century in a way quite unlike that of any other 'philosophical' book.[2] So, if we ask what *was* a philosophical book in this period, we can at least give an ostensive definition: Locke's *Essay concerning Human Understanding* was a philosophical book.

This much would be evident from a reading of *The Spectator* alone, with its numerous allusions to and explanations of Locke; indeed, Locke's *Essay* was one of the volumes that Mr Spectator found in the library of the fashionable lady, Leonora (*Spectator* 37). Addison doubtless did much to encourage the popularity of Locke: no philosopher has ever had a better publicity agent, and Addison himself had the professed intention of bringing 'Philosophy out of Closets and Libraries, Schools and Colleges, to dwell in Clubs and Assemblies, at Tea-Tables, and in Coffee-Houses' (*Spectator* 10).[3] Almost overnight, Addison made Locke in particular and philosophy in general not only respectable but fashionable.

The new appreciation of philosophy owed much to the new discoveries being made in the physical sciences, and it is worth remembering that in the eighteenth century the word 'philosophy' could also mean 'natural philosophy', or what we might call, in a loose sense, physics, but comprising optics, mechanics, astronomy, or any of the other physical sciences. This was also a phenomenon to which Addison addressed himself. Extolling the pleasures of the physical sciences, he writes, 'but among this Sett of Writers, there are none who more gratifie and enlarge the Imagination, than the Authors of the new Philosophy, whether we consider their Theories of the Earth or Heavens, the Discoveries they have made by Glasses, or any other of their Contemplations on Nature' (*Spectator* 420).

The use of the term 'natural philosophy' to cover the physical sciences has important implications for a more conventional or traditional use of the word 'philosophy'. For one thing, philosophy was being closely associated with natural phenomena and with an empirical method of thinking or reasoning. For another, in the description of the physical sciences as 'natural philosophy', a distinction was implied between the natural and the supernatural. This same distinction prevailed in philosophical discourses, and an eighteenth-century reader was increasingly being conditioned to expect a philosophical book to be one based on observation, documentation, and inference. A philosophical book was more and more one which took man as its chief subject and discussed man's relationship with the external world, with other human beings, and with his own mind. When Lady Mary Wortley Montagu wrote in 1754 to her daughter, Lady Bute, that 'Mr. Locke (who has made a more exact disection of the Human mind than any Man before him) declares he gain'd all his knowledge from the consideration of himselfe',[4] she spoke for her age: the acquisition of knowledge, the first step in philosophy, begins with one's self.

By the time Lady Mary was writing, it was also abundantly clear what a philosophical book was *not*. Empirical observations and inferences about human behaviour and the external world were philosophical; metaphysics was not. No one stated more emphatically than David Hume did, in 1748, what a philosophical book should not be:

> When we run over libraries, persuaded of these principles, what havoc must we make? If we take in our hand any volume; of divinity or school metaphysics, for instance; let us ask, *Does it contain any abstract reasoning concerning quantity or number?* No. *Does it contain any experimental reasoning concerning matter of fact and existence?* No. Commit it then to the flames: for it can contain nothing but sophistry and illusion.[5]

It is unlikely that Hume could or would have so described metaphysical books had he not been the beneficiary of the empiricism brought into British philosophy and the physical sciences by Locke on the one hand and Newton on the other. Yet it would be odd, if not incorrect, to think that Hume was largely responsible for the disavowal of metaphysics in the eighteenth century. Even those who might have been supposed to be sympathetic to the claims of metaphysics were quick to eschew a metaphysical method of thinking. For example, in translating and editing Bernard Neiuwentydt's *Het reg Gebruik der werelt Beschouwingen*, John

Chamberlayne wrote in the preface to his edition, 'I have not made use of the Metaphysicks',[6] and the readiness of a cleric to regard metaphysics as otiose doubtless owes much to the impact both of what Addison called the 'new Philosophy' and Locke's *Essay*.

As the idea of what constituted philosophical discourse began to change, readers began to reconsider their definitions of philosophical books as well as their attitudes towards them. Some, like Jonathan Swift, were not entirely sure about the good effects of Locke's pervasive influence. In his comments on Tindal's *Rights of the Christian Church Asserted* (1706), Swift takes an ironically dim view of Locke's innovations. Tindal had written that it would be necessary to show what was meant by the idea of government, and Swift comments,

> Now, it is to be understood, that this refined Way of Speaking was introduced by Mr. *Locke*: After whom the Author limpeth as fast as he was able. All the former Philosophers in the World, from the Age of *Socrates* to ours, would have ignorantly put the Question, *Quid est Imperium?* But now it seemeth we must vary our Phrase; and since our modern Improvement of Human Understanding, instead of desiring a Philosopher to describe or define a Mouse-trap, or tell me what it is; I must gravely ask, what is contained in the Idea of a Mouse-trap?[7]

Swift's ironic stance should not prevent us from seeing that he has correctly perceived the implications of the new methodology in philosophy. Part of his complaint is, to be sure, against the tergiversations that certain kinds of philosophical enquiry produced and the consequent deterioration in the clarity of the language that followed. Yet his formulation indicates just how much the 'new Philosophy' as well as the new kind of philosophical book that Locke and others were writing had affected the way in which men were going about inquiries into meaning, truth, virtue, and understanding. In the eighteenth century, a philosophical book became, more and more, one in which the author began by asking questions, either implicitly or explicitly, and moved by an inductive, empirical process towards an answer. No longer did one begin with certain imprescriptible, *a priori* truths from which various conclusions were deduced; instead, one began by collecting and sorting evidence.

2. 'TOO SPECULATIVE'

Swift's comments on contemporary philosophy and philosophical books are instructive in other ways, chiefly because Swift clearly was not in sympathy with the new philosophical procedures. Even his fellow countryman, Bishop George Berkeley, did not stir Swift as he had other readers of philosophical books. Writing to John Gay in 1732, Swift remarks of *Alciphron*, which had just been published, 'Pray how does Dr Berkeleys book pass amongst you; it is too Speculative for me . . .'. Gay also found the book too speculative.[8] To regard *Alciphron* as either 'speculative' or even 'too speculative' suggests that one goes to a philosophical book expecting to find solid and substantial, perhaps reassuring, conclusions. Certainly, some readers did, and perhaps Swift was one of them. There is also little doubt that he would not have found Berkeley's immaterialist notions acceptable in a Church of England divine.

Alciphron had its admirers, but otherwise the responses to it were almost all unfavourable, and Swift's comment is one of the milder ones. Within weeks of its publication two attacks were published, John, Lord Hervey's *Some Remarks on 'The Minute Philosopher'* and Bernard Mandeville's *A Letter to Dion*; in addition Peter Browne commented on the work in *Things Divine and Supernatural* (1733). These largely hostile reactions point to a change in public consciousness about what a philosophical book was or should be. Berkeley had professed as his aim, in the words of his sub-title, that the work should be 'An apology for the Christian Religion, against those who are called Free-Thinkers', and the late Professor Jessop described it as one of the 'three outstanding works of Christian apologetics'[9] in the eighteenth century, the other two being Joseph Butler's *Analogy of Religion* (1736) and William Paley's *A View of the Evidences of Christianity* (1794). These latter works, however, exhibit the methodology commonly found in more strictly philosophical works. Despite the growing division between philosophy and theology in the eighteenth century, a number of theologians incoporated into their writings the empirical procedures of the philosophers.

Berkeley's name is usually yoked together with that of Locke and Hume as one of the three 'great' philosophers of the eighteenth century, but in certain ways he is an anachronism. Both he and Locke were supporters of Christianity, but Locke was careful to keep his religion and his philosophy in more-or-less separate compartments. Berkeley's philosophy is, however, subordinated to his theological concerns. This is, to be sure, oversimplifying the matter, but as theology or religion and philosophy came to encompass quite different areas of enquiry in the later eighteenth century, so public expectations of what a philosophical book should be began to change. Berkeley's *Alciphron* produced the reactions it did because those expecting it to be a theological work were discomfited to find so much that was strictly secular in it, while those who thought it was a philosophical book found its preoccupation with the existence of God and its generally anti-deistic stance more suitable in a theological work.

Berkeley's works never achieved the popularity or currency of Locke's and Hume's. Several of his other most important works, namely his *Essay towards a New Theory of Vision* (1709), *A Treatise concerning the Principles of Human Knowledge* (1710), and *Three Dialogues between Hylas and Philonous* (1713), were reprinted several times, but the works which most excited the attention of his contemporaries were his tracts on tar-water.[10] Pope read the first of the tracts with a great deal of pleasure,[11] and Horace Walpole wrote to Horace Mann on 29 May 1744, 'We are now mad about tar-water on the publication of a book . . . by Dr Berkeley Bishop of Cloyne. The book contains every subject from tar-water to the Trinity; however all the women read it, and understand it no more than they would if it were intelligible.'[12]

Walpole's slighting comments were not untypical of his age and reveal many of the attitudes and assumptions that governed the reading of philosophical literature. Readers were not to be teased out of their 'common sense' by Berkeley's immaterialism. Boswell's story of Johnson's forcefully kicking a large stone in order to refute 'Bishop Berkeley's ingenious sophistry to prove the non-existence of matter' is well-known, but Boswell was not impressed: 'To me it is not conceivable how Berkeley can be answered by pure reasoning; but I know that the nice and difficult task was to have been undertaken by one of the most luminous minds [Edmund Burke's] of the present age, had not politicks "turned him from calm philosophy aside." '[13] Boswell's perplexity is genuine enough and seems to have been shared by others. Berkeley's immaterialism was not readily refutable in strictly logical or empirical terms, though it defied one's common-sense experience and expectations.

Berkeley tended to be taken more seriously by those with fairly strict notions of what philosophy was, in other words, by what we might call professional philosophers. Adam Smith had been very impressed by Berkeley's *Essay towards a New Theory of Vision* and termed it 'one of the finest examples of philosophical analysis that is to be found, either in our own, or in any other language'.[14] Smith's further comments on the book contain the same fulsome praise, but at this time he does not seem to have read the *Principles of Human Knowledge*. These comments on Berkeley probably stem from Smith's early career as a philosopher, before he knew and had read Hume, and his interest in strictly philosophical subjects waned as he developed his ideas on moral theory and on economics.

Adam Smith's acute early interest in Berkeley, and the failure of any mention or influence of Berkeley to appear except in the most minor way in his later works, illustrate pretty well the problems posed by Berkeley for a reader interested in philosophical literature in the eighteenth century. Very few of Berkeley's comments or arguments seemed to have a direct bearing on one's life, and in pursuing his immaterialist line of thought Berkeley left readers with little to do except expostulate. He had devoted much of his analysis to objects in the external world, if only to prove that they weren't 'really' there. In contrast, Locke and Hume were far more interested in the contents of the mind, in discovering how it worked, how knowledge was acquired, how experience enabled us to make inferences, and how we were affected by our perceptions and our reflections derived from these perceptions. They took the reader inside his own mind, as it were, and told him to look around and familiarize himself with the mind's operation. Berkeley was trying to convince the reader that the objects in the external world were perceived in the mind and nowhere else (except in the mind of God). Hume and Locke, arguing that the mind was a bundle of perceptions or a means of linking one perception or idea to another, offered a definition of the mind's ability to acquire knowledge that was at once more cogent and more 'reasonable'.

Berkeley did enjoy some popularity with other professional philosophers, most notably those Scottish intellectuals in the Rankenian Club, which was formed in Edinburgh around 1716 for the serious dicussion of new philosophy, literature, and rhetoric. They read Berkeley with some care and corresponded with him during the 1720s. In the memoirs of Robert Wallace published by his son, it was recorded that Berkeley had commented that 'no persons understood his system better than this set of young gentlemen in North Britain'.[15] Later, in 1739, David Hume remarked in his *Treatise of Human Nature* about Berkeley that

> A great philosopher has disputed the receiv'd opinion in this particular, and has asserted, that all general ideas are nothing but particular ones, annexed to a certain term, which gives them a more extensive signification, and makes them recall upon occasion other individuals, which are similar to them. As I look upon this to be one of the greatest and most valuable discoveries that has been made of late years in the republic of letters, I shall here endeavour to confirm it by some arguments. . . .[16]

What is clear from these remarks is, I think, that Berkeley appealed almost exclusively to professional philosophers and to those interested in what the general reader might reasonably regard as the minutiae of philosophy. The acuteness of Berkeley's mind and the graces of his literary style (often preferred by philosophers to that of Hume) did not recommend themselves to readers in the way that Hume's and Locke's writings did. Indeed, even Henry Home, Lord Kames, whose *Elements of Criticism* (of which Goldsmith remarked, 'It is easier to write that book, than to read it')[17] went through at least seven editions in the eighteenth century, proved to be more popular and accessible than Berkeley. Only the most intrepid soul would dare to argue that the *Elements of Criticism* is easy to read, and today most readers would be inclined to agree with Hume's assessment that 'there are some parts of the Work ingenious & curious: But it is too abstruse & crabbed ever to take with the Public.'[18] But the contemporary public took to it like ducks to water, and Hume later ruefully admitted, 'after his Elements of Criticism met with some Success, I shall never venture to make any Prophecy on that head'.[19]

3. 'ALL ENGLAND IN A FERMENT'

Hume's observation is both salient and sobering. Like many other percep-tive men, he proved to be impercipient when it came to estimating public taste and preference in philosophical works, his own as well as those of other writers. A remark in his autobiography, published in 1777 shortly after his death in 1776, not only highlights this difficulty but also draws attention to what the reading public could consider as a 'philosophical' book in the eighteenth century. For that matter, Hume does not regard the work as unphilosophical, to judge by his comment. Hume had published his *Enquiry concerning Human Understanding* in 1748 and had high hopes for it, but, as he notes, 'this piece was at first but little more successful than the Treatise of human Nature. On my return from Italy, I had the Mortifica-tion to find all England in a Ferment on account of Dr. Middletons Free Enquiry; while my Performance was entirely overlooked and neglected.'[20]

The book in question was Conyers Middleton's *Free Inquiry into the Miraculous Powers, Which are supposed to have subsisted in the Christian Church, From the Earliest Ages through several successive Centuries.* Reading the book today one admires the purity of the style, responds to the cogency of the argument, and concludes that it is totally irrelevant to any more compre-hensive philosophical topic. But this is a modern reaction and not that of the eighteenth-century reader. Middleton attacks the necessity of miracles in the Christian religion, as had Hume, asserting that they derive more from human testimony and human credulity than from anything else, and further challenging their historical validity:

> In a word; to submit our belief implicitly and indifferently, to the mere source of authority, in all cases, whether miraculous or natural, without any rule of discerning the credible from the incredible, might support indeed the faith, as it is called, but would certainly destroy the use of all history; by leading us into perpetual errors, and possessing our minds with invincible prejudices, and false notions both of men and things.[21]

Middleton's book was only one of many books, pamphlets, and essays in the 'miracles controversy' in the eighteenth century. Hume's essay 'Of Miracles', which forms section 10 of *An Enquiry concerning Human Understand-ing*, and Middleton's work were probably the two most formidable attacks on miracles published in the eighteenth century, one, ironically, from a Church of England divine, and the other from a notorious sceptic.

In the case of Middleton, we have a well-documented example of a reader who was profoundly influenced by the book, Edward Gibbon. Gibbon's initial reaction, however, was negative, in that he was temporarily converted to Catholicism, because of the evidence for miracles that Middleton had presented and then proceeded to demolish. Gibbon firmly believed that miraculous powers still belonged to the Church in the first four or five centuries of Christianity, and that miracles were the test of truth for the doctrines of the Catholic Church. His description of the effect of Middleton's book on his beliefs in his temporary conversion illustrates perfectly the collusion that could take place between philosophy and religion. His words have an almost Joycean ring: 'The marvellous tales, which are so boldly attested by the Basils and Chrysostoms, the Austins and Jeroms, compelled me to embrace the superior merits of Celibacy, the institution of the monastic life, the use of the sign of the cross, of holy oil, and even of images, the invocation of Saints, the worship of relicks, the rudiments of purgatory in prayers for the dead, and the tremendous mystery of the sacrifice of the body and blood of Christ, which insensibly swelled into the prodigy of Transubstantiation.'[22]

Gibbon's reaction to Middleton's *Free Inquiry* measures the co-extensiveness (and yet the ultimate irreconcilability) of religious doctrine and empirical philosophy in the eighteenth century, and Middleton's book found a ready audience in those whose faith was being tested by the new heterodoxical spirit of inquiry in philosophy. In practical terms, Hume and Middleton were not that far apart in their attitudes towards miracles: both regarded miracles as superstitious relics, but whereas Hume was arguing that a believing Christian had to accept the validity of miracles, Middleton was arguing that one did so at peril to one's faith! A troubled Christian, who had his doubts about miracles but not about the ultimate truth of Christianity, might prefer to side with a member of the Church of England rather than with the man regarded as the eighteenth century's most notorious infidel.

The popularity of Middleton's book, despite its heterodox conclusions, may be usefully contrasted with the relative unpopularity of Berkeley's works. Both were regarded as 'philosophical', though perhaps Berkeley would have been regarded as the better philosopher by other philosophers. Certainly the conclusions that Middleton reached, even if they did not contribute to the certainty of Christian theology, had more popular appeal than Berkeley's immaterialism. It was difficult to take Berkeley seriously, though he could not be easily refuted, a point that Lord Chesterfield noted in one of his letters to his son:

> Doctor Berkeley, Bishop of Cloyne, a very worthy, ingenious, and learned man, has written a book to prove that there is no such thing as matter, and that nothing exists but in idea: that you and I only fancy ourselves eating, drinking, and sleeping; you at Leipsig, and I at London; that we think we have flesh and blood, legs, arms, etc., but that we are only spirit. His arguments are, strictly speaking, unanswerable; but yet I am so far from being convinced by them, that I am determined to go on to eat and drink, and walk and ride, in order to keep that *matter*, which I so mistakenly imagine my body at present to consist of, in as good plight as possible.[23]

Berkeley's book could not be profitably discussed, because the logic of his argument could not be taken farther. Middleton's book, in contrast, offered scope for argument and discussion, and in fact it provoked a number of replies and thus helped to sustain the growing public demand for speculative, abstract, or theoretical books, in short, for books whose methodology and structure were philosophical.[24]

4. 'AN AUDIENCE NUMEROUS ENOUGH TO REWARD'

Middleton's and Hume's books, one successful immediately and the other latterly, came just at a time when the presses of Britain seemed to be groaning with philosophical books. It would be tedious to enumerate the philosophical books that were published in just one decade, the 1750s, but a decade which includes two or three books by Hume, one by Adam Smith, another by Burke, one by Lord Kames, as well as productions from a host of minor authors cannot be termed a philosophically reticent one. This was indeed the point to which Oliver Goldsmith drew attention in an essay published in 1761: 'I know no country but this where readers of learning are sufficiently numerous to give every kind of literary excellence adequate encouragement. On whatever subject the philosopher happens to treat, he may be sure of finding an audience numerous enough to reward, and sensible enough to discern his excellence.'[25] Goldsmith has no hesitation in finding the English (as distinct from the British) given to philosophy. In a series of essays on 'A Comparative View of Races and Nations', he made some generalized distinctions between the Irish, the Scots, and the English, observing that the last 'are distinguished from the rest of Europe by their superior accuracy in reasoning, and are in general called the nation of philosophers by their neighbours on the continent'.[26]

Goldsmith's latter comment appeared in the *Royal Magazine* for September 1760, when the epicentre of philosophical writing in Britain was surely in Scotland and, more specifically, in Edinburgh. Except for Joseph Priestley and Richard Price, who, for all their merits, cannot be termed major philosophical writers, there was hardly an Englishman in sight. Indeed, except for Locke and Shaftesbury, the names that one associates with the triumph of British empiricist philosophy in the eighteenth century are Irish or Scottish: Berkeley, Burke, Hume, Hutcheson, Adam Smith, Lord Kames, etc. Perhaps it was the presence of so many writers (mainly historians and philosophers) in Scotland that led Hume to comment, in a letter to Gilbert Elliot of 2 July 1757, that the Scots were the 'People most distinguish'd for Literature in Europe.'[27] Some allowance must be given for Hume's nationalistic leanings, but it is worth noting here how readily Hume had subsumed into the term 'literature' the disciplines of philosophy and history.

Hume regarded himelf primarily as a 'man of letters' and would not have been so ready to make the generic distinction between philosophy and literature that a later age would. Indeed, many readers in the eighteenth century would not have made such distinctions, and Hume would have had an unexpected ally in Samuel Johnson, who had defined literature in his *Dictionary* simply as 'learning; skill in letters'.

Hume's and Goldsmith's respective observations are, I think instructive, if only negatively, for a modern reader trying to understand or to isolate the assumptions that an eighteenth-century reader would have made in approaching a philosophical book. Goldsmith must be regarded as wildly wrong in asserting that the English, as distinct from the Scots, the Irish, or the Welsh, were 'distinguished from the rest of Europe by their superior accuracy in reasoning', if we think of 'superior accuracy in reasoning' as a feature uniquely philosophical. Equally, Hume was not entirely wrong in asserting that Scotland's writers, in 1757, were the 'most distinguish'd for Literature in Europe', if we regard philosophy and history as literature in its widest sense. Dr Johnson's definition of literature might be seen to exclude some of his own writings, if it were strictly interpreted, though many of us would want to regard a nation harbouring Dr Johnson in its midst as having in one man enough literary distinction for half a dozen nations and at least two or three generations. The interrelationship of concepts of philosophy and literature in the eighteenth century is complex, and readers as well as authors were only beginning to re-define and re-consider features of literature that might be peculiar to philosophical discourse.

In their wrongness, Hume and Goldsmith have nevertheless pointed to some of the assumptions and attitudes that lie behind reading in general and reading particular kinds of books. Because literature and learning were terms that readers used co-extensively, they tended to approach one genre of literature in much the same way that they would have approached another. Though generic and sub-generic distinctions could be made,[28] a philosophical book was not thought to require any special reading skills, a point which is perhaps illustrated by the remark Goldsmith made about Kames's *Elements of Criticism* (above, p. 170). The disparate and apparently contradictory remarks by Hume and Goldsmith reveal a disposition in the eighteenth-century author, as well as reader, to think of literature as a comprehensive and inclusive term, and to regard ideas and 'accuracy in reasoning' as the core of literary expression. If pushed, Goldsmith would doubtless have agreed that, in geographical terms if nothing else, England was not more heavily populated with philosophers than Ireland and Scotland were, nor would Hume have argued that the writings of Johnson and his circle were to be set at naught. Again, both could have turned to Johnson for elaboration and edification about the correlation between literature and philosophy in the mind of the eighteenth-century reader. Philosophy Johnson defined as 'knowledge natural or moral'. When one then turns in his *Dictionary* to look up the meaning of knowledge, and finds it defined first as 'certain perception; indubitable apprehension' and second as '*learning*; illumination of the mind' [my italics], one is made ineluctably aware not only of the inseparability of literature and philosophy to the eighteenth-century reader, but also of some of the hazards of generic definition.

It was left to another Scot to hazard a generic definition, or at least description, of philosophical writing and, by implication, of what was involved in reading a philosophical book. Hugh Blair in his vastly influential *Lectures on Rhetoric and Belles Lettres* (1783) devoted only a few pages to philosophical writing, but these pages give a better clue to the guidelines that readers of philosophical books were looking for than any other theoretical writings. Blair sees the object of philosophy as conveying instruction so that readers study philosophy 'for instruction, not for entertainment', but he argues that the rhetorical presentation is not to be neglected: 'The same truths, and reasonings, delivered in a dry and cold manner, or with a proper measure of elegance and beauty, will make very different impressions on the minds of men.' The suggestiveness of Blair's imagery here quite clearly implies something about the reader's expectations, and Blair indeed has a number of observations to make about an author's attention to 'the rules of Style and good Writing'. Of particular use to a philosophical writer and hence of particular value to a reader are examples from history and from men's characters. Such illustrations always improve a philosophical discourse, 'for they take Philosophy out of the abstract, and give weight to Speculation, by shewing its connection with real life, and the actions of mankind'. One can see the immediate applicability of this observation to Locke and Hume, but not perhaps to Berkeley, and one is once more reminded that the eighteenth-century reader expected his incursions into philosophical literature to have practical benefits and self-enhancing consequences. Blair is equally careful to caution that philosophical writing should not be decked out in the exotic flowers of euphuistic rhetoric: 'it is much better . . . to err on the side of naked simplicity, than on that of too much ornament'. Fortunately for the reader, Blair observes his own precepts and gives examples of both model philosophical discourse and that in which rhetorical embellishment exceeds philosophical acuity. Locke's 'celebrated Treatise on Human Understanding' is a model of 'the greatest clearness and distinctness of Philosophical Style, with very little approach to ornament'. In contrast, he cites the writings of Shaftesbury, which 'exhibit Philosophy dressed up with all the ornament which it can admit; perhaps with more than is perfectly suited to it'.[29]

It is difficult not to wish that Blair had been a little more expansive in his comments and had devoted more attention to what constituted philosophical writing, because he is clearly thinking of it as a genre or at least a sub-genre of literature. One must remember that these lectures began at the University of Edinburgh as early as 1759,[30] and that by the time they were published in 1783, many of his ideas had become received opinion. Before preparing his lectures, Blair had attended those of Adam Smith, but Smith seems not to have touched on the question of philosophical discourse in his lectures.[31] Given the widespread influence of Blair's lectures,[32] one is tempted to speculate that Blair helped turn a reader's attention towards the style of a philosophical discourse. As the century wore on, readers, whether pursuing the thread of knotty philosophical argument or unravelling the strands of narrative fabric, became more aware of the different kinds of discourse, and their expectations began to change. Coleridge was perhaps the last British author who attempted to keep philosophy within the stylistic boundaries of literature, and his uncertain reputation, as well as his failure to realize his potential, must in some measure be due to the development of a specifically 'philosophical' mode of expression which eventually led to a literature read only by specialists.

In citing Locke's *Essay* as a model of philosophical style, Blair was merely confirming the judgment that three generations of readers had already made. Yet Locke's popularity was not necessarily a measure of his clarity, and it seems reasonable to assume that Addison's commentaries on and paraphrases of Locke in *The Spectator* are prompted by an awareness that the density of Locke's writing could discourage readers less assiduous than himself. Addison's distinction between wit and judgment in *Spectators* 62 and 63, and the discussion of the pleasures of the imagination in *Spectators* 411–21, are consciously derivative, and they suggest the extent to which Addison felt that Locke required a plain man's guide to his philosophical writings. Hume's remark in his *Enquiry concerning Human Understanding* that 'Addison, perhaps, will be read with pleasure, when Locke shall be entirely forgotten'[33] might also be cited as evidence that Locke, for all his literary abilities and graces, was more hindered than helped by his style.

5. 'TOTAL ALTERATION IN PHILOSOPHY'

Hume was probably the first British philosopher who devoted more than routine attention to his style. Of course, no author is ever so insensitive to his readers' demands and expectations as to ignore completely whatever stylistic resources he may have, though I would be willing to make an exception to this generalization for the writings of Immanuel Kant (to go no further than the eighteenth century). Philosophers have ever been among those who are most sensitive to nuances of style: Quintilian records that

Plato left a number of versions of the beginning of the *Republic*.[34] Hume's earliest letters document his concern for his style, and a concern for style is a concern for the way one's book will be read. In 1737, the publication of his first book, *A Treatise of Human Nature*, was imminent, and he wrote to his friend Henry Home (later Lord Kames) about his excitement and apprehension, 'I began to feel some Passages weaker for the Style & Diction than I cou'd have wisht.' At the same time, he enclosed an early draft of what later became his notorious essay on miracles. Of this work, he says to Home,

> I once thought of publishing [it] with the rest, but . . . I am afraid [that it] will give too much Offence even as the World is dispos'd at present. There is Something in the turn of Thought & a good deal in the Turn of Expression, which will not perhaps appear so proper for want of knowing the Context: But the Force of the Argument you'll be judge of as it stands. Tell me your Thoughts of it. Is not the Style too diffuse? Tho as that was a popular Argument I have spread it out much more than the other Parts of the Work.[35]

In view of Hume's concern with his style and presentation, the reception of his work by the reading public was little short of humiliating. In his autobiography, he ruefully comments, 'Never literary Attempt was more unfortunate than my Treatise of human Nature. It fell dead-born from the Press; without reaching such distinction as even to excite a Murmur among the Zealots.'[36] Hume had been eager for the *History of the Works of the Learned* to review the volumes, and a review finally appeared in November and December, 1739. The reviewer's contemptuous opinion[37] was bad enough, but two particular observations must have been galling for an author so concerned about his style. The first says of Locke's *Essay* in comparison with the *Treatise*, 'A man, who has never had the Pleasure of reading *Mr. Locke's* incomparable Essay, will peruse our Author with much less Disgust, than those can who have been used to the irresistible Reasoning and wonderful Perspicuity of that admirable Writer.' Having compared Hume unfavourably with Locke, the reviewer now diminishes him to a mere exponent of Berkeley's theory of abstract ideas. But Berkeley's work, he observes, has not met 'with any favourable Reception among the Literati . . .; Its Fortune may now perhaps be more prosperous under the Auspices of its new Patron, who, we see, undertakes to raise it above all opposition.'[38] Few philosophers in the eighteenth century would have minded not being found equal to Locke, but for Hume to find himself interpreted as a disciple of Berkeley might very well indicate that he was right to be concerned about his style and about the presentation of his ideas.

After the failure of the *Treatise*, Hume published two slim volumes of essays in what he hoped was an imitation of Addison.[39] These were well received, and the first volume went into a second edition. Hume was thus encouraged to continue trying to get his revolutionary philosophical ideas into a form that would have widespread public as well as professional appeal. When he finally came to publish the result in 1748, under the title *Philosophical Essays concerning Human Understanding* (later changed to the more familiar *Enquiry concerning Human Understanding*), he addressed himself to the various kinds of philosophical discourse and the readers' demands and expectations in the first chapter, 'Of the Different Species of Philosophy'. The very fact that Hume chose to solicit the readers' interest and attention in the way and to the extent that he did points to a new awareness on the part of philosophical writers about their readers. There is almost a note of regretful irony in this chapter. Like many authors, Hume had expected his book to excite great public interest and even to produce a 'total Alteration in Philosophy'.[40] Ten years after the publication of the *Treatise*, he had realized that the audience for philosophy is neither so extensive nor so eager as he had assumed.

Positing two extremes in human character, the 'mere philosopher' and the 'mere ignorant', he finds that the most perfect character comes between those extremes, and in his reading finds nothing 'more useful than compositions of the easy style and manner, which draw not too much from life, require no deep application or retreat to be comprehended, and send back the student among mankind full of noble sentiments and wise precepts'. Yet Hume is worried that mankind in general might prefer 'the easy philosophy to the abstract and profound', and he proceeds to argue the case for the latter. One of the problems with abstract and profound philosophy lies in the crabbed metaphysics that dogs most theoretical enquiries. Even if a cogent reasoner can clear away mountains of intellectual rubbish, there are still problems. Proceeding with care '*and encouraged by the attention of the public*' [my italics], a philosopher may discover, if only partially, 'the secret springs and principles, by which the human mind is actuated in its operations'. For Hume, the task is not as hopeless as it seems, and the tone of his argument, now cajoling, now hectoring, prods the reader into accepting not only the necessity of the endeavour but also into anticipating the benefits to be achieved:

> Happy, if we can unite the boundaries of the different species of philosophy, by reconciling profound enquiry with clearness, and truth with novelty! And still more happy, if, reasoning in this easy manner, we can undermine the foundations of an abstruse philosophy, which seems to have hitherto served only as a shelter to superstition, and a cover to absurdity and error![41]

I have quoted from this introductory chapter fairly extensively because of the importance of the tone of Hume's argument, and the conduct of the argument itself. Hume is clearly aware of the need to persuade his reader to go along with him, and he deploys as much rhetorical embellishment and ornament as he decently can in what is, after all, a painstaking and intricate analysis of the phenomenology of the mind. The rhetorical stance is given away by the apostrophic use of 'happy', as happiness and still more happiness is not the emotion that immediately springs to one's mind as being consonant with the accomplishments that Hume hopes for. It does, however, contribute to a tone which invites the reader to conspire with the writer in a particular undertaking. A reader is obliged to admire and to succumb to Hume's deft use of metaphor here. First, one makes the topographical survey in order to determine and to unite boundaries, to make sure of the area in which one is working. Then one sets about with the author in demolishing the existing structures where superstition, absurdity, and error have taken refuge. Hitherto, Hume implies, philosophers and other seekers after truth have avoided these edifices and have strayed into philosophically undesirable areas. With the destruction of these safe refuges, superstition, absurdity, and error will have to yield their ground to the intrepid and fearless. Stirring stuff, even melodramatic if you like, but Hume was determined to compel his readers' complicity.

Throughout his correspondence Hume gives further evidence of his concern for his readers' reactions, and he often wrote to those who had disagreed with him or attacked him about points where he felt he had been misinterpreted. That is to say, he wrote to those for whom he had some respect. An example of the degree of interest that Hume took in readers' comments on his books, particularly the comments of his more able and more philosophically inclined readers, can be found in a letter to Dr John Stewart, Professor of Natural Philosophy at the University of Edinburgh, 1742–59. In 1754, Hume and Alexander Monro *secundus* were secretaries of the Philosophical Society in Edinburgh, and a volume of essays entitled *Essays and Observations Physical and Literary*, to which Hume probably wrote the preface, was issued under the auspices of the Society. One of the essays was by Stewart, who made some uncomplimentary references to Hume, provoking Hume into writing to him privately and saying that when he was 'abus'd by such a Fellow as [William] Warburton' he was unconcerned and probably disposed to laugh. In contrast, if 'Dr Stewart approaches any way towards the same Style of writing, I own it vexes me: Because I conclude, that some unguarded Circumstance of my Conduct, tho' contrary to my Intention, had given Occasion to it.' Stewart had also criticized an essay, 'Of the Laws of Motion', by Lord Kames in the same volume, in a ponderous and heavy-handed attempt at humour, and Hume suggested that his treatment of Lord Kames in such a manner was unnecessary, since Stewart's argument was superior: 'All Raillery ought to be avoided in philosophical Argument; both because it is unphilosophical, and because it cannot but be offensive, let it be ever so gentle.' Like any writer of philosophical discourse, Hume was keen not to be misunderstood, and asserted that if a 'man of Sense mistakes my Meaning, I own I am angry: But it is only at myself: For having exprest my Meaning so ill as to have given Occasion to the Mistake.'[42] This sensitivity to a reader's subjective reaction is not uniquely Hume's, but more than any British philosopher before him, he was conscious of the relationship between his style and his ideas. When he wrote the *Treatise of Human Nature*, he aimed to 'produce a total Alteration in Philosophy', but was aware that 'Revolutions of this kind are not easily brought about.'[43] Whether he was still hoping to effect this 'Revolution' in 1754 is doubtful, but he was perhaps even more susceptible to any criticism of his writings where that criticism might have ensued from his failure to make his meaning clear.

Hume obviously assumes that philosophical discourse is a special kind of discourse, and at the same time he wants to persuade his readers that this is the case. To do so means that he runs the risk of special pleading, and if he pleads too overtly that philosophy requires to be read in a special kind of way, he risks losing his audience, perhaps even before he has gained it. Failure to be understood is one of the hazards of philosophical writing, and philosophers must often forego the pleasures of rhetorical ingenuity for prosaic clarity. Like Hume, George Berkeley earlier in the century also experienced a good deal of humiliation at the reception of his first book-length excursion into philosophy.[44] His *Treatise concerning the Principles of Human Knowledge*, published in 1710, suffered a fate not much better than Hume's *Treatise* was to suffer in 1739–40.[45] Berkeley was 25 when the book was published; Hume was 28 when the *Treatise* appeared. Both authors did not spare their friends for opinions or news about their respective publications. Writing to Sir John Percival, to whom he had dedicated the earlier *Theory of Vision*, Berkeley states that he would be 'extremely obliged' if Percival could 'procure me the opinion of some of your ingenious acquaintances who are thinking men and addicted to the study of rational philosophy and mathematics.' Percival's reply could not have pleased him, as it was full of accounts of the ridicule and contempt with which the book had been greeted. Many would-be readers had been put off by the subject matter alone and had not ventured to read the work. Berkeley was discouraged, but not hopelessly so, particularly since those

> who have entered deepest into the merits of the cause, and employed most time and exactness in reading what I have written, speak more advantageously of it. If the raillery and scorn of those that critique what they will not be at the pains to understand had been sufficient to deter men from making any attempts towards curing the ignorance and errors of mankind, we should have been troubled with very few improvements in knowledge.

Just as Hume would be convinced that those of 'vulgar Sentiments' would never understand his philosophy, so Berkeley has in mind as his ideal reader a thinking man 'addicted to the study of rational philosophy'; if he is to be opposed, let it be done by 'reason and argument'. Percival could at least tell him that Samuel Clarke and William Whiston had read the book and had regarded it as fair and clear but, alas, wrong. Nevertheless, Berkeley was delighted, since there was nothing he desired more in his search for truth than 'the concurring studies of thoughtful and impartial men'.[46] One cannot help noticing that for Berkeley an *addiction* is going to be the means of effecting a *cure*. Obviously, the rewards of philosophical enquiry and exposition are significant enough to be worth the hazards of slight metaphorical inconsistency.

In the book, however, Berkeley declares that he aims at a wider audience, and his appeal to the reader is direct and straightforward: 'I entreat the reader to reflect with himself, and see if it doth not often happen either in hearing or reading a discourse, that the passions of fear, love, hatred, admiration, disdain, and the like arise, immediately in his mind upon the perception of certain words, without any ideas coming between.' This is both an appeal and a challenge to the reader either to accept Berkeley's account or to put forward good reasons for not accepting what he has to say. Berkeley is confident that the reader will be obliged to agree with him. This is not to say that he has any illusions about the difficulty of his task, but he does not set out to ensnare the reader quite so adroitly as Hume does. Consider the closing words of his introductory chapter: 'Whoever therefore designs to read the following sheets, I entreat him to make my words the occasion of his own thinking, and endeavour to attain the same train of thoughts in reading, that I had in writing them. By this means it will be easy for him to discover the truth or falsity of what I say. He will be out of all danger of being deceived by my words, and I do not see how he can be led into error by considering his own naked, undisguised ideas.'[47] The neatness by which Berkeley quickly makes his ideas the reader's is unmistakeable, but it lacks something of Hume's rhetorical seductiveness. Both authors, however, depend on the same vocabulary; both want, for example, to avoid leading their readers into error; both employ the same images of movement and concealment. But Berkeley puts the reader in his place and does not try to imagine how the reader is responding to his offerings and overtures, whereas Hume does. Hume is doubtless more ambitious and dramatic in putting forward the positive attraction of happiness, while Berkeley can promise only the negative consolation of not being deceived. Of course, one would not expect Berkeley to be as skillful a writer at 25 as Hume was at 37, when he published the *Enquiry concerning Human Understanding*; the kind of comparison I have been making is inherently unfair, but it nevertheless contributes to our perception of the way in which philosophical writers in the eighteenth century were developing new attitudes towards and new concepts of their readers.

6. 'A DEPTH OF REASONING, AND A SPLENDOUR OF LANGUAGE'

One of the attractions of Hume's writing in general lies in the absence of personal axes to grind. His views, particularly where they seemed to be theologically heterodox or to subvert Christianity, were frequently attacked in terms that do not always smack of temperance, good-will, and doctrinal disinterestedness. Hence, he was obliged to curry favour with a reader more assiduously and more subtly than other writers did. His chief antagonist – that 'bigotted silly Fellow, Beattie'[48] – appeared long after Hume's creative energies were expended. While I may be grinding my own axe here, I think that Beattie's representation of Hume and of himself to his readers, and his attitude towards them, give further valuable clues as to the ways in which philosophical writers expected readers to read philosophy.

Beattie's book, *An Essay on the Nature and Immutability of Truth, in Opposition to Sophistry and Scepticism* (1770), is perhaps his most famous publication and his least philosophically valuable. The popularity of the book was immediate, and it could number among its admirers Dr Johnson; writing to Boswell on 31 August 1772, he commented, 'Beattie's book is, I believe, every day more liked; at least, I like it more, as I look more upon it.'[49] In the journal that Beattie kept during his visit to London, he recorded another encomium by Johnson, this one by way of David Garrick: 'On this occasion he repeated a speech that Johnson once made to him in regard to my book on Truth. Garrick had been praising it highly as a most excellent work (which he always does when he speaks of it). Johnson seconded him warmly – "Why, sir, there is in it a depth of reasoning, and a splendor of language which make it one of the first rate productions of the age."' Beattie was also pleased by the fact that his book seemed to have had the effect of displacing Hume's essays. On 16 May 1773, dining with William Strahan, Hume's printer, he records that Strahan told him that 'my Essay has knocked up the sale of Mr David Hume's Essays'.[50]

The *Essay on Truth* came into existence as an answer to Hume and to the all-too-ready acceptance that his works were receiving by those who should have been more attentive to the destruction of Christianity that Beattie saw as the major purpose of Hume's writings, and probably of Hume's life as well. Beattie had commenced as an author at the age of 21, when some of his poems were printed in *The Scots Magazine* for 1756; his first book, a collection of *Original Poems and Translations*, was published in 1761, the year after he had been appointed to the chair of Moral Philosophy and Logic at Marischal College, Aberdeen. He began writing the *Essay on Truth* around 1765, about the time that he began work on his most famous poem, *The Minstrel*. By March 1767, he wrote to Robert Arbuthnot, 'I have also finished my essay on – I know not well how to call it; for its present title-page, "*An Essay on Reason and Common Sense*," must be altered.' Whether or not he should publish the work also exercised him, and he was reluctant to do so, 'for the principles are quite unfashionable; and there is a keenness of expression in some passages, which could please only a few, namely, those who are thoroughly convinced of the truth and importance of religion.'[51] It is difficult to believe that in the eighteenth century there were only a few among Beattie's potential readership who had such convictions about the 'truth and importance of religion', but the comment gives us some clue to Beattie's rhetorical strategy. I do not think he is being ironic; indeed, Beattie seems incapable of irony, though sarcasm comes easily to him. We have already seen that both Berkeley and Hume regard their works as too 'revolutionary' to be fashionable; that Beattie should unknowingly align himself with them in this way is one of the refreshing ironies of historical scholarship.

Uncertain whether to proceed with the work, though he himself had derived a good deal of satisfaction from writing it, Beattie continued to consult his friends, among them Dr John Gregory, author of the important and influential *Comparative View of the State and Faculties of Man, with those of the Animal World* (1765), and the immensely popular *A Father's Legacy to his Daughters* (1774). At one time, Gregory had been acquainted with Hume in a more or less friendly fashion, but he became convinced that Hume's writings were pernicious and that they must be opposed at all costs. When Beattie sent him a draft or a plan of the *Essay on Truth*, he responded with enthusiasm, encouraging Beattie to make his incursion *in partibus infidelium* and there defeat the enemy. Moreover, Gregory had some fairly emphatic ideas about what was necesary to counter the effects of Hume's writings and to make one's own attractive:

> In order, therefore, to be read, you must not be satisfied with reasoning with justness and perspicuity; you must write with pathos, with elegance, with spirit, and endeavour to warm the imagination, and touch the heart of those, who are deaf to the voice of reason. Whatever you write in the way of criticism will be read, and, if my partiality to you does not deceive me, be admired. Every thing relating to the 'Belles lettres' is read, or pretended to be read. What has made Lord Kaims's 'Elements of Criticism' so popular in England, is his numerous illustrations and quotations from Shakespeare. If his book had wanted these illustrations, or if they had been taken from ancient or foreign authors, it would not have been so generally read in England. This is a good political hint to you, in your capacity of an author; and certainly, if you write to the world, and wish to gain their approbation, you must write in such a manner as experience shows to be effectual for that purpose, if that manner be not criminal.[52]

Gregory's advice is more hortatory than instructive, but it gives abundant evidence of the kind of pains that potential readers thought putative authors ought to take with their philosophical works. Beattie could not take to heart Gregory's advice about quotations from modern authors, as his book was conceived on rather different lines from those of Lord Kames's *Elements of Criticism*. To a very large extent, the book is an attack on Hume, and specifically the *Treatise of Human Nature*, and many, if not most, of the quotations are drawn from Hume's writings. It is at least curious that Gregory feels that Beattie must use all his rhetorical skills and belletristic arts in order to insinuate the truth. After all, if the book is an essay on truth, it perhaps should not need these aids, and there is a certain ethical ambiguity about appealing to the hearts and imaginations of those who are impervious to reason if one is advancing the cause of truth.

Beattie's diffidence about his work and its merits was such that he left the arrangements for its publication to Robert Arbuthnot and his future biographer, Sir William Forbes. When they offered it to a publisher, it was refused, though the publisher intimated that he would have been willing to print it at the author's expense. Knowing that Beattie would not have accepted this arrangement (though very common practice in the eighteenth century), Arbuthnot and Forbes decided that they would have to be the underwriters of the first edition but that they would not disclose this harmless deception to Beattie. Accordingly, they wrote to him saying that they had accepted 50 guineas for the book and remitted that sum to him, while at the same time apparently guaranteeing the publishers, A. Kincaid and J. Bell in Edinburgh, against any losses. Beattie accepted these arrangements at face value (he had no reason to suspect anything), and Forbes recorded his satisfaction in his biography, saying that 'had it not been for this interference of ours in this somewhat ambiguous manner, perhaps the "Essay on Truth," on which all Dr Beattie's future fortunes hinged, might never have seen the light. It also strongly marks the slender opinion entertained by the booksellers at that period, of the value of a work which has since risen into such well-merited celebrity.'[53] The whims of fate are not more capricious than those of publishing, and the irony of the failure of Hume's *Treatise* (for which the publishers paid him £50) and the success of Beattie's *Essay*, which got into print almost by accident, is not easily missed. What the reading public will like is never an easy judgment to make, yet the history of philosophy owes more to the gamble of John Noon, Hume's publisher, than the contrivances of Sir William Forbes and Robert Arbuthnot.

One does not deny the merit of Beattie's work. As an exercise in Christian apologetics, it was successful, and it could be seen to provide a refutation of Hume's scepticism. However, Beattie's invitations to the reader and his manner of ingratiating himself with the reader are rhetorically far removed from those of Hume or Berkeley. The *Essay on Truth* had reached five editions by 1774, and it was felt that a collected edition of his works, to which readers could subscribe, was desirable. According to Beattie, 'some persons of distinction in England' persuaded him to consent to this edition, which had as its headpiece, of course, the *Essay on Truth*, plus some other works. In the preface to this edition, Beattie admits that he had been tempted to expand and lengthen the *Essay*, and perhaps to modify the language with which he abused Hume, but on reflection he decided to retain his original effort: 'it appears, not to me only, but to many other persons of far superior understanding, that my principles are founded on right reason, and on that way of thinking and judging, which has in every age been most familiar to the human mind.' Addressing himself specifically to the reader, he observes, 'A complete theory of evidence is not to be expected in this book. The attentive reader will see I never intended one.'[54] However inclined a reader might be to sympathize with or to criticize an author, he is placed at a disadvantage by comments such as these. If he asks for a 'complete theory of evidence' and expects to find one, he is judged 'inattentive'; the fault is his, not Beattie's. What if the reader fails to perceive Beattie's intention? Beattie has abjured any responsibility for the reader's shortcomings and failings. If the reader should decide, furthermore, that there are errors in Beattie's work, and that his principles do not meet the demands of right reason, then he aligns himself against those friends of Beattie's 'of far superior understanding' who have given the book their imprimatur. Only an intrepid reader would risk being judged 'inattentive' or would be willing to challenge those select few blessed with 'superior understanding'.

There are a number of other references in the introductory material to people with such superior capacities, superior, indeed, as Beattie says, to his own, who have admired and extolled the merits of the *Essay*. The reader who is not able to join this happy band may wonder what he is missing and feel that, unless he too admires Beattie's book unreservedly, he cannot count himself one of the intellectual cognoscenti. These self-denying disclaimers smack of false modesty, and a perusal of Beattie's other writings and letters reveals a constant pattern of such disclaimers. Rather than run the risk of intellectual arrogance, Beattie runs the greater one of false humility, and the resultant rhetorical stance is not likely to be one that will encourage a reader. For one thing, Beattie is too explicitly drawing attention to himself as author and hence as a being superior to his readers. Instead of entreating his readers to join him in a spirit of cooperative endeavour, Beattie presents the results of his lucubrations, complete with the endorsement of many with 'far superior understanding'.

Beattie also presents himself as merely doing his duty in attacking Hume and places himself emphatically on the side of angels and innocent little children:

> Being honoured with the care of a part of the British youth; and considering it as
> my indispensable duty (from which I trust I shall never deviate) to guard their

> minds against impiety and error, I endeavoured, among other studies that
> belong to my office, to form a right estimate of Mr Hume's philosophy, so as not
> only to understand his peculiar tenets, but also to perceive their *connection* and
> *consequences*.[55]

Not only does the poor reader who might be inclined to agree with Hume
now find himself opposed to Beattie, the superior beings who approved his
work, and the 'Noble and Learned Persons who conducted and
encouraged'[56] the book, but it also begins to look as if this putative reader
has nothing better to do than corrupt and deprave the young.

Beattie is, to be sure, an easy target for the kind of observation that I am
making, but I think his rhetoric, whether genuinely humble or piously
hypocritical, betrays a condescending attitude towards his readers. In
trying to appear helpfully authoritative, Beattie appears merely
authoritarian; he conducts his argument didactically, not dialectically, and
he assumes that his reader comes to his book with a specific purpose or goal
in mind. Readers of philosophical books in the eighteenth century were not
necessarily choosing them to read because they wanted to have old
hypotheses re-validated. Many of them were indeed interested in experimental enquiry, in analysis of philosophical problems, and in a new and
more correct understanding of old phenomena. Nevertheless, the popularity of Beattie's *Essay on Truth* proves that he was answering the needs of a
number of readers. Yet most of the comments on and reactions to the book
are notable for their emphasis on it as an antidote to Hume rather than on
its philosophical significance.[57]

7. 'A SORT OF ANTIPATHY BETWEEN PHILOSOPHICAL AND POETICAL GENIUS'

Though not in sympathy with Hume's treatment of philosophical and
theological issues, Beattie is in harmony with the general style of philosophical writing and the approach towards certain philosophical problems,
as is evidenced by the title he gave his book. In looking over the titles of
philosophical literature in the eighteenth century, one cannot help being
struck by the number of times words such as 'essay', 'treatise', 'enquiry',
etc. are used. Indeed, one is inclined to think that readers would have been
deterred from buying a philosophical book if it did not have one of these
talismanic words in the title. The prevalence of 'essay' also brings to mind
Dr Johnson's definition of the word as a 'loose sally of the mind; an
irregular indigested piece; not a regular and orderly composition'. Of
course, he also defined it as 'attempt; endeavour' and 'a trial; an experiment', definitions more in keeping with the senses in which philosophical
writers were using the word.[58] In writing an essay on truth, then, Beattie
was attempting something different from other writers using the term, who

composed essays on 'virtue', 'beauty', 'human understanding' or some other suitable abstraction.

The recurrence of these words is an easy and immediate pointer to one of the considerations a philosophical writer had to make, that of alerting his audience and preparing them for a particular kind of writing. Alexander Pope was clearly conscious of the philosophical utility and ubiquity of the word when he gave one of his last long poems the title *An Essay on Man*, which, he said, he wrote to 'please but a few, and (if I could) make mankind less Admirers, and greater Reasoners'.[59] (Occasionally, one feels that it would be at least a change to find an author who confessedly wrote to please the many.) Pope's excursion into the realms of philosophy in *An Essay on Man* is a measure of the enthusiasm of his time for ideas and the willingness of both author and reader to experiment with genres and forms in making new philosophical enquiries. Though *An Essay on Man* gave pleasure to more than the few that Pope had in mind, one has to doubt whether it improved the reasoning abilities of its readers. Pope was not the first to try to unite poetry and philosophy, but many authors had misgivings about doing so. One might have expected Beattie, whose *Minstrel* achieved such popularity, to make such an attempt, but he did not feel that philosophy and poetry could be yoked successfully together:

> Do you not think there is a sort of antipathy between philosophical and poetical genius? I question, whether any one person was ever eminent for both. Lucretius lays aside the poet when he assumes the philosopher, and the philosopher when he assumes the poet: In the one character he is truly excellent, in the other he is absolutely nonsensical. Hobbes was a tolerable metaphysician, but his poetry is the worst that ever was. Pope's 'Essay on Man' is the finest philosophical poem in the world; but it seems to me to do more honour to the imagination than to the understanding of its author: I mean, its sentiments are noble and affecting, its images and allusions apposite, beautiful, and new: its wit transcendently excellent; but the scientific part of it is very exceptionable. Whatever Pope borrows from Leibnitz, like most other metaphysical theories, is frivolous and unsatisfying: what Pope gives us of his own is energetic, irresistible, and divine. The incompatibility of philosophical and poetical genius is, I think, no unaccountable thing. Poetry exhibits the general qualities of a species; philosophy the particular qualities of individuals. *This* forms its conclusions from a painful and minute examination of single instances: *that* decides instantaneously, either from its own instinctive sagacity, or from a singular and unaccountable penetration, which at one glance sees all the instances which the philosopher must leisurely and progressively scrutinize, one by one. This persuades you gradually, and by detail; the other overpowers you in an instant by a single effort.[60]

Beattie's comments throw a good deal of direct as well as reflected light on the search for suitable literary forms for philosophical endeavour in the eighteenth century, and I think he has judged the weakness of *An Essay on Man* correctly. Poetry and philosophy may not be capable of being united in one enterprise, but no author (in English) has achieved so much as Pope has. In any case, *An Essay on Man* never laid any particular claims to philosophical innovation or revolution in the manner that the writings of Berkeley and Hume did, though generations of readers hostile to Pope have tried to insist that he was in fact trying to do just that. Pope's poem is more accurately seen as a restatement of 'old truths' attractively expressed, of a man thinking philosophically but employing the language and rhetoric associated with poetry. The popularity of the poem in the eighteenth century indicates that Pope had judged rightly his audience's taste for 'philosophy' presented in the more attractive disguise of poetry. I say 'disguise' deliberately, as the conclusive, consolidating nature of Pope's re-energizing of certain ideas is different in strategy and tactics from the efforts of philosophers to unpack the component parts of their perceptions, their experiences, and their inferences in order to reach a less imperfect understanding of human nature.

8. 'THE IDEAS WHICH ARE OFFERED TO THE MIND'

Beattie and Pope make strange bedfellows, either as poets or philosophers, but the popularity of their respective works gives us another clue to the development of interest in philosophical literature during their life-spans. To try to infer what readers in other centuries felt about the literature of their times is perhaps not so simple as it might seem, as the source to which one might turn most immediately, the correspondence of famous and not-so-famous authors, proves not so replete with data as one would like. For example, Pope's voluminous correspondence contains only one direct mention, and that a slight one, of Locke,[61] yet the whole of his writings, as well as his correspondence, is peppered with allusions to and dependencies upon Locke. Dr Johnson, who was undoubtedly the greatest reader of his age and perhaps of any age, makes only passing reference to Locke, though he draws upon Locke for quotations in the *Dictionary*. On the two occasions in his correspondence when he does mention Locke, on one he attributes to Locke a quotation that is proverbial, and on another he compares a manuscript 'Essay on Taste' by Frances Reynolds, the sister of Sir Joshua Reynolds, favourably to Locke and Pascal, assuring her that he is sincere. Yet, as reader, Johnson feels that the work is not ready for publication: 'Many of your notions seem not to be very clear in your own mind; many are not sufficiently developed and expanded for the common reader: it wants every where to be made smoother and plainer. You may by revisal and correction make it a very elegant and very curious work.'[62]

Johnson responds to this embryonic work both as writer and reader, seeing ways in which it has merit and ways in which it could be improved. Johnson's constant attention to the reader's psychological receptivity is, of course, a feature of all his writings, and few authors have ever made so emphatic a link between reading and behaviour. Even in a relatively light-hearted and easy essay such as *Adventurer* no. 137, Johnson can write, with unshakeable assurance, 'he that entertains himself with moral or religious treatises, will imperceptibly advance in goodness; the ideas which are often offered to the mind, will at last find a lucky moment when it is disposed to receive them'.[63] Johnson's emphasis on the extent to which reading can affect and determine behaviour is not an uncommon characteristic in the century, though it is one more often found in religious and theological writers than in poets, novelists, and essayists. Probably few eighteenth-century readers were as powerfully affected by literature as Johnson was, and his attitudes towards philosophical discourse are revealing. By no stretch of the imagination would one want to regard him as the 'common reader' to whom he alludes in his letter to Frances Reynolds, but he does provide an initial perspective from which one can make some tentative observations about readers of philosophical books in the eighteenth century.

That Johnson should choose to praise the work of Frances Reynolds by comparing it to the work of Locke and Pascal is in itself not only a measure of the esteem in which Locke and Pascal were held but reveals the extent to which philosophical ideas and philosophical writings had infused themselves into the consciousness of the reading public. In an age which sometimes assiduously sought and sometimes adventitiously found parallels in classical literature with its own accomplishments, the mere fact that Johnson chose to encourage Miss Reynolds by comparing her to modern philosophers rather than classical models indicates the readiness of the age to seek new ideas and to entertain new approaches. Johnson, for all his curmudgeonly defiance of writers like Hume and Bolingbroke, betrays in virtually every page of his writings a greater willingness to question received opinion and to reconsider old postulates than Beattie ever does. Nothing makes this clearer than his attitudes towards Berkeley and Hume. Berkeley he dismisses with comic gestures and with indifference, but Hume's method of reasoning, with its emphasis on experience and empirical enquiry, is too similar to his own for him to dismiss Hume's sceptical conclusions with equal equanimity. About most things, Johnson is willing to entertain the possibility that received opinions, or even his opinions, might be wrong, but not on the subject of religion. Like Beattie, he regards Hume as an enemy to religion, but, unlike Beattie, as an enemy with a good many arrows in his quiver. He never acknowledges directly the plausibility of Hume's scepticism, but the constant measures that he takes to reassure himself of the validity of Christianity are mute and moving testimonies to his doubts and fears.[64]

Johnson's reactions to philosophers and their writings cover a wide range. Boswell could always be certain of triggering off a printable outburst by bringing up a suitable name or topic. When the works of Henry St John, Viscount Bolingbroke, edited by Boswell's countryman, David Mallet, were published in 1754, Boswell recorded that

> The wild and pernicious ravings, under the name of 'Philosophy,' which were thus ushered into the world, gave great offence to all well-principled men. Johnson, hearing of their tendency, which nobody disputed, was roused with a just indignation, and pronounced this memorable sentence upon the noble author and his editor. 'Sir, he was a scoundrel, and a coward: a scoundrel, for charging a blunderbuss against religion and morality; a coward, because he had not resolution to fire it off himself, but left half a crown to a beggarly Scotchman, to draw the trigger after his death!'

Johnson's 'memorable sentence' might be more persuasive did we not know of his confession to Dr Charles Burney that he had 'never read Boling-broke's impiety'.[65] Nor did Bolingbroke escape Johnson's censure in the *Dictionary*, where he defined irony as a 'mode of speech in which the meaning is contrary to the words: as, *Bolingbroke was a holy man.*' Assuming that Johnson is not dissembling when he claimed never to have read Bolingbroke, one might reasonably infer that Johnson was as appalled by the testimonies to Bolingbroke's impiety as he was concerned about the pernicious effects that reading Bolingbroke's works might have. It is too facile to say either that Johnson was afraid of reading Bolingbroke or that he had furtively read Bolingbroke but wished to conceal having done so. It is somewhat less facile to say that, for Johnson, philosophical books which complemented and supplemented piety, religious decorum, and theological propriety could be safely read and recommended, but anything that tended towards heterodoxy or impiety could not even be allowed to satisfy curiosity.

Johnson's complex attitude towards authors and readers, ideas and actions, cannot be adequately summarized here, and, as anyone who has read, say, the preface to his edition of Shakespeare and *Rambler* no. 4 knows, his aesthetic criteria can often be at odds with his moral prerequisites. Moreover, he can be very specific in his abuse, as he is about Bolingbroke's collected works, but he can equally exercise charity when writing in more general terms about authors and the effects their writings can have. In *Rambler* no. 77, he admits that only a few men 'celebrated for theoretic wisdom, live with conformity to their precepts', but he acknowledges the corollary, i.e., that writers such as Bolingbroke may, for all their impiety, lead perfectly innocuous lives, only in an oblique way: 'The vicious moralist may be considered as a taper, by which we are lighted through the labyrinth of complicated passions; he extends his radiance farther than his heat, and guides all that are within view, but burns only those who make too near approaches.' Johnson is undoubtedly perplexed by the theoretical case of a writer whose works are full of moral wisdom yet whose own life and behaviour leave something to be desired, and perhaps even more perplexed by those whose debauched writings have not led to lives of unremitting wickedness. To be sure, Johnson comes down on the side of the former, but not without some misgivings: 'He, by whose writings the heart is rectified, the appetites counter-acted, and the passions repressed, may be considered as not unprofitable to the great republick of humanity, even though his behaviour should not always exemplify his rules.'[66] Such observations have an air of autobiography about them, as if Johnson were conscious that his moral precepts are struggling with his subjective inclinations.

Johnson's emphatic disavowal of any philosophical enquiry that might have subverted religion stems in part from a general lack of interest in philosophical topics. On several occasions, for example, Boswell tried to get him to discuss the concept of free will. One early attempt met with the well-known rejoinder, ' "Sir, (said he,) we *know* our will is free, and there's an end on't." ' On a later occasion, he 'avoided the question which has excruciated philosophers and divines, beyond any other'. Here, too, the topic is one with important theological overtones and consequences, and Boswell notes with regret his reluctance to be drawn into discussion: 'His supposed orthodoxy here cramped the vigorous powers of his understanding.' Some years later, in the presence of the nonconformist minister Dr Henry Mayo, Boswell was somewhat more successful and managed to elicit one or two observations from Johnson though he did not persist with the discussion: 'I was glad to find him so mild in discussing a question of the most abstract nature, involved with theological tenets, which he generally would not suffer to be in any degree opposed.'[67] What might have ensued had Boswell attempted to engage Johnson in a discussion of causality or of the operation of the understanding is probably a different matter. Johnson had little patience for abstract speculation, as Boswell dicovered, but when Boswell asked for guidance on various theoretical issues, Johnson would willingly recommend various books for his edification.

No doubt Johnson had settled many theological and philosophical issues in his own mind and, for many reasons, did not wish to disinter them. Boswell's interest in philosophical literature was greater than Johnson's, and he wanted guidance on such matters where Johnson would not have required it, indeed would have distrusted it. When Boswell had quizzed Johnson about Berkeley and had provoked the famous reply (above, p. 169), Boswell was not satisfied, nor could he see how Berkeley could be refuted. Johnson's reluctance to be drawn into discussions of philosophical topics or books, and Boswell's eagerness to do so measure not only the differences in the two men but differences in the way in which philosophical books could be read. For Johnson, books, of whatever kind, always had, or could be seen to have, practical consequences; for Boswell, books could sometimes, perhaps often, be theoretical exercises which one read for their novelty but which had no immediate effect upon one's day-to-day behaviour. The assumptions and attitudes that a reader brings with him to any book naturally and inevitably condition his estimation of the book's worth and prefigure its impact upon him. The differences between Boswell and Johnson as readers of philosophical books are not superficially great ones, but they point to a set of assumptions that values such books initially for their intrinsic, cognitive features and subsequently, if at all, for their utility. The topography of the intellectual landscape may be, or have been, the same, but the way in which readers like Boswell and Johnson could and did traverse it was certainly changing.

9. 'A CONTEMPT FOR THAT FICTITIOUS CHARACTER STYLED PHILOSOPHY'

The eagerness with which eighteenth-century readers turned to works of philosophy is also a witness to an unending quest for certitude, reassurance, or at least respectable company for one's fears and doubts. To read Hume was, perhaps, to be in the intellectual *avant-garde*; to read Beattie was, perhaps, to remind onself of the tactical hazards of being in that position. Beattie succeeded in comforting the afflicted, while Hume was more likely to afflict the comfortable. Yet both enjoyed more than common literary success. Any publisher who had suspected in the slightest that Beattie's *Essay on Truth* would sell like hot cakes would have jumped at the chance to publish it, and the success of many philosophical books suprised even those who had great philosophical gifts, as in the case of Hume and Lord Kames's *Elements of Criticism*. A turgid style was obviously no barrier to widespread acceptance by readers from a diversity of educational and cultural backgrounds; neither was clarity of style a guarantee of acceptance, as we can see in the example of Berkeley.

A troubled reader turning to philosophy in the eighteenth century would not have found much consolation for any deeply-held religious or theological beliefs. Even the most casual reader, whether modern or contemporary, would soon note that writers whose background was theological and whose profession was clerical often adopted not only the methodologies of the philosophers but their conclusions as well. The powerful and far-reaching effect of Joseph Butler's *Analogy of Religion* (1736) would have astonished a conventional clergyman from the seventeenth century, and even some of the more fundamentalist Christian sects today would find much in the work objectionable. The connection of philosophy and religion had been traditional, and readers in the eighteenth century might reasonably have expected to find a good deal more piety in philosophical works than they did. Equally, they would have found a good deal more 'philosophy' in theological works than they were aware of. The dissolution of the close intellectual relationship between philosophy and theology occurred almost unnoticed by most readers of philosophical literature in the eighteenth century, though it seems a fairly obvious one to us today.

Thus, a taste for reading abstract works and an inclination to piety might have led an eighteenth-century reader first to a theological book and then, by a sequence that hitherto would have been doctrinally unexceptionable, to a philosophical book. But philosophical books were opening up new areas of inquiry for newly literate readers. As a result, ideas that appeared inimical to Christianity, or at least to that form of Christianity advocated by Thwackum in *Tom Jones*,[68] began to infuse themselves into the consciousness of the newly literate. The various doctrinal controversies, e.g. the Bangorian controversy,[69] could only have undermined the autonomy of theology by illustrating to readers the potential for grave disagreement and misunderstanding in areas of intellectual endeavour that a reader might, not unreasonably, have associated with authority, rectitude, and propriety.

Philosophical books had the attraction for an eighteenth-century reader of offering both challenge and compromise, both adventurousness and accommodation. Traditional philosophical ideas and problems were explored from a diversity of angles and viewpoints, while the new emphasis on human understanding propelled readers into abstract consideration of themselves as among the more interesting and rewarding phenomena in the world. The variety of philosophical books available, the likelihood of yet another one appearing to catch the public's fancy, and the ease, the eagerness, and the respectability with which one could read philosophical books gave them a cachet that the imprimaturs of earlier philosophical books did not have. Horace Walpole, in one of his many characteristic dismissals of the value of philosophy, wrote to George Montagu (18 October 1766), 'I do not talk very sensibly, but I have a contempt for that fictitious character styled philosophy; I feel what I feel, and say I feel what I do feel.'[70] One would never regard Walpole as a man who put the reading of the latest philosophical book first on his list of priorities, but in his disparaging way, he has nevertheless measured out one of the motives that led other readers in the eighteenth century to philosophical books.

NOTES

1. Laurence Sterne, *Tristram Shandy*, ed. J. Work (New York, 1940), 85 (Bk 11, 2).
2. See the study by K. MacLean, *John Locke and English Literature of the Eighteenth Century* (New Haven, 1936). MacLean's pioneering work is indispensable, but much remains to be done on Locke's reputation and influence in the eighteenth century.
3. D. F. Bond (ed.), *The Spectator* (1965),

I, 44. All other quotations are from this edition. On Leonora cf. p. 215 below.

4. R. Halsband (ed.), *The Complete Letters of Lady Mary Wortley Montagu* (1967), III, 48. See John Locke, *An Essay Concerning Human Understanding*, ed. P. H. Nidditch (1975), IV, vi, 16; 591.

5. David Hume, *Enquiries Concerning Human Understanding and Concerning the Principles of Morals*, ed. L. A. Selby-Bigge, revised by P. H. Nidditch (1975), 165. The quotation is from the conclusion of the *Enquiry Concerning Human Understanding*, first published under the title of *Philosophical Essays Concerning Human Understanding*.

6. Bernard Nieuwentydt, *Het Regt Gebruik der Werelt Beschouwingen*, transl. John Chamberlayne, *The Religious Philosopher* (1718–19), I, vi.

7. Jonathan Swift, *Bickerstaff Papers*, ed. H. Davis (1957), 80.

8. H. Williams (ed.) *The Correspondence of Jonathan Swift* (1963), IV, 16, 23.

9. A. A. Luce and T. E. Jessop (eds.) *The Works of George Berkeley Bishop of Cloyne* (1948–57), III, 7.

10. Berkeley published the first of his tracts on tar water in 1744 under the title *Siris: A Chain of Philosophical Reflexions and Inquiries Concerning the Virtues of Tar Water*, and followed it with several pamphlets in the form of letters to his friends Thomas Prior and the Reverend Stephen Hales. See Luce and Jessop (eds.), *op. cit.*, V.

11. G. Sherburn (ed.), *The Correspondence of Alexander Pope*, (1956), IV, 514.

12. W. S. Lewis *et al.* (eds.), *The Yale Edition of the Correspondence of Horace Walpole* (New Haven, 1937–81), XVIII, 452.

13. James Boswell, *Life of Johnson*, ed. G. B. Hill and L. F. Powell (1934–64), I, 471–2.

14. Adam Smith, *Essays on Philosophical Subjects*, ed. W. P. D. Wightman and J. C. Bryce (1980), 148.

15. *Scots Mag.*, XXXIII (1771), 341. An adequate history of the Rankenian Club has yet to be written. E. C. Mossner suggests some sources in *The Life of David Hume* (1980), 617. The club is sketchily discussed in D. D. McElroy, *Scotland's Age of Improvement: A Survey of*

Eighteenth-Century Clubs and Societies (Pullman, 1969).

16. David Hume, *A Treatise of Human Nature*, ed. L. A. Selby-Bigge (1955), 17.

17. Boswell, *Johnson*, ed. Hill and Powell, II, 90; 16 October 1769.

18. J. Y. T. Greig (ed.), *The Letters of David Hume* (1932), I, 352.

19. *Ibid.*, II, 289–90.

20. Mossner, *Life of Hume*, 612.

21. Conyers Middleton, *The Miscellaneous Works* (1752), I, 187.

22. Edward Gibbon, *Memoirs of My Life*, ed. G. A. Bonnard (1966), 59.

23. B. Dobrée (ed.), *The Letters of Philip Dormer Stanhope, Fourth Earl of Chesterfield* (1932), 1232.

24. Middleton's book provoked a number of responses in the way of sermons, pamphlets, books, and letters. Oxford University, having slighted Middleton once, conferred a D.D. on Thomas Church for his *Vindication of the Miraculous Powers which subsisted in the Three First Centuries of the Christian Church* (1750) and conferred the same degree on William Dodwell for his *Free Answer to Dr. Middleton's Free Inquiry* (1749). John Wesley, who considered Middleton no better than a deist, criticized him in *A Letter to the Reverend Dr. Conyers Middleton* (1749). Middleton was preparing replies to the attacks upon him when he died on 28 July 1750.

25. A. Friedman (ed.), *Collected Works of Oliver Goldsmith* (1966), III, 161.

26. *Ibid.*, 85.

27. Greig (ed.), *op. cit.* I, 255.

28. A. Fowler, 'Genre and the literary canon', *New Literary History*, XI (1979–80), 106–8.

29. Hugh Blair, *Lectures on Rhetoric and Belles Lettres* (1783), II, 290–2.

30. R. M. Schmitz, *Hugh Blair* (New York, 1948), 62.

31. Smith devotes several lectures to historical writing, to rhetoric, and to stylistic analyses, to genres, etc., but says little about philosophical discourse *per se*, though he does comment on Shaftesbury's style. See J. M. Lothian (ed.), *Lectures on Rhetoric and Belles Lettres* (1963), 54.

32. For evidence of the popularity and influence of Blair's lectures, see Schmitz,

op. cit., 3, A. Hook, *Scotland and America* (1975), 75–92, and A. M. Williams, *The Scottish School of Rhetoric* (1897), *passim.*

33. Hume, *Enquiries*, ed. Nidditch, 7.

34. Quintilian records that Plato had written the first four words of the *Republic* in several different orders, so that the rhythm would be as perfect as possible; *The Institutio Oratoria of Quintilian*, tr. H. E. Butler (1953), III, 336–7 (VIII, 6, 64).

35. R. Klibansky and E. C. Mossner (eds.), *New Letters of David Hume* (1954), 2.

36. Mossner, *Life of Hume*, 612.

37. *Ibid.*, 122.

38. *History of the Works of the Learned* (1739), 359–90; 391–404.

39. N. Smith, 'Hume's "Rejected" essays', *Forum for Modern Language Studies*, VIII, 4 (October 1972), 354–71.

40. Klibansky and Mossner (eds.), *op. cit.*, 3.

41. Hume, *Enquiries*, ed. Nidditch, 16.

42. Greig (ed.), *op. cit.* I, 186–7.

43. Klibansky and Mossner (eds.), *op. cit.*, 3.

44. Berkeley's first book was *An Essay Towards a New Theory of Vision* (1709), but it might be more accurately described as a 'scientific' work rather than a philosophical one, although Adam Smith had described it as a philosophical work (see p. 169 above).

45. It was, however, one of the books that Hume wanted his friend Michael Ramsay to read in order better to understand his *Treatise of Human Nature.* See the letter to him in T. Kozanecki, 'Dawida Hume' a niezane listy w zbiorach Muzeum Czartoryskich (Polska)', *Archiwum Historii Filozofii i Mysli Sopolecznej*, IX (1963), 133–4.

46. Luce and Jessop (eds.), *op. cit.*, VIII, 35, 40.

47. *Ibid.*, II, 37, 40.

48. Greig (ed.), *op. cit.*, II, 301.

49. R. W. Chapman (ed.), *The Letters of Samuel Johnson* (1952), I, 279.

50. R. S. Walker (ed.), *James Beattie's London Diary, 1773* (1946), 47, 34.

51. W. Forbes, *An Account of the Life and Writings of James Beattie* (1806), I, 101.

52. *Ibid.*, I, 110–11.

53. *Ibid.*, I, 147–8.

54. James Beattie, *Essays: On the nature and immutability of Truth, in opposition to Sophistry and Scepticism* . . . [etc.] (1776), ix–x.

55. *Ibid.*, xii.

56. *Ibid.*, sig. a2^v.

57. M. Forbes, *Beattie and his Friends* (1904), 40–53.

58. See the discussion by G. Carnall and J. Butt in volume 8 of the Oxford History of English Literature, *The Mid-Eighteenth Century* (1979), 309–23.

59. Sherburn, *op. cit.*, III, 250.

60. W. Forbes, *op. cit.*, I, 93–4.

61. Sherburn, *op. cit.*, III, 433.

62. *The Letters of Samuel Johnson*, II, 433. Miss Reynolds revised the work, received further encouragement from Johnson, and eventually had 250 copies printed at her own expense in 1785; it was reprinted in 1789. Copies of the original 1785 edition disappeared without a trace (and copies of the 1789 version, slightly revised, were rare) until 1935, and in 1951 the Augustan Reprint Society reprinted it, with an introduction by J. L. Clifford.

63. Samuel Johnson, *The Idler* and *The Adventurer*, ed. W. J. Bate, J. M. Bullitt, L. F. Powell (The Yale Edition of The Works of Samuel Johnson, 1963), II, 491.

64. A similar point is made by E. C. Mossner in *The Forgotten Hume* (New York, 1943), 207.

65. Boswell, *Johnson*, ed. Hill and Powell, I, 268, 330; 6 March 1754, 15 April 1758.

66. Samuel Johnson, *The Rambler*, ed. W. J. Bate and A. B. Strauss (The Yale Edition of the Works of Samuel Johnson, 1969), IV, 40–41.

67. Boswell, *Johnson*, ed. Hill and Powell, II, 82, 104; III, 290; 16 and 26 October 1769; 15 April 1778.

68. 'When I mention Religion, I mean the Christian Religion; and not only the Christian Religion, but the Protestant Religion; and not only the Protestant Religion, but the Church of England.' Henry Fielding, *The History of Tom Jones*, ed. M. C. Battestin and F. Bowers (1974), I, 127 (III, iii).

69. In 1716, Benjamin Hoadly, Bishop of Bangor, published a pamphlet (and preached a sermon before the King to the same effect in the following year) in which he dismissed, among other things,

the need for an established church and
the authority of the Church over its
members; the pamphlet and the sermon

provoked over 200 replies within two or
three years.

70. Lewis *et al.* (eds.), *op. cit.*, x, 231.

8

Science books
and their readers in the
eighteenth century

G. S. ROUSSEAU

If science helped to give birth to the printed book, it was clearly the printed book
that sent science from its medieval habits straight into the boiling scientific
revolution. . . . It was of course the rapid dissemination of knowledge to whole
new classes that created the modern new attitudes to both science and religion
. . . (Derek de Solla Price, 'The Book as a Scientific Instrument', *Science*, CLVIII
(1967), 102–4[1]

. . . many books filled with profound philosophical [scientific] reasonings are
every day published in *England*; but correctness and elegance in Writing, and a
just taste in Architecture, Painting and Sculpture, are there still in their infant
state. (Madame du Bocage, 25 May 1750)

I. ENGLISH IDEOLOGY AND 'NATURAL PHILOSOPHY'

It is not surprising that natural philosophy – the study of the secular
natural world – should have begun to make its largest strides in the
Restoration period. Natural philosophy already possessed a significant
history by 1660 or 1680; this is clear merely from the repertoire of attitudes
held towards Aristotle, Bacon, Descartes and Malebranche.[2] And it was
discovering itself increasingly successful in deflecting students of moral
philosophy and theology, perhaps nowhere more evident than in the
remarkable career of Boyle, who had been attracted to both moral and
natural philosophy and who pronounced on both subjects, but who found
himself gradually enticed by the latter at the expense of the former. In the
Restoration period, natural philosophy enjoyed its own philosophy – what
we today would crudely call 'the philosophy of science': a belief that
increased study of the subject would eventually improve the lot of common

man. As a consequence of this 'philosophy of natural philosophy', and also because historians of natural philosophy then were often experimenters themselves – as were many of the early Fellows of the Royal Society – there was little interest in natural philosophy as a platform for political propaganda but great curiosity about it as an activity holding the potential for changing every aspect of man's sense of the universe about him. This new curiosity was more widespread among Britons than it had ever been before, and various explanations have been put forward to account for it. Puritanism in particular has been shown to have played a seminal role in the dissemination of the new curiosity about natural philosophy,[3] and the blend of social and political life in the years between the Great Revolution and the Glorious also contributed something distinctly unique,[4] as did the relation of the sexes and the notion that science was a masculine activity. Recently Simon Schaffer has brilliantly argued that the whole topography of natural philosophy in the Restoration can be attributed to monolithic interest in Newtonian matter-theory,[5] and in some fundamental sense this must be true. Others have persuasively shown that there is a sense in which 'natural philosophy' in the Restoration and early eighteenth century was a 'programme' *opposed* to progress in science, and that despite a shift in terminology the two types of 'natural philosophy' must not be viewed as similar in any way. Moreover, one school of natural philosophy – especially those who proposed universal language schemes – was clearly opposed to all thinking that was poetic and imaginative, and perhaps this group needs to be linked with the last. Finally, French scholars – Bachelard, Pecheux, Canguilhem, and especially Foucault – have argued that natural philosophy then was the *object* of an 'archaeology' aimed at unravelling significant world cosmologies, and no matter how hard one tries to combine this view with the previous three it is ultimately different.[6] These divergent approaches all have merit, and compel a modern student of 'eighteenth-century science and its books' to be vigilant when deciphering such a complex subject. Yet despite their differences, these three varieties of natural philosophy – as Newtonian matter theory, as hermetic pursuit, and as the object of an 'archaeology of knowledge' – share common ground. To the educated man in Restoration and eighteenth-century England, and perhaps to a few women, it was the most exciting of all subjects, ancient or modern, 'the genuine way to truth', as Malebranche had clearly decreed, and as Boyle repeated, the most certain means by which to understand the universe. But it was still 'God's' universe, and there was as yet no twentieth-century notion that what man does not understand – how the universe came into being and where it ends – he calls 'God'. Perhaps deism flourished for just this reason; and its popularity may have increased and waned in response to tensions felt and anxieties experienced over the degree to which the whole universe was 'God's'. What therefore began on the return of Charles II as an ideology to which a certain number of 'Baconians' adhered,[7] was transformed by the turn of the century into a widespread agreement about the soundness of natural philosophy – in whatever way it was construed – as the only route to 'truth'.

Once the scientific *via sacra* was established it also became fashionable. To cultivate 'natural philosophy', no matter how loosely defined, was to bring status to oneself, such as that enjoyed by the men who were collectors.[8] Yet these men and women collected specimens – rocks, shells, seeds, flowers, even instruments – in a religious and ideological climate which seemed incapable after 1660 of separating God and the natural universe. There was no inherent contradiction between religion and science, as there would be in the nineteenth century and even more emphatically in our own. Robert Boyle's best-known book, *The Christian Virtuoso*, renders this point patent even in its title: *Shewing that by being addicted to Experimental Philosophy, a man is rather assisted, than indisposed, to be a good Christian*, and the extreme notion of 'natural philosophy' as an 'addiction' is purposefully intended. Also, the rapid dissemination of deistic ideas in the Restoration period – and among all social classes – rendered it fashionable as well as 'pious' for men to explore the whole universe through which God had decided to reveal himself.[9] Furthermore, widely held if contradictory beliefs about the 'argument from design' – the notion that the more one understood the physical universe, the better one would then comprehend the wondrous planner who had brought all this universe into being – and the 'argument from the limitations of reason' – the idea that no matter how much man penetrated into the physical universe, his limited reason would never permit him to penetrate the deepest mysteries, not even with God's aid – ensured a common perception that God had aggressively invited men to try to unlock the secrets of the universe. Man consequently needed to cultivate humility and to implore the deity to assist him in two very distinct directions.[10] Exploration of God's creation was perhaps the best way to understand the moral as well as the physical universe; but no sooner had man begun to explore it, to experiment with its elements, than he began to align himself with other explorers, both amateur and professional. Man discovered the human element in the activities of 'natural philosophy', especially when he began to ponder and write about his experiences. The emphasis, therefore, of some recent students on the inferior quality of the 'new science' produced by the eighteenth-century *virtuosi* – those so-called amateurs who would be increasingly ridiculed after 1700[11] – is in a sense beside the mark. It is a 'whig' approach to cultural history that also errs by minimizing scientific activity as human experience – and we shall also see how it can cause modern scholars to misunderstand 'the rise of scientific books' after 1660. More consequential, surely, than the quality of science was the awakened interest of the *virtuosi* in a realm – the physical – in which they had been lethargic before.[12] For this reason the 'collections' of eighteenth-century men – of which books constitute a part – differ from those of their seventeenth-century predecessors. The 'Virtuoso-class', as Pope referred to himself,[13] now began to collect rocks and shells, telescopes and microscopes, books and pamphlets, instruments and clocks, and to gaze at the stars and planets, as well as to perform experiments of all types – to do everything to quench its wonder about this physical universe that was living proof of God's goodness. And fortunately, for the first time in economic history, a large segment of British society could afford to indulge this natural and relgious curiosity. 'Literary men' were as sedulous in these avocations as 'professional scientists' because they are never independent of the cultural environment, and also in part because it was now so fashionable to be part of Pope's 'Virtuoso-class'.[14] The Baconianism which derived from the *Novum Organum*, and which had figured so prominently in the manifestos of some serious experimenters in the Restoration period,[15] was now enhanced by current religious, ideological, social – even fashionable – factors. Not to endorse natural philosophy in some form or shape among the fashionable select few was to be a misfit, out of tune with the whole spirit of the age.

The Royal Society, which was formed in 1660 and received its charter shortly thereafter, also played a significant rôle in the common man's thinking about 'natural philosophy'. But books, not the Royal Society, as de Solla Price has also noticed in the epigraph of this essay, transformed the common man's attitude to science and shaped the 'modern' beliefs we have opposed to the 'medieval'. Historians have studied the influence of the Royal Society in greater detail than there is space for here,[16] yet sometimes without noticing to what extent interest in this 'colledge of learned men' itself evoked an interest in *books* about natural philosophy. The reading of books, as Sprat and other early historians of the Society reflected, was in no way a primary purpose of the organization; indeed, its motto, echoing Horace, *nullius addictus iurare in verba magistri* – 'bound to the word of no one' – mandated just the opposite: that the word counted for little and that language was too ambiguous to be trustworthy as evidence of anything.[17] Nevertheless, despite the anti-linguistic stand of the early Royal Society, its scientific and non-scientific members were addicted to books no less than Boyle's 'Christians' were addicted to 'experimental philosphy'. Both the professional scientists in the society, especially the physicians – of which there were many – and the literary men were book collectors, some collectors of note. Furthermore, the earliest Fellows themselves wrote papers and books which were recognized from the outset as of immense importance, and no contradiction between distrust of the word and application to it was seen. As early as 1679 Hobbes maintained that *The Philosophical Transactions* had veritably superseded academic textbooks, 'And as for Natural Philosophy, is it not remov'd from *Oxford* and *Cambridge* to *Gresham-College* in London, and to be learn'd out of their *Gazets?*'[18] These *Philosophical Transactions*, especially the *Abridgements*, continued to be reprinted throughout the eighteenth century – even Swift used a cheap 'penny edition' – and to find avid readers. They were widely advertised in newspapers and magazines, and aimed at large audiences. More important, the authors of these 'scientific' papers themselves read books – which we would call 'science books'.[19] If it is true that the largest single group of Fellows consisted of physicians, then the point about buying and collecting science books gathers even greater strength, for physicians were the one group, even more than university professors and scholars, who could afford to buy science books that were usually not cheap.[20] As the cults of 'natural philosophy' ideologically grew stronger and more fashionable, and as more men and women[21] began to dabble in as well as grow serious about them, the need for such books increased. Whether the period from 1660 to 1700 represents an unparalleled epoch in the demand for and subsequent production of science books is a topic to be explored below; at this point it is necessary only to understand why there was such a sudden increase of books published about 'natural philosophy' after the Restoration, and what rôle organized bodies such as the Royal Society played in this development.[22]

The ideology of a given culture is always elusive and difficult to gauge. Karl Mannheim has written that 'it is only when we more or less consciously seek to discover the source of [a collective society's] untruthfulness in a social factor, that we are properly making an ideological interpretation'.[23] This may be requisite, but there is no doubt that by 1700 or 1720 the various rôles of natural philosophy – even in its protean shapes – had altered from those demonstrated at the opening of the Restoration period, and that books lie at the centre of the change. The evidence to support the contention is abundant: the establishment of the Boyle Lectures is perhaps the weightiest, but it must not be forgotten that stipulated in the lecturer's agreement was a clause requiring him to submit a text, however much expanded over the original monthly sermon, which could be printed. The further fact that the most distinguished chemist of the age endowed lectures to establish a proper relationship between 'natural religion' and 'natural philosophy' speaks plainly for itself, as do the titles of the early lectures.[24] Margaret Jacob has shown that the Boyle Lectures 'were controlled by the latitudinarians and in particular by Thomas Tenison ... and John Evelyn', and, furthermore, that 'in the early eighteenth century the lectureship served as a podium for latitudinarian thought and for Newtonianism'.[25] No reason exists to doubt the assertion; yet even so, the Boyle Lectures in their *printed* version, as distinct from the monthly sermon, were a powerful collective weapon for disseminating Newtonian thought. Without the printed version, it is unlikely that the 'modern new attitudes to science' of which de Solla Price speaks could have been adopted in such a relatively brief period of time; and the Boyle Lectures – as we shall see – are but one of several examples. With powerful minds such as Boyle and Newton assisting, however indirectly, in the wedding of science and religion; with the diligence and industry of such men as John Martyn, the Royal Society's first printer; with the new literacy of the common man making gargantuan strides during the early decades of the eighteenth century;[26] and with the international reputation the British were establishing for themselves – as Madame du Bocage comments in her travel book – as the purveyors of science and reason over taste and elegance,[27] it is not surprising that by 1750 or so natural-philosophy books should have been the most sought after of all printed books. It is true, a few members of the literary establishment continued to savage and even sabotage the practitioners of the 'new science' and all they represented, but in almost every case – such as that of the Scriblerians – these attacks were made against pedantry and corruptions of learning rather than in defiance of the new widespread cults of natural philosophy.[28] Addison's attitude is typical of these attacks; a spiritual son of Dryden and a proponent of the new blend of Protestantism and Newtonianism, he nevertheless fears the 'dulness of the Royal Society' and fails to see the point of 'collecting Nature's refuse':

> they [the Royal Society] seem to be in a confederacy against Men of polite Genius, noble Thought, and diffuse Learning; and chuse into their Assemblies such as have no Pretence to Wisdom, but Want of Wit; or to natural Knowledge, but ignorance of everything else. . . . When I meet with a young Fellow that is an humble Admirer of the Sciences, but more dull than the rest of the Company, I conclude him to be a Fellow of the Royal Society.[29]

Yet Addison never minded that Newton had been 'a Fellow' of this society. Perhaps 'wit' is after all the clue: by 'wit' Addison designates 'quick natural ability expressed in refined language'; his objection about 'Want of Wit' centres on a lack of linguistic facility – the very facility against which so many early Fellows rebelled. Addison could not understand why learned men who could be cultivating their 'wits' were instead wasting precious time collecting specimens: 'It is indeed wonderful to consider, that there should be a sort of learned Men, who are wholly employed in gathering together the Refuse of Nature, if I may call it so, and hoarding up in their Chests and Cabinets such Creatures as others industriously avoid the Sight of.'[30] But if we remember that these scientists also wrote *books* about their activities, and even about the specimens they had 'hoarded', then it is not so hard to comprehend Addison's drift. A Fellow of the Royal Society is not dull because of the *source* of his wonder – Addison himself gazed in steady wonder at the stars night after night – but because of linguistic failure, because he cannot compose a good book. Pope and the Scriblerians made the very same charges in *The Memoirs of Martinus Scriblerus,* just as Pope and Warburton were to charge much later in their joint venture, *The New Dunciad: Notes and Variorum* (1742). Yet not one of these men can justly be said to be 'anti-science'. All these attacks on science – by Swift, Addison, Pope and many others – issue from a segment of the literary milieu worried about the infringement of 'natural philosophy' on 'the territory of wit', yet not out of any opposition to the pursuit of science itself or to the hopes for progress science was capable of offering mankind.[31] To what degree the attitudes to science held by literati of the early eighteenth century – both Grub-Street hacks and great writers – were shaped by their political ideology, is a subject that has not yet been studied.[32] But their acid criticism of 'natural philosophy' almost always occurs within the context of books, printed books. Had the scientists of the early eighteenth century not paraded their learning in treatise upon treatise, the Popes and Swifts would have left them alone. But they would not stop writing – making books. Pope's pronouncement on all pedants in the *Dunciad* could be made to apply as readily to them: 'Forever writing, never to be read.'

2. EDUCATION IN AND POPULARIZATION OF 'NATURAL PHILOSOPHY'

Such a state of affairs naturally changed the course of eighteenth-century education, but not at once. At the opening of the Restoration period, a student at any of the better schools – even old schools such as Eton and Winchester – would not be instructed in 'natural-philosophy' subjects except for arithmetic and geometry, which had been taught in English schools at least since 1500.[33] At approximately the same time the utility of the ancient languages was being called in question by educational propagandists who were increasingly seeking to instruct children through 'nature' and 'the concrete'. But they were a small minority and barely noticeable. The anonymous author of *An Enquiry into the Melancholy Circumstances of Great Britain* (1740), who advocated overthrow of the 'dead languages' in preference for more useful subjects like the principles of business and 'numbers', would not have found many followers in 1660, but as the seventeenth century wore out and the new century began, more and more educators were turning to this point of view.[34] Locke's philosophy also encouraged this point of view, as did the new needs of the expanding middle class; but actual reform and change proceeded slowly, as a survey of the whole period 1660 to 1800 demonstrates. As late as 1684 Reeve Williams clearly failed to be appointed master of the mathematics school in Christ's Hospital – then a leading school – because he was 'merely a mathematician' and not a classical scholar, on the premise that boys who studied maths ought to be thoroughly proficient in the grammar and vocabulary of the ancient tongues.[35] At most schools mathematics was not part of the normal curriculum, and there was consequently no need for mathematics textbooks. Dr Busby of Westminster, the London school attended by so many *virtuosi* in the Restoration period, taught maths throughout his tenure as headmaster, using Oughtred's *Clavis mathematicae* and Isaac Barrow's *Euclid's Elements*,[36] but he was unusual. In most other schools students could only learn mathematics by paying a tutor extra sums, as even Joseph Banks, the naturalist, found himself compelled to do a century later.[37] When Thomas James, the headmaster of Rugby who published a school edition of *Euclid* in 1791, reminisced about Eton College in the 1760s,[38] he used this occasion, as he had previous ones, to urge the College to include arithmetic and geography in the main curriculum on the grounds that they are crucial; and he advised that 'these sciences' be taught 'on a Holyday, or Half Holyday',[39] so that other subjects would not lose time. But around 1700 there was little sense of the belief Bentham would have in the next century that 'the sciences' are ultimately more useful subjects than any others because 'they strengthen the mind, preclude superstition and lay the basis for future employment'.[40] The problem of change was administrative as well as philosophical. The early inclusion of Locke in the syllabus at Cambridge shows that the university at least tried to modify its curriculum, whereas Oxford apparently did not. But even Cambridge did not alter its programme of studies enough, and the dissenting academies continued to attract all types of students who were not in fact dissenters precisely because of the altered shape of their curricula. The grammar schools, unlike Cambridge, were usually restricted by their charters and statutes – as is evident in some of the above instances – which required them to teach the classics. A celebrated eighteenth-century law suit involving the statutes of the Leeds Grammar School demonstrates how difficult it often was then to teach non-classical subjects such as 'science'. In view of this administrative state of affairs and educational philosophy, it is not surprising that few science textbooks for school use exist in our period, at least not until the late eighteenth century. Editions of Euclid were common, and they continued to increase as the eighteenth century wore on.[41] And texts in arithmetic, such as Oughtred and Barrow, and in algebra – especially John Wallis's *Treatise of Algebra* – followed as seconds in numbers of editions, but apart from these, what we would call 'science text books' for daily use in schools were not yet known.[42] The situation *vis à vis* science instruction in dissenting academies is somewhat different, certainly by the middle of the eighteenth century; but even in these schools students rarely purchased the books which their masters either read or on which they had based their lectures.[43] The facts then are these: certainly some books existed, but they were not used; masters and students alike complained of the unavailability of science books; and most schools did not teach subjects included under the heading 'natural philosophy' – not so old itself – so there was seemingly no need for the books. The situation was something of a Catch-22: science books for school use were not needed, and because they were not needed they did not exist in any great numbers.

Science instruction in colleges and universities was different, even if the universities had fallen into the decline about which much has been written. Christopher Wordsworth, the Edwardian Fellow of Peterhouse, captured the essence of academic life at the university when he described how Richard Watson became a professor of chemistry at Cambridge, and the point sheds light on science books at Cambridge and Oxford.[44] Watson had grown tired of mathematics and thought he could achieve fame – in the 1760s – by turning himself into a professor of chemistry, then the most fashionable of scientific subjects. 'He had never read a single word on the subject', Wordsworth comments using all sorts of reliable sources, 'nor seen a single experiment in it'. Therefore 'he sent for an operator from Paris, and buried himself . . . in his laboratory . . . and was soon able to interest a very full audience [at the university in Cambridge] of all ages and degrees'.[45] If the account appears hyperbolic, the substance of Watson's transformation probably is not; the episode supports the point that in a half century or so – from 1710 to about 1760 – science in Cambridge and Oxford had not altered. Gunther notes that in 1661, Newton came up to Trinity 'with nothing in mathematics',[46] and then cites an anonymous critic who accused the English universities of neglecting science except 'when some exceptional person has honoured the university'.[47] A century later, in 1759, Goldsmith made the same point, arguing that the English universities neglect learning, especially natural science, and exist merely to ensure 'the best chance of [one's] becoming great'.[48] Yet Goldsmith thought the real problem to be the schools rather than the colleges: 'might natural philosophy be made their pastime at school, by this means it would in college become their amusement'. Natural philosophy, then, was a problem after all, and had continued to be one for almost a hundred years. Hundreds of comments like those of Wordsworth and Goldsmith can be accumulated; there is no dearth of material. The issue about science and the science books students used in the universities is not whether the books were available, but rather the *extent* to which they were purchased and consulted and how they were read if they were read at all. No mystery exists about the titles and publishers of these science books: Christopher Wordsworth and others have carefully outlined the studies of typical students at Cambridge, the books they read and at what stage they read them: for example, 'Books in use at *Cambridge* about the year 1730, for *Arithmetic, Algebra, Geometry, Physics, Mechanics,* and *Hydrostatics*'; 'A list of Books used at Cambridge about the year 1730 for *Optics* and *Astronomy*'; 'Daniel Waterlands [sic] Advice to a Young

G. S. Rousseau

Cambridge Student With a method of study for the four first Years 1706–40'.[49] Certain books were used, but the issue, surely, is rather in what quantities these books were published, at what prices, and how far the economics of printing was a determinant of use. Wordsworth affirms without authority that by 1710 'the study of natural philosophy was extensively diffused in the university, and copies of the *Principia* were in such request that . . . one which was originally published at *ten shillings* was [now in 1710] considered cheap at *two guineas*'.[50] Two trends seem clear from the available evidence: first, as the eighteenth century progressed the sciences grew increasingly important at the universities and a certain expansion of the use of science textbooks occurred, and secondly, the adoption of Newtonian principles in the first decade of the century spurred the composition and publication of university textbooks.[51] If the first point seems apparent, the second is somewhat deceptive, at least so far as cause and effect are implicated. That is, was the dissemination of Newtonianism in the universities the excuse for composition of new texts based on these Newtonian principles, or was the sudden need for textbooks the excuse for merely inserting or intruding Newtonian principles? If one contends that the spread of 'natural philosophy' as a taught subject in universities in the early eighteenth century is but the master's – Newton's – campaign to have his principles universally adopted, then the problem is evanescent. But if not, then a question looms about an increase of science books after 1700 directly aimed at university students.[52] After the mid-century, the growth of 'life sciences' – especially botany and chemistry – is rapid and concentrated in the universities and, even more so, in dissenting academies such as the famous one in Warrington.[53] Historians of science have charted the terrain of the life sciences after 1750 rather well, but the puzzling question relates to the early century and to the so-called 'early books' of science published between 1700 and 1710, when a certain flowering is observed. There may indeed be other explanations for this surge than Newton and Newtonianism, but if Newton's campaign was as concerted as modern scholarship would have us believe, then the sociologists may be correct after all about the social origins of scientific knowledge.[54]

The availability and use of science textbooks in military schools is even more nebulous than in the universities. Early eighteenth-century military academies did not teach scientific subjects and required few books. Sir Herbert Richmond, the naval historian, comments that 'in the Navy, there was little in the way of book-learning', and that 'a boy's education depended on a captain under whom he served'.[55] This trend is confirmed by many sources, although sometimes the boy copied out of printed books as distinct from his master's lecture notes. In 1750 Robert Sandham wrote to his mother from Woolwich 'I have written [i.e. copied out] all Mr Muller's Artillery which is 40 octavo pages'.[56] But John Muller was then

206

the headmaster at Woolwich, a teacher called Boswell in the *Life of Johnson* 'the scholastick father of all the great engineers of this country', and the book referred to is his recently printed *Treatise Containing the Elementary Part of Fortification . . . for the Use of Royal Academy of Artillery at Woolwich* (1746). F. G. Guggisberg, a captain himself and later on a distinguished military historian, is more specific about the eighteenth century:

> The difficulty of teaching in these early days [the eighteenth century] was greater than at present, owing to the scarcity of printed books of instruction. The cadets themselves had none to guide them in military subjects, and could only learn by copying the masters' MSS. and drawings, making notes from their lectures, and carefully acquiring by memory the practical part of the sciences. In mathematics there was considerable improvement in this respect, as several treatises existed on the various branches.[57]

The 'scarcity of printed books' is curious, yet this is the strain constantly repeated among all types of educators of the period. Considering the subjects the young cadets needed to study – especially in mathematics and astronomy – there certainly were plenty of existing texts: editions of Euclid, Oughtred, all types of geometry textbooks, a variety of books about geography, cosmology and navigation. But the masters continued to complain that printed books were unobtainable, and that this is why the students must copy their assignments out of the masters' notes. In view of the disparity between fact and complaint, it may well be that the masters saw how they could advance themselves: what better reason to tidy up their lecture notes and peddle them to booksellers in the name of need?[58] Even if this is what actually happened, such publications cannot have found many students in military schools, for the Royal Naval Academy at Portsmouth Dockyard, for example, was started in 1729 with only a handful of students, the Royal Academy at Woolwich in 1741 with space for only 20 cadets, the Royal Military College at Sandhurst in 1799 with not many more.[59] Students in all military academies combined could not have totalled many more than 300 by 1800 – a figure that must give pause to the student of eighteenth-century book production. Furthermore, although instruction in mathematics and navigation apparently was required, this was of an elementary level only, and the Newtonian texts being adopted in colleges and universities were never used. Finally, more difficult scientific subjects such as hydrostatics, chemistry and physics were never introduced into the formal education of an English cadet until the mid-Victorian period,[60] so there can have been no need whatever for these books.

England's coffee houses, her 'penny universities' rather than her military academies, colleges, or universities, were the authentic source of the popularization of 'natural philosophy' in the eighteenth century, as well as the origin of many of its books. So much evidence exists to support the affirmation that it is impossible to compress it into a small space.[61] The epoch marks the heyday of the coffee house and neighbourhood academy as institutions of learning, and the primary reason may be that the new widespread literacy c. 1700 increased the demand – a veritable hunger – for knowledge among adults. Such is the contention of one historian of education,[62] and others have joined in the chorus. J. T. Desaguliers, the indefatigable popularizer of Newton and an erudite mathematician in his own right, has explained why there was a sudden demand in the early eighteenth century for published lecture notes. In the preface to his *Physico-Mechanical Lectures*, which he had delivered from 1712 to 1717 in a 'private academy' in Little Tower Street and later published, he wrote:

> the following papers being only minutes of my lectures for the use of such gentlemen as have been my auditors, were printed at their desire; to save the trouble of writing them over for every person. Therefore, I beg all such readers as have not seen my course of experiments, to pardon my want of method . . . and desire them not to expect a full account of all the experiments made in the course.[63]

The formula executed was straightforward: the printed book was a student's manual, and as such had to be brief, clear, simple, accessible to all readers, uncluttered by irrelevancies and remarks on methodology, and reasonably priced. Desagulier's success in both lecturing and then selling his 'lecture notes' as a printed manual – a 'science book' – was followed by others. Examples include Whiston, whose brilliant lectures dazzled Pope and whose similar albeit expensive illustrated manual, *The Copernicus* (1715), Pope purchased; Thomas Watts and Benjamin Worster who also lectured at the Tower Street Academy and who printed manuals; James Stirling at the Bedford Coffee House and many others.[64] These itinerant popularizers worked hand-in-hand with the printers and booksellers, often delivering the lectures on their (the printer's or bookseller's) premises, as in the case of some of these just mentioned.[65] Profit from this type of publication – perhaps the most significant form of popularization of natural philosophy – was obtained by all three entrepreneurs, lecturer or teacher, printer, and bookseller, and all three exploited a ready market. By the 1730s public lecturing was an established business, a profession with a modest guaranteed income for the teacher, as can be gleaned from several 'projects' and 'manuals' such as the *Proposals for a Course of Chemical Experiments with a View to Practical Philosophy* offered in 1731 by Shaw and Hauksbee,[66] who soon afterwards went on tour in the provinces with considerable success. By mid-century a large number of scientific societies and book clubs had come into existence, all of whose members demanded printed science books and could now afford one or two. The published lectures of 'the Professors of Gresham College' continued well into the eighteenth century and satisfied a small group of readers who had been lucky enough to obtain advanced training and who could understand technical language; the more typical adult reader who had not been fortunate enough to attend an academy or university, and whose total exposure to science derived from the public lectures of popularizers like Desaguliers and Whiston, wanted shorter and easier books than a lengthy treatise by a Gresham professor. Yet no books were so popular as the manuals used for courses of public lectures which the reader had already attended or which he was then in the process of hearing. Not even a repertoire of 'how-to-do-it' books for businessmen – works such as John Ayres's *Arithmetick: a Treatise Designed for the Use . . . of Tradesmen* (1710) – could compete with the coffee-house manuals. If only as much were known about the science books never intended for public lectures – books meant to be read in the solitude of one's own chamber – the scholar could speak with much greater authority on the subject of eighteenth-century science books.

The extraordinary aspect of the eighteenth-century coffee house – especially in the period before 1720 – is the clear way in which its proprietors and all those involved in its commercial life adopted *natural philosophy* as the chosen subject. Perhaps this reflects nothing more than popular taste, yet it is astonishing to learn that the general public preferred 'science' to all other subjects. Two recent social historians have attributed much of the scientific progress and industrial advance of the era to the men and women who convened in the 'penny universities': 'scientific advance came *mainly* from the activities of groups and societies meeting at first in the London coffee houses, and from public lecture courses given by scientists who were often of some note in their day'.[67] This was no doubt true, but if a significant number of the science books of the era were the published versions of these courses, in 'penny universities' and 'natural philosophy book clubs', then it is essential to understand the genesis of these books. The same social historians have provided a clue: 'these clubs', they note, 'were patronized largely by medical men, dissenting ministers and manu-facturers. . . .' They may have been 'patronized largely' by such men, but members of other professions frequented them as well. Moreover, all those who frequented the coffee houses and joined clubs for *social* in addition to scientific reasons – writers, artists and politicians – are omitted from this consideration, especially great writers such as Pope on whom the influence of Whiston was enormous. The crucial issue then is not numbers but types, and there is little doubt that for every Pope or Steele who became an habitué at Buttons to hear Whiston or Desaguliers lecture, dozens of other social types – men and women from many different walks of life – frequented the coffee houses to 'be seen' and to quench their curiosity, to familiarize themselves with the 'new science', and in many cases to apply this knowledge to commerce and industry.[68] The reasons for attendance are so different that it is impossible to condense them to two or three, and for just as many different purposes readers bought these 'coffee-house books'. From the instructor's point of view – whether speaking in a coffee house, private home, or small academy such as that in Tower Street – the task before him was equally manifold: first and foremost to fill the room and *sell* his published lectures (this is why the booksellers were so attentive to itinerant lecturers as a new professional type); then to cater to the most influential group in the audience, those genuinely capable of arranging for another set of lecture-demonstrations; and lastly to arouse more interest in natural philosophy so that all members of the audience would return next time.[69] As the eighteenth century wore on and the coffee-house audiences proliferated, various groups splintered: those interested only in the application of the new science formed clubs like the Spitalfields Mathematical Society (1717) where they could discuss and compare their 'inventions'; others concerned with one branch only – mathematics – established organizations such as the Northampton Mathematical Society (1721) and the Manchester Mathematical Society (1718); the Spalding Gentleman's Society (1717) was composed primarily of literary 'gentlemen' who reckoned themselves 'projectors' and virtuosi in their spare time. The most important development for science books is that in every case formation led to some type of publication, and this is why any account of the spread of science books that omits discussion of these penny universities is inchoate and can never satisfactorily explain why these books were suddenly in such great demand.[70] A new type of book had come into being for a brand new readership.[71] Much of the financial profit was divided between itinerant lecturer and bookseller, who were identical in certain instances, but there had been nothing like this new consortium – lecturer, bookseller, habitué or club member – in the previous century.

Viewed in the single dimension of 'content' this new book changed over the decades.[72] If the early (1700–20) species of the genre reflect an audience new and unaccustomed to natural philosophy, later specimens at mid-century do not. Mechanics, hydrostatics, pneumatics and optics continued to be popular throughout the century, but astronomy and mathematics waned as 'natural history' – botany, biology, and zoology – overtook and gradually supplanted it. Furthermore, all these books grew lengthier as the century wore on and as their authors assumed a readership far more adept in natural science than earlier readers had been. A comparison of these popular books with the Boyle Lectures, which continued to be published throughout roughly the same period (from 1691 to 1735), clinches the point: whereas the Boyle Lectures are large expensive tomes (the average volume cost over £2) filled with religious and metaphysical disquisitions and speculations, these popular lecture books are short, practical, accessible, adjusted to the literal-minded reader. Their style is usually clipped and plain, composed of short sentences and with figurative language played down as much as possible. The vocabulary employed is easy, and when technical or difficult words are used they are instantly defined. Experiments demonstrated in the coffee house are rehearsed and simplified, and mechanical instruments – such as Whiston's *The Copernicus*, a perpetual calendar of the skies permitting the user to predict precisely when future eclipses would occur – are diagrammed and fully explained. Engraved plates and other charts and diagrams contain clear legends and simple explications. The reader understands from the outset that the book in his hand is not a work of art or philosophy – nothing shaped and meditated upon – but a manual, a how-to-do-it book for those who have been attending the private demonstrations and listening to the lecturer.

The dissemination of natural philosophy – more accurately of 'cults of natural philosophy' of which popular science books constituted only one aspect – also intensified a need for dictionaries and almanacs of all types, inexpensive as well as dear, handy as well as decorative and handsome. Historically speaking, it would be false to contend that these widespread cults in themselves created a market for such books, for such dictionaries had also been written, although in fewer numbers, in the Restoration period: Richard Read's *Secrets of Art and Nature . . . being the Summe and Substance of Natural Philosophy* (1660); Richard Blome's *The Gentlemans* [sic] *Recreation* (1686); Richard Neve's *Apopiroscopy: . . . a Faithful History of Observations and Experiments* (1702); John Harris's instantly popular *Lexicon Technicum* (1704),[73] and several others. But the dissemination of natural philosophy after 1710 or 1720 caused an unprecedented consumer-interest in popular science books, a consumption that continued into the early nineteenth century and that stemmed from the typical Englishman's new commercialization of leisure, in Professor Plumb's phrase, and that could be witnessed after 1800 in such popular 'science books' as John Paris's *Philosophy in Sport Made Science in Earnest; Being an Attempt to Illustrate the First Principles of Natural Philosophy . . .* (1827). As several cultural historians have noted, the eighteenth century was an epoch of general dictionaries;[74] but it has not always been clear to what extent this propensity to compile dictionaries was actually channelled into the 'arts and sciences', that is, to dictionaries of scientific subjects as distinct from religious, historical, or other general types of dictionaries. From beginning to end, every decade of the eighteenth century brought to light an increase in the number of these compendious works – compiled by John Harris, Ephraim Chambers, Robert James – for reasons having as much to do with profit for the bookseller as with the public's craving for scientific knowledge. For example, both Ephraim Chambers and his publisher, David Midwinter, reaped huge profits from the *Cyclopaedia* – best described as a popular 'science dictionary' – which first appeared in 1728 and went through a dozen editions and revisions by 1779. William Strahan realized what a best seller this dictionary was, and bought the rights to reprint it in 1778, eventually adding to his fortune by doing so.[75] Robert James's *Medicinal Dictionary* (1743), to which Johnson contributed, reveals a similar history based on immediate success and subsequent reissue yielding vast amounts of money to the printer and bookseller, as do the various scientific dictionaries of Richard Brookes from which Goldsmith plundered so much, as we shall see, in his *History of the Earth and Animated Nature*. There is not enough space here to list even a fraction of the mid-century, let alone the late eighteenth-century, dictionaries; such a list, taken together with an analysis of the royalties gained by author and bookseller, would soon render evident to what extent the new literate public was buying these books.[76] By contrast the encyclopaedias of this period are perhaps not so prolific as the dictionaries, but they contain more scientific information than any previous compendia. As natural philosophy grew increasingly technical and specialized, dictionaries and encyclopaedias, like other popular works, grew more specialized too: no longer general compendia of 'arts and sciences', or even more narrowly of 'natural philosophy', dictionaries after 1720 or thereabout were more specifically dictionaries of mathematics, dictionaries of astronomy, dictionaries of geography, and so forth.[77] Medical dictionaries incorporating hard words – words unknown to the layman, such as those found in a handbook of diseases or in the pharmacopoeia – had appeared from the Restoration onward, so this continuation into the eighteenth century was not a new development, perhaps because medicine served a different social rôle, but the fragmentation of science dictionaries into specialized works marked the beginning of a publishing trend that continues to the present day. The rôle of the British press in this dissemination of science through popular dictionaries has not been fully explored, but scholars – even historians of science – are beginning to realize that the surge in science c. 1700–50 coincides with another development in publishing, namely 'the scientific press in transition'.[78]

If popular knowledge about natural philosophy was disseminated in dictionaries and encyclopaedias, it was also circulated in periodicals and magazines for which the eighteenth century has already become famous, and nowhere more so than in women's magazines such as the long-lived *Ladies' Diary* which commenced publication in 1704. It is true that a certain amount of 'women's science' had existed in the Restoration period. Marjorie Nicolson has demonstrated what a terrific impact 'Mad Madge' – the racy Duchess of Newcastle – had on the Fellows of the Royal Society, and has also demonstrated what an inspiration Lady Conway was to scientific thinkers.[79] But natural philosophy was nevertheless still a 'male endeavour' in the Restoration period and 'Madge' – called by G. D. Meyer 'the first English woman who wrote about science' – was the exception rather than the rule. Most serious scientists as well as *virtuosi* were men and conceived of scientific activity as 'male activity', perhaps as a consequence of the physiological reasons Malebranche offered in his *Search after Truth* (1694). Yet this situation began to change when John Tipper, an enterprising schoolmaster in Coventry who had grown tired merely of teaching students, launched an annual mathematical magazine for women in 1704 called the *Ladies' Diary*. Meyer – the most learned student of 'science for the fair sex' in our period – has written that 'Fontenelle, with some help from the Duchess of Newcastle, especially in her *Grounds of Natural Philosophy*, awakened in Englishwomen a dormant interest in science; afterwards, journalists like Dunton, Tipper and Philips fed that interest with natural history in general and with the findings of the microscope and telescope in particular.'[80] The key period is the two decades 1690–1710, for during this time women developed a new sense of themselves, despite Malebranche's verdict that they were biologically inferior to men. By 1710 English women were not merely reading more books; they also wanted to read books about 'male subjects', especially about science. Fontenelle catered to this need in *The Plurality of Worlds* (1715), a book ladies were reading at the same time they were scanning Pope's couplets about 'Belinda', and Fontenelle's lovely and inspiring Marchioness established the model of 'the scientific lady' for the eighteenth century. But even before this time male educators and philosophers emphasized that women ought to read science books. As early as 1677 Poulain de la Barre, a radical French priest, wrote in *The Woman as Good as the Man* (which may have been translated into English by Anthony Le Grand), that young women should study Descartes's *Discourse on Method* and Rohault's *Cartesian Physics*. By the end of the century science books written primarily for women had appeared; in the 1690s John Dunton's *Athenian Mercury* invited scientific questions from ladies; then in 1704 Tipper's *Diary* beckoned ladies to submit their poetry for publication, yet printed material far more mathematical than poetic;[81] finally in 1718 Ambrose Philips' *Free-Thinker*, a semi-weekly sheet, introduced a paragon named Sophronia who had immersed herself in books about natural philosophy – our science books. By approximately 1740 any literate woman, of low or high class, could select from a very large number of printed works – almanacs, broadsheets, weeklies, magazines, manuals, books – to quench her thirst for science, a trend that continued throughout the century, with a pronounced resurgence at the end. She could also choose from any number of books like the anonymous *Female Physician* (1739; reprinted many times) which told her how to care for herself. Perhaps this trend accounts for the criticism of *Pamela* held by George Cheyne, the fashionable physician; Cheyne had corresponded with Richardson during actual composition, and upon reading the novel was surprised that Pamela had studied so little natural philosophy: 'a good

Library of Natural Philosophy would be very proper for your Heroine, which you want and cannot otherwise procure I will help you.'[82] Surely Meyer is correct to notice that eighteenth-century ladies most certainly did not learn their science directly from the great scientists themselves – Newton, Huygens, Boyle, Hooke – or from their books: 'it was not to the primary works of these scientists that the ladies turned. Instead, professional expositors simplified and popularized for lay consumption the major scientific advances of the time.'[83] Yet the leading printers and booksellers of the day (about which more must be said) did not exploit this available market without injury to the fair sex. Although science as an activity designed for women as distinct from men was becoming increasingly popular in the early period from 1700 to 1720, there was a natural resistance that elicited a number of printed satires written by both men and women; however peripheral they are, these works deserve to be considered as 'science books' together with the popularizations described above.[84] If it is not altogether clear, as Meyer suggests, to what degree the English bluestockings were genuinely interested in science, they were nevertheless reading and buying books about this subject. They may have bought them and subscribed to journals and magazines without digesting the contents, but until further evidence is brought to light, it must be assumed that the sheer volume of popular scientific literature written explicitly for women was consumed by them because they possessed a vigorous interest in the subject.[85]

3. NEWTON AND 'THE TRADE IN BOOKS': THE SCIENTIFIC WITS

All these developments would have been inconceivable without the advent of a Newton. In an important essay already cited,[86] Simon Schaffer has gone so far as to argue that the rise of natural philosophy in the Restoration period was nothing other than 'Newtonian matter theory' and a whole series of responses to it, and there is certainly a sense in which this is the case. If the scientific movement of the seventeenth century was essentially Baconian, and if that great age of scientific discovery, encompassing Harvey's discovery of the circulation of the blood, Leeuwenhoek's invention of the miscroscope, Willis's brain theory, Boyle's discovery of the chemical laws in mechanics, Hooke's hydrostatics and so forth, owed its primal impulse to Bacon's teachings – hence its common designation as 'the Bacon-faced generation'[87] – the next three generations from 1690 to 1780 were indebted to Newton and perhaps ought to be known as 'the Newton-faced generations'. Surely this is not the appropriate place to argue for Newton's rightful succession to Bacon; besides, others have already done so more adequately than I could.[88] But however excellent their argument, they have rarely been vigilant to the effect of this succession on the book trade and the readers to whom it catered. Abundant evidence exists to support the contention that from roughly 1680 to 1750 science, or natural philosophy, *meant* Newton. Whether agreeing or disagreeing with his physical laws;[89] whether delivering physico-theological sermons or university lectures or popular coffee-house talks to disseminate his ideas; whether discussing his ideas in recently formed science clubs and reading groups; whether simplifying and expatiating on these Newtonian laws in almanacs, dictionaries and encyclopaedias that laymen could understand; or – in areas not yet touched upon – whether applying his laws to non-physical areas such as the disparate realms of civil government, painting, medicine, and so forth;[90] the student was always in effect talking or writing about Newton. In *Newton Demands the Muse* (1946) Marjorie Nicolson demonstrated how the *Opticks* were versified in dozens of poems throughout the century, and a similar book could be written for the *Principia*. Yet only recent compilations – such important works as Peter and Ruth Wallis's *Newton and Newtoniana 1672–1975* (1976) – have demonstrated to what an extent this 'Newton-faced generation' was writing and reading books about the man who had changed everyone's concept of the universe about him. When I. B. Cohen and Marjorie Nicolson wrote about Newton 20 or 30 years ago they wrote perceptively, but neither scholar could then have known to what degree the century 1680–1780, bibliographically considered, ought to have been called 'the century of Newton'.[91] That century itself provided numerous clues, not merely in the literally hundreds of popularizations to which I have been referring – works such as Elizabeth Carter's *Newton's Philosophy Explain'd for the Use of Ladies* (1739) and the dozens of published and unpublished poems invoking Newton as their muse – but also in the less obvious patterns of book-reading and book-collecting that constituted such an important aspect of eighteenth-century life.[92] It ought not to be forgotten that early in the century Addison, an ardent Newtonian himself, had laid down in a popular periodical that 'Sir *Isaac Newton's* Works' ought to be found in every lady's library; indeed this is the only 'science book' required for 'Leonora's library'.[93] And if Leonora had to read Newton, then one should not be surprised to discover Elizabeth Carter and her 'Saturday-correspondent' Catherine Talbot, and many other women, reading him; perhaps not the mathematical sections, but surely the Scholia to the *Opticks* and other popular works Newton had written. As the eighteenth century wore on, writers of all types, high and low, serious and in jest, assumed that a vast readership existed in Britain that wanted information about the greatest scientific genius who had lived, and consequently poured forth printed material in unprecedented amounts – a cornucopia of printed works in different genres that has still to be taken into account in major discussions of the spread of secular knowledge in Western civilization.[94]

Most of Newton's own writings, especially the *Principia* and *Opticks*, did not lie at the centre of this dissemination. They continued to be reprinted and reissued in small quantities, and translated into many languages,[95] but were read by relatively small numbers and in any case were not the books that support the above generalizations. Nor were the more easily grasped interpretations of Newton's system by Samuel Clarke, John Keill, Colin Maclaurin, Henry Pemberton, Cadwallader Colden, and many others; although these books attempted to present Newton's system to literate readers they were not always successful.[96] Far more influential were the outright popularizations – simple works in almanacs, dictionaries, and poems – that made no pretension whatever to be faithful to their original. This is why two types of Newtonian books need to be distinguished: the interpretations, or reinterpretations, and the popularizations. The authors of the second type were often hacks and wrote for financial gain; yet, almost paradoxically, they were capable of effecting cultural secularization by reaching large audiences. In this connection the 'scientific poem' begs to be considered. Upon occasion even Pope, Gray, Cowper, and later on Blake and Wordsworth, wrote in this vein; more commonly, though, its authors were poets of lower ranks, the Akensides, Armstrongs, Jagos, Beatties, and Erasmus Darwins who were far more sedulous in their aim to versify scientific ideas than to discover an original 'poetic voice'. Modern discussions of 'the scientific poem' in England have imposed judgments of value in the relation of aesthetic considerations to didactic aims that were foreign to the original poets involved.[97] A Thomson or Akenside – both 'bestselling poets' in their day – naturally sought to write as well as possible and to whet the reader's imagination by a marriage of form and content, craft and ideas; but science, especially Newtonian science, had been the poet's original source of inspiration, and he generally considered it unlikely that his readers would not be as excited about his subject as he was. Precisely why Newtonian science should have seemed such a likely topic for versification when there were so many others from which to select is a matter to be debated by historians and sociologists of eighteenth-century English culture; what is important for the production of science books is the relation of these writers – and by implication their readers – to their chosen subject. In almost every instance it is apparent that 'science' meant Newtonian science, even among writers who understood little of the substance of the *Principia* and *Opticks*. It is as if 'Newton' were a vast region of the literate imagination even in the most remote of English shires. To write a quasi-popular 'science book' in 1720 or 1740 meant to write about Newton, even if the author's debt were oblique; and the science books of this period demonstrate a universal lag of time between original scientific idea and popular or semi-serious adoption. The universities and their presses, as well as certain houses in the English and Scottish metropolis, continued to publish science books such as William Jones's *An Essay on the*

First Principles of Natural Philosophy (Oxford, 1762), and Robert Greene's *The Principles of the Philosophy of the Expansive and Contractive Forces* (Cambridge, 1727), which none but a handful of scholars could read or understand. But these, no more than the original *Principia* or *Opticks*, were not the books that changed the thinking of the common man.

The influential books were those that popularized Newtonianism. As we have seen, Newton's ideas were rapidly applied to domains other than the physical universe; moreover, authors unfamiliar with Newton's actual texts were often unaware of the debt they owed to these applicators. By the end of the seventeenth century, for example, books both endorsing and rebutting Locke swelled into a major industry; but many of these books were attempts to reconcile Locke's 'science of the mind' with Newton's physics.[98] The same was true, though to a lesser degree, of books by Cheyne, Whiston and Hartley later in the eighteenth century. Whatever else these writers may be called, they were first and foremost 'science writers' – that is, authors whose 'systems' had been radically changed by recent Newtonian science more than by any other sphere of knowledge. Cheyne was a trained physician with a deep understanding of religion and art who grew increasingly mystical as he aged. The remarkable aspect of his career is the uncanny way in which he engaged the public's attention: almost anything he wrote or said was quickly 'consumed' by the public after knowledge spread of his unparalleled reduction of weight, especially as recounted in his autobiographical book *An Essay of Health and Long Life* (1724). For years after 1724, his books about diet and health permitted Cheyne to sustain a reading public enjoyed by few other English authors of the day.[99] Yet Newtonian science more than any other sphere of thought – even more than the theology to which he was so devoted – had inspired his most serious reflections, especially *Philosophical Principles of Religion* (1705), an extended meditation on God's place in a Newtonian cosmos. Similar generalizations can be made and supported for Hartley's brilliant *Observations on Man* (1749). This popular and didactic large book attempted to demonstrate that virtually all man's ideas are formed by 'mystical vibrations' conducted from the sensory and 'vibrating' organ to the brain; yet without the heritage of Newton and Locke, Hartley's system would have been impossible. Hartley, also a physician like Cheyne, probably read Newton's original works rather than one of the many available popularizations. The more significant point is that many readers in the 1750s learned their 'Newtonianism' from Hartley's *Observations* rather than from a book written by Newton himself. Much earlier the same had been true of Whiston's *Astronomical Principles of Religion* (1717), which Whiston, Newton's successor as Lucasian Professor of Mathematics at Cambridge, had written after being deprived of the Chair. Throughout the 1720s there are references to this work as a vast source of knowledge about Newtonianism, rendering it clear that Whiston had brought Newton's ideas to the common reader. In different ways all these books were responses to Newton, as well as meditations upon cosmology; in this sense they are similar to the more apparent 'translations' of Newton's system in more technical books such as Rohault's *System of Natural Philosophy* (1723) and other 'systems of natural philosophy' that do not pretend to simplify or interpret Newtonian hypotheses.[100] This variety of printed responses raises a further important question about the *diversity* of 'science books' in the first part of the eighteenth century: while many historians of science have recognized that most 'systems' of natural philosophy were directly or indirectly replying to Newton, it has not been evident to what an extent derivative 'science books' such as those by Cheyne, Whiston, and Hartley owed their origins to Newton. Such a theory of origins may not sit well with certain historians because it lays such great weight on Newton's ideas and minimizes those of his forebears and contemporaries.[101] Yet if viewed from the vantage of the eighteenth-century common reader – an angle to which I have repeatedly returned in this essay – these derivative books are the ones capable of teaching what Newton's ideas actually were, and this is the reason such works are reprinted more frequently than Newton's own books.

4. NATURAL HISTORY: THE 'BOOKISH SPORT'

Yet if Newton was the spring of much, if not most, of the printed natural philosophy of the first half of the century, natural history – which, unlike natural philosophy, cannot be traced to a single monumental scientist – was the well for the second half. The reasons for this precise succession are immensely complicated and cannot be reduced to generalizations compressed into a few sentences.[102] Furthermore, the specific reasons proffered will depend on the analyst's view of the history of scientific thought in the Enlightenment, and whether he adopts a linear, dialectical, synchronic or other approach. Necessarily complicated though this matter of attribution is, some aspects are plain, and those that directly apply to science books and their readers ought not to be omitted. By 1750 the Newtonians had won their war – certainly at home – and there was no longer any reason to continue to campaign vigorously. Further popularizations and interpretations for students could still be produced, indeed they were,[103] but it was no longer necessary to proselytize as frantically and sedulously as the army of Newtonians did in the first three decades of the century. Moreover, as natural history increasingly attracted readers from 1700 onwards, natural philosophy gradually lost them: it was not a swift progression, but as the one continued to lose, the other continued to gain. Jacques Roger, perhaps the most learned student of Enlightenment natural history, has attributed much of this inverse succession and discontinuity to gradual 'abandonment of the Cartesian philosophy' and to the literary abilities of natural history writers: in England John Ray, William Paley, William Derham, Oliver Goldsmith, Gilbert White; on the Continent Pluche, Fabricius, Lesser, Buffon, Bonnet and many others.[104] Roger's two reasons are no doubt the right ones, especially if one realizes to what an extent abandonment of Cartesianism meant adoption of Newtonianism and to what degree this adoption had succeeded in England by 1750: 'that whole corpus of [natural history] literature, whose success was enormous, has not yet been studied in its own right, perhaps because it has been considered as an accident in the history of science'.[105] 'Accident' it may or may not have been, but its effect nevertheless was to steal the very readers of natural philosophy who had been taught to crave knowledge about their terraqueous globe. The dynamic antagonism of natural philosophy and natural history, suspected by Roger, was never more evident than at mid-century. As Roger has written, because 'a "history of nature" is opposed to a "natural philosophy", which is the search for the causes of the phenomena',[106] it is consequently unthinkable that both could coexist at mid-century – or in any period – and be read by the same readers.

The triumph of natural history over natural philosophy was ultimately based, as Roger has argued, on a set of theological, intellectual and literary assumptions, yet the victory also had marked effects upon book production in the second half of the eighteenth century. In a certain simple sense the consequence is only arithmetical: all that was printed about natural philosophy before 1750 is transferred after 1750 to books about natural history. Stated in this way, though, the succession is deceptive insofar as it implies an absolute equality among both types of books. Yet the exchange was disparate, as Roger has suggested and I shall attempt briefly to develop, for natural-history books were far better written and much more beautifully produced than their predecessors in natural philosophy had been; and their success consequently derives more directly from a relationship between book and reader, as distinct from merely writer and reader, than had been the case for natural philosophy.[107] In a sense it is almost as if the British readership at mid-century was ready for an elegant *and* readable factual book which natural history could supply. Also, if one recollects that English natural-history books begin with John Ray, enjoy a number of sumptuous editions in the 1720s and 1730s, then pass on to popularizers such as Richard Brookes and Oliver Goldsmith, and culminate in Gilbert White's *Natural History of Selborne* (1789), then Roger's point as well as my own readily makes itself; for there are no books *qua* books in the other sphere – natural philosophy – that can vie with these, not even the 'scientific poems' (Thomsons's *Seasons*, Blackmore's *The Creation*, Pope's *Essay on Man*, Darwin's *Botanic Garden* – which is a 'natural history' poem) which had, of course, a certain following in the eighteenth century.[108] Both types of books centred on the rôle of God in his creation, and on the 'natural' as distinct from supernatural or socio-economic aspects of their subject; but whereas books on natural philosophy were often technical, dry, repetitive, and written by authors who had no sense of literary form or style, those about natural history tended to be simple, elegant, beautifully illustrated (sometimes in colour) and often endowed with an architectural shape that enticed readers. But there were other differences as well, differences pertaining to innate elements of the subjects themselves. A 'natural history' of birds or insects, fossils or shells, genuinely lent itself to simplicity, elegance and illustration in ways that natural philosophy did not; such a 'history' naturally divided into symmetrical units which would seem artificial if imposed on natural philosophy. And natural history was blessed in attracting masterful prose stylists who were not discouraged by the technical rigours and difficult vocabulary of natural philosophy. A Goldsmith could master the best classification schemes of animals or birds in a relatively short time; it is doubtful whether Goldsmith would have understood Newton's fluxions (calculus) or physics well enough to write brilliantly about them (the historian ought never to assume that the common reader perusing popularizations of Newtonianism c. 1700 or 1720 understood them well enough to explicate them to others). Therefore while a dynamic approach to the triumph of natural-history books over those about natural philosophy is valid, these less recondite reasons existed to ensure the greater success of natural history with an audience composed of intelligent but non-scientific readers.[109]

Buffon's remarkable popularity in Britain and among English-speaking readers documents the point in a nutshell. His books on natural history began to appear in 1749 in French, and in 1762 in English, the year when *The Natural History of the Horse* was first published. No previous books on natural history were sought after so eagerly. Roger has argued that Buffon's popularity in France and elsewhere in the second half of the eighteenth century can be attributed to the common man's interest in global exploration – the sense Goldsmith had felt in *The Traveller* of a world composed of 'lakes, forests, cities, plains, extending wide'; and Foucault has attributed the same widespread popularity to the zeal with which naturalists from Ray and Lhuyd onwards were then collecting and reclassifying the entire kingdom of nature as a consequence of a new separation of 'words' and 'things'.[110] Both these arguments are no doubt valid, but however metaphysical their concerns, something must have been owing to the average Englishman's Francophilia and to the public's reading habits. After all, natural history had flourished in the Renaissance, and there is no surer proof of its vitality then than the number of books about the symbolism of the natural world (animals, vegetables, minerals). In the Restoration period, the natural history of wonders was commonly found in children's books, as were the natural histories of countries just slightly later. What was lacking throughout this period from approximately 1600 to 1750 was a writer genuinely capable of engaging the attention of the common reader, and a readership sufficiently large in numbers and leisured in the economic sense, to benefit from such natural-history books. Buffon provided all this for a ready audience. He also appealed by the lucid style in which he wrote and the pictorial format his publishers used. It is not surprising that Buffon, who gave the world its most celebrated definition of style – the notion that style can never be anything less than 'the man himself'[111] – employed an elegant and polished style in French which his English translators admirably captured. Yet the success of Buffon's works in Britain, as Charles Waterton commented in his own *Essays on Natural History* (1838), owed as much to his publishers; for Buffon was not merely lucky, and the unparalleled enthusiasm for his books derived from a collaboration between author and bookseller-printer that veritably ensured his niche as a best-selling author for four decades. The anonymous writer of an early review in the *Monthly* has captured some of the dramatic excitement he sensed upon reading the first English translation of Buffon's *Natural History* by William Kenrick, the dramatist. Likening the reader's experience in the *Natural History* to that of the reader in Swift, the reviewer argues that '[Buffon] has made a voyage through our system, seated in the magnetical steel chair of his countryman, *Cyrano de Bergerac*, the adventurous Prototype and Precursor of our Lemuel Gulliver'.[112] The exhilaration of 'taking the voyage' with Buffon was achieved by a rhetorical and pictorial eloquence that even Johnson noticed, according to Boswell, and which almost every reviewer in England discoursed upon in the eighteenth century. And while criticism of Buffon's scientific 'system' or 'knowledge of his subject' abounds, his excellence as a stylist remains a constant in the chorus of eighteenth-century approbation. In England the reader of weeklies and monthlies continued to hear about 'the beauty of the Author's style, which is always enchanting, even where it betrays marks of negligence'.[113] One reviewer of the Kenrick 1775 translation in three volumes went so far as to contend seriously that Buffon was a sorcerer capable of bewitching his readers: 'let the reader decide whether his fame be owing to the solidity of his investigations and discoveries, or to those sublime flights, and that magic power, energy, and grace of style, that have astonished and *bewitched* a considerable part of Europe.'[114]

If Buffon 'bewitched' his readers, he accomplished this by an attitude to nature as well as a glowing pen. In the words of another anonymous reviewer – actually Buffon's first reviewer in England – he mesmerized them 'not by contracting the sphere of nature within a narrow circle, but by extending it to immensity, so that we can obtain a true knowledge of her proceedings'. Linnaeus was a more venerated naturalist than Buffon during the period 1750–1800; he was the Newton of that age; yet he was utterly incapable of 'bewitching' readers anywhere. If Buffon's *Natural History* ranks as one of the ten most popular books in the second half of the eighteenth century,[115] nothing Linnaeus ever wrote attained the status of a 'natural-history bestseller'. Linnaeus's impact, especially his systems of bisexual classification and natural taxonomy which were altering the course of serious science, was more consequential than any 'system' generated by Buffon; yet Linnaeus was important as a *scientist* rather than as an author, and the distinction is crucial for an understanding of 'science books'.[116] No serious botanist or naturalist in England could afford to overlook Linnaeus at mid-century, no matter in which language he read Linnaeus's works; he would do very well, as Johnson assured Boswell, to overlook Buffon.[117] Johnson seems to be intimating the very distinction between 'scientific systems' and 'scientific thought' which I have been attempting to make throughout this essay. Ideas and books differ, and granting that here and there in Linnaeus are light touches of wit and humour and elegance, nevertheless there is none of the literary sophistication that pervades every page of Buffon.[118] This is why the English reviews of Linnaeus constitute an important collective document: they demonstrate how Linnaeus came to be viewed as a 'genius' worthy to be ranked among the greatest scientists of all time, in the words of Raymond Hirons, one of Ralph Griffiths' frequent reviewers of books on natural history for the *Monthly*, a giant worthy of comparison with other giants: 'the same science [botany] which has been disgraced by a butterfly-catcher, or a hunter after cockle-shells, is immortalized by the labours of a Bacon, a Boyle, and a Linnaeus'.[119] Buffon is not in the list; he was never viewed as a major scientist; yet he, rather than Linnaeus, held sway among the many readers active in the cults of natural history. A point about language also needs to be made. Others than Hirons recognized that natural history was altering the English language far more than natural philosophy had done in the previous half century.[120] Hirons himself had attributed much of the change to the introduction of the Linnaean system into England: 'Linnaeus has totally reformed the language of botany, and indeed, in great measure, introduced a new language into the science'.[121] But scientific genius such as Newton possessed and linguistic ripples such as Linnaeus clearly caused are distinct from the books the common reader then wanted to consume. If the demand for editions of Newton was small before 1750 in relation to the demand for books by his staunch popularizers, the same is true of Linnaeus after 1750. Benjamin Stillingfleet, Richard Pulteney, William Withering, John Hill, Erasmus Darwin – all popularizers of Linnaeus – are the authors whose books sold, not Linnaeus or the members of the 'Norfolk Linnaean group' whose books were too serious for popular consumption. Pulteney's *General View of the Writings of Linnaeus* (1781) proved so popular that his publisher

Tom Payne claimed 'not to have a copy in his hands after the year 1785'. The point then is that whereas Linnaeus was more important than Buffon for the record of science, he could not write a single scientific book everyone could understand. He would not do what Freud decided to do at a major turning-point in his career: popularize the serious in at least one readable book.

Goldsmith's *History of the Earth and Animated Nature* stands somewhere between the enormous popularity of Buffon on the one hand and the serious scientific attitude of Linnaeus on the other. Goldsmith plundered both authors as models, Linnaeus for his system of sexual classification and Buffon for his descriptions of animals and birds, but with a difference. Goldsmith, unlike these authors, was a native English writer whose refined prose style had been noted long before *Animated Nature* appeared on 1 July 1774, seven weeks after his death. The reader could expect a 'natural history' from his pen that was a prose classic, something not even the translators of Buffon (Kenrick *et al.*) ever hoped to achieve.[122] Furthermore, Goldsmith had already written successful poetry, drama and fiction, and he knew how to appeal to the taste of a broad cross-section of the populace, especially to its relatively recent demand in prose for authorial sentimentalism and continuous sympathy. When these qualities, everywhere engraved on the stamp of *Animated Nature*, were wedded to a description of the *whole* terraqueous globe that quenched the reader's own lust for travel and exploration in unknown places, the result was a popular set of 'science books' that ran to almost a dozen editions by 1800 and at least 22 editions by 1876.[123] The argument then of some recent critics, to the effect that *Animated Nature* is *not* an important work of Goldsmith's, needs to be re-evaluated. It was reprinted 'by popular demand' as often as *The Vicar of Wakefield* and *The Citizen of the World*, and was rivalled in the genre of popular science books only by English editions of Buffon. Paul Kaufman, mentioned earlier, has discovered that this popularity of Buffon and Goldsmith was as evident in cathedral libraries as in other lending libraries. No other writers on a scientific subject rivalled these two, if numbers of editions and documented borrowings are an appropriate yardstick.

But *Animated Nature* demonstrates another tension between scientific ideas and scientific books that has been a *leitmotif* of this essay. Indeed it casts light on the public's reading habits by demonstrating that a book like *Animated Nature* could be lionized *despite* its reviewers. So well did the public know what it wanted to read, and the booksellers – in this case John Nourse – how to feed that hunger. Edward Bancroft, a young American then resident in London with his growing family, considered *Animated Nature* a poor performance in every way *save* one: 'Our Author has adopted no methodical arrangement'; 'his work is to be considered as a compilation'; 'his descriptions . . . are almost wholly employed upon their more amusing properties'; and in his conclusion: 'however well qualified he was to excel in works of *imagination*, his talents appear to be ill-suited to those of *science*'.[124] There again lay the old dichotomy: *science* and *imagination*. But the novice reviewer had missed the larger truth: scientific 'bestsellers' had excelled in all ages for precisely this reason – that they had been 'works of *imagination*' – and not because they promulgated radical theories. This was as true in the Renaissance as it has been in our own century. Johnson in the capacity of a reviewer was far more perceptive: he chided Goldsmith for plundering Buffon so mercilessly and for propagating the old saw about cows shedding their horns at three years of age, but concluded that *Animated Nature* was nevertheless 'an excellent performance'.[125] Johnson knew that scientific 'bestsellers' are less comprehensive than scientific 'dissertations' and always borrow from serious writers. This is precisely what Goldsmith had done: he lifted from Buffon while applying the best aspects of Linnaeus's theory. Yet Goldsmith, like smaller fry in Grub Street, knew what he was about in *Animated Nature*; he knew he wanted to write a popular as opposed to a scholarly book, a book, as Johnson might have said, that mankind would actually read. Goldsmith's assessment of Richard Brookes's *Natural History* (1763), to which Goldsmith himself contributed all the introductions, remains the best commentary on *Animated Nature*. 'We could wish', he lamented, 'that he [Brookes] had thrown more life and variety into his manner, and imitated those Painters who, to give their pieces greater force, throw all their animals into action'.[126] Goldsmith had certainly ensured that 'the art of contrast' figured prominently in his narrative and for good reason: when he described animals in *Animated Nature*, he sentimentalized them by pervading his book with rhetorical personification, authorial sensibility, and human sympathy, especially when strong animals prey upon weak ones.[127] And he did so with prudence and and taste in mind: by 1774 the cults of natural history abounded, as did books (by the dozens) on the subject. Anyone then could write about natural kingdoms, but only a few could capture everyone's attention.

Books about natural history shared a vast readership eager to learn about living creatures in nearby and remote places. This accounts for the eagerness of booksellers to enlist the best authors to write on the subject. Andrew Millar had paid Fielding the 'huge fortune' of £600 for exclusive rights to publish *Tom Jones*, and as recently as 1771 – only a few years before *Animated Nature* appeared – Smollett's publisher offered £210 for *Humphry Clinker*; but William Griffin paid Goldsmith £840 for *Animated Nature*, a very large sum by any measurement. Natural history was the universal British pastime, if not the national sport, by mid-century: Why else would the influential *Critical Review* claim in 1763 that 'Natural History is now, by a kind of *national establishment* . . . the favourite study of the time', and a few years later, in 1785, its rival, the *Monthly*, ask why 'all nations of refinement especially, should forward this species of knowledge [natural history] in their own tongue'?[128] Such an abundance of similar pronouncements is found that no reason exists to doubt their collective validity. Yet if the cults of natural history were expanding, so too was the 'book craze', as one commentator noted. As early as 1720 the naturalist William Sherard wrote to Richard Richardson, the Yorkshire scientist, that 'Natural History of all sorts is much in demand' (he meant 'the demand for books'), and in 1746 the Quaker merchant and naturalist Peter Collinson commented in a letter to Linnaeus that 'we [English] are very fond of all branches of Natural History; they sell the *best of any books* in England'.[129] This was a pre-Buffonian 1746; by 1760 or 1770 the public was caught, the time was ready for bestsellers among a readership thirsting for them: books almost everyone could understand and afford, not merely finely illustrated coffee-table productions for the fashionable and the rich. A steady 'progress' of natural-history books had appeared: in the 1740s George Edwards, one of the most gifted naturalists of the time, brought out a four-volume *History of Birds* that was sound and sold well,[130] and two decades later Thomas Pennant's *British Zoology* appeared, which the poet Gray owned and regularly consulted and which Goldsmith often read while writing *Animated Nature*.[131] In this continuum the trend was towards reasonably priced books written in a language and style the educated layman could understand.[132] This lineage culminated in such masterpieces of the mode as Erasmus Darwin's *Botanic Garden* (1789) and *Zoonomia: or the Laws of Organic Life* (1794–6), and Gilbert White's *Natural History of Selborne* (1789). Procrustean as it seems, it is nevertheless true to claim that by 1770 or so the natural-history book outdistanced all other science books, and did so irrespective of the reader's social class. The wealthy adorned their Chippendale tables with John Hill's magnificently illustrated *Vegetable System*, a 26-volume set that is aesthetically more pleasing than it is scientifically accurate; from 1759 onwards it usually appeared in biennial instalments at the price of £1 11s. 6d. per volume.[133] Those in less fortunate circumstances could buy Richard Brookes's set of *Natural History* in six volumes, which Newbery brought out cheaply in 1763 for only 18s;[134] those in the middle economic bracket could afford Goldsmith's set, though they might also read Buffon. And the booksellers and printers were not worried that after 1774 Buffon would spend another 14 years (1774–88) dressed in full-court costume composing 'natural history' eight hours every day and writing a total of 44 volumes![135] So secure had the English 'trade' in natural-history books grown. Immense as was Buffon's popularity in England, it was still *Animated Nature*, not Buffon's books, that the British public read and bought. There were, of course, other competing books: dozens, even hundreds, of books too long to list here,[136] but even if they were discussed one strain would be salient: the idea that natural history finally prevailed on the bestseller market. Goldsmith and Buffon shared this market, and to a lesser extent certain hacks, though neither writer was scientifically solid and though neither received complete academic approbation from his contemporaries.[137]

Although no other bookish 'sport' could compete with 'the natural history craze', a few tried. Marjorie Hope Nicolson has traced the growth of popular interest in books about the microscope and telescope in the Restoration period, and discovered how this enthusiasm shaped scientific activity then.[138] Books about microscopes and other instruments could not vie with books on natural philosophy and natural history, but the works of writers such as Henry Baker, author of the very popular *Microscope Made Easy* (1742) and *Employment for the Microscope* (1753),[139] and Benjamin Martin, the prolific instrument-maker who delivered lectures that required handbooks for attendance,[140] were runners-up. The reason for widespread enthusiasm about these books is not difficult to fathom: as natural philosophy and, later on, natural history made their impact on the layman's imagination, the notion spread that the naked eye could perceive the intricacies and fine details of 'Nature's kingdom' only with the aid of instruments such as the microscope and telescope. There was, of course, an ancillary and more abstract reason that Marjorie Hope Nicolson has isolated in connection with the ancients-moderns controversy:[141] that 'the moderns' paraded their interest in the new science by flaunting their mechanical instruments. But this penchant for modernity among scholars could not vie with the common man's need to see Nature's kingdom with his own eye. A similar state of affairs existed for books about other types of instruments and clocks. The search for the longitude, for example, had been important at least since 1676 when the first Astronomer Royal, Sir John Flamsteed, moved into Greenwich; after 1707, discovery of the longitude grew more pressing than it had been for the previous quarter of a century: ignorant of their longitude, a flotilla of nearly 2,000 British sailors ran aground in the Scilly Islands and was destroyed with heavy loss of life. The government became panic-stricken – especially in view of the importance of the navy to England's global might – and offered maximum rewards of £20,000 for proposals that would lead to discovery.[142] Schemes were devised and published,[143] and by the 1720s readers could find them in all sorts of libraries and purchase them at bookstalls, but books about the longitude never approached the numbers of books in natural history. The market for printed material about marine instruments was steady but small; perhaps the same was true of books about clocks, although these books were read by a more diverse audience. Early in the century William Derham's classic was popular and continued to be reprinted,[144] but clocks really came into their own c. 1760 when marine chronometers were being much discussed as the only instruments capable of accurately determining the longitude at sea.[145] All sorts of books about clocks appeared in this decade, books serious and staid as well as light and newfangled, books such as *The Clockmakers* [sic] *Outcry* (1760) which parodies *Tristram Shandy* and is not a 'scientific book' at all except insofar as it invokes clocks all the way through, and 'mechanical books' such as Benjamin Martin's *The Description and Use of a Table Clock upon a New Construction, Going by a Weight Eight Days* (1770).[146] Technology in the home as well as on the road and at sea was then expanding; it was not yet, however, in a league to be compared with natural history, the 'Sunday pastime' of the British Isles.

5. SCIENCE BOOKS AND THE LITERARY IMAGINATION

The impact of so many concomitant scientific trends – philosophical, theological, technological, social – was reflected on the contemporary literary imagination. It could not have been otherwise. To the degree that this influence is attributable to science *books* as distinct from scientific *talk*, the literary man responded primarily in three ways: insofar as science books were shaping his general world view; in his impulse to collect these science books; and in the myriad ways in which he was invoking science in his own writing. The first – world view – is subtle and elusive, rarely perceived by writers on a conscious level, and even when perceived it is not always clear what difference this angle of vision resulting in a *gestalt* makes to a writer's final text.[147] Most great English writers alive in the period from 1680 to 1740 were aware of the immense proliferation of science books. Certainly Swift and Pope and the Scriblerians were, and if they had been alive in the decade 1650–60, they might have compared this surge to the proliferation of books about alchemy and magic then. Furthermore, most of these English authors – not merely 'the greats' but lesser talents as well – took political positions and defended ideological stands, but certainly not all seem to have been aware of the degree to which science, and science books, were shaping their *perception* of the whole world about them. Consciousness of alteration was probably more manifest on the level of collecting: whereas 'the ancients' had been collectable in 1680, now, in 1740, the party of 'the moderns' was winning on library shelves. Documentation of this phenomenon is not impossible for the assiduous researcher: abundant catalogues are extant for seventeenth- as well as eighteenth-century writers, and types of titles and numbers of volumes on shelves can be counted. The appendix (p. 235) provides some indication of the distribution of science books among the major English writers of the period, and it is important to notice how many different scientific books appear. No comparable pattern exists for English writers in the same period of the two previous centuries: 1480–1540 and 1580–1640. The last evidence of influence – explicit invocation of science – is, of course, a more uncertain terrain but certainly not a no-man's land. Donald Davie is on firm ground when he challenges Mallarmé and Professor R. L. Brett for objecting to early eighteenth-century poetry, for example, because this body of verse has paid *too much attention* to science and to the mechanical metaphors of a scientific world view.[148] What greater proof of evidence of influence could possibly exist? This is surely not the place to engage in polemics about the merits of eighteenth-century poetry except to notice that Davie – a consummate poet himself – has not been the only apologist for this body of literature. Other champions include Auden and Eliot and scholars such as Marjorie Nicolson, Maynard Mack, G. S. Fraser, I. A. Richards, Reuben Brower, and dozens of others who agree that such scientific metaphors and scientific language strengthened rather than weakened it.[149] But these metaphors and tropes would never have been invoked in the first place if science books had not proliferated in unprecedented numbers. Cause and effect are relatively clear in this instance, and it does not matter if some poets assimilated their knowledge from newspapers.[150] What counts for more is the undeniable fact that the largest upswing in the publishing history of scientific books had occurred.

Evidences of this fact were apparent everywhere, in high society as well as low, certainly throughout the adult world. Two instances – one among the rich, the other the young – may suffice to show how widely disseminated science books were becoming. Aristocratic librarians had collected some technical 'science books' throughout the Middle Ages, and continued throughout the Renaissance. The Knyvet brothers – Thomas and Sir Henry – collected so many scientific books at Ashwellthorpe in Norfolk at the end of the sixteenth century that 'the medical books alone occupy ten folio pages of the list'.[151] But the Knyvet brothers were exceptional: even in the next century one would expect to find some science books in every aristocratic library, yet these were rarely a large percentage of the whole, and what is more, it was uncommon to discover a large collection of current science books. In the eighteenth century this trend changed, and the librarians of such great Whig lords as the dukes of Devonshire, Newcastle, and Norfolk ardently bought up science books. No one to my knowledge has systematically studied the percentage of science books in aristocratic libraries 1500–1800, but it is fair to assume that such a survey would reveal a very marked increase for the eighteenth century.[152] Science books for children show an equally amazing increase in our period. When L. F. Gedike, a German schoolmaster who professed to have visited the Leipzig bookfair 'every year of his adult life', returned home in 1787, he noted that 'no one other form of literary manufactory is so active as [scientific] book-making for young people of all grades and classes . . . a flooding tide [of] . . . geography for children, history for children, physics for children'.[153] Many of the books Gedike saw were written in English, and the British were publishing and exporting them as a consequence of the revolution in childhood then taking place, as well as an unprecedented craving for information among the young. All types of fables and allegories – by Aesop, Perrault, and others – were available for children in the Restoration period but 'science books', no matter how simplified, were almost impossible to find. Yet a notion persists among some historians of education that these books continued to be scarce until the late eighteenth century, a generalization the facts will not support except for a few isolated cases such as military schools and remote colleges in outlying provinces.

As early as 1710 such a book appeared, published both in English and French: *A Short and Easie Method to Give Children an Idea or True Notion of Celestial and Terrestrial Beings.* Containing 38 plates reproducing many figures drawn from the heavens, it combined the educational principles of Comenius and Locke while attempting to inculcate both French and English in order 'to teach the arts and sciences, plants, fruits, and living creatures'.[154] Despite an emphasis on terrestrial as distinct from celestial life, these early books for children were spurred by a hunger for knowledge about astronomy. This may be why Isaac Watts, such a popular voice a decade later, would compose his very first science book for 'young adults' and call it *The Knowledge of the Heavens and the Earth Made Easy, or the First Principles of Geography and Astronomy Explained*, which appeared during the same year as *Gulliver's Travels* and which commented upon 'the heavens and the earth' in remote places, albeit not in Swiftian manner. By the 1730s Thomas Boreman initiated the 'publishing industry' that would make him a rich man: the printing of natural-history books for children.[155] This progression from natural philosophy to natural history paralleled the movement in 'adult science', and was a development Boreman exploited to its utmost. A decade later, in the 1740s, John Newbery, the printer about whom so much has been written and so little is yet known, began to issue *The Circles of the Sciences . . . in Ten Volumes for Children*, books for children that went through many editions over the next three decades and which opened up the plenitudinous world of science.[156] Dedicating one volume to 'one science', Newbery published each book in octavo and each was written in the simplest language imaginable to educate the beginning reader. For three more decades he and his firm continued to write and publish children's books such as *Tom Telescope's Newtonian System of Philosophy*, being 'the substance of six lectures read to the Lilliputian Society', which first appeared as *The Philosophy of Tops and Balls*.[157] Populated by intriguing concatenations such as 'Master Telescope', 'Countess of Twilight' and 'Duke of Galaxy', the book, which bears so many Goldsmithian traces that it could have been written by him, reveals the heavens to 'the little gentry' just as Fontenelle's dazzling Marchioness had opened them up to an adult audience in *A Plurality of Worlds*. This is not the place to explain how 'the aesthetics of the infinite' were communicated to children in the eighteenth century or the proper moment for a detailed history of science books for children, but such a survey would no doubt show how these books increased and how their quality improved with every decade.[158] Women such as Anna Barbauld and Sarah Trimmer wrote these books as did their male counterparts,[159] thereby paving the way for the Jane Marcets who would capture 'the hunger for science among children' in the next century.[160] Every decade brought new titles, the best reprinted over and again in new editions: in the 1780s John Aikin's *Calendar of Nature*[161] and the anonymous *Jack Dandy's Delight*; in the 1790s several English versions of Arnaud Berquin's *Looking-Glass for the Mind* – the popular English translation of a 'science book' for children written by a master of the genre who had been influenced by Rousseau's theories in *Émile*; at the turn of the century Jeremiah Joyce's *Scientific Dialogues . . . in Six Volumes for Children*, a more serious science book than any of these others which covered the main branches: mechanics, astronomy, hydrostatics, pneumatics, optics, magnetism, electricity and galvanism.[162] If this survey had been extended beyond 1800, the trend towards better and cheaper books would be readily evident.[163] The fortunes of the book trade were not surprising in view of the amazing growth of eighteenth-century science, conceived as activity, knowledge, and ideology'. No matter what one's social class, every literate man, woman and child had thirsted by 1800 for knowledge about the natural world which the booksellers in England were quenching as Napoleon conquered Europe.

6. SCIENCE IN GRUB STREET

'The buzzing tribe', the class of booksellers, printers and publishers denounced by Pope in *The Dunciad*, was altogether aware of this new market and ready to exploit it greedily. Yet before the 'dunces' – usually 'depressed' writers – could compile saleable anthologies and compilations of 'science', the booksellers had to be ready and willing to print these books. The cause and effect of this state of affairs, and the internal structure of these 'publishing houses', are matters few scholars have been willing to tackle because so few actual facts are known. It may be that the right questions have not even been put as yet. The questions that fall into the domain of science books are fortunately specific and capable of partial solutions, although much more research will be needed before authoritative generalizations can be made.

Certainly by mid-century, the houses of Davis, Dilly, Hodges, Innys – a very large house that published many of the works of Newton and Boerhaave – Millar, Murray, Nourse, Rivington, and Robinson were printing large numbers of science books, large, that is, in relation to the number printed before c. 1720 and as a part of the total number of published titles. John Nourse's publishing establishment is especially germane here. He was one of the first scientific booksellers in England, specializing in popular treatises on mathematics, and mathematically-based books from hack writers who produced pot-boilers partly based on learned treatises and on the theories of others, just as Goldsmith did with natural history. But unlike Davis, Millar and Rivington, Nourse paid his hacks well, and he also cornered a whole segment of the technical-books market, as a consequence of which his enterprise was profitable.[164] On the other hand, equally large and prominent houses – Dodsley and Lintot – published so few science books that it may be said that certain houses were 'science houses' and others not. Why, then, were certain houses enthusiastic, and others most unreceptive? Plomer provides no clue, nor do more specialized recent studies.[165] The direction most houses took may reflect the interests of their proprietors, or it may have been based on chance: a book falling into the bookseller's lap, as it were. For every William Innys who cared about the new science, who had genuine interest in medicine and who had actually sought out Boerhaave.[166] dozens of other booksellers ranging from the notorious Curll to Pope's *bête noire*, Lintot of *Dunciad* fame, could not be persuaded unless there were assurance of a quick pound. Given the enthusiastic reception of natural philosophy in the early eighteenth century and the number and types of science books available by 1730 or 1740, it is reasonable to wonder why houses devoted exclusively to science books did not spring up. Could they not have made a good living from these books, perhaps printing as well a few other types of titles? The questions, however, may be poor – may suffer from 'telescopic history' that glances backwards. Furthermore, so many documents (contracts, ledgers, bank accounts) have disappeared that it may not be possible to retrieve answers. In almost every specific case, only tentative generalizations are possible because of the disappearance of these documents. For example, Innys had published the first English translation of *Boerhaave's Aphorisms* in 1715, and continued to reissue it in 1722, 1724, and 1728. Sometime after 1728 Bettesworth bought the copyright from Innys and brought it out in 1735 in the same version.[167] Why did Innys sell? Purchase of such copyright from Innys is not commonplace in this period, and whereas it is impossible to learn how many copies Innys had sold in the four editions, the book itself must have been among the dozen or so most popular science titles of the time. Can Bettesworth, who published few science books, have hoped to expand his own science titles and establish himself as something of a 'science bookseller'? Was Innys reaping small returns on the *Aphorisms* and only too glad to sell out to Bettesworth on London Bridge or any other bookseller? It is tempting, but risky, to hazard guesses.

John Hill's publishing manoeuvres also pose a challenge to the student of eighteenth-century science books, although they shed much light on the history of publishing, because Hill catered to such a different reading audience from Boerhaave's and because Hill, unlike Boerhaave, was such a prolific popular-science writer.[168] So far as can be learned, Hill published 96 books with 29 different publishers during his lifetime.[169] The house of Baldwin at 47 Paternoster Row printed 25 of these titles, with Hill often holding total or partial copyright; Thomas and Mary Cooper printed nine titles, as did Thomas Osborne, and C. Davis five. All were well-known and prolific houses at mid-century. Yet the firm of Baldwin did not specialize – in our modern sense – in science books, and published few scientific titles other than Hill's. The Baldwins primarily printed political literature, especially in pamphlets, and c. 1750 did not have the copyright for the works of any acclaimed scientists. Why, then, did Baldwin, as distinct from any number of other large, leading houses take on a quarter of Hill's books? And why did Hill, having established such rapport and effective arrangements with the Baldwins, offer the other three-quarters to other houses? Hill's correspondence reveals no particular friendship with any of these publishers,[170] and there is no value in speculating about Hill's reasons for approaching one bookseller over another. If this avenue of exploration were extended to many London booksellers, it would be evident that at mid-century there was no such publishing organism as a 'science house'. Until further evidence is brought to light, it is probably more accurate to believe that all houses considered suggested titles on the basis of economic (and sometimes political) success, and that the 'science list' – in our current nomenclature – was not yet a category in which the booksellers and publishers cared or hoped to specialize.

The structure of prices is another matter, although less irksome to sort out and settle. During the sixteenth and seventeenth centuries the book trade was flooded with cheap handbooks on English science, hastily compiled by greedy booksellers eager to tap a steadily growing market. This state of affairs has deftly been summarized by F. R. Johnson: 'Most of these books were, like [Thomas] Hill's,[171] translations and compilations; but they were poorly printed, written in atrocious English style, and translated with so little regard for accuracy and clarity that no reliable knowledge – scientific or pseudo-scientific – could be derived from them.'[172] These books, moreover, were cheap, perhaps all selling for under a shilling, and were written by incompetent hacks who knew little if anything about science. After the establishment in the Restoration period of the Royal Society and the new spur given to natural philosophy, more knowledgeable writers of science began to compile these books, and their prices steadily rose. By 1720 a Londoner eager to own a science book would have been fortunate to discover one for under three or four shillings.[173] Yet 'as late as the third quarter of the [seventeenth] century £12 a year were still thought sufficient for the year's pay of a schoolteacher, who of all others might be expected to show an interest in books',[174] and the average earning power did not climb so much in the next 50 years (1675–1725) to invalidate the point about the cost of science books in relation to annual earnings.[175] By 1730 or 1740 the disparity between the cost of a work of fiction, poetry or imaginative prose – a book of 'literature' – and a science book, whether theoretical or applied, was considerable. Whereas readers eager to purchase books could choose from any number of literary, historical or theological titles for a couple of shillings, most science books averaged from four to ten shillings and there were many that were much more expensive.[176] Dodsley's science books were cheaper than most others, yet even Dodsley offered no science book, other than the odd pamphlet on herbal medicine or a 'penny cure' for venereal disease, for less than two shillings.[177] When Dodsley brought out in translation Anthony Cocchi's popular *Pythagorean Diet* (1745), he charged 1s. 6d., and Robert Douglas's more theoretical *Heat in Animals* (1747), a work 'of natural philosophy', cost 2s. 6d.: in relation to other science books these were inexpensive. The reader who wanted to purchase Rice Charleton's *Bath Waters* (1754) – a balneological work about the medicinal value of spas – could have bought it in 1754 for 1s. 6d., but a year earlier would have had to pay six shillings for Thomas Gataker's *Operations on Venereal Complaints* (1753; second edition) and 18 shillings – almost a tenth of his annual salary if he had been a school teacher then – for Robert Hooke's *Micrographia* (1745).[178] After mid-century these books were gradually reduced in price, and by the 1770s and 1780s literary and science books cost roughly the same amount. While the precise reasons for this trend are not clear, they must have depended, in whatever degree, on the demand for these books as well as the copyright amount or other advance royalty paid to authors. So far as can be learned, authors were paid smaller sums to write and compile science books than were literary writers, and this was as true for renowned authors as well as unknowns in Grub Street. Joseph Johnson, the late eighteenth-century bookseller and publisher, issued over 2,700 imprints in the 48 active years of his career, many of which were scientific titles, including almost all the works of Joseph Priestley and Erasmus Darwin, and William Cowper's *Poems*, yet he paid rather small sums to his science writers: only £40 to George Walker for a *Treatise on the Sphere* (1777)[179] and £150 – the largest amount I can discover – to William Nicholson for an *Introduction to Natural Philosophy* (1782),[180] an elementary science textbook that soon superseded John Rowning's *System of Natural Philosophy* (1735). Expectation of sales, the number of actual buyers, the price paid to the author – all these influenced the publishers of science books and contributed to the way in which the new demand for science books was altering the eighteenth-century book trade.[181]

Libraries of every type – circulating, non-circulating, proprietary, community, school, university, cathedral, and other public types – were the natural resort of those who could not afford to purchase science books at these prices. Two questions about these libraries especially need to be asked: first, precisely which titles and about how many science books could a borrower expect to find in a library in our period, and secondly, do the lists of borrowings of these libraries afford any clue about the popularity of certain titles over others? The answers are influenced by the fact that the nature and function of these libraries have only been distinguished in the last few decades and even the most recent research does not permit altogether satisfactory answers.[182] What is nevertheless clear is that all libraries irrespective of type contained *some* science books even at the very beginning of the century, and that sometime in the decade of the 1770s these books (calculated as a percentage of the total number) dramatically began to increase.[183] Furthermore, even in their primitive way borrowing records demonstrate that although there was a steady demand for science books throughout the century, it was small in comparison to borrowings in history, *belles lettres* and travel until the 1770s; after this time, science books gradually began to outstrip others, theology and philosophy notwithstanding, and by the end of the century science (all branches) became the top competitor to literature and travel.[184] The materials thus far brought to light also indicate that these trends are as valid for Scotland and Ireland as for England and they apply, moreover, to provincial libraries as well as urban.[185] According to most historians, the eighteenth century marked the rise of 'book clubs'; yet when book-club lists are scrutinized it becomes patent that the trends just delineated for public and commercial libraries apply to them as well.[186] What is surprising is the extensiveness of science books in the small circulating libraries such as Philpotts' in Bristol: here the borrower would expect to discover mostly works of non-fiction, in accord with the general taste of the provincial reading public, but would he think to find in such a small row of books Buffon's *Natural History*, Goldsmith's *Animated Nature*, Patrick Boyne's *Tour Through Sicily and Malta* – a work containing serious scientific discussion of the antiquity of the crust of the earth – and Sir William Hamilton's geological *Observations on Mount Vesuvius?*[187]

The evidence is not yet sufficient to reply with any degree of certainty, for to answer in the affirmative may seem to stack the deck in favour of science, and it may appear to some that the deck has already been sorted too far. Nor is the evidence positive enough to know if urban borrowers demanded more science titles than provincial, or if certain regions of the realm varied in their demand for this type of non-fiction; but one thing is clear: by the 1780s imaginative literature and history (including travel) had to share the limelight with all manner of science books, including the sciences of the globe as well as the even newer sciences of man. This fact in itself ought to reveal something significant about eighteenth-century intellectual pluralism: the way that knowledge was in a ferment and rapidly exploding; and it demonstrates beyond any shadow of doubt how the 'new science', as Boyle and his contemporaries called it a century earlier, was now directly 'translating' into the public's actual reading taste in its thirst for knowledge about the practical and applied – even the technological – aspects of theoretical science. Perhaps this is why the first catalogue of the London Library – the precursor of the present library – was prefaced with these words: 'It is intended that the London Library shall contain all those great works in *science and literature*, which it is difficult for individuals to procure. . . .'[188] The charter of a new lending library formed in the 1680s, a century earlier, might have contained the same words, but the words themselves would have been gratuitous inasmuch as few of the borrowers would have possessed enough literacy to understand even the simple science books. There was nothing arbitrary in 1772 about the pronouncement of Dr James Ramsay, the Enlightenment philanthropist who was so important in the abolition of slavery: 'Natural History is, at present, the favourite science all over Europe, and the progress that has been made in it will distinguish and characterize the eighteenth century in the annals of literature in the future'.[189]

Natural history had eventually carved that niche, yet less is known about the tides of reading tastes in natural history than is thought. As Paul Kaufman has written, 'few important areas of literary history, in the broad sense, remain so nebulous and undeveloped as the description of reading vogues',[190] and these vogues encompass science books as well as literary. If, then, any single direction for the future study of books in the eighteenth century emerges from this essay, it is the author's desideratum that these 'reading vogues' will eventually be studied in and of themselves, for they would no doubt shed much light on everything herein discussed. I suspect, furthermore, that a detailed exploration of eighteenth-century medical books would reveal many of the same patterns and trends noticed above. But the precise curve of the development of medical books – its intellectual domain as well as it social exigencies and reading vogues – must be told elsewhere.

APPENDIX

SCIENCE BOOKS IN THE LIBRARIES OF SOME EIGHTEENTH-CENTURY AUTHORS

The catalogue that follows provides information about the libraries of a select group of prominent literary figures in Restoration and eighteenth-century England: Addison, Burke, Congreve, Defoe, Gibbon, Goldsmith,

Johnson, Newton, Pope, Sterne and Swift. While the number of figures is necessarily small owing to limitations of space, there is no reason to believe that a larger sample would change the essential nature of the patterns found below or, indeed, any conclusions that may be drawn from this tabulation. Newton is included because recent scholars have shown that he was far more prominent in literary capacities than was previously thought, and also on the assumption that the contents of his admittedly large library would point to important contrasts with the holdings of the purely 'literary' figures of the times.

The uses here of the terms 'science' and 'scientific' are admittedly problematic, but if the above essay has shown anything it has demonstrated that no satisfactory definition of a 'science book' can be made, precisely because the age itself did not draw fine distinctions between 'science' and 'non-science' – or between 'science' and 'literature' – upon which sub-sequent centuries seem to have insisted. This definitional failure of the eighteenth-century notwithstanding, I have applied the same rule here that I applied in the essay, and have included – among other types of 'natural philosophy' – eighteenth-century books dealing with natural history, geography, and anthropology.

Furthermore, I have included pre-1700 scientific authors in the survey because they provide an excellent context in which to interpret the scientific libraries of these literary writers. By including ancient, medieval and Renaissance scientific books, one can see at a glance the prevalence of eighteenth-century scientists in the library of an individual writer; and students working on a particular author – whether Swift or Pope or Johnson – will eventually be grateful for learning, for example, that the works of Galen are to be found in only a few of the libraries studied here whereas the books of Thomas Burnet, the author of *The Sacred Theory of the Earth*, are found in almost every writer's library. Such information is often obscure and not easily gathered, but it is quickly found in the chart below. However, comparisons of this type would be impossible if the compilation had been limited to eighteenth-century scientific writers. The same reasons explain why the list of scientific authors is not restricted to English nationality.

Conclusions to be drawn from this compilation must await study elsewhere; but certain trends are already apparent, and their identifica-tion is essential for understanding the literary writer involved, as well as the particular scientist. For example, it is now patent that a large part of Sterne's library is devoted to medical books – especially French medical books – with a physiological bent, and that the same Sterne who wrote so brilliantly in *Tristram Shandy* about 'Tristram *Trismegistus*' never owned a copy of any of the works of 'Hermes Trismegistus' whose books were so often reprinted in Sterne's lifetime; that Luigi Cornaro's works – whose books on health underwent so many reprints and in so many languages in the eighteenth century – are found only in Newton's library whereas the writings of Dr George Cheyne, who is discussed so prominently in the above essay, are found in many libraries; that not one of our writers had a book by John Freke, the scientific author referred to many times in *Tom Jones*; that Johnson's library, which contained many science books, had no copy of the works of William Cadogan, the popularizer of children's care, although Johnson's is the only library with any of Linnaeus's books, and that Defoe's library is the only one to possess any works by Athanasius Kircher whose *Mundus Subterraneus* inflamed Coleridge's imagination; that only Newton owned copies of the books of his most ardent popularizer, J. T. Desaguliers; that the best-known writings of the Newtonians were widely represented in the libraries of literary men, and, finally, that Defoe had many science books whereas Pope owned few. These and many other interpretations will be drawn from the compilation.

Nevertheless, the limitations of such a list must not be minimized or neglected. The mere fact that a book appears in a library does not mean the owner has read the book, or even that he is aware of its contents. Moreover, the lack of information here about the numbers of these science books in relation to other types of books in any individual library, and the further lack of dicussion about the circumstances in which the owner obtained the book, will inevitably raise questions about the validity of such an approach. But it has not been my purpose here to interpret the compilation or draw significant conclusions from its patterns. I shall be happy if others engage in that work.

Finally, a word about the sources – primary and secondary – upon which I have drawn. I have used sales catalogues, both published and unpublished, whenever possible, and in cases in which no authoritative sales catalogue was available I have attempted to verify that the books listed here were actually in the library of the owner. Such verification, however, has not been possible in every case, and questions are bound to be raised about the actual appearance of the book in a particular library. I have also drawn upon secondary studies of individual literary figures and their reading.

In the format of the compilation, the number in parentheses indicates the number of different titles by the scientific writer; i.e. Cheyne (4) means that the owner of the library had four different titles by Cheyne in his library. Duplicate copies of the same book are not listed. Thus an owner whose library contained three copies of Cheyne's *English Malady* and no other books by Cheyne is listed as owning merely 'Cheyne' – that is, one book only. An author's first name is given only if the Christian name is necessary to distinguish him or her from other scientific authors with the same initials.

G. S. Rousseau

CATALOGUE

Acosta, J. de Newton
Adams, George Gibbon
Adanson, M. Gibbon
Aelianus, C. Gibbon (3)
Agricola, Georgius Johnson, Newton (3)
Albineus, Nathan Newton
Albinus, B. S. Gibbon (2)
Aldrovandus Goldsmith
Alimari Newton
Alipili Newton
Allen Sterne
Alpinus, Prosperus Defoe, Johnson
Amatus Newton
Anderson, Robert Newton (2)
Anville, J. B. Gibbon (12)
Apollonius Pergaeus Defoe
Apperley, Thomas Johnson
Arbuthnot, John Congreve, Gibbon, New-
    ton (2), Sterne, Swift
Archimedes Defoe, Johnson, Newton (2)
Aretaeus of Cappadocia Johnson (2)
Astruc, Jean Gibbon, Goldsmith, Johnson,
    Sterne
Aurelianus, Caelius Gibbon
Avicenna Swift

Bacon, F. Addison, Goldsmith, Newton,
    Pope, Sterne, Swift
Baglivi, G. Defoe
Bailly, J. S. Gibbon (6)
Baker, Henry Gibbon (2)
Baker, Thomas Newton
Balam, Richard Newton
Barba, Alvardo Newton (2)
Barrow, Isaac Johnson (4), Newton (2)
Bates, T. Congreve
Bauhinus, C. Defoe
Bayle, P. Sterne
Baylies, W. Sterne
Béardé de L'Abbaye Johnson
Beaumont, J. Swift
Becher, Johann Johnson, Newton
Bedford, Arthur Gibbon (2)
Bellini, L. Defoe
Belon, P. Gibbon
Belot, Jean Newton
Bernoulli, Johann Newton (4)
Bidloo, Govard Newton (2)
Birch, Thomas Johnson
Birkenhout, J. Goldsmith
Bizot, Pierre Newton
Blackmore, R. Defoe (2), Sterne

Blair, Patrick Newton
Blanckaert, S. Defoe
Blegny, N. de Defoe
Bochart, S. Defoe
Boerhaave, H. Johnson (4), Newton (3),
    Sterne
Bolletti, G. G. Gibbon
Bonet, Théophile Sterne
Bonnet, Charles Gibbon
Borel, Pierre Newton
Bordelli, Giovanni Johnson, Newton (3)
Borrichivs, Olaus Newton (2)
Bossche, G. Defoe
Bowles, William Gibbon
Boyle, R. Addison, Burke, Defoe, Gibbon
    (3), Goldsmith, Johnson (5), Newton (22),
    Pope, Sterne, Swift
Bradley, Richard Defoe, Newton (4)
Brahe, T. Defoe
Brice, A. Sterne
Briet, P. Gibbon (2)
Brookes, R. Goldsmith, Sterne
Brown, G. Defoe
Brown, J. Defoe
Browne, John Newton
Browne, Thomas Congreve
Bruno, J. P. Defoe
Buchan, William Gibbon
Buffon, G. L. Burke, Gibbon (8),
    Goldsmith
Burnet, Thomas Addison, Congreve, Defoe,
    Gibbon (2), Johnson, Newton (4), Sterne,
    Swift
Burton, Robert Johnson, Sterne
Buesching, A. F. Gibbon (13)

Cadogan, William Gibbon
Caesalpinus, Andreas Johnson
Caesivs, Bernardus Newton
Caius, John Defoe, Johnson
Cardanus, H. Defoe, Johnson (10), Sterne,
    Swift
Carré, L Defoe
Cawood, Francis Newton
Celsus, Aurelius Congreve, Defoe, Johnson,
    Newton, Swift
Chauvin, E. Defoe
Cheselden, William Johnson, Sterne
Cheyne, George Defoe (4), Johnson, Newton
    (4), Sterne (3)
Clarke, James Newton (2)

238

Cockburn, William   Defoe
Cooper, William   Newton
Cornaro, Luigi   Newton
Cowper, William   Newton
Croker, T. H.   Goldsmith, Sterne
Cronstedt   Johnson
Crousaz, J. P. de   Defoe
Culpeper, N.   Congreve

Dale, Samuel   Congreve
Dale, Thomas   Newton
Davisson, William   Newton
Derham, William   Goldsmith, Sterne
Desaguliers, J. T.   Newton (2)
Descartes, R.   Defoe, Newton (7)
Diemerbroeck, I. de   Congreve, Defoe
Digby, Sir K.   Goldsmith, Newton
Dionis, P.   Sterne
Ditton, Humphrey   Newton
Douglas, James   Newton, Sterne
Dover, T.   Sterne
Drake, J.   Sterne
Du Chesne, Joseph   Newton (3)
Duhamel, J. B.   Johnson (2), Newton

Edwards, George   Goldsmith (4)
Eschuid, Joanne   Swift
Eschuid, Joannes   Swift
Euclid   Burke, Defoe, Gibbon (3), New-
  ton (6), Sterne

Fabri, Honoratus   Newton (2)
Fabricius, Hieronymus   Johnson (2)
Fallopius, G.   Johnson
Fatio de Duillier, N.   Newton (3)
Ferguson, James   Gibbon, Johnson (3), Sterne
Fermin   Goldsmith
Fernel   Swift
Fevillée, Louis   Newton
Fida, Abu al   Gibbon (2)
Flamsteed, John   Newton
Floyer   Sterne
Fontenelle, Bernard   Addison, Congreve,
  Sterne
Foster, Samuel   Newton
Fracastaro, Girolamo   Congreve
François Marie, Père   Newton
Freind, John   Defoe, Newton
Frénicle de Bessy, B.   Newton
Fréret, N.   Gibbon
Fromondus   Newton
Fuller, Thomas   Newton, Sterne

Gale, T.   Defoe, Sterne

Galen   Burke, Defoe, Johnson (2), Swift
Galileo   Newton
Gassendi   Congreve, Defoe, Johnson,
  Newton
Gautruche   Newton
Geer, Carl de   Goldsmith
Gellibrand   Newton
Geoffroy, E. F.   Sterne
Gerard, J.   Johnson, Sterne
Gerhard, Johann, M. D.   Newton
Gesner, J.   Gibbon, Goldsmith, Johnson (3)
Gibson, T.   Swift
Gilbert, William   Johnson
Glaser, Christophe   Newton
Godfrey, Ambrose   Newton
Goodall, Charles   Defoe
Gordon, George   Newton (2)
Gouan   Goldsmith
Graaf   Defoe
Grandi, Guido   Newton (4)
Gravesande   Defoe, Gibbon (4), Johnson,
  Newton (9)
Greaves, John   Defoe (2), Gibbon (2),
  Johnson (2), Newton (2)
Gregg, Hugh   Newton
Gregory, David   Newton (4)
Gregory, James   Newton (4)
Gregory, John   Sterne
Grew, N.   Defoe
Guidott   Defoe
Gumilla, J.   Gibbon (3)
Gunter, E.   Newton

Hales, Stephen   Johnson (2)
Haller   Gibbon (15), Johnson
Halley   Newton (3)
Hamilton, Sir William   Gibbon (2)
Harris, John   Defoe (2), Newton (2)
Harris, Walter   Defoe
Hartley, David   Johnson (2)
Hartlib   Newton
Hartmann, Johann   Newton
Harvey, W.   Burke
Hatton   Johnson, Newton
Hauksbee, Francis   Newton (3)
Heister, L.   Defoe, Sterne
Helmont   Johnson, Newton
Helsham   Johnson
Hermann, Jacob   Newton, Sterne
Hertzberg, E. F.   Gibbon
Hill, John   Gibbon (2), Goldsmith, John-
  son (2), Sterne (2)
Hippocrates   Burke, Congreve, Gibbon (3),
  Johnson, Swift

G. S. Rousseau

Hobbes Addison, Defoe, Newton, Sterne, Swift
Hoffmann, Friedrich Johnson, Sterne
Holbach Gibbon (2)
Hollandus, J. Newton
Hooke Defoe, Newton (4)
Horrocks, Jeremiah Newton
Huxam Johnson

James, Robert Johnson (4)
Jones, William Newton (2)
Johnston, John Newton

Kaempfer Gibbon
Keill, John Defoe, Gibbon (3), Newton (4), Sterne
Kemp, W. Defoe
Kendal Newton
Kennedy, Peter Defoe, Newton (2)
Kepler, J. Defoe (2)
Kersey, John Newton
Kircher Defoe (2)
Kirwan Gibbon
Klein, Jacob Goldsmith
Knowles, G. Defoe, Sterne
Koenig, Emanuel Newton

La Hire Defoe, Newton (2), Sterne
Lawrence, Thomas Johnson
Leadbetter Sterne
Le Clerc, Daniel Defoe, Johnson, Newton
Ledran Sterne
Lémery, Nicolas Defoe (2), Newton (2)
Lemort Newton
Leow, J. F. Newton
Lesser, F. C. Gibbon (2)
Lewis, William Johnson
Lhuyd, Edward Newton, Sterne
Lilly, William Congreve
Linnaeus Goldsmith (3)
Lister, Martin Defoe, Newton
Long, Roger Sterne
Lowe, Peter Sterne
Lull, R. Defoe

Maclaurin, Colin Gibbon, Newton (3), Sterne
Macquer Johnson (3)
Malcolm Johnson
Manilius Congreve, Defoe, Gibbon (4), Johnson, Pope
Marggraf Johnson
Martin, Benjamin Sterne
Maubray Sterne (2)

Maupertuis Johnson
Mayerne, T. T. de Defoe
Mead, Richard Gibbon (3), Johnson (2), Newton (2), Sterne
Melanchthon Sterne, Swift
Menuret de Chambaud Sterne
Michelotti, P. A. Newton
Miller, P. Sterne
Moffett, T. Defoe
Moivre Newton (7)
Molyneux, W. Defoe
Monro, A. Burke, Sterne
Moore, Jonas Newton (4)
Morgagni Newton
Morin, J. Swift
Moxon, J. Defoe, Newton, Swift (2)
Mudge, John Johnson (2)
Musschenbroek Johnson, Newton (3), Sterne
Mylius, J. Newton
Mynsicht Newton

Newton Addison, Burke, Congreve, Defoe, Gibbon, Johnson (5), Newton (21), Pope, Sterne, Swift
Norwood, Richard Newton (2)

Oughtred Defoe
Owen, Charles Goldsmith

Palfyn Newton
Paracelsus Defoe, Johnson (3), Newton (5), Swift
Paré Defoe
Parkinson, John Newton
Paxton, P. Sterne
Payne, William Johnson (4)
Pemberton Congreve, Sterne
Pennant Gibbon (9), Goldsmith (4)
Petiver Newton (4)
Pitcairne, A. Defoe, Johnson, Newton
Place, E. Newton
Plat, H. Defoe
Pliny the Elder Congreve, Defoe (2), Gibbon (20), Goldsmith, Johnson (3), Sterne
Plot Newton
Pluche Goldsmith (4), Sterne (2)
Porterfield, R Sterne
Pott, Percivall Johnson (3)
Pringle, John Sterne
Pysegur, A. M. J. Gibbon

Quincy, John Burke, Congreve

Randolph, G. Sterne

240

Ray Congreve, Gibbon (2), Goldsmith, Newton (2)	*Templeman, P.* Sterne
Réaumur Gibbon (20), Johnson	*Tolet, F.* Defoe
Ripley Newton (3)	*Tournefort* Goldsmith
Riverius, L. Johnson	*Towne, R.* Defoe
Robinson, N. Defoe	*Trembley, A.* Gibbon, Goldsmith
Rohault, J. Gibbon, Newton, Sterne	*Tunstall* Johnson
Rudd, Thomas Newton	*Turner, Daniel* Sterne
Ruysch Newton, Sterne	
Rzaczynski, G. Johnson	*Valsalva, A. M.* Defoe
	Verheyen Sterne
Salmon, William Congreve, Defoe, Johnson, Newton (2)	*Vesalius* Defoe, Johnson
Sanctorius Congreve	*Wallis, John* Defoe (2), Newton (2)
Schelhamer(us) Johnson, Newton	*Ward, Seth* Newton
Scultetus, J. Defoe	*Watson, Richard* Johnson (3)
Sénac, J. B. Gibbon (2)	*Webster, John* Newton
Sendivogius Newton (3)	*Whiston, William* Addison, Defoe (2), Newton (5), Sterne
Spallanzani Gibbon (4)	*Whytt* Burke
Sprat, Thomas Gibbon, Newton, Sterne	*Wilkins, J.* Congreve, Sterne
Stahl Johnson	*Willis, Thomas* Congreve, Defoe, Johnson, Newton, Sterne
Starkey Newton (8)	*Willoughby, Francis* Goldsmith
Stephens, J. Sterne	*Wingate, Edmund* Newton (3), Sterne
Stone, E. Newton	*Winslow, J. B.* Gibbon (4)
Strother Defoe	*Wintringham, C.* Sterne
Stuart, Alexander Newton	*Wolfius* Johnson (11)
Stukeley Sterne	*Woodward, John* Johnson, Newton (3), Swift
Swammerdam Goldsmith, Sterne	
Sydenham Congreve, Defoe (2), Sterne	

NOTES

I am grateful to Professor R. Hambridge, as well as Dr J. P. Feather and Dr I. Rivers, the editor of this volume, for commenting on this essay at various stages of its preparation, although I myself am responsible for any gaps the reader may discern. I must also thank Mrs Leila Brownfield for her unrelenting energy in ferreting out some of the obscure details in the appendix.

1. Quoted in E. L. Eisenstein, *The Printing Press as an Agent of Change* (1979), II, 691. Madame du Bocage's remark is found in her *Letters Concerning England* (2 vols., 1770), I, 34, written while she was a visitor in London.
2. As evident in Richard Helsham, M.D., *A Course of Lectures in Natural Philosophy* (1743). See also A. Ferguson (ed.), *Natural Philosophy through the Eighteenth Century* (1972).

3. See R. K. Merton, 'Puritanism, pietism, and science', in *Social Theory and Social Structure* (New York, 1957), 574–606; *idem, Science, Technology and Society in Seventeenth Century England* (1970); C. Webster, *The Great Instauration* (1975); S. B. Barnes, *Scientific Knowledge and Sociological Theory* (1974); S. Shapin and S. B. Barnes (eds.), *Natural Order* (1979). For deism, see N. Torrey, *Voltaire and the English Deists* (New Haven, 1930) and P. Gay, *Deism: an Anthology* (Princeton, 1968).
4. C. Hill, *Puritanism and Revolution* (1958); *idem, Society and Puritanism in Pre-Revolutionary England* (1964); *idem,* 'Mechanic preachers and the mechanical philosophy', in *The World Turned Upside Down: Radical Ideas during the English Revolution* (1972), 287–305; K. Thomas, *Religion and the Decline of*

Magic (1971); P. M. Mathias (ed.), *Science and Society 1600–1900* (1972); B. Easlea, *Witch Hunting, Magic and the New Philosophy* (1980).

5. S. Schaffer, 'Natural philosophy', in *The Ferment of Knowledge: Studies in the Historiography of Eighteenth-Century Science*, ed. G. S. Rousseau and R. Porter (1980), 55–92.

6. For example M. Foucault, *The Archaeology of Knowledge* (1972) and *The Order of Things* (1970); see also Schaffer, *op. cit.*, who discusses this matter at some length.

7. See the discussion of 'Baconianism' in M. Purver, *The Royal Society: Concept and Creation* (Cambridge, Mass., 1967), 20–62, and R. Frank, *Harvey and the Oxford Physiologists* (Berkeley, 1981).

8. See W. Houghton, 'The Engish virtuoso in the seventeenth century', *J. History of Ideas*, III (1942), 51–73, 190–219; R. Porter, 'Gentlemen and geology: the emergence of a scientific career, 1660–1920', *Historical J.*, XXI (1978), 809–36; S. F. Cannon, *Science in Culture* (1978).

9. L. Stephens' *History of English Thought in the Eighteenth Century* (2 vols. 1876) remains the classic study of deism in England during this period.

10. The common man in the period 1660–1720, so far as one can generalize, would hear the 'argument from the limitations of reason', in biblical, allegorical, moral and psychological versions, every Sunday from the pulpit and read about it in printed sermons.

11. See the subsequent two pages and J. M. Levine, *Dr Woodward's Shield: History, Science and Satire in Augustan England* (Los Angeles, 1977).

12. The extent of this awakening has been shown by M. H. Nicolson in *Pepys' Diary and the New Science* (Charlottesville, 1965); Evelyn, Dryden, Butler, Waller, Denham, Cowley, the Duchess of Newcastle and many other literary figures, male and female, are treated in addition to Pepys.

13. G. Sherburn (ed.), *The Correspondence of Alexander Pope* (5 vols., 1956), II, 264. Pope had a great deal to say, of course, about this 'class'; see, for example, the

Dunciad: Book Four, which expatiates on these *virtuosi*-scientists who 'Impale a Glow-worm, or Vertu profess,/Shine in the dignity of F.R.S.' (IV, 569–70).

14. See D. Stimson, *Scientists and Amateurs: a History of the Royal Society* (New York, 1948); L. S. Feuer, *The Scientific Intellectual* (New York, 1963); D. S. L. Cardwell, *The Organisation of Science in England* (rev. edn, 1972); M. Berman, ' "Hegemony" and the amateur tradition in British science', *J. Social History*, VIII (1975), 30–50, who studies aspects of class-structure and fashion.

15. And even in histories of natural philosophy. Bishop Thomas Sprat – the historian of the Royal Society, high churchman, Bishop of Rochester and 'believer' in the new science of natural philosophy – explains in his *History of the Royal Society* (1667) how a new '*Systeme of Natural Philosophy*' (327) had been built up: 'one great Man [Bacon], who had the true Imagination of the whole extent of this Enterprize [the new science], as it is now set on foot' (35). By 'this Enterprize' Sprat means the Royal Society, as it had developed before 1667, but his monolithic attribution to one man of the whole development of 'new science' in the seventeenth century is of course no longer credited. Yet credit to Bacon thunders down throughout the eighteenth century in books about the development of the Royal Society and in biographies of Bacon; see D. Mallet, *The Life of Francis Bacon* (1740); T. Birch, *The Life of the Hon. Robert Boyle* (1744).

16. See Purver, *op. cit.*; the useful introduction by J. I. Cope and H. Whitmore Jones to *Sprat's History of the Royal Society* (St Louis, 1966); Stimson, *op. cit.*; H. Lyons, *The Royal Society, 1660–1940* (1944); Frank, *op. cit.*

17. One hundred years later Samuel Johnson selected the same motto as the epigraph for *The Rambler* (1752), almost ironically and without any of the resistance to language felt by the early Fellows of the Royal Society.

18. Thomas Hobbes, *Behemoth* (1679), 155, quoted in Purver, *op. cit.*, 73.

19. For analysis of the authors of these

papers, see H. Lyons, *The Royal Society* (1944), 126; M. Hunter, 'The social basis and changing fortunes of an early scientific institution: an analysis of the membership of the Royal Society, 1660–1685', *Notes and Records of the Royal Society of London*, XXXI (1976), 9–114; *idem*, *Science and Society in Restoration England* (1981).

20. The point is supported further by material gathered by P. Laslett in 'The foundation of the Royal Society and the medical profession in England', *British Medical J.*, 11 (1960), 167. Sir G. Clark, *A History of the Royal College of Physicians of London* (3 vols., 1962–71), 11, 435–6, discusses the income of physicians and the style of life they enjoyed; so far as I am aware the libraries of physicians 1660–1760 have not been studied in any depth except for those of a few physicians of note, such as Richard Mead, who amassed about 30,000 volumes, and the surgeon John Hunter, whose vast library formed the basis of the Hunterian Collection in Glasgow University. See also P. G. M. Dickson, *The Financial Revolution in England* (1967), for some discussion of the incomes of physicians in relation to other incomes then, and J. F. Fulton, *The Great Medical Bibliographers* (1951), for a study of these physicians as collectors.

21. See the section on 'ladies' philosophy' below and, for a witty and early treatment of women and 'natural philosophy', Nicolson, *Pepys*, ' "Mad Madge" and the "The Wits" ', 101–76.

22. The internal ideological wars of the Fellows and of outsiders in the book trade with whom they quarrelled also played a rôle, but delineation of this matter lies beyond the scope of this essay; see R. F. Jones, *Ancients and Moderns: a Study of the Rise of the Scientific Movement in Seventeenth-Century England*, (St Louis, 1961, rev. edn.). Joseph Priestley, the so-called 'father of chemistry' and ingenious student of rhetoric, writing at the end of the eighteenth century thought in retrospect that the early Royal Society had done more to foster publication of science books and pamphlets than any other

group; see *The Theological Repository* (2 vols., 1769), I, vii–viii.

23. See K. Mannheim, *Ideology and Utopia* (New York, 1936), 61; a fine discussion of Bacon's concept appears on 61–2.

24. E.g., William Derham, *Physico-theology, or a Demonstration of the Being and Attributes of God from his Works of Creation* (1713), which went through 12 editions by 1754.

25. M. C. Jacob, *The Newtonians and the English Revolution 1689–1720* (1976), 33.

26. No account of science books in the eighteenth century can omit this factor and hope to treat the subject adequately, yet even J. L. Thornton and R. I. J. Tully are silent on literacy in *Scientific Books, Libraries and Collectors: a Study of Bibliography and the Book Trade in Relation to Science* (3rd edn., rev. 1971). For important background, see also L. Rostenberg, *Literary, Political, Scientific, Religious and Legal Publishing, Printing and Bookselling in England 1551–1700* (New York, 1965).

27. From the Restoration down through the end of the eighteenth century the perception is found in the diaries of foreigners as well as natives: see S. Sorbière, *Voyage to England* (1664), together with T. Sprat's *Comments upon S. Sorbière's Voyage* (1665), and P. J. Grosley's *Tour to London* (2 vols., 1772), I, 185–90.

28. As D. J. Greene has shrewdly argued in 'Swift: some caveats', *Studies in the Eighteenth Century*, 11 (Sydney, 1973), 354–8.

29. *The Tatler*, no. 236 (1710) containing the 'Will of a Virtuoso', Addison's most extended satire on *virtuosi*. See also *Tatler*, 119, 216, and 221 for other attacks. Only M. C. Jacob (*op. cit.*) has commented, albeit briefly, on the political and ideological aspect of Addison's response to science.

30. See D. Bond (ed.), *The Spectator* (5 vols, 1965), I, 191; further discussion of Addison's attacks on the *virtuosi* and other natural philosophers is found in M. H. Nicolson, *Science and Imagination* (Ithaca, 1962), 174–6.

31. Much of the criticism was that naturalist-philosophers were not

Baconian *enough*, and had allowed themselves to be deflected from their calling, i.e. the discovery of techniques with clear social utility. See Feuer, *op. cit.*, 44–6. But literary men were not the only group to attack science. John Sergeant's (1622–1707) *Method of Science* (1696) objects to the philosophy of 'natural philosophy' on the grounds that it is incapable of establishing 'the truth' about reality and that it is therefore an altogether limited form of knowledge; approaching both truth and knowledge from an Aristotelian realist position, Sergeant, who was vigorously opposed to Locke's views, argues that the truth produced by 'natural philosophy' is incommensurate with innate ideas; see my forthcoming essay 'Sergeant's neo-Aristotelian *Method of Science* (1696) and "the way to truth" '. Commentaries on Malebranche and prefaces to his works are also revealing for the relation of 'natural philosophy' to 'truth': see, for example, the 1694 English edition of the *Treatise Concerning the Search after Truth* . . . (1694).

32. Actual ridicule has been surveyed in Nicolson, *Science*, and in P. Rattansi, 'Satire on science in the seventeenth and eighteenth centuries' (Ph.D. thesis, University of London, 1971), but not the extent to which the literati embraced aspects of the new latitudinarian ideology.

33. See F. Watson, *The Beginnings of the Teaching of Modern Subjects in England* (1909), 288; see also M. L. Clarke, *Classical Education in Britain 1500–1900* (1959); A. M. d'I. Oakeshott, 'English grammar schools 1660–1714' (Ph.D. thesis, University of London, 1969); W. A. L. Vincent, *The Grammar Schools 1660–1714* (1969); M. Seaborne, *The English School* (1971); R. S. Thompson, *Classics or Charity? the Dilemma of the Eighteenth-Century Grammar School* (1971). Useful comments about the lack of 'science books' are also found in contemporary works on education: see Gilbert Burnet, *Thoughts on Education* (1668, repr. 1761); N. Carlisle, *A Concise Description of the Endowed Grammar Schools in England* (2 vols., 1818).

34. Perhaps Daniel Defoe's *Complete English Tradesman* (1726) ought to mark the dawn of a new era for the stress laid on 'natural philosophy' in a 'young gentleman's education'; see also E. C. Mack, *Public Schools and British Opinion 1780–1860* (New York, 1939), 57; and G. C. Brauer, *The Education of a Gentleman: Theories of Gentlemanly Education in England 1660–1775* (New York, 1959).

35. Quoted in Vincent, *op. cit.*, 215, whose source is E. H. Pearce, *Annals of Christ's Hospital* (1908).

36. J. Sargeant, *Annals of Westminster School* (1898), 135. By 1751 Barrow's edition of Euclid had gone through six editions in Latin and at least four in English, and other scholars prepared other editions, totalling more than 50 by 1780.

37. A. C. Babenroth, *English Childhood* (New York, 1922), 173. D. E. Allen notes in *The Naturalist in Britain: a Social History* (1976), 16, that Banks could not find books about botany even when he went up to Oxford.

38. A. K. Cook, *About Winchester College* (1917), 316. A. C. Benson, *Fasti Etonenses* (1899), makes no mention of science education at Eton.

39. Quoted in W. Birch, *The School Master; a Tribute to the Memory of Thomas James . . . with a Short Memoir* (1829), 14.

40. Bentham's *Chrestomathia* (1816), his philosophy of education, has no eighteenth-century equivalent; Locke's *Thoughts Concerning Education* (1693) is the closest approximation but is remarkably silent on the matter of textbooks, and however 'modern' Aubrey's *Idea of Education of Young Gentlemen* claimed to be in the 1690s, it nevertheless placed little emphasis on 'natural philosophy'.

41. See D. M. Simpkins, 'Early editions of Euclid in England', *Annals of Science*, XXII (1966), 225–49.

42. We tend to forget for how long 'science' was excluded from the curriculum of English schools, whether endowed or unendowed: as late as the Regency Charles Darwin claims to have been incapable of learning anything about

'science' at Dr Butler's school in Shrewsbury and equally unable to obtain science textbooks there; see C. Darwin, *His Life Told in an Autobiographical Chapter* (New York, 1893), 9, and P. Kaufman, *Libraries and their Users: Collected Papers in Library History* (1969), 132–3, who confirms Darwin's statement with hard evidence.

43. I discuss the economics of this state of affairs below. For dissenting academies see ch. 6 above and J. W. A. Smith, *The Birth of Modern Education: the Contribution of the Dissenting Academies 1660–1800* (1954).

44. C. Wordsworth, *The Undergraduate* (1928), 13.

45. *Ibid.*, 13; Wordsworth is quoting here from *Scholae academicae* (1877, repr. 1968), 189–90.

46. R. W. T. Gunther, *Early Science in Cambridge* (1937), 226.

47. *Ibid.*, 226; presumably Gunther means a student of superior talent. Gunther notes in *Early Science in Oxford* (14 vols., 1945), XIV, 3–4, that science teaching there was no better, yet he maintains that 'mathematics and natural philosophy are so generally . . . understood, that more than 20 in every year of the Candidates for a Bachelor of Arts Degree [at mid-century] are able to demonstrate the principal Propositions in the *Principia*'; see *Early Science in Cambridge*, 59.

48. See A. Friedman (ed.), *Collected works of Oliver Goldsmith*, 5 vols. (1966), I, 334, and for the passage cited below, I, 463; the passages quoted are respectively from *An Enquiry into the Present State of Polite Learning in Europe* (1759) and *The Bee:* no. 6, 'On education'.

49. C. Wordsworth, *Scholae academicae* (1877; repr. 1968), 78–81, 248–9, 330–7; in his other appendices Wordsworth gives reading lists, the names of textbooks required on examinations, the reading lists of the schools, the lecture notes of several tutors, etc.; see also D. A. Winstanley, *Unreformed Cambridge* (1935); A. D. Godley, *Oxford in the Eighteenth Century* (1908); Gunther, *Early Science in Oxford*; and W. A.

Pantin, *Oxford Life in Oxford Archives* (1972). The situation at Oxford was similar to that at Cambridge, with the exception that 'natural philosophy' was adopted even more slowly there, and this may be why the Oxford University Press printed so few 'science books' between 1700 and 1800, as H. G. Carter, *A History of the Oxford University Press* (1979), has shown.

50. Wordsworth, *Scholae academicae*, 69.

51. The spread of Newtonianism in the early eighteenth century, and the means by which it was adopted, has acquired an ocean of scholarship that cannot be treated here. What is of interest is the degree to which the adoption depended on printed books.

52. A large percentage of these 'books' are merely printed versions of the lecturer's notes, but this fact does not alter the matter of origins.

53. See J. Crellin, 'Chemistry and eighteenth century British medical education', *Clio Medica*, IX (1974), 21, and the discussion below of natural history books.

54. Especially T. S. Kuhn, *The Structure of Scientific Revolutions* (1962; rev. edn. 1970) and the various books of M. C. and J. R. Jacob, especially 'The Anglican origins of modern science', *Isis*, LXXI (1980), 251–67.

55. 'The navy', in A. S. Turberville (ed.), *Johnson's England* (2 vols., 1933), I, 57.

56. Quoted in Sir J. Smyth, *Sandhurst* (1961), 33.

57. F. G. Guggisberg, '*The Shop*': *the Story of the Royal Military Academy* (1900), 26.

58. John Muller's publishing career demonstrates the point: he was one of the first to complain about the need for military science textbooks (see p. 206 above) and then exploited the argument of need to persuade London booksellers to continue to print his textbooks: works such as *A Treatise of Fortification* (1746) – the book Sandham was copying and which went through three editions by 1774; *A Treatise Containing the Practical Part of Fortification* (1755), which also went though several editions in a few years; *A Treatise of Artillery* (1768); *A New System of Mathematicks [for the Use of*

Military Students] (1769); *The Attack and Defence of Fortified Places* (1770) – many of which were assigned in his classrooms at the Royal Academy at Woolwich.

59. See H. Barnard, *Military Schools and Courses of Instruction in the Science and Art of War*...(New York,1969), 525–8, 559–65.

60. *Ibid.*, 628–9.

61. I have presented some of the evidence in an essay entitled 'Immortal Doctor Cheyne and the "Scientific Wits": aspects of science and millenarianism in the eighteenth century', in *Messianism and Millenarianism in Eighteenth-Century England*, ed. R. H. Popkin (Berkeley and Los Angeles, forthcoming).

62. N. Hans, *New Trends in Education in the Eighteenth Century* (1966), on whose book I have heavily drawn in this section.

63. J. T. Desaguliers, *Physico-Mechanical Lectures* (1717), i.

64. As Hans notes (*op. cit.*, 141) many well-known persons attended these lectures, including famous poets and writers, financiers, politicians, physicians, courtiers, foreigners, and other dignitaries. If as diverse a group bought these science books as attended the coffee-house lectures, then the dissemination of these books indeed penetrated almost all segments of society. Attendance at these courses was then as fashionable as it was educational, and purchase of the lecturer's manual was a status symbol.

65. Desaguliers, Watts and Worster worked in collaboration with the Innys brothers, the successful family of booksellers whose premises were in the northwest alley behind St Paul's Church. See also below, p. 231.

66. In 1713–14 Pope attended Whiston's lectures at Button's coffee house and bought the course-manual, *A Course of Mechanical, Optical . . . Experiments . . . the Explanatory Lectures read by William Whiston* – for only 6s.; in 1731 Shaw's lecture course cost 5 guineas and the printed lecture notes 6s.

67. J. Lawson and H. Silver, *A Social History of Education in England* (1973), 219; italics mine. Passages discussed below are also found on p. 219.

68. No one has undertaken a prosopographical study of the English coffee houses in which those who are known to have attended and their backgrounds are studied.

69. A failure to distinguish the various professions of the audience of the early coffee houses is the chief weakness of A. Ellis's otherwise informative *The Penny Universities: a History of the Coffee Houses* (1956).

70. The matter is further complicated by the relation of these itinerant lecturers and their 'science books' to Grub Street, a relation which no one seems to have studied in any detail; even our finest student of Grub Street – Pat Rogers – is silent on the matter in *Grub Street: Studies in a Subculture* (1972), as were his predecessors: A. S. Collins, K. Hornbeak, E. E. Kent, and E. A. Bloom.

71. And it is crucial to note about this readership that no similar books were then being prepared for 'courses' or 'demonstrations' on other subjects, i.e., history, literature, politics.

72. The contrasts discussed in this paragraph derive from study of a representative group of each type of book, including but not limited to: F. Hauksbee, *Physico-Mechanical Experiments* (1709); W. Whiston, *A Course of Natural Philosophy* (1715?); W. Vream, *A Description of the Air Pump* (1717); Desaguliers, *Lectures*; B. Worster, *The Principles of Natural Philosophy* (1722); W. Whiston, *Astronomical Lectures* (1728); P. Shaw and F. Hauksbee, *Proposals for a Course of Chemical Experiments* (1731); and then, later on, J. Ferguson, *Astronomy* (1756); *idem, Lectures on Select Subjects* (1760); *idem, An Epitome of Natural and Experimental Philosophy* (1769); A. Walker, *An Analysis of a Course of Lectures* (1770); J. Banks, *An Epitome of a Course of Lectures* (1775). A complete list of the Boyle Lectures from their inception in 1691 to their demise in the 1730s is found in G. S. Rousseau, 'Science', in *The Contexts of English Literature: the Eighteenth Century*, ed. P. Rogers (1978), 160.

73. A fifth edition was brought out by 1736 'with very considerable additions . . . from later discoveries in mathematicks and philosophy'. In 1744 a supplement appeared as prepared 'by a Society of gentlemen who were studying science'. Perhaps David Abercromby's compendium ought to be added to this list: see *Academia Scientarum: or the Academy of Sciences, being a Short and Easie Introduction to the Knowledge of the . . . Sciences* (1687). Trained as a physician, Abercromby also wrote a crisp *Discourse on Wit* (1686) and was praised by the prestigious and influential Haller for anticipating the ideas of the Scottish School of Common-Sense Philosophy.

74. W. T. Starnes and G. E. Noyes, *The English Dictionary from Cawdrey to Johnson 1604–1755* (Chapel Hill, 1946); M. Segar, 'Dictionary making in the early eighteenth century', *Rev. English Studies*, VII (1931), 230–8; and several articles studying the impact of Bayle's dictionary. See also M. H. Nicolson, 'English almanacs and the new astronomy', *Annals of Science*, IV (1939), 1–33; A. Hughes, 'Science in English encyclopaedias, 1704–1875', *Annals of Science*, V (1940), 220–39; D. A. Kronick, *A History of Scientific and Technical Periodicals: the Origins and Development of the Scientific and Technologic Press, 1665–1790* (New York, 1962); D. Layton, 'Diction and dictionaries in the diffusion of scientific knowledge: an aspect of the popularization of science', *Brit. J. History of Science*, II (1965), 221–34.

75. See the Strahan ledgers 1775–90.

76. A small sample shows that at mid-century these books averaged £1 1s. so the common man could not readily afford them; but aristocrats, libraries, colleges, and other institutions bought them. It may not be going too far to affirm that 'dictionary-reading' became a national pastime among the new leisured class; see also J. H. Plumb, *The Commercialisation of Leisure in Eighteenth-Century England* (1973).

77. E.g., S. Blankaart, *The Physical Dictionary* (1702); E. Stone, *New Mathematical Dictionary* (1726); W. Hooson, *The Miner's Dictionary*

(1747); John Hill, *A New Astronomical Dictionary* (1768), a re-issue of his earlier *Urania* (1754); Richard Brookes, *General Gazeteer, or a Compendious Geographical Dictionary* (1762); G. Smith, *A Universal Military Dictionary . . . Explanation of the Technical Terms* (1779). Stone was a popularizer of mathematics, but many of the authors of these dictionaries were physicians who had the leisure and cash to prepare such compendious works.

78. J. E. McClellan III, 'The scientific press in transition: Rozier's journal and the scientific societies of the 1770s', *Annals of Science*, XXXVI (1979), 425–49.

79. Nicolson, *Pepys*, 101–75 and *idem*, *Conway Letters* (New Haven 1930); see also S. Mintz, 'The Duchess of Newcastle's visit to the Royal Society', *J. English and Germanic Philology*, LI (1952), 168–76.

80. G. D. Meyer, *The Scientific Lady in England 1650–1760* (Berkeley, 1955), 49. See also Hans, *op. cit.*, 'Education of women', 202–7.

81. From the start Tipper's strategy contributed to the financial success of the periodical: women were invited to submit their scientific questions 'in verse', which Tipper promised to publish; yet he printed only a fraction of the poems he received, reserving most available space for his *own* scientific questions. Nevertheless, the enticement impelled his female readers (were there any males?) to buy each issue, thereby ensuring the solvency of the *Diary*.

82. C. F. Mullett (ed.), *Letters of Dr George Cheyne to Samuel Richardson (1733–1743)* (Columbia, Mo., 1943), 70. Hans (*op. cit.*) lists the relevant printed works but does not speculate about the causes for the revival; yet it may be that the scientific individualism displayed by courageous women from the time of 'Mad Madge' and Fontenelle was now sentimentalized by a new generation of young women in the 1790s who had read or heard about these female pioneers. Valuable comparisons can be made between scientific women c. 1690, 1790, and in the Regency, e.g., Jane Marcet's *Conversations on Natural*

G. S. Rousseau

Philosophy (1819) and her many other popular science books for ladies.

83. Meyer, *op. cit.*, viii.

84. Meyer concentrates on Susannah Centlivre's *The Bassett-Table* (1705), Thomas Wright's *The Female Vertuosos* (1705), and James Miller's *The Humours of Oxford* (1730), but others should also be considered. In *A Treatise on Female, Nervous, Hysterical . . . Diseases* (1780), William Rowley considers excessive application to 'natural philosophy' a cause of madness and eventual suicide. A further detailed study of this subject needs to be made.

85. Their interest in natural philosophy c. 1690 was related, of course, to the widespread secularization of culture about which so much has been written; yet the part played by scientific women in this emancipation of the religious and philosophic imagination has been overlooked. There are many books about female writers before 1800; see M. R. Mahl and H. Koon (eds.), *The Female Spectator: English Women Writers before 1800* (Bloomington, 1977); but none on scientific women.

86. Schaffer in *The Ferment of Knowledge*, 58–71.

87. See Jones, *op. cit.*, 'The "Bacon-faced generation"', 237–67.

88. Among cultural historians see: Feuer, *op. cit.*, 411–19; P. Gay, *The Enlightenment* (2 vols., 1963–9); Kuhn, *op. cit.*; G. Buchdahl, *The Image of Newton and Locke in the Age of Reason* (1961); F. Manuel, *A Portrait of Isaac Newton* (1968). Among historians of science: A. Thackray, *Atoms and Powers* (1970); M. C. Jacob, *op. cit.*; and the secondary works discussed by Schaffer in *The Ferment of Knowledge*, 58–71. Indispensable also are G. J. Gray, *A Bibliography of the Works of . . . Newton* (1888) and P. and R. Wallis, *Newton and Newtoniana 1672–1975 (1977)*.

89. The disagreements were studied by H. Guerlac, 'Where the statue stood; divergent loyalties to Newton in the eighteenth century', in *Aspects of the Eighteenth Century*, ed. E. Wasserman (Baltimore, 1965), 317–34.

90. Examples include: (for government)

J. T. Desaguliers, *The Newtonian System of the World, the Best Model of Government* (1728); (for painting) *anon.*, *The Geometry of Landskips and Painting . . . Useful to Line Limners in Drawing and Gentlemen in Choosing Pictures* (1735); (for medicine) N. Robinson, *A New Theory of Physick and Diseases, founded upon the Principles of the Newtonian Philosophy* (1725).

91. I. B. Cohen, *Franklin and Newton* (1956) and M. H. Nicolson, *Newton Demands the Muse* (1946).

92. Especially in the new age of leisure as J. H. Plumb has shown in *Commercialization of Leisure* and *Georgian Delights* (1979).

93. Addison, *Spectator* 37 (cf. p. 165, above) D. Bond comments in his Clarendon Edition (5 vols., 1965, 1, 154, n. 6) that Addison may have been thinking of Newton's recently published *Arithmetica Universalis* (1707); but 'young ladies' could have learned simple arithmetic from any number of available books in 1711, especially those by Isaac Barrow, and did not need this work. Probably Addison was thinking of the *Opticks* and *Principia*. Culpeper's *Directory for Midwives* (1651), reissued many times by 1711, is also mentioned in Addison's list.

94. D. Knight has rightly stressed the cultural importance of science books in the development of western civilization, in *Natural Science Books in English 1600–1900* (1972) and in *Sources for the History of Science 1660–1914* (1975), but has not enquired into the spur Newton gave to the book trade.

95. See P. and R. Wallis, *op. cit.*, *passim*.

96. These Newtonians are studied by Schaffer in *The Ferment of Knowledge*, 58–71; Manuel, *op. cit.*; and in various papers by Peter Heimann.

97. See R. Cohen, *The Art of Discrimination* (1964); a sounder treatment, more faithful to the original intentions of these poets, is found in A. D. McKillop, *The Background of Thomson's Seasons* (Minneapolis, 1942).

98. See Buchdahl, *op. cit.*; and an important series of articles by G. A. J. Rogers demonstrating the various ways in which Locke's works ought to be

interpreted as a direct response to Newton and vice-versa. Of especial importance is Rogers' 'Locke's *Essay* and Newton's *Principia*', *J. History of Ideas*, XXXIX (1978), 217–32. It would be interesting to learn whether the banning of Locke's *Essay* in Oxford University in 1703 had any effect on either the reading or sales of Locke's book then.

99. The precise size of this readership has never been and perhaps cannot be determined, but few books sold as well as Cheyne's *Essay of Health and Long Life* (1724) which went through four editions in just the first year, and his *English Malady* (1733) which, although not as sought after as its predecessor, nevertheless went through several reissues by mid-century. Even the more concrete *Observations on the Gout* (1720) reached a fifth edition by 1723, and was in a 'ninth corrected edition' by 1738, destined to go through many subsequent editions. *Philosophical Principles of Religion* (1705) was in a 'fifth corrected' edition in 1736. Both Cheyne and his publishers – principally the house of Strahan – reaped vast profits from these reprints.

100. Many other similar titles are discussed by Schaffer in *The Ferment of Knowledge*, 58–71.

101. It also suggests that scientific revolutions – and, more generally, revolutions in knowledge – occur as the result of one man's work rather than a whole change in world view or socio-economic organization; see Kuhn, *op. cit.*, 'Revolutions as changes of world view', 111–35. Aspects of Cheyne's and Whiston's debt to Newton have been treated by H. Metzger in *Attraction universelle et religion naturelle chez quelques commentateurs anglais de Newton* (Paris, 1938).

102. Important discussions of the problem include: J. Roger, *Les sciences de la vie* (1963) and *idem*, *The Ferment of Knowledge*, 'The triumph of natural history', 263–70; M. Foucault, *Les mots et les choses* (Paris, 1966), translated into English as *The Order of Things*; W. Lepenies, *Das Ende der Naturgeschichte*

(Munich, 1976); for the social and economic aspects see J. M. Chalmers-Hunt, *Natural History Auctions 1700–1792* (1976). An important contemporary book that provides still another point of view is William Smellie's *Philosophy of Natural History* (1790).

103. Lists of these books and secondary studies of them are found in P. and R. Wallis, *op. cit., passim*.

104. See Roger, *Ferment of Knowledge*, 263–4.

105. *Ibid.*, 263.

106. *Ibid.*, 264.

107. *Ibid.*, 263. Roger does not state that the reason for the success is 'literary', but this is his implication, especially when he urgently sends the reader to C. V. Doane, 'Un succès littéraire du XVIIIe siècle: le *Spectacle de la nature de l'abbé Pluche* (Dissertation, University of Paris, 1957). See also my own discussion below.

108. The poems were often reprinted and reissued and were clear money-makers. Their contents have been analysed by several scholars (A. D. McKillop, M. H. Nicolson, R. Cohen, *et al.*), but I am unaware of any study that examines them from the reader's point of view, that is, from his expectations while consulting a didactic-scientific poem.

109. I certainly do not wish to imply that after 1750 books about natural philosophy ceased to be published, or that readers of natural history books were preeminently amateurish; there is a certain overlap in both directions, but for the sake of generalization I have epitomized the evolution of each province of book – natural philosophy and natural history – in extreme terms. D. E. Allen's approach to the rise of natural history is social; see *The Naturalist in Britain*. Yet, excellent as this study is, it says little about the reasons for the sudden craze for natural history in the eighteenth century, except that the phenomenon expressed itself 'in social activities' from the beginning.

110. J. Roger, *Buffon: les époques de la nature* (Paris, 1962) and *Ferment of Knowledge*, 262–8; M. Foucault in *The Order of Things* (1970).

111. See Buffon, *Discours sur le style* (Paris, 1753).

112. *Monthly Rev.*, LII (1775), 616, a review of the three-volume *Natural History of . . . Animals, Vegetables, Minerals* (1775) translated by William Kenrick. This edition was followed in 1781 by a nine-volume set translated by William Smellie, the Scottish naturalist and printer who must not be confused with the Scottish physician who lived at the same time. Containing 260 plates, the edition is a landmark in the evolution of eighteenth-century science books for its remarkably low price of £3 12s. The three-volume Kenrick set (1775) had cost twice this, and the current (i.e. 1781) edition of Buffon in French was available in 16 volumes for 16 guineas. Smellie's firm, known as 'Creech and Smellie', became printers to the University of Edinburgh and published many scientific and medical books from 1770 to the end of the century, including William Buchan's *Domestic Medicine*, the first edition of the *Encyclopaedia Britannica* (1771), a popular *Philosophy of Natural History* (2 vols., 1790), sometimes referred to as Smellie's *Natural History*, a reissue of Benjamin Stillingfleet's *Tracts Relating to Natural History* (1762; and a now scarce 1778 edition), the works of Blair, Beattie, George Campbell, William Cullen, John Gregory – all important 'scientific writers' – and the translations of Buffon. Information about Buffon in England is found in O. E. Fellows and S. F. Milliken, *Buffon* (New York, 1972), much of which is based on S. F. Milliken, 'Buffon and the British', (Ph.D. thesis, Columbia University, 1965).

113. *Monthly Rev.*, LXII (1780), 400. Nangle was unable to identify this reviewer or the one discussed in n. 116.

114. *Monthly Rev.*, LXI (1780), 531. Many similar comments can be compiled in the literally dozens of reviews that appeared from 1762 onwards, when Ralph Griffiths, editor of the *Monthly Review*, brought out the *Natural History of . . . the Horse* (1762). By the 1790s English readers could choose from at

115. least five sets of Buffon's works in translation.

115. See Kaufman, *Libraries*, 156, where the point is documented for Scotland; there is no reason to believe it is not equally valid for England.

116. The distinction was clearly recognized in Linnaeus's own lifetime or shortly after his death in 1778; see Thornton and Tully, *op. cit.*, 192–5; B. Henrey, *British Botanical and Horticultural Literature before 1800* (3 vols., 1975), II, 650–2.

117. See L. F. Powell (ed.), *Boswell's Life of Johnson* (6 vols., 1934), III, 84.

118. F. A Stafleu, for example, writes in *Linnaeus and the Linnaeans* (Utrecht, 1971), 123, of Linnaeus's 'sardonic humour', and others have noticed a witty vein, but these qualities are minimal in the whole *oeuvre*.

119. *Monthly Rev.*, XLV (1772), 258.

120. This fascinating subject is not treated in D. Davie's *Science and Literature 1700–1740* (1964) which terminates before the 'natural history' movement had advanced very far; for some discussion see T. Savory, *The Language of Science* (1953).

121. Raymond Hirons, *Monthly Rev.*, XLV (1772), 259.

122. As early as 1762, before anyone had read Buffon in English, William Rider announced in *An Historical and Critical Account of the Lives and Writings of the Living Authors of Great Britain* (p. 14) that while Goldsmith 'is surpassed by few of his Contemporaries with Regard to the Matter which his Writings contain, he is superiour to most of them in Style, having happily found out the Secret to unite Elevation with Ease, a Perfection in Language, which few Writers of our Nation have attained to'. I have learned much from J. H. Pitman's *Goldsmith's Animated Nature* (New Haven, 1924) and from mounds of notes I collected in the British Library while compiling *Goldsmith: the Critical Heritage* (1972), where the Rider passage is cited on p. 158.

123. Pitman, *op. cit.*, 9; since Pitman published his study several other editions of *Animated Nature* have come to light.

124. *Monthly Rev.*, LII (1775), 310–14; most of Bancroft's reviews in 1775 were harsh, for example, his savage attack on the English translation of Bienville's *Treatise on Nymphomania*. Light on Goldsmith's relation to the book trade and on his reviewers is found in E. E. Kent, *Goldsmith and his Booksellers* (Ithaca, 1933).

125. Powell (ed.), *op. cit.*, III, 84.

126. *Monthly Rev.*, XXIX (1763), 285; elsewhere on the same page Goldsmith chastises Brookes for unrelentingly 'dry descriptions' and extols 'the flowing manner of the French Naturalists' – a 'manner' he himelf invoked in *Animated Nature*.

127. One of the literary triumphs of *Animated Nature* is enticement of the reader into believing he is reading about outlandish animals in distant exotic places; while engaging the reader by this device, Goldsmith at the same time loses no opportunity to philosophize and extemporize about *man*. The reader thus gains the impression (given nowhere in Linnaeus or Buffon) that 'natural history' is a province of knowledge about *familiar mankind* as well as animals.

128. See *Critical Rev.*, XVI (1763), 312 and *Monthly Rev.*, LXXII (1785), 403.

129. Quoted without reference in Allen, *op. cit.*, 36.

130. The first three volumes cost 2 guineas apiece, and the fourth may have sold for the same amount; there was also a cheap pocket edition in two volumes for 6s. Three more volumes appeared from 1758 to 1764 priced at a total sum of £6 6s. These prices are inexpensive compared to the prices of many other natural-history books.

131. *British Zoology* began to appear in 1766 at a price of £2 2s. 6d. and continued to be regularly issued until 1812; for Gray's reading of Pennant, see P. Toynbee and L. Whibley, *The Correspondence of Thomas Gray* (3 vols., 1935), III, 1163ff. and C. E. Norton, *The Poet Gray as a Naturalist* (Boston, Mass., 1903), 27. Goldsmith's indebtedness to Pennant is discussed in Pitman, *op. cit.*, 138–9.

132. Especially 'how-to-do-it' books for those who were 'Sunday naturalists', but as these books often appeared in the form of chapbooks rather than science books, I have not discussed them in any detail here.

133. An entire set of 26 volumes cost 38 guineas 'with 1600 copper plain plates' and 160 guineas 'with coloured plates and 26,000 figures' in 1775 when the last volume appeared. Volume 1 (1759) with copper plates cost £1 11s. 6d., volume 2 (1761) £2 12s. 6d.; thereafter, the volumes continued to cost £1 11s. 6d. for the next two decades. Curiously, the first three volumes fetched only 17s. 6d. in 1794 at the auction of the library of the Earl of Bute (Hill's patron), and 'an elegant copy, the plates beautifully coloured, 27 volumes' fetched £79. See the *Sales Catalogue of the . . . Rt. Hon. the Earl of Bute 1794* (BL 1255. c. 15.1–3). Hill's *Essays in Natural History and Philosophy* (1752), a cheaper book, is worth consulting for contemporary reflections on the popularity of natural history as distinct from natural philosophy. After 1760 the market was flooded with books on the *Florae Britannicae*.

134. A second edition appeared in 1772 for the same price. The copper plates in Brookes's volumes are inferior to Hill's in the *Vegetable System*, yet illustration in the 1760s was an important aspect of the public's attraction to natural-history books. See W. Blunt, *The Art of Botanical Illustration* (1951), and D. Knight, *Zoological Illustration* (1977). Knight maintains that Hooke's depiction of specimens seen through the microscope led the way to the beautiful illustrations of the eighteenth century, but he does not comment on the social history of interest in science.

135. For editions of Buffon in England 1750–1800 and Buffon in relation to the book trade, see Milliken, *thesis*.

136. The reader who is curious about the extensiveness of these books should consult Henrey, *op. cit.*, III: *the Eighteenth Century: Bibliography* (1975). There was even a big trade in children's natural-history books and demand for

books such as *Jack Dandy's History of Birds and Beasts* (c. 1781).

137. For example, Sir William Watson, a leading Fellow of the Royal Society at this time, judged Linnaeus's *Systema Naturae* 'the masterpiece of the most compleat naturalist the world has seen' (*Gentleman's Mag.*, xxiv (1754), 558), and by comparison considered the natural histories of Buffon and Goldsmith the products of amateurs. Yet Watson judged as a scientist without any interest in these men as writers of books. A study such as S. E Hyman's *The Tangled Bank: Darwin, Marx, Frazer and Freud as Imaginative Writers* (New York, 1962) has curiously not as yet been written for these 'imaginative writers' who moulded the taste of their century.

138. 'The telescope and imagination', *Modern Philology*, xxxii (1935), 233–60 and *The Microscope and English Imagination* (Northampton, Mass., 1935).

139. *The Microscope Made Easy* went through 5 editions by 1769, its brilliant success owing something to the simple manner in which Baker explained how to prepare and observe specimens. For the popularity of this book see also G. L'E. Turner, 'Henry Baker, F.R.S.', *Notes and Records of the Royal Society of London*, xxix (1974), 53–79.

140. Martin wrote dozens of books and tracts about instruments that have now been studied by J. R. Millburn in *Benjamin Martin, Author, Instrument-maker, and 'Country Showman'* (Leyden, 1976). Millburn has appended a useful bibliography of these works on pages 193–207; of interest are *Micrographia Nova . . . a New Treatise on the Microscope* (1742); *All Sorts of Philosophical, Optical and Mathematical Instruments* (1756); *An Essay on Visual Glasses* (1756); *Horologia Nova* (1770), all of which were published in England and went through frequent reprints. The elder George Adams' *Micrographia Illustrata* (1746) underwent 4 editions by 1771.

141. The controversy is worthy of reference because of the light it sheds on other types of 'scientific' books and their readers. See Nicolson, *Science*, 200–1.

142. The prize was awarded in 1753 when it was shared by John Harrison, Tobias Mayer and others. See E. G. Forbes, 'Tobias Mayer's claim for the longitude prize', *J. Navigation*, xxviii (1975), 77–90; H. Quill, *John Harrison* (1966).

143. In great numbers, for example: Whiston and Ditton, *A New Method of Discovering the Longitude* (1714); an anonymous *Longitude to be found out with a New Invented Instrument* (1715); numerous satires on the Whiston-Ditton book by the 'Club of Scriblerians'; Arbuthnot's satire *To the Right Honourable the Mayor and Aldermen of the City of London* (1716), in which the author ironically asserts that the reward for discovery of the longitude has had beneficial effect on 'common folk' because it has obliged 'Cooks, and Cook-maids to study Opticks and Astronomy', and to 'throw the whole Art of Cookery into the Hands of Astronomers and Glassgrinders'.

144. *The Artificial Clockmaker, or a Treatise of Watch and Clock Work, Showing to the Meanest Capacities the Art of Calculating Numbers to All Sorts of Movements . . . with the Ancient and Modern History of Clockwork* (1696) was in a fourth edition by 1734, each time having been reprinted by 'the author', after which time it began to appear in 'corrected editions'.

145. For discussion of clocks and chronometers see Millburn, *op. cit.*; H. Michel, *Scientific Instruments in Art and History* (1967); C. M. Cipolla, *Clocks and Culture* (1967); M. Dumas, *Scientific Instruments of the . . . Eighteenth Century* (1972); O. Kurz, *European Clocks and Watches in the Near East* (1975); S. L. Macey, *Clocks and the Cosmos* (Hamden, Conn., 1980).

146. To the reader it must have seemed that interest in clocks was peaking in this decade; as much is announced in the preface of A. Cumming's *Elements of Clock and Watch-work* (1766).

147. On this subject – especially the rôle of ideology in literature – see M. Bradbury, *The Social Context of Modern English Literature* (1971), and although it deals with a period just after ours, R. D. Altick, *The English Common Reader:*

a *Social History of the Mass Reading Public* (Chicago, 1957). But also see Barnes, *Scientific Knowledge; idem, Interest and the Growth of Knowledge* (1977); M. C. Jacob, *op. cit.*; J. R. Jacob, *Robert Boyle and the English Revolution: a Study in Social and Intellectual Change* (New York, 1977).

148. D. Davie, *The Language of Science and the Language of Literature 1700–1740* (1963), 2–3.

149. The attack on this literature in our time has been made by neo-Romantic critics such as H. Bloom and G. Hartman who argue that this body of verse possesses *no* tropes, only *topoi* that have been substituted for tropes. But the assessment must not be ambiguous: Auden, Eliot *et al.* have praised these writers – Pope, Swift, Gray, Thomson, Johnson, Churchill – for their use of scientific metaphor, but *not* because they are 'scientific poets' or 'scientific writers'. A poet must invoke more than 'scientific' language and mechanical tropes before he becomes 'a scientific poet'; for this he must at least versify scientific topics as a large part of his programme. Whereas Akenside, Armstrong and Thomson are 'scientific poets', Pope and Churchill are not. *An Essay on Man* is an exception.

150. See n. 74 above for the dissemination of science in newspapers.

151. Quoted in A. Maclean, *Humanism and the Rise of Science in Tudor England* (New York, 1972), 220. See also D. McKitterick, *Sir Thomas Knyvet* (1977).

152. Here one wonders if any light on this matter will be shed by the studies of subscriptions to books on which Peter Wallis and his team at Newcastle are engaged. It may also be that the percentage change is also evident in other types of libraries, such as those of curates and naturalists; see J. Salter, 'The books of an early eighteenth-century curate', *Library*, XXXIII (1978), 33–46 and R. A. Harvey, 'The private library of Henry Cavendish', *The Library*, II (1980), 281–92. Valuable material is also found in M. Plant, *The English Book Trade* (1939), 55–64.

153. Quoted without source in P. Muir, *English Children's Books 1600 to 1900* (New York, 1954), 67.

154. This rare work is no. 261 in William Sloane's checklist of *Children's Books in England* (New York, 1955); for further discussion see M. F. Thwaite, *From Primer to Pleasure* (1963), 208.

155. Almost nothing is known about Boreman and the financial records of his firm seem to have disappeared.

156. In accord with the *utile-dulce* ethic of the age, Newbery intended this series to be both instructional and delightful, as the first advertisement I have been able to locate states: 'the Whole will seem rather an Amusement than a Task'; see *Penny London Post*, 18 January 1745. C. Welsh, *On Some of the Books for Children of the Last Century* (1886) and *A Bookseller of the Last Century* (1885) has been replaced by S. Roscoe's *Provisional Check-list of Books . . . Issued under the Imprints of John Newbery* (1966) and *John Newbery and his Successors* (1973).

157. Essentially a popularization of Newtonian science, this is also a children's book and succeeds by understanding the structure of curiosity of a child's astronomical imagination. From 1761 to 1794 it went through seven editions.

158. Improvement in illustration is described by J. Whalley in *Cobwebs to Catch Flies: Illustrated Books for the Nursery . . . 1700–1900* (1974).

159. E.g., Sarah Trimmer's *An Easy Introduction to the Knowledge of Nature* (1780) went though 10 editions by the turn of the century, having been composed 'to supply the *lack* of natural history knowledge' in Anna Barbauld's *Lessons for Children* (1778).

160. Begun in 1806, Miss Marcet's series was successful in its rhetorical habit of casting each book in the form of 'conversations': *Conversations on Chemistry* (1806) reached 16 editions by 1853, *Conversations on Natural Philosophy* (1819) reached 20 by 1880, and so forth.

161. The same John Aikin who wrote the more 'adult' *Essay on the Application of Natural History to Poetry* (1777) and who was the only serious scientist then who

approved of Goldsmith's *Animated Nature*.

162. Comparison of this book published at the end of the century with *A Short and Easie Method* (1710), discussed above, shows how much more information about science children were now expected to possess.

163. J. A. Paris's *Philosophy in Sport Made Science in Earnest* (1827) was another bestseller after 1800. See also C. Meigs, 'Roots in the past up to 1840', in *A Critical History of Children's Literature* (1953; rev. edn. 1969), 105–10.

164. For Nourse, see J. P. Feather, 'John Nourse and his authors', *Studies in Bibliography*, xxxiv (1981), 205–226. J. P. Feather and Giles Barber have in preparation a full-length biography of Nourse.

165. Such studies as R. Straus, *Dodsley: Poet, Publisher and Playwright* (1910); A. Briggs (ed.), *Essays in the History of Publishing . . . the House of Longman, 1724–1974* (1974); P. Hernlund, 'William Strahan's ledgers 1738–1785', *Studies in Bibliography*, xx (1967), 89–111; I. Maxted, *The London Book Trades 1775–1800* (1977).

166. See G. A. Lindeboom, *Boerhaave and Great Britain* (Leyden, 1974), 19.

167. But Innys bought back the copyright, and in 1742 he issued it again in an identical version to that of the 1735 Bettesworth edition; C. Hitch was a partner in both the Innys and Bettesworth editions.

168. Some idea of this audience is gained by examining my 'Chronological checklist of the works of John Hill', in *The Renaissance Man in the Eighteenth Century*, ed. D. J. Greene (Los Angeles, 1978), 107–29.

169. Based on the findings of the above checklist; the *DNB* list is highly incomplete.

170. See G. S. Rousseau (ed.), *The Letters and Private Papers of Sir John Hill* (New York, 1982), Introduction *passim*.

171. Not to be confused with John Hill, just discussed. See F. R. Johnson, 'Thomas Hill, an Elizabethan Huxley', *Huntington Library Quarterly*, vii (1944), 329–51.

172. *Ibid.*, 341.

173. The price applies to popular handbooks as well as theoretical science books by Boyle, Locke or Newton, all which types had greatly improved since the times of Pepys. An English translation of Burnet's *Sacred Theory of the Earth* cost 12s. in the early eighteenth century; Fontenelle's 1757 edition in English of the *Plurality of Worlds* cost 6s.

174. Plant, *op. cit.* (1974 rev. edn.), 54.

175. See E. S. Gilboy, *Wages in Eighteenth-century England* (Cambridge, Mass., 1934). Some information is also found in M. S. Rosen, 'Authors and publishers: 1750–1830', *Science and Soc.*, xxxii (1968), 218–32.

176. Based on a survey I have made of representative science books for each decade of the eighteenth century.

177. The prices on Dodsley's lists at mid-century divide between theoretical science books and practical handbooks for the home. Books on the nursing of children or the suppressing of hemorrhages are usually under 2s. and cheap in contrast to science books without practical application.

178. Some of Dodsley's prices at mid-century are quoted by T. F. Dibdin in *Bibliomania; or Book Madness* (1876, rev. edn.).

179. According to George Walker in *Essays on Various Subjects* (2 vols., 1809), i, lxxx; see also L. Chard, 'Bookseller to publisher: Joseph Johnson and the English Booktrade, 1760 to 1810', *Library*, xxxii (1977), 138–54.

180. See Henry Crabbe Robinson, *Diary* (2 vols., 1872), i, 194–5.

181. One other consideration ought to be mentioned: the practice, common by about 1720, of booksellers and printers of keeping in stock current pills and potions for sale. Scholars have continued to be perplexed at the origin of this practice, but it seems to be clearly related to the distribution of goods in the period. Because well-established networks provided a ready-made distribution system, some publishers – notably Newbery – bought into medicine patents to maximize their profits: see J. Alden, 'Pills and

publishing; some notes on the English book trade, 1660–1715', *Library*, VII (1952), 21, and P. S. Brown, 'Medicines advertised in eighteenth-century Bath newspapers', *Medical History*, XX (1976), 152–68. The traditional explanation has been that the practice worked to the profit of both parties: the booksellers (e.g. Newbery) received a commission on all sales in return for advertising the panaceas in their newspapers and selling them in their shops; the medical-pharmaceutical profession gained free advertisement in newspapers and had low overhead costs. Booksellers also carried in stock a large number of scientific instruments, especially those sold in coffee houses by itinerant lecturers. The booksellers Jonah Bowyer and Jonas Brown carried tickets as well as instruments used for Desaguliers' lecture-demonstrations which began on 14 December 1713 at the Bedford coffee house. This date is written in an eighteenth-century hand in the BL copy (551.d. 19. 81) of J. T. Desaguliers, *A Catalogue of the Experiments in Mr Desaguliers Course* (1713). I greatly profited from J. P. Feather's 1981 lecture at the University of California, which dealt with some of this material.

182. See H. M. Hamlyn, 'Eighteenth-century circulating libraries in England', *The Library*, 5th ser. I (1946–47), 197–222; F. Beckwith, 'The eighteenth-century proprietary library in England', *J. Documentation*, III (1947), 81–98; T. Kelly, *Early Public Libraries: a History of Public Libraries in Great Britain before 1850* (1966); C. Parish, *History of the Birmingham Library: an Eighteenth-Century Proprietary Library* (1966); Kaufman, *Libraries*, and 'Readers and their reading in eighteenth-century Lichfield', *The Library*, 5th ser., XXVIII (1973), 108–15, dealing with cathedral libraries.

183. In the catalogues and borrowers' lists surveyed by Kaufman, 'Readers', the crucial decade is the 1770s.

184. Kaufman goes even further when he observes that by the 1780s 'there is a preponderance of scientific works'; see P. Kaufman, 'The Westminster library', *The Library*, 5th ser. XXI (1966), 243.

185. Kaufman, *Libraries*, 'Scotland as the home of community libraries [in the eighteenth century]', 134–47 and R. C. Cole, 'Community lending libraries in eighteenth-century Ireland', *Library Quarterly*, XLIV (1974), 111–23.

186. See P. Kaufman, 'English book clubs and their role in social history', *Libri*, XIV (1964), 1–31, and Beckwith, n. 184, 94–5.

187. Kaufman, *Libraries*, 31–2; Goldsmith's *Animated Nature* continued to be one of 'the ten most popular books' in public libraries down to the end of the century.

188. *A Catalogue of the Books of the London Library Instituted in the Year 1785*, a manuscript quoted by Kaufman in *Libraries*, 19.

189. *Scots Mag.*, XXXIV (April 1772), 136.

190. Kaufman, *Libraries*, 28.

Index

Index

Berkeley, James, Earl of, 53
Berquin, Arnaud, *Looking-Glass for the Mind*, 230
Bettesworth, Arthur, 32, 34, 36, 231, 254
Bible, the, 98–122, 135, 149
Bion, 79
Blackmore, Sir Richard, *The Creation*, 219
Blackwall, Anthony, *Introduction to the Classics*, 91; *The Sacred Classics Defended and Illustrated*, 113
Blackwell, Samuel, *Several Methods of Reading the Holy Scriptures*, 99–100
Blair, Hugh, *Lectures on Rhetoric and Belles Lettres*, 175–6
Blake, William, 216
Blome, Richard, *The Gentleman's Recreation*, 211
Blount, Sir Thomas Pope, *Characters and Censures*, 84
Bocage, Mme du, 197, 202
Boerhaave, Herman, 230, 231, 232; *Aphorisms*, 231
Bolingbroke, Henry St John, Viscount, 59, 189, 190
Bolton, Robert, 150, 152
Bond, Donald F., 64–5
Bonnet, Charles, 219
Bononcini, Giovanni, 55; *Cantate e Duetti*, 55
bookbinding, 7–8, 9
booksellers and bookselling, 8–20, 230–2, 254–5
Boreman, Thomas, 229
Borrow, George, *Lavengro*, 41
Boswell, James, 29–30, 40, 182, 190, 191–2, 221; *Life of Johnson*, 71, 103, 169, 190, 191, 207, 222; *London Journal*, 29
Bowyer, Jonah, 14, 255
Boyer, Abel, *Royal Dictionary, French and English*, 17
Boyle, Robert, 197, 198, 202, 214, 222, 235; *The Christian Virtuoso*, 199
Boyle Lectures, the, 201–2, 210, 246
Boyne, Patrick, *Tour through Sicily and Malta*, 234
Brainerd, David, 147–9, 152; *Journal*, 148–9; *Mirabilia Dei inter Indicos*, 148
Bray, Dr Thomas, 128
Brett, R. L., 228
Breval, John, 55–6; *Remarks on Several Parts of Europe*, 56
Brindley, James, 76
Brodrick, Thomas, *Complete History of the War in the Netherlands*, 63
Brooke, Henry, 58, 61, 62; *Gustavus Vasa*, 58

Brookes, Richard, 212, 219; *Natural History*, 224, 225, 251
Brotherton, John, 32
Brower, Reuben, 228
Brown, Jonas, 14, 255
Browne, Peter, Bishop of Cork, *Things Divine and Supernatural*, 168
Brueggemann, Lewis, *A View of the English Editions . . . of the Greek and Latin Authors*, 76–7, 79, 94
Brumois, Pierre, *Greek Theatre*, 70, 81
Buckley, Samuel, *Third Letter to Dr Mead*, 57, 63; *Thuani Historiarum sui Temporis*, 57
Buffon, Georges Louis Leclerc, Comte de, 219–23, 224, 225, 226, 250, 251, 252; *The Natural History of . . . Animals, Vegetables, Minerals*, 222, 234, 250; *The Natural History of the Horse*, 220, 250
Bull, George, 162
Bunny, Edmund, *Christian Exercise, appertaining to Resolution*, 135
Bunyan, John, 27, 29, 149, 152; *Doctrine of the Law and Grace*, 147; *Grace Abounding*, 147; *The Pilgrim's Progress*, 29, 30, 44, 144
Burder, George, 29
Burke, Edmund, 169, 173, 236, 239–41
Burkitt, William, *Expository Notes, with Practical Observations, on the New Testament*, 17, 99, 103, 105, 107, 111–12, 114–15
Burlington, Richard Boyle, third earl of, 61
Burmann, Petrus, 85
Burnaby-Greene, Edward, 88–9; *Odes of Pindar*, 75
Burnet, Gilbert, Bishop of Salisbury, 59, 61, 135, 156; *A Discourse of the Pastoral Care*, 138; *History of His Own Time*, 42, 59, 63, 64; *Thoughts on Education*, 244
Burnet, Thomas, *The Sacred Theory of the Earth*, 236, 254
Burney, Dr Charles, 190
Burns, Robert, 27
Burton, John, *Pentalogia*, 78–9
Busby, Dr Richard, 94, 204
Bute, Countess of, 166
Bute, John Stuart, third earl of, 251
Butler, Joseph, Bishop of Durham, *Analogy of Religion*, 117, 168, 192
Byron, Henry J., 43

Cadogan, William, 237
Calamy, Edmund, 135, 152; *An Abridgment of . . . Baxter's . . . Life*, 147
Calmet, Dom Augustin, *Dictionary of the Holy Bible*, 101

Index

Camden, William, *Britannia*, 42
Caroline, Queen, 59, 60
Carte, Thomas, 47
Carter, Elizabeth, 72; *Newton's Philosophy Explain'd*, 215
Cartwright, Edmund, 83
Caslon, William, 19
catalogues, library sale, 70, 76, 237; trade sale, 15, 16, 18
Catullus, 92
Chalmers, George, 38, 39
Chamberlayne, John, *The Religious Philosopher*, 166-7
Chambers, Ephraim, 211; *Cyclopaedia*, 211-12
chapbooks, 8, 13, 20, 23, 27-44
Chapman, George, *A Treatise on Education*, 92
Charleton, Rice, *Bath Waters*, 233
Chaucer, Geoffrey, 16
Chesterfield, Philip Dormer Stanhope, Earl of, 69, 76, 77, 85; *Letters*, 69, 172
Cheyne, Dr George, 213-14, 217, 218, 237, 249; *English Malady*, 237, 249; *Essay of Health and Long Life*, 217, 249; *Observations on the Gout*, 249; *Philosophical Principles of Religion*, 217, 249
children's books, 20, 228-30
Chiswell, Richard, 13
Choudard-Desforges, P.-J.-B., *Tom Jones à Londres*, 28
Church, Thomas, *Vindication of the Miraculous Powers*, 194
Churchill, Charles, 253
Churchill, John, 13, 14
Cicero, 130
Clapp, S. L., 48
Clark, Samuel jr, 136
Clark, Samuel sr, 136, 137
Clarke, John, 92; *Dissertation upon the Usefulness of Translations*, 81
Clarke, M. L. 90
Clarke, Samuel, 137, 181, 216; *A Paraphrase on the Four Evangelists*, 99, 104, 105
Claudian, 71, 91
Clements, Henry, 14
Clockmakers Outcry, The, 227
Cobham, Richard Temple, Viscount, 53, 65
Cocchi, Anthony, *Pythagorean Diet*, 233
Cohen, I. B., 215
Colden, Cadwallader, 216
Cole, Christian, *Historical and Political Memoirs*, 56
Cole, William, 53
Coleman, D. C., 55

Coleridge, Samuel Taylor, 76, 176, 237
Coles, Elisha, *Dictionary, English-Latin, and Latin-English*, 17
Collier, Jeremy, 54, 61
Collins, Anthony, 121; *A Discourse of the . . . Christian Religion*, 116; *The Scheme of Literal Prophecy Considered*, 116-17
Collinson, Peter, 225
Collyer, David, *The Sacred Interpreter*, 101, 102, 108
Collyer, Mary, 72
Colman, Benjamin, 148
Colman, George, 84
Comenius, Johannes Amos, 229
congers, book trade, 13-15
Congreve, William, 18, 236, 238-41
Conway, Anne, Viscountess, 212
Conyers, George, 12
Cooper, Elizabeth, *Muses Library*, 72
Cooper, Thomas and Mary, 232
copyright, 10-11, 13, 15, 17, 18, 20, 21
Copyright Act (1709), 10, 11, 16, 32, 33
Cornaro, Luigi, 237
Cornish, Joseph, 73-4; *An Attempt to Display the Importance of Classical Learning*, 74
Cosin, John, 60
Cosin, Richard, *Regni Angliae . . . Reginae Elizabethae*, 60
Cowper, William, 216; *Poems*, 233; *The Task*, 28
Cox, Thomas, 32, 42
Critical Review, The, 89, 95, 224
Cromwell, Oliver, 104
Cudworth, Ralph, 152
Cumberland, Richard, 137
Curll, Edmund, 231

Dacier, André, 80, 83
Dacier, Anne, 80, 87, 88
Darwin, Charles, 244-5
Darwin, Erasmus, 216, 222, 233; *The Botanic Garden*, 219, 225; *Zoonomia*, 225
Davidson, Joseph, 81, 84, 94; edn of Virgil, 81
Davie, Donald, 228
Davis, Charles, 230, 231, 232
Defoe, Daniel, 27-41, 236, 237, 238-41; *Complete English Tradesman*, 244; *Farther Adventures*, 32, 38, 39; *Moll Flanders*, 29, 30, 39-41; *Serious Reflections*, 32, 33, 36, 39; *Life and Strange Surprizing Adventures of Robinson Crusoe*, 22, 28-39, 40, 42, 43, 44
Deloney, Thomas, *Jack of Newbury*, 27; *Thomas of Reading*, 27

Index

Index

Index

20, 234; private, 2, 70, 235–41, 243; public, 2, 99, 234

Licensing Act, expiration of (1695), 6, 8, 10

Licensing Act (1737), 58

Lightfoot, John, *Horae Hebraicae*, 103, 108

Lillo, George, *The London Merchant*, 18

Lindsay, John, *A Critical and Practical Commentary on the New Testament*, 106, 107

Linnaeus, 221–3, 224, 225, 237, 250; *Systema Naturae*, 252

Lintot, Bernard, 12, 13, 17, 18, 85, 231

Locke, John, 72, 165–7, 168, 169, 170, 173, 175, 188, 189, 203, 204, 217, 229, 244, 248–9; *An Essay Concerning Human Understanding*, 42, 151, 165, 167, 175, 176, 177, 249; *Paraphrase and Notes on the Epistles of St Paul*, 106; *Thoughts Concerning Education*, 244

London book trade, 9–11, 12, 13–16, 20

London Library, the, 235

Longinus, 89; *On the Sublime*, 88

Longman, Thomas, 13

Louis XIV, 82

Lowth, Robert, Bishop of London, 78; *Lectures on the Sacred Poetry of the Hebrews*, 112, 113, 120

Lowth, William, 103, 112; *A Critical Commentary and Paraphrase of the Old and New Testaments*, 104–5; *Directions for the Profitable Reading of the Holy Scripture*, 99, 100, 102

Lowther, Anthony, 58

Lucan, 70, 71, 91

Lucian, 71

Lucretius, 79, 187

Lukin, Henry, *An Introduction to the Holy Scripture*, 113

Luther, Martin, 100

Lyttleton, George, Lord, 124; *Dialogues of the Dead*, 85

McEwen, William, *Grace and Truth*, 102

Machin, I. W. J., 'Popular religious works of the eighteenth century', 98

Mack, Maynard, 228

Maclaurin, Colin, 216

Maitland, William, *History of London*, 56, 62, 64

Malebranche, Nicolas, 197, 198, 213; *Treatise Concerning the Search after Truth*, 213, 244

Mallarmé, Stéphane, 228

Mallet, David, 190

Mandeville, Bernard, *A Letter to Dion*, 168

Mann, Horace, 169

Mannheim, Karl, 201

Marcet, Jane, 230, 247–8, 253

Marchant, John, 106; *A Commentary on the New Testament*, 107

Marlborough, John Churchill, Duke of, 55

Martial, 74

Martin, Benjamin, 226, 252; *The Description . . . of a Table Clock*, 227

Martyn, John, 202

mathematical societies, 210

Mayer, John, *Commentary upon . . . the Old Testament*, 104

Mayer, Tobias, 252

Mayo, Dr Henry, 191

Mead, Richard, 243

Meadows, W., 32

Mears, William, 14

Meyer, G. D., 212–13, 214

Middleton, Conyers, 194; *Free Inquiry into the Miraculous Powers*, 171–3, 194

Midwinter, Daniel, 14

Midwinter, David, 211

Midwinter, Edward, 32

Millar, Andrew, 13, 224, 230, 231

Milton, John, 16, 61; *Paradise Lost*, 21, 140; *Poetical Works*, 53

Mist's *Weekly Journal*, 31

Mitchell, Joseph, 56–7, 61; *Poems on Several Occasions*, 56, 64

Monro, Alexander, *secundus*, 179

Montagu, Elizabeth, 84

Montagu, George, 193

Montagu, Lady Mary Wortley, 72, 166

Monthly Review, The, 72, 75, 78, 82, 83, 84, 87, 89, 93, 94, 95, 99, 221, 224–5, 250

More, Hannah, 27

More, Henry, 152

Morgan, Joseph, 48, 49, 50, 53, 64; *A Complete History of Algiers*, 48, 53

Mortimer, John, 17

Moschus, 79

Motley, John, *History of Peter I of Russia*, 64

Motte, Benjamin, 42

Muller, John, 206–7, 245–6; *Treatise Containing the Elementary Part of Fortification*, 207

Mumby, F. A., 7

Murray, John, 230

Musgrave, Samuel, 89

Neal, Daniel, *History of the Puritans*, 147

Neal, Nathaniel, 162, 163

Neiuwentydt, Bernard, *Het reg Gebruik der werelt Beschouwingen*, 166

Neuburg, Victor, 27

263

printers and printing, 8–9, 10, 19, 99
Prior, Matthew, 17, 49, 60, 61; *Poems on
Several Occasions*, 60
Project for Historical Biobibliography
(PHIBB), 50, 51, 52
Propertius, 74
provincial book trade, 9, 11–13
Pulteney, Richard, 222; *General View of the
Writings of Linnaeus*, 222–3
Pulteney, William, 52, 53, 60
Pye, Henry James, 80, 94

Quintilian, 176

Ramsay, Allan, 27; *Poems*, 54
Ramsay, Dr James, 235
Ramsay, Michael, 195
Randall, C., 35
Rankenian Club, the, 170, 194
Ray, John, 219, 220
Read, Richard, *Secrets of Art and Nature*, 211
Read, T., 40, 41
Reed, Joseph, 28
Remarkable History of Tom Jones, The, 29
Reynolds, Frances, 188–9; 'Essay on Taste',
188, 195
Reynolds, Sir Joshua, 188
Richards, I. A., 228
Richardson, Richard, 225
Richardson, Samuel, *Sir Charles Grandison*, 22,
119; *Clarissa*, 22; *Pamela*, 28, 213
Richmond, Sir Herbert, 206
Rider, William, 250
Rivington, Charles, 13, 230, 231
Robertson, William, 22
Robinson, Ranew, 14, 230
Roche, Michael de la, *New Memoirs of
Literature*, 81
Roger, Jacques, 218–19, 220
Rogers, Pat, 51, 56
Rohault, Jacques, *Cartesian Physics*, 213;
System of Natural Philosophy, 218
Rollin, Charles, *The Method of Teaching and
Studying the Belles Lettres*, 78
Rousseau, Jean-Jacques, 29; *Émile*, 30, 230
Rowe, Nicholas, 49, 55, 61; *Jane Grey*, 18;
Pharsalia, 55; *The Royal Convert*, 55; *Jane
Shore*, 18; *Tamerlane*, 55
Rowley, William, 248
Rowning, John, *System of Natural Philosophy*,
233
Royal Magazine, The, 173
Royal Society, the, 200–1, 202, 212, 232,
242, 243

Ruffhead, Owen, 85

Sacheverell, Henry, 53
Sanadon, Noël Étienne, 83; *Horace*, 81
Sanderson, Robert, 152
Sandham, Robert, 206
Sappho, 79, 92
Sarpi, Pietro, *Histoire du Concile de Trente*, 63,
64
Saunders, Thomas, 136, 138
Scaliger, J. C., 85, 87
Schaffer, Simon, 198, 214
school books, 74, 81, 204
Scots Magazine, The, 182
Scott, David, *History of Scotland*, 64
Scott, Thomas, 122
Scougal, Henry, 138, 149, 150, 152, 156, 157;
Discourses on Important Subjects, 156; *The Life
of God in the Soul of Man*, 146, 156
Scriblerians, the, 202, 203, 227, 252
Sebright, Sir Thomas, 52
Seneca, 140
Sergeant, John, *Method of Science*, 244
Seven Wise Men of Gotham, 29
Shackleton-Bailey, D. R., 87
Shaftesbury, Anthony Ashley Cooper, third
earl of, 137, 173, 175
Shakespeare, William, 16, 18, 183
Shaw, P. and Hauksbee, F., *Proposals for a
Course of Chemical Experiments*, 208
Sherard, William, 225
Sheridan, Richard Brinsley, *The School for
Scandal*, 28
Sheridan, Thomas, 72
Sherlock, Thomas, Bishop of London, *The
Use and Intent of Prophecy*, 121
Shippen, William, 52
Short and Easie Method to Give Children, A, 229,
254
Shuckford, Samuel, *The Sacred and Profane
History of the World Connected*, 101
Shuter, Ned, 28
Sibbes, Richard, 150, 152
Silius Italicus, 71, 91
Sketchley, J., 36
Smalridge, George, 54
Smart, Christopher, trans. of Horace, 80, 82
Smellie, William, 250
Smith, Adam, 169, 173, 176, 194
Smith, John, 152
Smollett, Tobias, 22, 95; *Humphry Clinker*, 28,
115–16, 118, 224; *Peregrine Pickle*, 28;
Roderick Random, 28

Index

Society for Promoting Christian Knowledge, the, 128, 148–9, 163
Somerset, Countess of, 145
Sophocles, 91
Sorbière, S., *Voyage to England*, 243
Spenser, Edmund, *The Faerie Queene*, 17
Sprat, Thomas, Bishop of Rochester, 200, 242, 243; *History of the Royal Society*, 242
Stackhouse, Thomas, *A New History of the Bible*, 101
Stanhope, George, trans. of à Kempis, 154–5; *A Paraphrase and Commentary*, 99, 106
Stanley, D., *Sir Philip Sidney's Arcadia Modernised*, 64
State Trials, 42
Stationers' Company, the, 8, 10, 19, 41
Statius, 71, 91
Steele, Sir Richard, 17, 61, 209; *The Lucubrations of Isaac Bickerstaff*, 55, 65; *Tatler*, 65
Steffers, J. H., 28; *Thomas Jones*, 28
Stephanus, 76
Stephens, William, *Sermons*, 54
Sterne, Laurence, 22, 236–7, 238–41; *A Sentimental Journey*, 90; *Tristram Shandy*, 1, 28, 165, 227, 236
Stevens, John, *History of Ancient Abbeys and Collegiate Churches*, 59
Stewart, John, 179
Stillingfleet, Benjamin, 222
Stirling, James, 208
Stirling, John, 81, 83, 94
Stockdale, Percival, 101
Stone, J., 41, 42
Stonhouse, James, 145
Strahan, William, 182, 212, 249
Strype, John, 53; *History of the Life and Acts of . . . Edmund Grindal*, 50, 53
subscription, publication by, 13, 47–66, 70
Sunderland, Charles Spencer, Earl of, 55
Swift, Jonathan, 42, 54, 62, 167–8, 201, 203, 221, 227, 236, 238–41, 253; *Bickerstaff Papers*, 167; *Gulliver's Travels*, 27, 29, 32, 41–4, 229
Sykes, Arthur Ashley, *An Essay upon the Truth of the Christian Religion*, 117, 118

Talbot, Catherine, 215
Talmud, the, 107
Taylor, Jeremy, Bishop of Down, 152, 155; *The Great Exemplar*, 109, 119; *Holy Living*, 128, 146, 155; *Holy Dying*, 155
Taylor, William, 14, 31, 32, 33, 34, 36, 42

Tenison, Thomas, Archbishop of Canterbury, 50, 201
Terence, 70
Theatre of Fun, The, 28
Theed, Richard, *Sacred Biography*, 108
Theocritus, 70, 78, 79, 83
Thomson, James, 56, 61, 70, 216, 219, 253; 'To the Memory of Sir Isaac Newton', 56; *The Seasons*, 28, 56
Tibullus, 74, 79, 80, 89
Tickell, Thomas, 53, 59
Tillotson, John, Archbishop of Canterbury, 98, 138, 150, 152, 161, 163
Tindal, Matthew, *Rights of the Christian Church Asserted*, 167
Tipper, John, 213, 247; *The Ladies' Diary*, 212, 213
Tonson, Jacob, 11–12, 13, 14, 16, 17, 18, 53
Tonson, Jacob jr, 59
Trapp, John, *Commentary on the Old and New Testaments*, 104
Trapp, Joseph, 51, 79–80, 88; trans. of *Aeneid*, 48, 51, 56, 72, 88; *Praelectiones Poeticae*, 88
Trimmer, Sarah, 230: *An Easy Introduction to the Knowledge of Nature*, 253
Twining, Thomas, *Aristotle's Treatise on Poetry*, 94, 95
typology, 102, 116–18, 121–2, 125
Tyrtaeus, 79, 94

Universal Bible, The, 106
universities, 205–6, 245
Ussher, James, Archbishop of Armagh, 139
Utrecht, Treaty of, 60

Varnam, Thomas, 14
Virgil, 69, 70, 71, 74, 76, 78, 79, 81; *Aeneid*, 48, 51, 56, 71, 72, 88; *Georgics*, 94; *Pastorals*, 94
Voltaire, François Marie Arouet de, 29; *La Henriade*, 59–60, 63, 66
Voyages and Travels, 34

Walker, George, *Treatise on the Sphere*, 233
Wallace, Robert, 170
Wallis, John, *Treatise of Algebra*, 204
Wallis, Peter and Ruth, *Newton and Newtoniana*, 215
Walpole, Horace, 76, 169, 193
Walpole, Sir Robert, 51, 52, 56–7, 58, 59, 60, 61, 62, 65